# HISTORIC W
## —IN—
# SAN FRANCISCO

# HISTORIC WALKS

## —IN—

# SAN FRANCISCO

## 18 Trails
## Through the City's Past

## Rand Richards

Heritage House Publishers
San Francisco

Sixth Printing, Updated November 2008

Readers of this book should not trespass on private property nor disturb occupants of private homes or dwellings referred to herein. The author and publisher assume no responsibility or liability for any such action by readers of this book nor for any injuries or damage sustained on any of the walking tours. Since some of the walks are strenuous, users of this book should check with their physicians before embarking on any of these walks if they have any doubts about their health or fitness.

Cover Design by Larry B. Van Dyke and Rand Richards

Front cover photo: Market Street looking east near Powell Street, c.1898. Courtesy Presidio Army Museum Photo Collection, Golden Gate National Recreation Area, National Park Service. Back cover photo: Bush Street near Kearny, 1870s. Courtesy California Historical Society, FN-04021.

Printed in the United States of America

Heritage House Publishers
P.O. Box 194242
San Francisco, CA 94119
www.HeritageHouseSF.com

## Library of Congress Cataloging-in-Publication Data

Richards, Rand
    Historic walks in San Francisco : 18 trails through the city's past /
    Rand Richards
       p. cm.
    Includes bibliographical references and index.
    ISBN 1-879367-03-3 (pbk.)
      1. San Francisco (Calif.)–Tours. 2. Historic sites–California–San
Francisco–Guidebooks. 3. Historic buildings–California–San Francisco–
Guidebooks. 4. Walking–California–San Francisco–Guidebooks. 5. San
Francisco (Calif.)–History. 6. San Francisco (Calif.)–Biography. I. Title.

F869.S33 R53 2001
917.94'610454–dc21

                           2001024944

# Contents

## The Walks:

In Memory of a Gentle Soul
my Uncle Bill

William R. Ledermann
(1933–1999)

# Preface / Acknowledgments

There were two great pleasures in doing the research for this book. One was that I uncovered a lot of grand stories that I had not previously known, and the other was in the new friends I made as I knocked on doors and asked questions while walking the City's streets. I was pleasantly surprised by the widespread love of and interest in San Francisco history. Many people, I discovered, had done research on their own dwellings and buildings and they were generous in sharing the fruits of their research with me. Some even gave me private tours.

I must start my list of people and organizations to thank by mentioning three individuals whose advice I have relied upon for years. Peter Browning of Great West Books did his usual fine job of copyediting the manuscript, and helped me typeset and prepare the final product for the printer. I also relied upon him for advice on publishing matters large and small, especially on the production aspects of publishing. My friend Malcom E. Barker of Londonborn Publications also provided wise advice and counsel. And I thank my father, Robert C. Ledermann, for his review of the manuscript and his helpful comments.

I also wish to thank Paul Yamazaki of City Lights Books, for his encouragement and support of my books over the years, and Bill Kostura for directing me to several productive research sources and for his permission to re-publish a photo from his book *Russian Hill: The Summit.*

Richard F. Tolmach of Sacramento drew the maps and prepared the lists of sites on the facing pages. I thank him for the fine job he did and for his patience during the necessary back-and-forth while they were being brought to completion. My thanks also to Larry B. Van Dyke for his appealing cover design.

I did the majority of my research at the San Francisco History Center on the sixth floor of the New Main Library. I spent many a pleasant afternoon there reading and making notes. I must thank Pat Akre, Susan Goldstein, and all of the following staffers who helped me ferret out many useful items—Jason Baxter, Tom Carey, Selby

Collins, Mitzi Kanbara, Greg Kelly, Christina Moretta, Tami Tsuzuki, and Tim Wilson. Thanks also to the backroom staff—John, Katherine, Chris, and Elise.

I also wish to acknowledge the help and assistance I received from Wendy Welker, Tanya M. Hollis, and the rest of the staff at the California Historical Society, Ellen Harding and the staff at the California State Library at Sacramento, Kim Sulik and the staff at the Presidio Park Archives & Records Center of the Golden Gate National Recreation Area, Patricia Keats, Susan M. Haas and the Society of California Pioneers, the J. Porter Shaw Library of the San Francisco Maritime National Historic Park, Bill Buettner and San Francisco's Architectural Heritage, and Robert J. Chandler and the Wells Fargo History Room. Thanks also to the San Francisco Performing Arts Library and Museum, and to the Japanese American History Archives. And a special thanks to Kathleen Manning and Prints Old and Rare of Pacifica for the loan of several images reproduced herein.

I also paid visits to a number of City agencies and departments. Foremost among them was the office of the Landmarks Advisory Board where Andrea Green and Patricia Gerber provided case reports that contained in-depth information on buildings in San Francisco's official historic districts. I also made use of information at the San Francisco Planning Department and the Department of Public Works. Thanks also to Debra Lehane and the San Francisco Arts Commission, in whose files I learned a lot about the City's "street furniture"—its public statues and monuments. And Gregory J. Diaz, the Chief Deputy Assessor at City Hall, showed me how to find public records in the Assessor's and Recorder's Office (not always an easy task).

Many individuals and other organizations made contributions to this book in one way or another. In mostly alphabetical order they are: Father Dan Adams and St. Benedict/St. Francis Xavier Church; Advance Camera; photographer Robert Altman; Alex Andreas of the Boom Boom Room; Cloe Azevedo; Elaine Barbieri and Fr. Gabriel Zavattaro, S.D.B. of Saints Peter and Paul Church; Bay Photographic Lab; Chris Berlin, John Graham, and Micah Mann of the Sherman House; Jason Bley; Heather Clisby; Andrea Davis and the Federal Reserve Bank of San Francisco; Ward Dunham of Enrico's Café; Michael Feno of Lucca Ravioli; Lawrence Ferlinghetti and Nancy

Peters of City Lights Publishing; Dan Flynn; Sister Gayatriprana and the Vedanta Society of Northern California; Donal Godfrey, S.J.; Reverend Richard Grange of Kokoro Assisted Living; Susan Johnson; Trevor Hailey; Kit Haskell; Jeremy Hollinger of the Coming Home Hospice; Gary Holloway; Jack Hornor, M.D.; Lilli Kalis, M.D.; Freda Koblick; Don Langley; Enid Ng Lim; Lisa S. Lowy, Esq.; Lindy Luoma; John Maguire and John Cingolani of the San Francisco Fire Department; Brian Mavrogeorge; Jim McGrath; Mark Mendenhall of the Judicial Council of the Ninth Circuit at the U.S. Court of Appeals Building; Sharon Moore; Ben Nerone; Ernie Ng; photographer Daniel F. Nicoletta; Zulma Oliveras of the Women's Building; Reggie Pettus of the New Chicago Barbershop; Chris Phaeton of the Harvey Milk Civil Rights Academy; Isabell Questell of Mercy Services Corp. at Notre Dame Plaza; Gerald S. Sample of the St. Andrews Society of San Francisco; John Schnorr; Wolfgang Schubert; Star Consulting at the Abner Phelps House; Sarah Stocking; Rocky N. Unruh, Esq.; John Valentini of A. Cavalli & Co.; Mariquita West; Vinnie Wetzler; Bob Woodman; and John Yengich at Most Holy Redeemer Church.

A heartfelt thanks to all of the above.

# Introduction

This book contains walking tours of eighteen San Francisco neighborhoods. Each chapter begins with practical information about the walk including the approximate length and time it takes. Each walk is also rated Easy, Moderate, or Strenuous depending on the steepness of the streets on the route. San Francisco is a city of hills; there is no getting around it. Parts of some tours will be difficult for those with limited mobility, or even impossible for those in wheelchairs. In the information box at the head of each chapter I have indicated under "Hills" the streets that might pose a problem.

Another problem is getting to the locales themselves and, if you're driving, finding parking. It is certainly better to take public transportation if you can and avoid the hassle and expense of parking. I have indicated the major San Francisco Municipal Railway bus and streetcar lines for each neighborhood, but it would be best to pick up a transit map. Muni publishes its own map, entitled "The Official San Francisco Street and Transit Map," which sells for $2.00 and can be found at newsstands and similar outlets. You can also call Muni at (415) 673-6864 and get specific help from an operator in terms of telling you how to get from where you are to where you want to go. If you do drive, I have given information on where to best find parking. Always check street signs for posted regulations. You don't want to return to your car to find that it has been towed away. Note also that most residential neighborhoods have two-hour time limits for those without a requisite parking sticker on the bumper. A few tours, especially in the downtown area, are located near BART stations, so I have mentioned those stations where appropriate. (BART is Bay Area Rapid Transit, and in downtown San Francisco is a subway running under Mission and Market streets.)

I have also listed where public restrooms are on each route. Fortunately, the City recently struck a deal with a private firm to install public toilets in heavily traveled areas. They are big, oblong, green-painted things that are generally clean and easy to use. Put 25 cents in the slot and the door slides open and then closes automatically behind you. Just press a large button by the door to exit. These green booths have the added advantage of having easy-to-read maps of the city on their exteriors in case you get lost or wonder where you are in terms of the bigger picture.

After the block of practical information that starts each chapter, an introduction provides an overview of the history of that neighborhood, to help set the scene for the sites you will be visiting. Then the numbered locations start. All directions, in terms of where to walk and which corner a particular building is found on are in italics. If you are having trouble finding a place, ask a passerby. Most residents know their neighborhoods well.

# San Francisco: A Brief History

San Francisco's first inhabitants were Indians whose ancestors arrived more than five thousand years ago. They lived undisturbed for millennia until a troop of Spanish soldiers under the command of Captain Gaspar de Portolá arrived in 1769. He and his band were the first Europeans to see San Francisco Bay. Portolá's expedition was followed in 1776 by a settlement party under the command of Juan Bautista de Anza. On June 29 of that year the settlers, including several priests, celebrated a mass near present-day Mission Dolores, thus marking what is considered the official founding of San Francisco.

Spain's rule over San Francisco and the rest of California lasted less than two generations. Spain's crumbling empire led Mexico, which included California, to declare independence in 1821. The San Francisco Bay Area then was nothing more than a backwater at the northern end of the new republic of Mexico. In 1835 William Richardson, a former British seaman, became the first permanent resident at Yerba Buena Cove, a sheltered curve in the shoreline on the northeast corner of the peninsula that later became the heart of downtown San Francisco. He was joined the following year by Jacob Leese, who built a home next door. By 1839 there was enough in the way of population and dwellings for resident Jean Vioget to lay out a few streets around the central plaza. He used the prevailing Spanish unit of measurement, the vara (one vara equals 2.75 feet, so 50 varas—a common lot size—equals 137.5 feet), which became the standard for the blocks and lots used in San Francisco.

In 1846, clashes between the U.S. and Mexico led to war. American naval forces under the command of Captain John B. Montgomery came ashore on July 9 of that year, raised the American flag over the plaza—soon to be called Portsmouth Square after his ship the *Portsmouth*—and claimed San Francisco for the United States. The following year the new government changed the town's name from Yerba Buena to that of the bay it fronted—San Francisco. A few months later surveyor Jasper O'Farrell corrected the Vioget plat, which was off by a few degrees, and greatly expanded it, mapping out a real city with plenty of room to grow. He also created Market

Street, San Francisco's broad main boulevard.

On January 24, 1848, James Marshall, who was directing the construction of a sawmill in Coloma, a camp on the American River in the Sierra foothills, found a gold nugget in the mill's tailrace. This discovery kicked off the famous California gold rush. It took a couple of months for the news to reach San Francisco, but soon after it did the town's few hundred residents departed almost en masse for the gold fields. They were the vanguard of the multitudes that would soon descend on the hamlet on the shore of Yerba Buena cove. By 1849 San Francisco was a boomtown caught in the full cry of the gold fever. The population mushroomed. Gambling, prostitution, and other entertainments flourished. Construction boomed and real estate rocketed upward in value. San Francisco was on its way to becoming a real city.

But the huge influx of people led to growing pains. San Francisco suffered six major fires in an 18-month period starting in December 1849. Tents and shaky frame dwellings were soon replaced by buildings of brick and stone. A few of these, mainly in the Jackson Square district, still survive.

Physical upheaval was accompanied by social upheaval. Due to perceived threats to public order, a Committee of Vigilance was formed in 1851 by the town's leading merchants to combat what they saw as a crime wave. Five years later a second committee was organized when a prominent newspaper editor, James King of William, was shot down in the street by James Casey, a corrupt politician who had stolen an election to the Board of Supervisors. Casey and several other victims were hanged and a number of other undesirables were banished before the Committee disbanded.

The 1860s saw the rise of a select group of men who became fabulously wealthy and dominated the City's affairs. Leland Stanford, Charles Crocker, Mark Hopkins, and Collis P. Huntington—who became known as the Big Four—were the majority shareholders in the Central Pacific (later renamed Southern Pacific) Railroad, which built the western half of the transcontinental railroad between 1863 and 1869. They profited largely from the labor of Chinese immigrants, who despite their unstinting efforts faced racism and discrimination in their quest for a better life in their adopted country. Severely proscribed in where they could live and what occupations they could practice, they withdrew into their own enclave, the forerunner of today's Chinatown. The Big Four, meantime, built showplace mansions atop prominent Nob Hill.

The discovery of silver in western Nevada led to other fortunes being amassed in the 1860s and 1870s. William C. Ralston and Darius O. Mills, who founded the Bank of California in 1864, were the initial beneficiaries of what was called the Big Bonanza—the richest silver discovery ever. Ralston, with his share, built the Palace Hotel and a number of other edifices before his untimely death in 1875.

The two bankers were soon superceded by a quartet known as the Bonanza or Silver Kings: James G. Fair, James C. Flood, John Mackay, and William O'Brien. Fair and Flood, in particular, left their mark on San Francisco, Fair by accumulating a great deal of real estate, and Flood (and later his son) in building ego-gratifying mansions.

The wealthy lived in splendor up on the heights, but down below near the waterfront, the bottom of the heap existed in a cesspool of vice known as the Barbary Coast. A hangout for criminals of all kinds who profited from prostitution and shanghaiing of the unwary for forced sea duty, the Coast had its heyday during the latter half of the 19th century. But when the Red Light Abatement Act, which was passed to close down the ubiquitous brothels, was finally upheld by the California Supreme Court in 1917, the raucous district faded away.

The Barbary Coast is gone, but two other San Francisco institutions that started in the 19th century are still going strong today: Golden Gate Park, where the planting of greenery among the sand dunes began in 1870; and the cable cars, which were first launched in 1873. The latter proved ideal for overcoming the City's steep hills. At the peak in the late 1880s, a dozen cable car lines extended 112 miles all over San Francisco. Today, a reduced back system of three city-owned lines covers 10.5 miles in the northeast corner of town.

Shortly after the page turned from the 19th to the 20th century, San Francisco underwent a radical change. On April 18, 1906 the city was struck by one of the largest earthquakes ever recorded in North America. Damage was initially moderate, but the shaking left the city's water mains broken. A number of small fires soon blazed out of control and merged into one huge conflagration. The fire raged for three days and destroyed almost the entire downtown as well as South of Market and parts of the Mission District. The losses were staggering: 28,000 buildings burned and 250,000 people, or roughly two-thirds of the population, were left homeless.

Once the debris was cleared the City was quickly rebuilt, even though it had to contend with a messy corruption trial that targeted the mayor, Eugene Schmitz, his advisor and fixer, Abe Ruef, and the entire Board of Supervisors. The graft-influenced and shoddily built City Hall, which suffered heavy damage in the earthquake, was demolished and replaced by a beautiful Beaux-Arts structure that now forms the centerpiece of a grand Civic Center complex. These fine government buildings are about all that was effectively realized from a grand plan for San Francisco that had been proposed by the leading urban planner of his day, Daniel H. Burnham. Burnham had drawn his inspiration from the "City Beautiful" movement, which incorporated classically inspired public buildings into city plans featuring parks and boulevards.

As the 20th century progressed, San Francisco continued to grow. Despite the Great Depression of the 1930s both the Bay Bridge and the Golden Gate Bridge were pushed through to completion. The decade ended with San Francisco hosting a world's fair, the Golden Gate International Exposition, more commonly called Treasure Island, after the island in the bay on which it was held.

When the United States entered World War II in 1941, San Francisco started its transformation into the highly diverse and open society it has become today. The war brought a huge influx of newcomers to the City as soldiers poured in to man the many military bases in the Bay Area. African Americans came in large numbers from the South to work in defense plants and settled in the Japantown/Fillmore area—replacing the Japanese Americans who been unjustly removed as potential enemy aliens.

After the war, change became the order of the day as first the Beats, in North Beach in the 1950s, started a counterculture revolution, which was followed by the flowering of the hippies in Haight-Ashbury in the 1960s. The Summer of Love in 1967 was chronicled the world over. In the 1970s, gays settled in large numbers in Eureka Valley—known today as The Castro—and established their own community. The postwar changes continue to be felt today as San Francisco has built an enduring reputation as a city of diversity of all kinds: racial, ethnic, religious, and sexual.

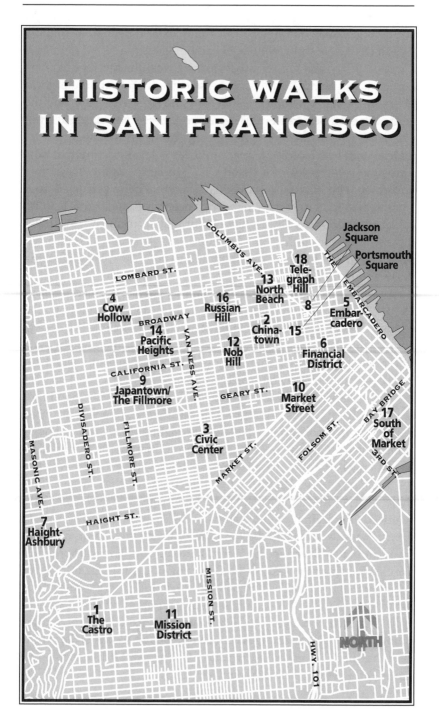

# HISTORIC WALKS IN SAN FRANCISCO

Jackson Square

Portsmouth Square

18 Tele-graph Hill

13 North Beach

LOMBARD ST.

4 Cow Hollow

16 Russian Hill

8

5 Embar-cadero

BROADWAY

14 Pacific Heights

2 China-town

15

VAN NESS AVE.

12 Nob Hill

6 Financial District

CALIFORNIA ST.

9 Japantown/ The Fillmore

GEARY ST.

10 Market Street

DIVISADERO ST.

FILLMORE ST.

3 Civic Center

FOLSOM ST.

BAY BRIDGE

17 South of Market

3RD ST.

MASONIC AVE.

MARKET ST.

7 Haight-Ashbury

HAIGHT ST.

1 The Castro

11 Mission District

MISSION ST.

HWY. 101

NORTH

# The Castro/Eureka Valley

**Length:** 1.1 miles / 1.8 kilometers.
**Time:** 1¼ hours.
**Walk Rating:** Easy to Moderate.
**Hills:** Castro Street between 19th and 20th, on the way to stop 4, is a moderate climb.
**Public Transit:** The Castro is well served by public transit. Muni's Castro Street station, served by streetcar lines K, L, and M, is located underground at Harvey Milk Plaza at the intersection of Market and Castro streets. In addition, surface streetcar line F runs along Market Street from the Plaza all the way to the Ferry Building. Muni bus lines 24 and 33 traverse Castro and 18th streets respectively.
**Parking:** Street parking can be difficult to find. The farther away you look from the commercial hub at 18th and Castro the better your chances of finding a space.
**Restrooms:** There is a coin-operated (25 cents) public toilet on Market Street just off 17th Street across the sidewalk from the gas station. You will pass by it between stops 11 and 12 and again near the end of the tour.

Eureka Valley, as The Castro was previously known, was originally part of an 1846 land grant belonging to José de Jesus Noé, the last Mexican alcalde of San Francisco. Noé sold off chunks of his more than 4,400-acre rancho in the 1840s and '50s, but it was only several decades later when the land was subdivided into lots by homestead associations that residential development really started. A cable-car line installed on Castro Street in 1887 provided the spur that kicked off growth in earnest. Most of the early residents were Irish, Germans, and Scandinavians who established homes, farms, brickyards, and other small businesses in the area. For almost a century this neighborhood of pleasant Victorian and Edwardian homes remained a working-class, family-oriented community centered around the local businesses, churches, and schools.

Change came in the first two decades after World War II when families moved to the suburbs to take advantage of newer and roomier housing. In San Francisco this migration was fueled by the loss of blue-collar jobs when commercial activity at the port of San Francisco declined and manufacturing jobs left South of Market for suburban industrial parks. The hippie invasion in the nearby Haight sealed the

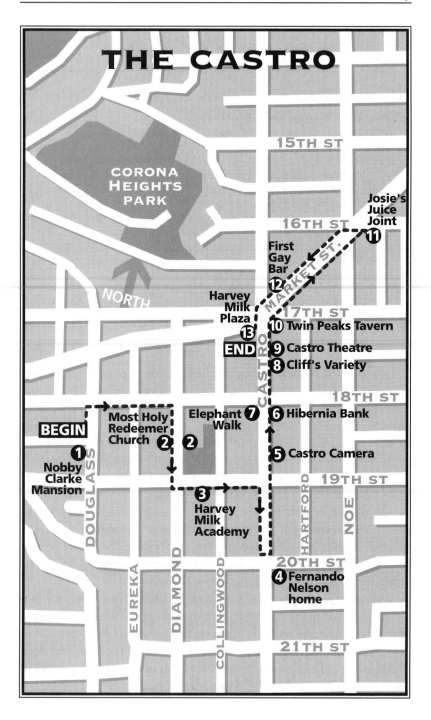

# THE CASTRO

CORONA
HEIGHTS
PARK

15TH ST

Josie's
Juice
Joint
⑪

16TH ST

First
Gay
Bar
⑫

NORTH

MARKET ST.

Harvey
Milk
Plaza

17TH ST

⑬

⑩ Twin Peaks Tavern

END

⑨ Castro Theatre

⑧ Cliff's Variety

CASTRO

18TH ST

BEGIN

Most Holy
Redeemer
Church ②

Elephant ⑦
Walk

② 

⑥ Hibernia Bank

❶
Nobby
Clarke
Mansion

DOUGLASS

⑤ Castro Camera

19TH ST

❸

HARTFORD

NOE

Harvey
Milk
Academy

EUREKA

DIAMOND

COLLINGWOOD

20TH ST

❹ Fernando
Nelson
home

21TH ST

# THE CASTRO

**1** 250 Douglass Street - Nobby Clarke Mansion

**2** 114 Diamond Street - Most Holy Redeemer Church

**3** 4235 19th Street - Harvey Milk Civil Rights Academy

**4** 701 Castro Street - Fernando Nelson Home

**5** 575 Castro Street - Location of Harvey Milk's Castro Camera

**6** 18th and Castro streets - SE corner - former Hibernia Bank

**7** 18th and Castro streets - SW corner - Location of Elephant Walk Bar

**8** 479 Castro Street - Cliff's Variety store

**9** 429 Castro Street - The Castro Theatre

**10** 401 Castro Street- Twin Peaks Tavern

**11** 3583 16th Street - Location of Josie's Juice Joint and Cabaret

**12** 2348 Market Street - Location of The Castro's first gay bar

**13** Market and Castro streets - SW corner - Harvey Milk Plaza

decision for many of the remaining old-line families in Eureka Valley. They sold out in increasing numbers, driving real estate prices down to bargain levels in the late 1960s and early 1970s.

Gay baby boomers, drawn to the City by its reputation for tolerance and by the white-collar jobs available in the new office towers going up downtown, migrated to Eureka Valley to take advantage of cheap rents and real estate. By the early 1970s the neighborhood had become a gay enclave as gay-owned businesses swiftly replaced long-established neighborhood stores. Dee's Dress Shop, for example, became the All American Boy—boots and muscle shirts replaced maternity clothes. Eureka Valley became "The Castro."

A new sense of liberation born of sexual freedom and growing political clout led to a high-water mark for The Castro in 1977 with the election of gay activist and local resident Harvey Milk to the Board of Supervisors. But Milk was assassinated a year later. And the identification of the AIDS virus in 1981 brought a sobering new reality to the neighborhood as the disease ate its way into the gay community.

The Castro's population is still heavily gay today, but with the devastation of AIDS and changing times—gays now feel more accepted and free to live where they choose in San Francisco—the district has, in recent years, seen more of an influx of straights, primarily families with young children who like the sense of community and who feel safe there. Gay residents today complain more about the high rents that are displacing small local businesses with chain store outlets than about straights moving in.

---

*Start this tour on Caselli Avenue near the northwest corner of Douglass Street and Caselli. Across Douglass Street is:*

---

### ❶ 250 Douglass Street – Nobby Clarke Mansion (1891).

This grand house, so out-of-scale with everything around it, was built in 1891. At the time it stood in splendid isolation as the manor of a 17-acre spread owned by Alfred E. "Nobby" Clarke (1833–1902). Clarke was an Irish immigrant who had come to San Francisco in 1850, and after a stab at gold mining and then working as a stevedore he became a policeman. He earned a law degree during his two

decades on the force and eventually became chief legal advisor to the department. When
he retired in 1887 (after having
been dismissed once and then
reinstated) he was said to be
worth $200,000, a tidy bankroll
for a police officer. How he
amassed this sum is unclear,
but he developed a reputation
in later years as a litigious sort,
suing on behalf of his clients

**The Nobby Clarke Mansion, 1890s.**

and himself over all sorts of things. He once filed suit against the
California Supreme Court for $500,000 for imprisoning him on con-
tempt charges. In 1894 Clarke himself was sued by his creditors. It
must have had a telling effect because two years later Clarke declared
bankruptcy and had to leave his mansion.

Shortly after Clarke's death, in 1902, his Douglass Street house,
which architecturally is a mix of Queen Anne and Classical Revival,
was converted into a hospital. By the mid-1920s it had been subdivided into apartments. It remains apartments today.

---

*Walk north on Douglass Street the half block to 18th Street and turn right.
Go one full block to Diamond Street and turn right. The large building two
doors down is:*

---

### ❷ 114 Diamond Street – Most Holy Redeemer Church (1901).

Most Holy Redeemer Church was built in 1901 to serve the growing population as the neighborhood developed. It remained a focal
point for local Catholic families for nearly three generations. But
starting in the 1970s, single gay parishioners began to make up more
and more of the congregation as the families departed. As AIDS hit
full force in the 1980s the church's funerals and memorial services
quadrupled and the average age of those being buried dropped by
about forty years.

During Pope John Paul II's visit to San Francisco in 1987 it was
suggested that he visit Most Holy Redeemer to show his good will
toward AIDS sufferers. But the Pope in The Castro would have been

just too good a story, so he went instead to Mission Dolores where he met with AIDS patients and their caregivers. A photo of him there embracing a four-year-old boy with AIDS was widely published.

The church building itself was extensively remodeled inside and out in 1998. A prime alteration was the addition of a new entrance pavilion at the north side in place of the center door (which is still used for latecomers to services). The original 1901 structure, made of redwood, was covered over with stucco sometime after 1936. One of its twin towers was also removed during that remodeling.

Across the street are two buildings, both built in the 1920s, that were once part of the church complex. Directly across from the church is the former convent. Since 1987 its has been a hospice for terminally ill patients, but not just for those with AIDS. It operates under the auspices of California Pacific Medical Center. A few years ago, with no fanfare, movie star Elizabeth Taylor, who has made AIDS one of her causes, dropped in at the 15-bed facility to visit the patients.

Next to the convent is the former parish school. Due to declining Catholic enrollment it closed in 1980. It is now San Francisco Friends School, a Quaker school. It draws students from all over the city and the Bay Area.

---

*Continue on Diamond for half a block and cross over Diamond and 19$^{th}$ Street. The school building on the south side of 19$^{th}$ between Diamond and Collingwood is:*

---

## ❸ 4235 19$^{th}$ Street – Harvey Milk Civil Rights Academy.

One of the City's elementary schools, Harvey Milk Civil Rights Academy is an alternative school whose special charge is to teach tolerance and non-violence. Many of the students, who are bused here from all over the city, have parents who are gay or lesbian.

For 105 years this school was known as Douglass Elementary (the building dates from 1954). The name was changed in 1996 to honor Harvey Milk, who not only was a strong champion of tolerance and civil rights but who also had a personal interest in the school since he fought to keep it open when it was threatened with closure in the 1970s.

While changing the name to honor the slain supervisor might

seem obvious and appropriate, nothing in San Francisco happens without sparking controversy; the naming of this school was no exception. Back in the 1980s, school officials, when they thought about honoring Milk by changing the name, were at first reluctant since they believed that the school was named for Frederick Douglass, the great African American Civil War abolitionist. When they discovered it was named instead for Stephen R. Douglass, an early California secretary of state, they suddenly had no qualms. But local parents, some of whom had attended Douglass Elementary, opposed the idea and it died. In 1996 however, the school board approved the change and it went through.

**At the dedication ceremony in November 1996, held at the playground across the street, when local politician Tom Ammiano said in his speech that he could see the spirit of Harvey Milk rising over the building, all the children in the audience looked to the sky—searching for Harvey.**

Before leaving the school, note the interesting and unusual mural on the building to the left of the main entrance. It's entitled "a good book is a good friend" and it is made up of hundreds of pieces of glued-together clear glass shards behind which are drawings and writings by the students about reading and books. The mural was done by a parent of one of the students.

---

*Continue on 19<sup>th</sup> Street to Castro. Go right on Castro and up the hill one block to the corner of 20<sup>th</sup> Street. Across the intersection on the southeast corner is:*

---

### ❹ 701 Castro Street – Fernando Nelson home (1897).

This corner Queen Anne Victorian with the witch's-cap tower was once the home of Fernando Nelson (1860–1953), likely the most prolific builder of houses in San Francisco. He claimed to have built more than 4,000 houses in his long lifetime, many of them in Eureka Valley, Noe Valley, and the Mission. They were affordable single-family houses of established types that were purchased by clerks, laborers, policemen, and other workingmen. Selling prices ranged from $500 to $2,000 and buyers' choices of amenities were limited to paint or wallpaper in the parlor; or a "fancy door" could be had for $5.00 in place of a $1.25 plain front door.

Nelson built this house for himself in 1897 and lived here with his wife and sons (who joined him in the business when they were of age) for a dozen years. The house then stood at the back of the lot. In the basement, Nelson kept a horse named Bill who worked a treadmill at night that powered a saw used to cut studs and other lumber for his houses. Nelson moved to Presidio Terrace in 1909, and a subsequent owner moved the house to the front of the lot and added the garages underneath.

---

*Cross over Castro Street and walk down the east side of the street for almost a block and a half to:*

---

## ❺ 575 Castro Street – Location of Harvey Milk's Castro Camera (1973–1977).

**Location of Harvey Milk's Castro Camera.**

This Victorian, with a modernized first floor storefront, was built in 1894 by Fernando Nelson. Its historical significance, however, lies in its connection with the life and career of Harvey Milk. He opened Castro Camera here in 1973 shortly after moving to San Francisco. Never much interested in business, Milk left the operational details to his partner, Scott Smith, while he used the premises as his de facto political headquarters. He kept a comfy couch by the front window to encourage neighborhood residents to come by and chat about whatever was on their minds. Milk and Smith had to move both the camera store and themselves—they were living upstairs—to new quarters in 1977 when their rent nearly quadrupled. (The couple split up at the same time; Harvey found a new companion and moved a few blocks away.)

Harvey Milk is memorialized at this location by a painting of him on the second floor along with his trademark quote "You gotta give 'em hope," and by a bronze plaque embedded in the sidewalk near the curb, which notes that he was the first openly gay elected official in California.

---

*Continue down Castro to the corner of 18th Street.*

---

## ❻ 18th and Castro streets – SE corner – former Hibernia Bank (1929).

The intersection of 18th and Castro streets is the main crossroads of the Castro, and this corner has long served as a community rallying and rendezvous point. The building on the corner, now a Bank of America, was once a branch of Hibernia Bank, an Irish-founded institution that served the neighborhood long before the arrival of gays. The sculpted out corner of the bank building—which perhaps was the original entrance—provided Harvey Milk's volunteers with space to set up tables to organize voter registration drives during his political campaigns.

**The southeast corner of 18th and Castro is sometimes known as "Hibernia Beach" because it's a popular spot for shirtless gays to show off their pecs and get some rays on sunny afternoons.**

---

*Across Castro Street on the opposite corner is:*

---

## ❼ 18th and Castro streets – SW corner – Location of Elephant Walk Bar (1975–1996).

The Elephant Walk was the scene of a nasty confrontation between San Francisco police and gays in the early morning of May 22, 1979 (it would have been Harvey Milk's 49th birthday). On the afternoon of May 21 the jury had delivered its verdict of manslaughter in the trial of former supervisor Dan White for assassinating George Moscone and Harvey Milk. Although the killings struck almost everyone as outright murder, the jury returned the lesser verdict, which led to outrage in the gay community. Thousands marched to the Civic Center that evening to protest the decision, and the rally there turned ugly as protesters smashed doors and windows at City Hall and set fire to police cars.

Shortly after midnight, police cars crammed with cops rode out to the Castro to get revenge. The police captain in charge was quoted at the scene as saying: "We lost the battle at City Hall. We aren't going to lose this one." With that, police officers in full riot gear waded into to the crowd swinging their nightsticks. Some people took refuge in the Elephant Walk but to no avail. The cops followed them in, clubbing people indiscriminately and smashing glass and furniture. Ten minutes of mayhem left victims with broken ribs, collapsed lungs, and ugly lacerations on their scalps. Later that day after the broken glass had been swept up, residents gathered in the intersection to sing a poignant "Happy Birthday" to Harvey Milk.

---

*Cross over 18^th Street and continue up Castro Street to:*

---

### ❽ 479 Castro Street – Cliff's Variety store (since 1936).

A family-run business, Cliff's Variety started as a traditional 5 and 10 cent store. When the neighborhood changed in the early 1970s it was one of the first straight businesses not only to hire gays but to actively solicit their business. It recognized that the new residents were renovating the neighborhood's Victorians, and it stocked the necessary tools, hardware, and other materials. A neighborhood institution, it has continued to prosper.

---

*Just up the street a few doors is:*

---

### ❾ 429 Castro Street – The Castro Theatre (1922).

The Castro Theatre is the last of the great movie palaces of the 1920s still in business in San Francisco, and one of the few left in the country. Even more remarkable is that other than the revamped marquee and the neon blade sign, which were added in 1937 (and refurbished in 1997 for the 75^th anniversary), the theater has undergone relatively little change. The free-standing ticket office—still in use— and the handmade blue and yellow Moorish tiles are original to the building. The interior, although refurbished, with a cast plaster ceiling designed to represent a tent and an attached large lantern with multiple reflectors, is also virtually unchanged.

The Castro Theatre opened in 1922 under the ownership of the Nasser Brothers, sons of a Syrian immigrant who came to San Francisco in 1901. (The Nasser family still retains ownership to this day.)

The architect was Timothy Pflueger (1894–1946), a local boy who never went beyond high school and was largely self-taught. The Castro was the first of eight movie theaters Pflueger designed; he also did the Alhambra on Polk Street and the grandiose Paramount in Oakland.

---

*Continue up Castro Street to the corner of 17$^{th}$ Street.*

---

### ⑩ 401 Castro Street – Twin Peaks Tavern.

In 1972, as The Castro's population shifted toward gays, new owners purchased the Twin Peaks Tavern, which had been long been a hangout for the local blue collar workers who lived in the neighborhood, and it became a gay watering hole. But what made the changeover distinctive were the full-length plate-glass windows that were installed all around on this highly visible corner. It amounted to a virtual declaration that things were now different, that gays didn't need to hide anymore.

---

*Cross 17$^{th}$ Street and head east on Market past the gas station. At Noe and 16$^{th}$, cross Noe and go a short distance down 16$^{th}$ Street to:*

---

### ⑪ 3583 16$^{th}$ Street – Location of
### Josie's Juice Joint and Cabaret (1990–2000).

Now the location of a Zao Noodle Bar restaurant, part of a local chain, this was the site in the 1990s of Josie's Juice Joint and Cabaret, a gay comedy club. Local politician Tom Ammiano, who started as a standup comedian, used Josie's as his informal campaign headquarters during his runs for a seat on the Board of Supervisors. The building has been totally remodeled inside and out since Zao took over.

The loss of the quirky Josie's illustrates the changing nature of The Castro—and of many other San Francisco neighborhoods as well. The lament is heard that as chain outfits replace local businesses a uniqueness and certain special identity is lost.

*Retrace your steps to Market Street and cross over to the north side of Market. Walk west up most of the block toward Castro Street and stop in front of the bar at 2348 Market Street.*

## ⑫ 2348 Market Street – Location of The Castro's first gay bar (1963).

This was the address of The Castro's first gay bar. Called the Missouri Mule, it opened in 1963. Before it closed ten years later, nearly 30 gay bars had come and gone in the neighborhood. It was by no means the first known gay bar in the city; a bar called the Dash in the Barbary Coast on Pacific Avenue in the 1890s probably claims that distinction. And The Castro was not the first gay enclave in San Francisco. North Beach, the Tenderloin, Polk Street, and South of Market all preceded The Castro as having had homosexual enclaves. What made The Castro unique was the intense concentration—it was made into a neighborhood by, of, and for gays.

*Continue up Market to Castro. Cross over to the southwest corner of the intersection to:*

## ⑬ Market and Castro streets – SW corner – Harvey Milk Plaza.

In 1986 a bronze plaque memorializing the life and achievements of the late Harvey Milk was attached to the concrete column at the entrance of the underground Muni station on this corner, and this area was designated Harvey Milk Plaza. To create a more fitting memorial, and one that would encompass the whole intersection of Castro, Market, and 17th streets, a design competition was recently held. Elements of the winning designs include cafes, seating, a pavilion, and such things as mist emitters and skyward directed lasers. No one firm has been chosen to carry out such a plan and no date for completion has been set.

If you arrived here by Muni streetcar to start this tour you have now come full circle and can catch a return car from this same location.

# Harvey Milk

## (1930–1978)

Known as "The Mayor of Castro Street" for his interest in local politics, Harvey Milk is the gay equivalent of Martin Luther King for San Francicso's gay community. A resident of the City only in the final few years of his life, he was largely responsible for the gay community's political awakening.

A native of Long Island, New York, he had a traditional middle-class suburban upbringing. He was a good student in high school and played on the football team. He joined the U.S. Navy after majoring in math at Albany State University and quickly made the officer corps. He had known he was gay since the age of 14 but, as was the custom in the conservative 1950s, kept his affairs discreet.

After his military service he became a financial analyst for the Bache & Company brokerage firm in Manhattan. He wore three-piece suits to work and was so conservative that he supported Barry Goldwater for president in 1964. But he had a less buttoned-down side. When the social upheavals of the late 1960s arrived he quit Wall Street and became an associate producer for the musical *Hair*. He came to San Francisco for the first time in 1968 with the troupe, but stayed

**Harvey Milk outside his camera store, circa 1977.**

only briefly before returning to New York.

He came back to San Francisco for good in 1972 and settled on Castro Street, as part of the first wave of gays that would transform the once Irish working-class neighborhood into a gay mecca. In 1973 Harvey and his partner, Scott Smith, opened a camera shop on Castro Street. That same year, as an openly gay candidate, he ran for a seat on the local Board of Supervisors. A born politician who was a tireless campaigner and gifted public speaker, he lost that race and two subsequent ones, but on his fourth run for office in November 1977 he finally was elected to the Board of Supervisors, thus becoming one of the first openly gay elected officials in the country.

During his short term in office, the restless, driven, and always passionate Milk pushed not just for gay causes: he championed the downtrodden, the elderly, and those who had no natural constituency at City Hall. And he didn't neglect the small things that help make a city more livable for all its inhabitants: he authored the "pooper scooper" law which requires dog owners to pick up their pets' droppings.

Harvey Milk was a man of destiny, but that destiny included his strong premonition that he would be assassinated. He even tape recorded a will in which he said "Should a bullet enter my brain. . . ." On November 27, 1978 that tragically came to pass when disgruntled former supervisor Dan White, who thought Harvey was responsible for blocking his reappointment to the Board after he had resigned in haste, shot and killed him at City Hall after first assassinating the mayor, George Moscone.

One of the most frequent refrains in Harvey Milk's speeches was "You gotta give 'em hope." He was referring mainly to young, closeted gays who feared going public with their homosexuality. But his lasting legacy is that he gave the gay community something much more important—political power. Openly gay men and women have now served not only on the Board of Supervisors but on the Superior Court, in the state legislature, and in other high political offices.

# Chinatown

**Length:** 1.2 miles / 1.9 kilometers.
**Time:** 1½ hours.
**Walk Rating:** Easy to Strenuous.
**Hills:** If you can't abide steep streets you may want to skip stops 8 and 9, since there is a steep ascent on Sacramento Street from Stockton to Joice and an equally steep descent on Clay from Joice back to Stockton. California Street between Kearny and Grant is a moderate uphill as is the block of Sacramento between Grant Avenue and Stockton Street.
**Public Transit:** Muni bus line 1 runs east on Clay Street and west on Sacramento through Chinatown. The 15 bus runs north on Kearny past Portsmouth Square.
**Parking:** The city-owned garage under Portsmouth Square (entrance is on Kearny Street via Clay) is relatively inexpensive. Pricier is the St. Mary's Square garage on the south side of California Street between Kearny and Grant. On weekend mornings street parking in the nearby financial district is usually easy to find, but look carefully at curbside signs since some streets are tow away zones at certain times.
**Restrooms:** There is a free public restroom in Portsmouth Square.

Chinatown's origins go back to the early 1850s when Chinese merchants and businessmen began to coalesce on Sacramento Street near Kearny and along Dupont Street (now Grant Avenue) from Sacramento to Jackson. The first Chinese had arrived in San Francisco in 1848, but it was only in the 1850s—after the gold rush was well under way—that they began to arrive in appreciable numbers. Virtually all of them came from the Canton area in the coastal province of Guandong. (Immigrants from this one area of China constituted the bulk of Chinatown's population until as late as the 1960s.) As more and more continued to arrive, particularly to work on the western half of the transcontinental railroad in the 1860s, they became targets for abuse and discrimination. By the 1870s, racism had reached a fever pitch. Various laws were enacted that excluded Chinese from most occupations where they would compete with whites, and they withdrew into the blocks bounded by California, Stockton, Broadway, and Kearny streets – the predecessor of today's larger Chinatown. The buildings they inhabited were inherited largely from whites who had moved closer to the water-

# CHINATOWN

❶ Sacramento Street

❷ 600 California Street

❸ Old St. Mary's Church

❹ 717 California St. - Sing Fat Co. & 601 Grant Ave. - Sing Chong Co.

❺ 827 Stockton Street - Victory Hall

❻ 843 Stockton Street - "Chinese Six Companies"

❼ 830 Stockton Street - Kuomintang Building

❽ 920 Sacramento Street - Donaldina Cameron House

❾ 965 Clay Street - YWCA Building

❿ 925 Stockton Street - Chinese Presbyterian Church

⑪ Duncombe Alley

⑫ Beckett Alley

⑬ 620 Jackson Street - Site of the "Municipal Crib"

⑭ Cooper Alley

⑮ Wentworth Alley

⑯ 743 Washington Street - Old Chinese Telephone Exchange

⑰ 955 Grant Avenue

⑱ St. Louis Alley

⑲ Ross Alley

⑳ 819 Washington Street - Site of "Little Pete" Assassination

㉑ Waverly Place

㉒ 125 Waverly Place - Tin How Temple

㉓ Commercial Street

㉔ 761 Commercial Street

㉕ 755 Commercial Street - Rube Goldberg property

㉖ 748 Commercial Street

㉗ 742 Commercial Street - Location of the Parisian Mansion

㉘ 736 Commercial Street

㉙ 731-743 Commercial Street

front as Yerba Buena Cove was filled in and the main business district moved farther east and south.

Chinatown was leveled by the earthquake and fire of 1906, as was all of downtown San Francisco. The Chinese were still faced with hostility from leading white businessmen and politicians, and there was talk of moving Chinatown out of its prime location to Hunters Point. But the Chinese were adamant about staying put. Chinatown was a major tourist attraction, and had been since the 1860s, and the possibility of losing that business to Oakland or elsewhere led local leaders to refrain from pushing the issue.

Thus Chinatown was rebuilt in the same location but the architectural style changed. Led by Look Tin Eli, a leading Chinese businessman, the new buildings were given a more colorful "Oriental" look, the idea being that this would help erase Chinatown's unsavory opium-den and slave-girl reputation and further enhance the quarter's appeal as a tourist destination. The white architects who were hired proceeded to decorate basic Edwardian-style buildings—particularly the upper stories—with upturned eaves and pagoda-style roofs in vibrant reds, greens, and yellows. These decorative touches were modeled after the imperial palaces and temples of Beijing rather than the much simpler native architecture of villages in Guandong. The style took hold and many buildings were remodeled along these lines, especially in the 1920s by family associations that typically occupy upper floors.

One innovation of Chinatown's early dwellers was an alteration of the city's grid street pattern. Residents carved pedestrian thoroughfares into and through a number of blocks of their densely packed community. This was a direct borrowing from their villages back home, where such venues provided ease of access and more privacy. These alleys were also used as main entrances to dwellings, a feature they continued to have in their new surroundings. (This contrasts with alleyways elsewhere in the City, which are usually just used as secondary access—residential entrances are on the main streets.)

Chinatown's alleys, virtually from their founding until about the mid-1910s, were prime locations for vice—in particular gambling, opium, and prostitution. As to the latter, both white and Chinese prostitutes operated from brothels within Chinatown's confines, but while the former tended to be "volunteers," Chinese harlots were much more likely to be virtual slaves, forced into the trade by their owners. Most had been procured in China and had either been kidnapped, sold by their parents, or tricked aboard ships bound for San Francisco. Once arrived they were smuggled in and sold or auctioned off to brothel owners. The luckier ones became concubines for merchants or served as household domestics.

This tour will take you past most of Chinatown's important institutions, past and present, as well as to the locations, and in some cases the actual buildings, that were once hotbeds of vice.

---

*Start this tour at the southwest corner of Sacramento and Kearny streets.*

---

### ❶ Sacramento Street (1839).

Sacramento Street between Kearny and Grant Avenue can be considered the birthplace of Chinatown. It was here in the early 1850s that Chinese merchants first started to congregate—establishing grocery, dry goods, and similar businesses. They called the street Tong Yen Gai or "Street of the Men of T'ang," the T'ang Dynasty having been one of China's most eminent. More colloquially, Sacramento was simply known as "Chinese Street."

---

*Walk south one block to California Street. If you are here during business hours enter the lobby of the building on the northwest corner of California and Kearny streets.*

---

### ❷ 600 California Street (1990).

During the excavation for this building in 1988 local archeologist Allen Pastron unearthed the foundation of a Chinese store that once stood near the northeast corner of this block. It was destroyed during the fire of May 3-4, 1851, which wiped out much of San Francisco's business district. All that remained of the store was the redwood floor covered with the remnants of many artifacts, including a gold coin dated 1851. The high degree of fragmentation of the pieces recovered and the relative lack of burn marks led to speculation that the store was dynamited in an attempt to establish a firebreak to prevent the further spread of the flames.

A small sampling of the recovered artifacts can be seen in the hand-crafted wooden case in the southeast corner of the lobby of this building. Among them are an orange stoneware opium bowl, a polychrome porcelain spoon, a bone toothbrush, and two reconstructed objects—a handsome blue and white porcelain vase, and a large brown ware egg jar.

---

*Walk up California Street to the northeast corner of Grant Avenue.*

---

### ❸ Old St. Mary's Church (1854, 1909) – California Street and Grant Avenue – NE corner.

Old St. Mary's—originally St. Mary's Cathedral—is one of San Francisco's most historic structures. It was constructed during 1853–54 on land donated by John Sullivan, an Irish immigrant and early pioneer (he arrived in 1844) who made a fortune in San Francisco real estate. The building was designed by local architects Craine and England. Catholic Archbishop Joseph S. Alemany (1814–1888) had requested that it be modeled after the chapel in his native town of Vich, Spain, but the architects gave him something that more nearly resembled an English country church. Since building materials were scarce in gold-rush San Francisco, the granite blocks used as trim for the foundation were imported from China and the bricks came around the Horn from New England. A steeple planned for the bell tower was never built due to the threat of earthquakes. When the cathedral was opened, on December 25, 1854 with a celebratory Christmas mass, it was the largest building in San Francisco and dominated the skyline.

By the mid-1880s vice from Chinatown had spread to the area around St. Mary's; brothels dotted adjoining Dupont Street. Archbishop Patrick Riordan, who had replaced the retired Archbishop Alemany, wrote in December 1885: "The location of the present Cathedral is such that it can scarcely be approached from any direction without a shudder at the sinfulness and filth of its surroundings…" Accordingly, plans were made to erect a new cathedral in a better neighborhood, and in 1891 a new St. Mary's Cathedral was dedicated at Van Ness and O'Farrell. Old St. Mary's—as it was soon called—became a parish of the Paulist order.

Prostitution remained rife in the area, and in the 1890s a group of wives and mothers successfully petitioned city officials to move the harlots out of their Dupont Street bagnios. To the distress of the Paulist Fathers the prostitutes set up shop right across California Street in buildings on what is now known as St. Mary's Square. Church officials pressured the City to condemn the land and convert it to a park, but nothing had been done by the time of the 1906 disaster. The fire destroyed the brothels, the prostitutes did not return, and soon after that the park of St. Mary's Square came into being. St. Mary's Square as it's constituted today dates from 1950, reduced from its former size when the City allowed a parking garage to be built below it. The park has a statue of Chinese leader Dr. Sun Yat-sen by Beniamino Bufano, and across from it is a memorial with a bronze plaque dedicated to Chinese Americans who gave their lives in World Wars I and II.

> The church's bell tower sports the biblical quote "Son, Observe the Time and Fly from Evil," but it was there before prostitutes moved into the area.

Old St. Mary's, although not totally destroyed by the 1906 calamity, was gutted by the fire. Except for the back wall, the façade and main walls remained standing, and the church was rebuilt and rededicated in 1909. In 1929 the church was extended 50 feet to the north on the Grant Avenue frontage as the sanctuary was enlarged and a transept added. Final changes came in 1966 when a four-alarm fire damaged the former cathedral. Reconstruction took over a year. The church as it stands today is not the 1854 structure, although it closely resembles it. It still rests on its original foundation, and some of the bricks are likely ones that came around the Horn.

---

*On the southwest and northwest corners respectively of the intersection of California Street and Grant Avenue are:*

---

## ❹ 717 California Street – Sing Fat Company (1907) and 601 Grant Avenue – Sing Chong Building (1908).

These two structures, with their crowning pagoda-like towers, are prime examples of the new, elaborately decorated buildings that went up after the 1906 earthquake. They were the forerunners and were meant to be showcase examples of the new Chinatown. Positioned near the southern entrance to the quarter, their four floors were meant

to serve as a shopping
mecca and kind of
Oriental bazaar. Large
picture windows (some
now bricked up) dis-
played their wares. Both
buildings, like the vast
majority of Chinatown
real estate at that time,
were owned by whites
and were leased to Chi-
nese tenants.

**Sing Chong Building.**

The manager of Sing
Chong was Look Tin Eli,
a prime promoter of the
new-look Chinatown.
Look, a local businessman who with his brother founded the Canton
Bank, the first Chinese-run bank in the U.S., was at the center of a
famous court case in 1884. Born in the town of Mendocino in northern
California, he made a trip to China—and when he returned to the U.S.
he was denied admission under the federal 1882 Exclusion Act, which
greatly restricted entry for all Chinese. He filed suit, and won when
the U.S. Circuit Court ruled that a Chinese born in the U.S. was
indeed a U.S. citizen.

The Sing Fat ("Living Riches") Company and the Sing Chong
("Living Prosperity") Company are no longer rich or prosperous.
Although their namesake buildings still stand, both companies are
long out of business. Sing Fat couldn't weather the Depression, closing in 1931; Sing Chong lasted until 1970.

---

*Go north one block on Grant Avenue into the heart of Chinatown. Turn left
on Sacramento and go up one block to Stockton Street. This stretch of Sacramento Street in the 1880s was lined on both sides with brothels housing
white prostitutes. Turn right on Stockton and stay on the east side of the
street to better see the next two buildings which are on the west side of this
busy boulevard.*

---

**❺ 827 Stockton Street – Victory Memorial Hall** (1914, 1970).

The two-story stucco building (third from the corner) across the street with a green tile roof capping the first floor is Victory Hall, an all-Chinese high school. Because of discrimination it was many years before Chinese could attend school with white children, so separate all-Chinese schools were established within the confines of Chinatown. The first such school for the upper grades opened in 1884. Victory Hall, whose name was changed from Chinese Central School after World War II to honor Chinese Americans who had been killed in that conflict, is the descendant of that first school.

The two-story building in back with the gabled towers is the original building, constructed in 1914. The one-story building in front of it with the main entryway was added in 1951.

**❻ 843 Stockton Street – "Chinese Six Companies"** (1908).

Set back slightly from the sidewalk and wedged in between two other buildings is the headquarters of the Chinese Consolidated Benevolent Society, more popularly known as the "Chinese Six Companies." The organization was established in 1854 as a society to aid new Chinese immigrants.

*Although a seventh "company" was added in 1876, the original six associations led to the name Six Companies, which has stuck.*

Acting as a kind of quasi-governmental agency the Six Companies served as a bridge between the larger white society and the Chinese community. The group's aim was to combat discrimination by the white community, to mediate disputes among the Chinese themselves, and to promote Chinese business affairs. Up until 1913, when a separate organization was established for the purpose, the association had also been responsible for stopping tong wars. Tongs had started innocently enough in mining camp towns during the gold rush as social organizations, but in San Francisco's Chinatown they evolved into criminal gangs taking a cut of much of the illicit gambling and prostitution trade. Tong-generated violence and an occasional street melee continued in Chinatown into the 1920s.

Although the Six Companies' influence has lessened in the modern era as discriminatory barriers have fallen and as the Chinese have become more assimilated, the group continues to serve some of its original functions and still has a good deal of prestige.

---

*Walk to the end of this block of Stockton to Clay Street and cross over to the other side of Stockton. As you walk back toward Sacramento Street you will be able to get a better look at the two buildings just mentioned above. At the northwest corner of Stockton and Sacramento look across Stockton at the three-story building in the middle of the block with the sign "Dr. Sun Yat-sen Memorial Hall of San Francisco" over the first floor.*

---

**❼ 836 - 838 Stockton Street – Kuomintang Building** (1915).

This rather nondescript building has been the headquarters in Chinatown since 1915 of the Kuomintang, a political party founded by Dr. Sun Yat-sen (1867–1925). Sun dedicated himself to the over-throw of the monarchy in China, and shortly after that occurred, in October 1911, Chinatown's Chinese celebrated by dropping their traditional style of dress in favor of western clothing and by cutting off their queues. The queues had been a symbol of subservience to the ruling Manchu dynasty.

Chiang Kai-shek (1887–1975) succeeded Sun, and in 1949 re-treated to the island of Taiwan after being routed on mainland China by Mao Zedong and the Communists. The elders in Chinatown today are still strong supporters of the Nationalists—the followers of Sun and Chiang—and their flag, the 12-pointed white star on a red and blue background, can still be seen fluttering atop major buildings in the area today.

---

*Walk up steep Sacramento Street a half block to Joice Alley. On the northeast corner of Sacramento and Joice is:*

---

**❽ 920 Sacramento Street – Donaldina Cameron House** (1908).

The Chinese Presbyterian Mission Home, more popularly known today as the Donaldina Cameron House after its most influential di-rector, was established as a home for Chinese girls seeking refuge from enforced prostitution and abusive employers.

The Mission Home began in 1876 in a small, wood-frame house across the street at what was then 933 Sacramento Street. There was a real need for such a refuge: Chinese women and girls had few legal protections then, and unmarried ones were practically looked on as chattel. Once at the home, girls would be taught English, written Chinese—most were illiterate—and practical skills such as sewing. And since this was a Christian rescue mission, Bible classes were also held. Some of the girls then found legitimate employment, others got married, and some returned to China.

**Donaldina Cameron House, circa 1920s.**

In 1893 the Mission Home moved to its present location in a much larger brick Romanesque Revival structure with a gable roof and a corner tower. Donaldina Cameron joined the staff in 1895. Under her leadership the Chinese Presbyterian Mission House developed a national reputation; Theodore Roosevelt visited the home in 1903.

The 1906 earthquake and fire damaged the 1893 structure to the point where it could not be salvaged, so in 1908 the present building was erected to replace it. Its clinker brick façade is made up of bricks blistered by the heat of the 1906 fire that were gleaned from the rubble.

The slave trade in Chinese girls continued into the 20th century, but by the 1930s had been pretty much eliminated. The Donaldina Cameron House—so named in 1942 to honor its long-time director—continued serving the Chinese community by taking in battered wives, women with immigration problems, and girls remanded to its custody by the juvenile court. Today the house no longer houses abused women—they are referred to shelters—but it still serves Chinatown's youth by offering counseling, language classes, and various educational programs.

*Walk down Joice Alley to Clay Street. On the southwest corner of Clay and Joice is:*

## ❾ 965 Clay Street – Former YWCA (1932).

This fine building was designed by noted architect Julia Morgan (1872–1957). One of the few female architects of her day, she was the first woman to graduate from U.C. Berkeley's School of Engineering (in 1894), the first to receive a master's degree from the prestigious Ecole des Beaux Arts in Paris, and the first of her sex licensed to practice architecture in California. She studied with legendary local architect Bernard Maybeck after her return from Paris. Her signature building is San Simeon, William Randolph Hearst's baronial estate south of San Luis Obispo.

As part of the bread and butter part of her practice she designed a lot of YWCAs throughout the state of California, but this one is arguably one of her finest—especially given the nature of its site on a steep slope. She did a lot of research on Asian design before even starting. The effort paid off. There is no tacked-on imperial grandeur here as there is elsewhere in much of Chinatown, no curled eaves, no multi-tier pagodas. Just an understated but beautifully designed and delineated building well suited for its site.

Some of the details worth taking a closer look at are the cement arch over the door with a waving serpent design, the bronze and glass lantern with a finely wrought decorative metalwork on top of and below the base, and the recessed industrial sash windows with the cut-out keystones.

The arched-roof structure right on the corner of Clay and Joice was the Y's gymnasium. The main entrance, to the right with finial-topped turrets—designed to resemble a Chinese city gate—leads to a courtyard that connects with the YWCA residence hall around the corner at 940 Powell Street. It was designed by Julia Morgan as well, and also was built in 1932.

The former YWCA recently was converted to office and exhibit space for the Chinese Historical Society of America. Their museum documents the Chinese experience in America, although the emphasis is on Chinese immigrant life in and around San Francisco.

*Walk down Clay Street and turn left on Stockton. Part way down the block on the west side of the street is:*

**⑩ 925 Stockton Street – Chinese Presbyterian Church** (1907).

Despite the several Chinese temples scattered around nearby, most Chinatown residents today are Christians. Churches such as this one are an outgrowth of work begun by white missionaries in China in the 19<sup>th</sup> century. When they returned to San Francisco the missionaries continued their proselytizing among the residents here.

This undistinguished Classical Revival building, which makes no concessions to "Oriental" design, is the outpost of the Presbyterian church—the sponsor of the Donaldina Cameron House—in Chinatown. (The Catholics, the Baptists, and others have their own missions.) The structure looks totally out of place here, sandwiched in between two other buildings on this now highly commercial street.

*Walk north a block and a half on Stockton Street to Jackson and cross over Stockton if you haven't already done so to the northeast corner of Stockton and Jackson streets. A short distance down Jackson on the north side is:*

**⑪ Duncombe Alley** (c.1870s).

The west side of this dead-end alley, now cordoned off by a private metal security gate, was, in the 1870s and 1880s, lined with opium dens, most of them in basement rooms. Illuminated only by lamps fed with nut-oil, they were dark, smoky confines that helped contribute to Chinatown's sinister reputation. In most, furniture was minimal and was usually comprised of no more than wooden shelves covered with blankets that were affixed bunk bed-like to the walls. There Chinese and sometimes white men and women, after deep inhalations of opium smoke drawn through a long pipe, would lie in a glassy languor oblivious to the world and its cares. One writer of the time having witnessed such scenes described an opium den as resembling a "sepulcher for the dead."

*Walk down Jackson Street past Grant Avenue and stop at Beckett Street, an alley leading in from the left that cuts through to Pacific Avenue.*

**⓬ Beckett Alley** (by 1849).

In the1880s local doctors started reporting that boys as young as ten were contracting venereal diseases. With Chinatown the probable source of the problem, as sex could be had there for as little as 25 cents, the Board of Supervisors commissioned a report to shed light on the extent of vice in the district. A map, which accompanied the report, published in 1885, showed the primary business of each structure. Virtually every building in Beckett Alley at the time was labeled "C.P." for "Chinese Prostitution."

The brothels here were some of the lowest in Chinatown. The prostitutes occupied "cribs," which were no more than cubicles separated by cheap partitions spaced maybe six feet apart. Girls would typically entertain dozens of customers a night. Because of the coercive conditions that most of them worked under, the average girl lasted five years or less in the trade. Fading beauty and sexual and other diseases left them burned out and discarded at an age when most women were just getting started in life.

---

*Walk a little farther down Jackson Street toward Kearny.*

---

**⓭ 620 Jackson Street – Site of the "Municipal Crib"**
(1904–1907).

Civic graft and corruption were an integral part of much of early San Francisco's history. One of the most egregious examples was found in a brothel that once stood in about the middle of this block. (620 Jackson as an address no longer exists.) It was dubbed "the Municipal Crib" by *San Francisco Bulletin* editor Fremont Older, who suspected that Mayor Eugene Schmitz and his close associate, political boss Abe Ruef, shared in its profits. Older's hunch was later proved correct, and after sensational trials both men were found guilty of extortion and sentenced to prison.

The Municipal Crib—or Standard Lodging House as it was officially known—opened in May 1904 as a three-story building with 90 cubicles. Rebuilt after the 1906 fire, it was enlarged to four stories with 130 cubicles and was nicknamed "the Big Ship" after its shape. Unlike many brothels which housed only Chinese or white women the Municipal Crib had women of various races and ethnicities.

French women occupied the third floor and were the most expensive at $1.00; black women lodged on the fourth floor and were less expensive; Mexican women at 50 cents were even cheaper and were found in the basement. The Municipal Crib closed in September 1907 after the mayor's conviction for extortion.

In the years prior to the Municipal Crib's existence there was a courtyard in back of the site called "the Palace Hotel." It was a derisory tag of course, since it was just the opposite of the real Palace Hotel and all of its luxury. This Palace Hotel was a squalid courtyard with an open sewer. Located in one of the most densely packed parts of an already crowded Chinatown, it was surrounded by tenements filled with elderly and mostly unemployed Chinese men who shared a communal kitchen in the center of the courtyard.

---

*Cross Jackson Street and look for the entrance to a narrow alley between 641 and 647 Jackson.*

---

### ⓮ Cooper Alley (c.1860s).

Before the Christian missions established their shelters in the 1860s and 1870s, in this vicinity was located a "hospital," in which elderly women and diseased prostitutes too sick to be of further service were brought and left to die. A *Chronicle* reporter visited the scene in December 1869 and described the "hospital" as a foul, windowless basement where the "patients" were placed on rice mat covered shelves attached to the wall. There they were left to die either by starvation or by their own hands. After a few days a watchman would return and smother or strangle anyone still living.

If you care to walk down dead-end Cooper Alley, which believe it or not is not the narrowest in Chinatown, it will give you a sense of the cramped conditions Chinatown still operates under today and by extension what it must have been like in the 19<sup>th</sup> century. The alley serves as a service corridor for a restaurant as well as the entry for Chinese residents who live in a small brick building near its end.

---

*Walk west a very short distance on Jackson Street to Wentworth Street, an alley that goes through to Washington Street.*

---

**⓯  Wentworth Alley** (by 1849).

The Chinese typically had their own names for streets and alleys: Wentworth Alley they knew as either "Tuck Wo Gai" — Harmony Street — allegedly for the harmonious look this venue had in the 19ᵗʰ century when it was decorated with paper lanterns, or as Fish Alley because of a number of fish markets that once stood here. Fish Alley also deserved its moniker, because many of the rooftops above were used to dry fish for export. Fresh fish would be carried to the roofs in baskets, where they were spread across bamboo drying frames.

Also worth noting about Wentworth is that a few of the existing buildings were brothels in the decade after 1906. The two on the east side of the street are #32, which was built in 1907, and #42, which dates from 1908. Number 42 especially has been so severely remodeled (in 1963) that it is impossible today to get any sense of its original character. On the west side, neighboring buildings 15 and 19 Wentworth (both 1907) were once bordellos. The ground floor facades have been refaced over the years, but the upper stories, particularly that of #15, appear to look much as they did originally.

---

*Walk through Wentworth to Washington Street. Across Washington and a little up the grade is:*

---

**⓰  743 Washington Street – Old Chinese Tel. Exchange** (1909).

One of the most fancifully decorated buildings in the district, this structure with the triple pagoda roof — multiple pagodas are a sign of importance and dignity — served as Chinatown's telephone exchange until 1949. The exchange started in 1894 in a building next door on the southeast corner of Jackson and Grant, and in 1901 moved to the present site where it initially occupied just the second floor of its new home. The present

**The Old Chinese Telephone Exchange.**

structure was erected after the 1906 fire.

The Chinese style may seem unusual construction for a conservative company such as the Bell System but to its credit it has a history of designing buildings to fit their neighborhoods. The interior, which was open to visitors, also featured Chinese decorative themes. There was lots of carved wood, the walls were of black lacquer trimmed in red and gold, and two large golden dragons perched above the ebony switchboard.

The exchange served only Chinatown, and the operators (only Chinese women were hired after 1906) had to be fluent in English and five dialects of Cantonese. They mostly relied on their memories to route calls to local residents, who usually requested people and businesses by name rather than number. But the Chinese Telephone Exchange did produce a directory—America's only hand-painted telephone directory—in which all names, addresses, and phone numbers were inscribed in Chinese characters in a 30-to 40-page book. The exchange ceased operations in 1949 due to the advent of direct-dial technology.

The building now houses a bank.

---

*Go up to Grant Avenue, turn right, and go most of the way down the block for a look at a building on the west side of the street:*

---

### ❼ 955 Grant Avenue (1907).

At six feet, ten inches wide this building is believed to be the narrowest commercial storefront in Chinatown, possibly in the city. The reason it is so narrow is that it occupies what was once an alley that connected to St. Louis Alley behind it. St. Louis Alley is accessed from Jackson Street and is the next stop on this tour.

Originally a candy store, in recent years it has been home to a jewelry concession.

---

*Walk around the corner and up Jackson Street a short way to St. Louis Alley.*

---

### ❽ St. Louis Alley (c.1860s).

This now placid walkway was once the site of a notorious slave market where Chinese girls were stripped naked and auctioned off to begin a life of involuntary prostitution. In later years it was home to migrant farm workers on leave from picking produce in California's rich agricultural valleys. Those times are now a world away. Today only the clatter of mah-jongg tiles, a popular game resembling dominoes, echoes down this now peaceful dead-end.

---

*Walk up Jackson Street a short distance to Ross Alley, which connects to Washington Street at the end of the block.*

---

### ⓳  Ross Alley (c.1870s).

Ross Alley, previously known as Stouts Alley, has been tagged with a couple of other appellations. It was once known as Old Manila Alley—Gow Lo Sun Hong to the Chinese—because the brothels and gambling dens here were favorites of Filipinos and Latinos. The street was more commonly known as the "Street of the Gamblers" after an Arnold Genthe photograph of the same name. Gambling dens predominated here in the late 19$^{th}$ century. Their entrances were fortified with iron boiler plate to thwart police raids. Many bore dent marks from SFPD sledgehammers.

Worth a look here is the Golden Gate Fortune Cookie Company at 56 Ross. It's open to the public, usually offers free samples as well as bags of cookies for sale. And 37 Ross, the address of a family association, is also of interest. Look up to the second and third floors at the beautifully crafted gold lettering on black background sign boards.

---

*At the southern end of Ross Alley cross over Washington Street to the start of Waverly Place. The building on the southeast corner of Washington and Waverly is:*

---

### ⓴  819 Washington Street – site of "Little Pete" assassination.

Few Chinese were known outside Chinatown, but one of them who was was the gangster Fong Ching, aka "Little Pete." The baby-faced racketeer ran a legitimate business, a shoe manufacturing enterprise, for which he employed white salesmen to cover for the fact that his shoes were manufactured by Chinese (whites typically boycotted Chinese-made goods that competed with those made with white labor). But Pete made his real money from extorting protection money from area brothels and shopkeepers. His other passion was fixing horse races. He made sure his horse won by bribing the jockeys of all the other horses to lose.

Like many gangsters, Little Pete made plenty of enemies: rivals put a price on his head. He lived above 819 Washington, and on January 23, 1897 at about 9 p.m. he descended for a shave to the barber shop below that then stood at this corner. Normally security conscious, he sent his only bodyguard that night out to get a paper with the day's racing results. Seconds later two gunmen from a rival tong, who had been waiting for just such an opportunity, walked in and blew Fong Ching's brains out as he sat in a barber chair. The once dirt-poor immigrant who had arrived friendless and penniless in San Francisco at age 10 was 32 years old when he died.

**㉑ Waverly Place** (c.1849–1852).

This wide alley seems to have not been as much as a haven for vice as its narrower and more hidden brethren. Not that it didn't have some; the southern end of Waverly near Sacramento Street in the 1880s did have a concentration of brothels staffed with white prostitutes.

In April 1879 Waverly Place was the scene of a bloody battle between two tongs over the ownership rights to a Chinese slave girl. Over fifty participants engaged in hand-to-hand combat, and at least four men were killed. But the street was best remembered by its Chinese inhabitants for a more mundane reason. It was known as "Fifteen Cent Street" because of the many barber shops that lined both sides in the 19th century. Fifteen cents was the price of a haircut that also included a rebraiding of the queue.

---

*About halfway down this first block of Waverly Place on the west side is:*

---

**㉒ 125 Waverly Place – Tin How Temple** (1911).

Located atop a four-story building—so as to be closer to heaven—is Chinatown's most historic temple or joss house, the Tin How. Tin How is an anglicized version of T'ien Hou, the goddess of sojourners and seafarers. Since all Chinese immigrants arrived at San Francisco by sea in the early days it is easy to understand why, among all the gods whom Chinese worship, she would assume such importance. (Unlike the organized group religion familiar to Christians, Chinese faithful pray privately to individual gods. Their religious beliefs incorporate elements of Taoism, Buddhism, and Confucianism along with a bit of ancestor worship.)

The oldest Chinese temple in the United States, the Tin How has occupied this location since 1852. That first temple was replaced by a successor in 1875, which in turn burned in 1906. Part of the altar that dates from the 1870s was saved from the fire and is incorporated into the temple today. Other highlights include the array of wooden gods along one side wall; ceremonial wands, or battle axes, designed to do battle against evil spirits; and the rows of oranges at the back, which represent offerings by those praying to the god of Wealth. Also worth noting is the profusion of red lanterns suspended from the ceiling. The red cards attached are from parishioners expressing their wishes for long life, happiness, and so forth.

If you are on this tour during business hours it is worth the climb up four flights of stairs—there is no elevator—to see the Tin How Temple and get a glimpse of this ancient form of Chinese worship.

---

*Walk ahead on Waverly to Clay Street and take a left to Grant Avenue. On Grant cross over and turn right. Go a half a block to:*

---

## ㉓ Commercial Street (1850).

Standing virtually in the shadows of the Financial District's high rises, the 700 block of Commercial Street still manages to retain the feel of a now vanished era. This modest block has a great deal of history associated with it. Almost all of the mostly two- and three-story buildings you see here were once houses of prostitution.

This block was laid out in 1850, probably as a land-based extension of Long Wharf, which began at the present-day intersection of Commercial and Leidesdorff streets in 1849. Initially, French immigrants established themselves here, but by the early 1860s Chinese settled into the few blocks on the west end of Commercial while the white population gravitated toward the waterfront as wharves were extended further into the bay. Chinese predominated here until the

1906 earthquake. They operated a variety of general merchandise shops as well as a few manufacturing enterprises dealing in such things as shoes and cigars.

After the 1906 earthquake and fire leveled this area the 700 block of Commercial Street quickly took on a different character. Two-and-three story brick houses went up—virtually all of them in 1907—which quickly filled with white prostitutes. For the next decade this block was an active red-light district.

Some of the buildings worth noting here are:

### ㉔ 761 Commercial Street (1907).

On the north side of the street, 761 Commercial is of an unusual design, having a second-story iron mansard roof punctuated by five dormer windows. The Sanborn Company, which published maps used by fire insurance firms to evaluate properties, shows that in 1912 this building housed "female boarders," a euphemism for prostitutes.

### ㉕ 751 Commercial Street (1907) – Rube Goldberg property.

Rube Goldberg (1883–1970) the owner of a house of ill-fame? It's true. To be precise, the Pulitzer-Prize-winning cartoonist famous for his drawings of complex contraptions designed to perform simple tasks didn't own or run the brothel itself, but he did own this building while it was used as a house of prostitution.

Goldberg, who was born in San Francisco, attended U.C. Berkeley, where he earned an engineering degree in 1904. He worked briefly for the City designing sewer systems, then pursued his ambition — a job for $8 dollars a week at the *Chronicle* as a janitor/cartoonist.

**751 Commercial Street.**

He purchased this property in November 1906, and the following month he signed a contract to pay almost $7,500 to an architect and contractor to erect this two-story-with-a-basement brick building.

As a struggling cartoonist making eight dollars a week he obviously could not have afforded to buy such a building on his own. The money to bankroll such an endeavor apparently came from his father, a wealthy banker and real estate speculator who, perhaps not coincidentally, had his office around the corner on Kearny Street.

Goldberg moved to New York in October 1907, where he went on to fame and fortune. Rents derived from 755 Commercial Street apparently provided income for him while he established his career in the Big Apple. He left San Francisco just as this block of Commercial Street was getting into full swing as a red-light district, so it's not certain that he knew what this building was being used for, but he no doubt was happy to pocket what must have been steady and lucrative income. He sold the place in 1916, which coincided with his signing a new contract (with his father acting as his agent) with the *New York Evening Mail,* which one source estimated at a princely $1,000 a week. He no longer needed the income from 755 Commercial.

Goldberg returned to San Francisco for visits from time to time, and in 1919 on one of his trips to his hometown he penned an article for the *Bulletin* in which he wrote: "I know many things that would startle the world if I ever divulged them." He was speaking satirically about the birth of the League of Nations having just returned from a trip to Europe, but in retrospect, if indeed he knew what his building was being used for, this might have been a sly reference to his erstwhile ownership of a San Francisco bordello.

---

*Across the street are:*

---

**❷❻ 748 Commercial Street** (1907).

This French Baroque design house is the only one on the street that actually looks the part of a parlor house. It was the most architecturally interesting of the 700 block until a recent renovation removed a garlanded cartouche keystone that adorned the archway over the second-floor window. The insensitive alteration has lessened its visual appeal. "Female boarders" once held sway in this 19-room, one-bath townhouse.

### ㉗ 742 Commercial Street – Location of the Parisian Mansion (1907-1917).

This address housed one of the more famous bagnios of early 20th-century San Francisco—the Parisian Mansion. It could be considered a parlor house—meaning that had pretensions of refinement; it charged $3 for sex instead of $1 like most of the other establishments on the block. It also likely had a front parlor on the main floor where there was a bar and where the madam greeted customers.

It was also noted for its "Virgin's Room" where a gullible newcomer would pay double or triple the price to have sex with a "virgin." The "virgin" was usually one of the younger girls who had a youthful enough face and the skills to act the part of an ingenue. Meanwhile the house increased its take in these exhibitions by charging other customers $5 to $10 to watch the action through peepholes in the mirror-lined chamber.

The Parisian Mansion was run by a Madam Marcelle and her partner, Jerome Bassity—one of the sleaziest figures in the history of San Francisco vice. Described in contemporary accounts as a "divekeeper" and "nabob of the underworld," Bassity was the City's leading pimp during the first decade of the 20th century. A flashy dresser, the portly Bassity was an assiduous patron of the fleshpots himself. Frequently drunk and free with his use of a revolver, he sometimes amused himself by shooting out the lights or at the feet of his girls to make them dance. Bassity's reign as a brothel owner came to an end about 1910 when a reform movement started gaining steam and the grand jury turned up the heat on him.

Architecturally this building is an odd mixture of Mission Revival with a bell-shaped roofline and Chinatown Chinese with a decorative tile roof cornice, which was probably put on after its brothel heyday. The alternating white tile and brick rounding the entrance adds visual interest. The building has 19 rooms and six bathrooms.

### ㉘ 736 Commercial Street (1907).

The most notable architectural feature here is the elaborate cornice with stone wreaths above the second story. Originally this was only a two-story building; the top two floors were added in 1928. The architects—Lansburgh and Joseph—also designed the house for Rube Goldberg across the street.

This brothel was one of the last to close. Most shut down soon after the California Supreme Court upheld the Red Light Abatement Act in January 1917, but 736 Commercial managed to stay open until May of that year. Stella Hayes, Jerome Bassity's mistress, lived here for a spell but seems to have been long gone by the time it closed.

---

*Back on the south side of the street is:*

---

**❷❾ 731–743 Commercial Street** (1906).

In 1933 Herbert Asbury wrote a classic book about San Francisco vice called *The Barbary Coast*. In it he describes how on December 17, 1906 Jerome Bassity gave a grand opening party for a newly rebuilt Commercial Street brothel. The affair was described as a "wild debauch" in which all comers for that night only were serviced for free.

Asbury unfortunately did not give the address. A *San Francisco Call* reporter was on the scene, however, and the following day's paper gave a brief account, indicating that the police made no effort to close the place and quoting Bassity as saying he had "fixed it with Ruef and Schmitz," a reference to Abe Ruef, a corrupt political operator, and Eugene Schmitz, the graft-grasping mayor. The reporter noted that Madam Marcelle had opened a resort at 730 Commercial that same evening (a building now replaced by the present one, which dates from 1929) but gave the address of "Bassity's house" as 731 Commercial. It seems almost certain this was the location of that wild party.

The original ground-floor storefronts of this structure retained their architectural integrity until the late 1990s, when misguided remodeling destroyed the continuity. Only 731 itself with its decorative pilasters appears to remain unaltered.

# Donaldina Cameron

## (1869–1968)

Called by one writer "China-town's Angry Angel," Donald-ina Cameron waged a life-long crusade in San Francisco's Chi-natown rescuing Chinese girls from virtual slavery. A few were domestic servants mis-treated by their owners, but most were prostitutes held in bondage by brothel owners. To her charges Donaldina was af-fectionately known as "Lo Mo" or "The Mother," but to her adversaries she was "Fahn Quai" or "White Devil."

She was born on a New Zealand sheep ranch in 1869, the youngest of six children of Scottish parents. At age two

**Donaldina Cameron.**

the Camerons moved to the San Francisco Bay Area where Don-aldina grew up in various locales. As a young woman she had handsome good looks and a regal bearing; she could have been taken for a headmistress of an elite girls school. In 1895 she heard of an opening with the Presbyterian Mission House, a Christian social service agency involved in helping young Chinese women and girls escape conditions of servitude in Chinatown. When the director, Miss Culbertson, died two years later, Cameron took over and for the next 40 years earned a reputation as the Carrie Nation of the yellow slave trade.

Backed by her strong Christian faith, an iron will, and her own considerable personal courage, Lo Mo, a couple of policemen armed with axes and sledgehammers, and an interpreter—Cameron never learned to speak Chinese—would sally forth to locations in Chinatown where she had been tipped that a girl was being held against her will. Employing the element of surprise, the group would break down doors if necessary to claim a usually frightened young woman, who likely as not had been hastily hidden away in a closet or under floorboards by her master. If the girl's keeper could not prove a filial relationship, the rescued girl would be taken back to the Mission's home at 920 Sacramento Street.

The Chinese slave owners not infrequently retaliated. Armed with warrants alleging minor law violations on the part of the girl, they would try to reclaim their property. But Lo Mo employed the same dodges her adversaries used against her—she would hide rescued girls behind the boiler in the basement of 920 or under large sacks of rice. She sometimes received death threats, and on at least one occasion dynamite was discovered on the front steps of the home. But her constant raids on Chinatown were effective. One slave owner once called on Cameron to make sure that she would not seize his legitimate wife whom he was bringing in from China.

Lo Mo retired in the mid-1930s, by which time active slavery for the prostitution trade had pretty well subsided. During her tenure she is estimated to have rescued over 2,000 Chinese women and girls from squalid situations and put them on a path to a better life.

Donaldina Cameron never married, and in 1942 moved with two of her sisters to a cottage in Palo Alto. Reserved and independent, she lived on alone after her sisters' deaths and died at the ripe old age of 98 in 1968, a light-year removed from her days waging war against the slave owners of Chinatown.

# Civic Center

**Length:** 0.8 miles / 1.3 kilometers.
**Time:** 1 hour.
**Walk Rating:** Easy.
**Hills:** None.
**Public Transit:** Muni bus lines 47 and 49 run along Van Ness
Avenue. The F streetcar line goes along Market Street. The Civic
Center BART station is located on Market Street between Hyde and
Leavenworth streets.
**Parking:** There is a city-owned garage underneath Civic Center Plaza
(entrance is on McAllister Street). Metered street parking – one hour
limit – is found around the plaza and on nearby streets. For free
street parking – two hour limit – you have to go to Franklin Street
or farther west.
**Restrooms:** There are public restrooms in the New Main Library and in
the basement of City Hall. There is also a coin-operated (25 cents)
public toilet on the southeast corner of Civic Center Plaza.

San Francisco's Civic Center, on the National Register of Historic Places since 1978, is home to the City's grandest public buildings. This showcase area, comprising city, state, and federal offices, was, at the City's birth, literally a backwater. At the time gold was discovered it was a sandy, swampy wasteland watered by springs and creeks. One writer at the time described it as "among the most dreary and melancholy spots that surround the city."

The area was far from the original settlement at Yerba Buena Cove, and the city fathers considered it suitable only as a graveyard, which is what the triangular section of land between Larkin, McAllister, and Market streets became starting in 1850. Yerba Buena Cemetery, as it was called, was full by about 1860. A decade later, with the city rapidly expanding, it was decided to build a new city hall here, since the local government had outgrown its home on Kearny Street at Portsmouth Square. As many as 9,000 bodies were removed and reburied at the City Cemetery out in Lincoln Park in the Richmond District. (In the course of digging up the graves, some coffins were discovered to contain rocks, not skeletons. This was due to apparent greed on the part of the coroner, who received payment for burying corpses of transients and unknown persons. To increase his income

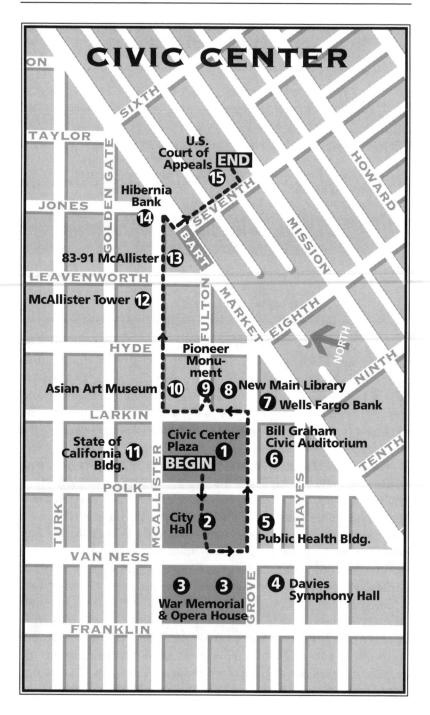

# CIVIC CENTER

**❶ Civic Center Plaza**

**❷ City Hall**

**❸ The Veterans War Memorial and Opera House**

**❹ Louise M. Davies Symphony Hall**

**❺ Public Health Building**

**❻ Bill Graham Civic Auditorium**

**❼ Wells Fargo Bank**

**❽ New Main Library**

**❾ James Lick Pioneer Monument**

**❿ Asian Art Museum / Old Main Library**

**⓫ State of California Building**

**⓬ 100 McAllister Street - McAllister Tower**

**⓭ 83-91 McAllister**

**⓮ Hibernia Bank**

**⓯ U.S. Court of Appeals Bldg.**

the coroner would recycle the body so that it would be found in a different spot—while he buried a load of rocks instead of the victim.)

In 1871 construction started on the "new" City Hall. After twenty-seven years of work—it was financed on a year-to-year pay-as-you-go system—it was finally finished in 1897. It was a rather uninspired Classical Revival structure capped by a slender dome. Due to graft-induced shoddy construction most of the edifice was reduced to an utter ruin in seconds when the 1906 earthquake hit.

The earthquake actually proved fortuitous because it came at a time when America's civic leaders were looking at their increasingly dense and crowded cities and were envisioning something better. It was called "The City Beautiful Movement" and its architects dreamed of replacing cluttered city streets and dilapidated tenements with broad boulevards and imposing, classically inspired public buildings and monuments. Daniel Burnham, the noted architect of the influential Chicago Columbian Exposition of 1893, had submitted just such a redevelopment plan for San Francisco just before the 1906 quake struck. Burnham's plan proposed a civic center with nearby Market Street and Van Ness Avenue as its axis. This placement never occurred and most of Burnham's plan never came to fruition, but its value lay in that it stretched city planners' thinking about what a new civic center could be. As a result it was decided not to build a new city hall on the exact same site as the old. Several square blocks of land were purchased just to the west of the old site, and a new configuration arose around a central plaza.

Many cities were similarly inspired by the City Beautiful Movement, but San Francisco's Civic Center complex is one of only a handful that was ever brought to fruition. What led to it being completed in a city known for its fractious political climate was a rare confluence of factors: the city rallied around Mayor James ("Sunny Jim") Rolph Jr., a consensus candidate of integrity who succeeded a notoriously corrupt regime; San Francisco was eager to showcase itself with the upcoming Panama Pacific International Exposition which it would host in 1915; and the excellence of the design of the major buildings, especially City Hall. These factors, falling into place as they did in the few years after the 1906 disaster, led to the birth of this beautiful array of buildings. Many architects and historians consider the San Francisco Civic Center to be the country's premier example of a Beaux-Arts style municipal government complex.

---

*Start this tour across the street from City Hall in Civic Center Plaza at the head of the green lawn.*

---

## ❶ Civic Center Plaza (aka Joseph L. Alioto Performing Arts Piazza).

While it seems only natural in the present scheme of things that the open space of Civic Center Plaza forms an obvious centerpiece of the whole Civic Center complex, when the project first got rolling a building occupied the southern half of the square. Now known as Commerce High School, it was a large, tan brick building erected in 1909. Rather than demolish it, in 1913, in a gargantuan moving job, it was hauled a few blocks to the west and still stands today on the northeast corner of Fell and Franklin streets.

Before gazing up at City Hall look carefully at the sidewalk in front of you. You will see three manhole covers embossed with "Cistern SFFD." San Francisco, ever cautious about fire, has over two dozen cisterns below ground scattered around the city. Below this plaza is the largest of all of them, a 500,000-gallon repository that the city's fire department can tap in an emergency.

## ❷ City Hall (1916) – 1 Dr. Carlton Goodlett Place (Polk Street).

City Hall, the crown jewel of the Civic Center, opened in March 1916 after a construction job that lasted two and half years. It was designed by the local architectural firm of Brown & Bakewell, who were awarded first prize in a competition. Both men were graduates of the prestigious Ecole des Beaux Arts in Paris but their main claim to fame prior to this commission was the design for the Berkeley City Hall, a much less grand structure.

The San Francisco City Hall was their crowning achievement; it is hard to conceive of a more beautiful public building than this one. The eye-catching dome, echoing the Italian Renaissance in general and St. Peter's Basilica at the Vatican in particular, is not only taller than that of the U.S. Capitol but it is also one of the largest in the world. The gilt adorning it and the front doors and the balconies is of 23.5 carats, nearly pure gold.

---

*If you are here during City Hall's normal weekday business hours or on Saturday or Sunday afternoons when it's also open (from noon to 4 p.m.), cross the street and enter the building. If not, walk north to McAllister Street and then west to Van Ness Avenue.*

---

City Hall's interior is just as impressive as its exterior. The grand staircase with its steps fanning out at the base has served as the backdrop for a number of movies and wedding pictures. Presidents of the United States have been received here in the rotunda; Mayor Moscone and Supervisor Harvey Milk lay in state here after they were assassinated in 1978.

If City Hall looks almost new it's because it was recently refurbished and seismically upgraded. The lighted interior of the dome never fails to impress. The soft white hand-carved plaster decorative flourishes adorning the upper stories and ceiling nearby look as if they were just made yesterday. In the wings on the main floor, the North and South Light Courts, which had their glass skylights papered over, have once again been opened up to natural light. The offices formerly located here have now been given over to a museum exhibit space and to a café and retail store.

The building suffered damage in the 1989 Loma Prieta earthquake. It was closed in 1995, and when it reopened in January 1999 it had been seismically reinforced using a new technique called base isolation. Three-foot-wide rubber and steel disks called base isolators were installed under each of the structure's 600 columns to absorb shocks from earthquakes. In addition, an underground four-foot-wide moat around the building allows it to move up to twenty-seven inches in any direction, further reducing the likelihood of damage. San Francisco's City Hall now holds the distinction of being the largest building in the world secured by a base isolation system.

---

*After viewing the interior, exit City Hall on the Van Ness Avenue side. From the steps here you will see two handsome buildings across Van Ness*

*Avenue. To the right is the Veterans Building and to the left is the Opera House.*

### ❸ War Memorial Veterans Building and Opera House (1932) – 401 Van Ness Avenue.

These two buildings have a tortured history spanning more than a two-decade period before they were finally built. After the 1906 earthquake destroyed most of the city's theaters and the Grand Opera House on Mission Street, support started growing for a new home for the Opera, preferably on city-owned land. But an unfavorable California Supreme court ruling in 1911 scotched the proposal to donate city land for the purpose. It was not until after World War I when a veterans group started casting about for a permanent home, that the project finally gained some momentum.

Since a building supporting a veterans organization would be an easier sell for fundraising, the opera lovers joined forces with the veterans in 1920, inasmuch as neither could make a go of it alone. The veterans and music lovers did not mix well; the groups disagreed over the design of the building, its management, and the apportionment of the funds raised. The original site for their building was the southwest corner of Van Ness and Grove where Davies Symphony Hall stands now. But the fact that a single lot was considered too small, combined with the acrimony between the two groups, led the City to purchase the present two blocks of land. Each group could then have its own building. This wrangling lasted throughout the 1920s. Ironically the stock market crash of 1929 and the subsequent decline in wages and prices of materials speeded the project to conclusion—construction funds had previously been set aside, which allowed the project to be brought in on budget. The cornerstones were laid in 1931 and the buildings opened the following year. They harmonize with City Hall across the street so well because architect Arthur Brown Jr. had a hand in the design of all three.

The Veterans Building was home to the San Francisco Museum of Modern Art from 1935 to 1994; it occupied the third and fourth floors. The Performing Arts Library and Museum now occupies the fourth floor. Offices of various veterans organizations continue to occupy the first two floors. The Opera House had its premiere on October 15, 1932 with performance of Puccini's *Tosca* conducted by Gaetano

Merola. The glittering first night audience included the City's leading businessmen and socialites, among them A. P. Giannini, the Zellerbachs, and Mrs. Sigmund Stern. In 1945 the Opera House hosted the historic signing of the U. N. Charter. President Harry Truman signed on behalf of the United States. Both the Veterans Building and the Opera House are still city-owned.

---

*Walk to the corner of Van Ness Avenue and Grove Street for a look across the street at:*

---

### ❹ Louise M. Davies Symphony Hall (1980) – Van Ness Avenue and Grove Street – SW corner.

The block where Symphony Hall now stands was once the site of the home of Thomas C. Hayes, who settled here in the early 1850s. His Victorian house boasted a surrounding lawn studded with trees and fountains. Hayes died in 1868 and his house was demolished soon after. In early 1880 a grand Italianate edifice, St. Ignatius College and Church, opened here; it occupied the whole block. (They moved here from their original location on Market Street where the old Emporium building is today.) The main entrance was on Van Ness Avenue; the front steps led into the building between two twin landmark towers. The structure was destroyed by the 1906 earthquake and fire. St. Ignatius reestablished itself in the Lone Mountain area, and in 1930 changed to its current name of the University of San Francisco.

In 1924, after the High School of Commerce was built on the other side of Hayes Street (the building is now the headquarters of the San Francisco Unified School District), this block became the school's athletic field and remained so until 1952. Subsequently it became a parking lot. Symphony supporters started stirring in the 1960s. They initially coveted the Marshall Square lot in the Civic Center (where the New Main Library is now) but lost out to library boosters. In the late 1970s, after prodigious fund raising, with several million dollars pledged by Louise M. Davies, construction started. The hall opened in 1980 to general acclaim, although the acoustics initially needed some fine tuning. This contemporary building, with its wraparound glass promenades, blends nicely with its neighbor the Opera House without echoing its historical style.

*Walk one block east on Grove and cross Polk Street to the southwest corner of Civic Center Plaza. Catty-corner on this intersection is:*

## ❺ Department of Public Health Building (1932) – 101 Grove Street.

Part of the original 1912 plan for the Civic Center, this fine understated and often overlooked building, with its third-floor windows capped by alternating triangular pediments, and its rooftop classical balustrade, would not look out of place in Paris or Rome. It blends nicely with its neighbors City Hall and the Bill Graham Civic Auditorium and maintains the unity of the entire Civic Center design.

*Walk half a block farther east on Grove on the plaza's perimeter. The building across Grove Street is:*

## ❻ Bill Graham Civic Auditorium (1915) – Grove Street between Polk and Larkin streets.

Prior to the structure before you there stood here another large building—the Mechanics Pavilion. (The main entrance was on Larkin Street.) Erected in 1882, it was intended as the permanent home for a series of fairs sponsored by the Mechanics Institute, an organization

The Mechanics Pavilion, circa 1885.

still going strong today (its headquarters is at 57 Post Street). These fairs, designed to promote mechanical arts and crafts, had been held almost annually since the 1850s at various San Francisco locations. After a number of moves a large wooden hall was constructed here. It served not only its intended purpose but also functioned as a general interest meeting hall and sports arena. On April 18, 1906 it fulfilled its final function—serving as a hospital for San Franciscans injured in the earthquake and fire. As the flames approached and devastated this area the patients were hastily moved to the Presidio, and the building, like so many others, burned to the ground.

With the upcoming Panama Pacific International Exposition of 1915 coinciding with the planning for a new civic center, sponsors of the PPIE decided to make a gift to the City of a meeting hall and auditorium. In 1913 construction started on the Exposition Auditorium (you can see the lettering carved in the top center of the building between the two main flagpoles). It was finished in January 1915 just in time for the fair's opening in February, and was in fact the only Civic Center building open to the public at the time the fair ended in December.

The Civic Auditorium (as it has been popularly known for most of its existence) has hosted a wide variety of events, including concerts, trade shows, balls, circuses, and prize fights. Before Moscone Convention Center opened in 1981, it also hosted national conventions, including the 1920 Democratic National Convention.

**It was at the 1920 convention that a young, relatively unknown politician named Franklin Roosevelt was nominated for vice-president. FDR could walk then; this was before he was stricken with polio.**

The Exposition Auditorium's name was changed to the Bill Graham Civic Auditorium, after the rock impresario who was killed in a helicopter crash in 1991. Appropriately, the annual Bay Area Music Awards (the Bammies) are usually held here.

---

*Continue east to the southeast corner of Civic Center Plaza. Catty-corner is a two-story brick building:*

---

### ❼ Wells Fargo Bank (c.1908) – Grove and Larkin streets – SE corner.

While there is nothing historic about this building per se, what makes it noteworthy is its odd angle in relation to the corner. The reason for this is that the configuration for the old City Hall and its neighbors included a two-block long boulevard called City Hall Avenue, which paralleled Market Street and stretched from the intersection of Grove and Larkin streets to the intersection of McAllister and

Leavenworth. Since that City Hall's ruins were not removed until 1909 and the new Civic Center's plan was not set until 1912, businesses started to rebuild along the already established street lines. The new Civic Center moved City Hall a block farther west and erased City Hall Avenue, leaving this building and one other—at 83–91 McAllister—standing in odd juxtaposition to their neighbors.

### ❽ New Main Library (1996) – Larkin Street between Grove and Fulton streets.

The block where the new main library now stands, long known as Marshall Square (after James W. Marshall, the discoverer of gold in 1848), was a bone of contention for a long time in terms of what would ultimately get built there. In the Civic Center plan of 1912 this plot was reserved for the opera house. Mayor James Rolph, Jr. vetoed that idea however, in an apparent attempt to please some political supporters who opposed it.

The block lay vacant until 1941 when a small, one-story Streamline Moderne-style building was erected here. During World War II the building served as a USO for servicemen on leave. In the 1950s new court buildings were proposed for the site, but bond issues to fund them were defeated three times during that decade—which was a good thing, since unharmonious steel and glass boxes out of proportion with the rest of the Civic Center were planned for this lot.

Finally the library, which had outgrown its previous headquarters (right across Fulton Street from where it is now) and had long had its eye on Marshall Square, received its due when a 1988 bond measure passed, thus providing the necessary funding. The small Streamline Moderne building, which had served as various government offices over the previous few decades, was torn down and construction was started on the New Main Library in 1992. It opened in 1996, thus finally bringing to completion the grand plan for the Civic Center as envisioned in 1912. The building's main façade, with its silver stainless steel recessed columns and understated ornament, makes for a kind of postmodern updating of Classicism that blends well with its much older neighbors.

---

*Cross Larkin Street and go north one block to Fulton Street and then walk
half a block east for a look at the large monument in the middle of the street.*

---

**❾ Pioneer Monument** (1894) – **Fulton Street between Larkin
and Hyde streets.**

This oversize granite and bronze monument was a gift to the City
by pioneer James Lick, who when he died in 1876 left a bequest of
$100,000 for a monument that would depict California's early history.
It took almost 20 years before the bequest was honored—this rococo
monolith is the result. The female bronze statue with her shield and
spear and the bear atop the main column symbolize California. The
four other tableaux radiating out from the center depict other aspects
of California history. The most controversial of these is the one depict-
ing an Indian fallen at the feet of a Franciscan missionary and a
Spanish vaquero, the latter two emblematic of the groups that started
the devastation of the Native Americans and their culture. Sensitivity
to ethnic pride has changed since this monument was created, so in
1996 a plaque was added giving Native Americans their due.

The Pioneer Monument originally stood on the southeast corner
of Marshall Square near the intersection of Grove and Hyde streets.
When erected it sat in the middle of a traffic island on a thoroughfare
that was the main entrance to the pre-1906 City Hall from Market
Street. The 1,000-ton monument remained in place until 1993, when it
was moved here. It now sits just about where the center of the old City
Hall was. (Fulton Street between Hyde and Larkin did not exist at
that time.)

---

*Walk back to Larkin Street for a look at:*

---

**❿ Asian Art Museum – former Old Main Library** (1917)
**– Larkin Street between Fulton and McAllister.**

This classical edifice, designed by architect George Kelham and
probably modeled after the Detroit Public Library, which had opened
a few years previously, was the first permanent home of the San
Francisco Public Library. The library's origins go back to the late
1870s when a group of civic-minded citizens organized a free library
in a hall on Bush Street in downtown San Francisco. In 1888 the

library moved into a wing of City Hall (of which this was the site), and in 1893 moved again to a larger location within the same building. Most of the library's books were destroyed in the 1906 fire. It started afresh, and in 1917 moved into its new home. The Old Main Library reached capacity in the mid-1940s. The overcrowding was not alleviated until the New Main Library opened in 1996. (In 1985, workers digging in the basement of the Old Main discovered parts of a human skeleton, a legacy of the former Yerba Buena burial ground.)

After several years of remodeling and seismic upgrading the Old Main reopened in 2003 as the new home of the Asian Art Museum. Despite the incongruity of displaying Asian art in a building built as a library, the new forum provides the AAM with a larger and more open space in which to showcase its collection. The museum moved here from a wing it inhabited in the M. H. de Young Museum in Golden Gate Park, where it had been located since it first opened to the public in 1966. The core of the AAM's collection of 12,000 objects was donated by Avery Brundage, a Chicago millionaire. It comprises the finest collection of Asian art outside of Asia. The museum's official name today is the Chong-Moon Lee Center for Asian Art, after a local benefactor who provided funds for the conversion of the Old Main Library into this new home for the collection.

---

*From the intersection of Larkin and McAllister streets you can get a good look at:*

---

### ⓫ State of California—Earl Warren Building (1926) – McAllister Street between Larkin and Polk.

One of the four original Civic Center buildings, this one was the last completed. It was funded through a bond issue in 1914, and construction was supposed to start in 1917. But the U.S. entry into World War I that year cancelled the start date and more delays after the war ended pushed things back even further. So unlike City Hall, the Civic Auditorium, and the Library, which all opened in the mid-teens, the State Building wasn't completed until 1926.

The building suffered enough damage in the 1989 Loma Prieta earthquake that it had to be closed for almost ten years. It reopened in December 1998 after refurbishing and seismic upgrading. And it was renamed the Earl Warren Building after the late former governor of California and Chief Justice of the U.S. Supreme Court. It houses offices of state officials, including chambers of the California Supreme Court which meets here when in session in San Francisco.

Behind the Earl Warren Building is a new 14-story addition, the Hiram W. Johnson Office Building, completed in 1998. Named also for a former governor of California, it replaces a seven-story state office building that dated from 1958. Although not of an historical design and taller than the other buildings facing the plaza, it nicely complements the smaller Earl Warren Building. Even better, as seen from the Civic Center, it nicely blocks the view of the dark, unattractive Federal Building behind it on Golden Gate Avenue.

---

*Walk east along the south side of McAllister Street for almost two blocks for a look across the street at:*

---

**⑫  100 McAllister Street – McAllister Tower** (1930).

This relatively unknown tan brick tower has an intriguing and unusual history. In the 1920s several Methodist churches joined together with the aim of building a church in a downtown location. Because the costs of doing so were prohibitive they came up with the idea of combining it with a hotel. The idea was that the hotel would bring in revenues that would defray the costs of operating the church.

This 28-story tower, (originally designed by Miller and Pflueger and completed by Lewis Hobart), a combined church and apartment hotel, was the result. Called the William Taylor Hotel (after a gold rush-era street preacher) it opened in 1930 and billed itself as the tallest hotel in the West. Hotel rooms took up floors 5 to 14 while floors 15 through 26 were reserved for residents and longer term guests.

The William Taylor Hotel couldn't weather the Depression, however. It closed, and in 1936 it reopened as the Hotel Empire. To help make it pay, the new owners needed to put a bar on the premises. Because of "blue laws" at the time no bars were allowed within 200 feet of a church. Since there was a church on the ground floor the only way to go was up. Thus the Sky Room, San Francisco's first rooftop bar, with a 360-degree panoramic view, opened on the 24th floor. (It's commonly thought that the Top of the Mark was the first, but it didn't open until 1939.)

One former resident of the Hotel Empire was Sally Rand, the noted "fan dancer" and stripper whose "Nude Ranch" was one of the most popular attractions at the 1939–1940 Treasure Island World's Fair. She stayed in the hotel in 1939—very likely in one of the two penthouses above the Sky Room— at the start of her run at the fair.

In 1942, with the war on and with office space at a premium, the U.S. government took over the hotel and converted the rooms into offices. The Internal Revenue Service set up shop in the former church. IRS employees, mindful of their surroundings, would joke that visiting taxpayers had come "to get religion."

McAllister Tower.

Number 100 McAllister remained a government office building until the early 1960s, when the new Federal Building opened at 450 Golden Gate Avenue. In the 1970s Hastings College of Law bought it and in 1982 turned it into student housing, which it remains today. (It is not open to the public.)

As you face the building the triple doors with the Gothic arches to the left mark the entrance to the former church, which inside rose four stories high. You will be able to get a better look at the Sky Room from Seventh Street as you approach the last stop on this tour.

*A little farther east on the south side of McAllister Street is:*

### ⓭ 83–91 McAllister Street (1908).

Like the previously mentioned Wells Fargo Bank this building too with its odd angle to the street was erected on the line of the now disappeared City Hall Avenue, and marked its eastern end.

---

*Continue on McAllister to its end where it intersects with Jones Street.*

---

## ⑭ One Jones Street – Hibernia Bank Building (1892).

Designed by Beaux-Arts trained Albert Pissis (1852–1914), this was the first classical banking temple built in San Francisco. Grand but not grandiose, it's a steel-frame, granite-clad two-story-with-a-basement structure with a copper dome. It is a wonderful design for this corner—the building's symmetry and proportions hold one's eye. Architect Willis Polk called it the most beautiful building in San Francisco.

The Hibernia Bank was a local institution founded in 1859 by John Sullivan, an Irishman who made a fortune in San Francisco real estate. Targeted originally at Irish immigrants, it broadened its reach to all San Franciscans as the years passed and opened other branches around town. The One Jones Street office served as the bank's headquarters from the time it opened in 1892 until 1980. The Hibernia Bank was merged out of existence in 1982 after being purchased by a Hong Kong bank.

Closed since the mid-1980s, the building has been sadly neglected in recent years. San Francisco police operated a substation out of the basement in the 1990s but they moved out in 2000 as the premises lacked cells for prisoners and other amenities.

The neighborhood, on the edge of the Tenderloin, is rather scruffy so keep a close watch on your valuables.

---

*Walk around the corner to Market Street and go the half block to Seventh. Cross Market and head south on Seventh Street toward Mission Street to see the large white building on your left. If you look back at McAllister Tower from here you can more easily see the plate glass windows of the Sky Room on the 24$^{th}$ floor near the top.*

---

## ⑮ U.S. Court of Appeals Building (1905) – 95 Seventh Street.

The phrase "They just don't build them like that anymore" was never truer of any building in San Francisco than this one. The interior would do a Florentine Renaissance palazzo proud. It is one of the most lavishly furnished public buildings in the United States. Today it houses the federal Court of Appeals for the Ninth Circuit, which comprises the nine western states including Alaska and Hawaii.

The large lot it stands on was purchased by the federal government in 1891 for a little over a million dollars as the location for a combined office building and post office. The site was an odd choice—it was far from downtown and was not close to anything else of significance. Political pressure may have influenced the selection. Leland Stanford lobbied the Postmaster General to choose this site over several others under consideration; postal carriers would have to ride the adjacent Market and Mission streetcar lines, which were owned by Stanford.

Construction did not begin until 1898, and the building wasn't finished until August 1905. The solidly built structure survived the 1906 earthquake with only minor damage. The southwest corner sank a few feet; unbeknownst to the builders an old stream bed had once run down Mission Street. More miraculously the building also survived the fire. Postal workers inside, despite being ordered by troops to leave, refused to do so, and using water-soaked mail bags they managed to beat back the flames that had entered the north end of the building.

The building also fared well during the 1989 Loma Prieta earthquake, suffering little structural damage. The interior terra cotta ornamentation, however, was rendered so unsafe that the building had to be closed. After a major renovation, including seismic upgrading, the Court of Appeals Building reopened in January 1997—minus the post office.

The interior is what makes this building so special. On the main floor deeply veined white Carrara marble lines the hallways. Overhead a groin-vaulted ceiling is finished with rough-cut mosaic tiles. The upper floors, especially the courtrooms, are finished with various kinds of marble: Tennessee Imperial Pink, Vermont Verde, Black Belgian, Pacific Coast Salmon Pink, African red Numidian, and several Italian marbles including white Carrara and Siena yellow. These are complemented by a number of rare and exotic woods: white and dark Mexican mahogany, East Indian red mahogany, antique oak, and carved California redwood. The latter is noteworthy because redwood is difficult to carve; it splinters easily. Several courtrooms also have colorful tile mosaics and walls inlaid with decorative designs of Venetian glass.

Why did the government go to such expense? It is partly explained by the fact this was America's imperial age. The U.S. was becoming a world power, and richly endowed federal buildings provided tangible evidence of that. But a more prosaic explanation can be found for this particular building: it seems that the original plans called for a five-story building, but when it was determined that the soil could not support such a structure the money that would have gone for the upper two floors was spent on decorating the interior instead.

The main floor of the Court of Appeals Building is open to the public weekdays during business hours.

# Thomas C. Hayes

## (1823–1868)

Born in Ireland in 1823, Tom Hayes emigrated with his family at age five to the U.S. They settled in upstate New York, but at age 18, lured by the attractions of a big city, Hayes moved to Manhattan. He was attracted to politics at an early age and was elected assessor while only in his early twenties. When gold fever swept the East Coast he, like so many other young men, booked passage to California. In mid-1849 he arrived in San Francisco and quickly resumed his passion for politics. He first served as an assistant alderman; subsequently he served two two-year terms as county clerk, starting in 1853.

Hayes, who served in a local militia, was described by a contemporary as "a tough, muscular Irishman"—and he had a taste for violence. He served as a second in several duels including the famous Broderick-Terry duel (he was a second to Terry; both men were pro-Southern and pro-slavery) and he engaged in a duel of his own. After John Nugent, editor of a local newspaper, accused Hayes of malfeasance in office, Hayes challenged him to a duel. On June 9, 1853 the two men met on vacant land next to the Sans Souci roadhouse, a tavern at Fulton and Divisadero streets described as "a favorite pleasure resort for 'bloods' and sporting men." The weapons chosen were rifles rather than the usual pistols. Hayes emerged from the contest unscathed but he shattered Nugent's left arm with one shot. The editor took over a year to recover and never regained full use of his arm.

**Thomas C. Hayes.**

After the Broderick-Terry duel in 1859, Hayes's political aspirations waned as the pro-union, anti-slavery forces became ascendant in San Francisco. Hayes had acquired a large tract of land—roughly the area bounded by Van Ness Avenue, Haight, Fillmore, and Fulton streets—and had built himself a home in the northeast corner of his tract (in the block where Davies Symphony Hall stands today). He retired there to devote himself to his real estate and to business. In 1861 he opened a resort at Hayes and Laguna streets called Hayes Park Pavilion. Open to the public, it put on variety shows and other entertainments. He even built a steam railroad that ran from Second and Market streets and out Hayes to Laguna to bring people in from downtown. The park did not last long however, since it was soon superseded in popularity by Woodward's Gardens in the Mission District, a much larger and more successful endeavor.

In 1868, after the passions stirred by the Civil War had cooled, Hayes reentered politics. He was elected a delegate to the Democratic National Convention in 1868, and took passage to New York via the Isthmus. He died at sea, apparently of natural causes, on the way. His body was offloaded at Panama. Due to legal wrangles it was not returned to San Francisco until 1870, where he was buried after being eulogized in a public ceremony by the mayor and other city officials.

Both Hayes Street and Hayes Valley—once part of his land holdings—are named for pioneer Thomas C. Hayes.

# Cow Hollow / Union Street

**Length:** 1.8 miles / 2.9 kilometers.
**Time:** 1½ hours.
**Walk Rating:** Easy.
**Hills:** The last block of the tour, up Pierce Street to see the Casebolt House, is a mild uphill.
**Public Transit:** Muni bus lines 41 (peak hours only) and 45 run the length of Union Street in both directions. The 47 and 49 lines traverse Van Ness Avenue, one block from the Franklin Street start of this tour.
**Parking:** There is a parking lot on Union Street between Octavia and Laguna streets. Street parking can be tight in this neighborhood, but the metered spaces along the commercial strips of Union and Fillmore streets create turnover.
**Restrooms:** There are no public restrooms, but commercial establishments abound along the route of this tour.

Cow Hollow, now one of the most desirable residential districts in San Francisco, was once one of its least attractive locations. At the time of the founding of Yerba Buena in 1835 the area was mostly a sandy waste with a few fresh water springs but little vegetation. The ragged shoreline, located north of where Lombard Street is today, was unsuitable for ship anchorage.

The first person to take an interest in Cow Hollow was Benito Diaz, a resident of Yerba Buena. He was given a land grant to the area in 1845 after petitioning the Mexican governor, but the following year, probably in response to the American takeover, he sold it to Thomas O. Larkin (for whom Larkin Street is named.) Larkin, a bit of a visionary, thought that the section, located as it was right on the bay near the Golden Gate, would make a fine little town separate from Yerba Buena. With the transition to American rule however, land titles to much of San Francisco became clouded. Larkin sold the property to a colleague, but in 1855 the courts ruled that Diaz's original claim was invalid. Larkin's dream town never materialized; in the meantime, squatters had settled in on certain parcels.

Two of Cow Hollow's most distinctive features for many years were the trail that led to the Presidio from Yerba Buena cove, (the path widened into the Presidio Road and ran for most of its length be-

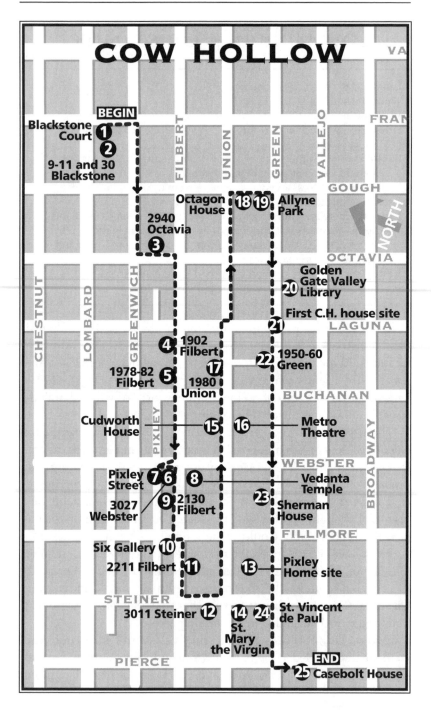

# COW HOLLOW

**BEGIN**

Blackstone Court **①**
**②**
9-11 and 30 Blackstone

2940 Octavia **③**

Octagon House   **18 19** Allyne Park

Golden Gate Valley **20** Library

First C.H. house site **21**

**④** 1902 Filbert   1950-60 **22** Green

1978-82 Filbert **⑤**   **17** 1980 Union

Cudworth House   **15** **16** Metro Theatre

Pixley Street **7 6**   **8** Vedanta Temple
3027 Webster   **9** 2130 Filbert   **23** Sherman House

Six Gallery **10**
2211 Filbert **11**   **13** Pixley Home site

3011 Steiner **12**   **14 24** St. Vincent de Paul
St. Mary the Virgin

**END**
**25** Casebolt House

# COW HOLLOW

**❶** Blackstone Court

**❷** 9-11 and 30 Blackstone Court

**❸** 2940 Octavia Street

**❹** 1902 Filbert Street

**❺** 1978-82 Filbert Street

**❻** 3027 Webster Street

**❼** Pixley Street

**❽** 2963 Webster Street - Vedanta Temple

**❾** 2130 Filbert Street

**❿** 3119 Fillmore Street - Location of the Six Gallery

**⓫** 2211 Filbert Street

**⓬** 3011 Steiner Street

**⓭** Site of Frank Pixley Home

**⓮** Episcopal Church of St. Mary the Virgin

**⓯** 2040 Union Street - Cudworth House

**⓰** 2055 Union Street - Metro Theatre

**⓱** 1980 Union Street

**⓲** Octagon House

**⓳** Allyne Park

**⓴** 1801 Green Street - Golden Gate Valley Library

**㉑** Site of the first house in Cow Hollow

**㉒** 1950-60 Green Street

**㉓** 2160 Green Street - Sherman House

**㉔** St. Vincent de Paul Roman Catholic Church

**㉕** 2727 Pierce Street - Casebolt House

tween Union and Filbert streets), and Washerwoman's Lagoon, a large lake fed by freshwater springs. It sat in the area now bounded by Franklin, Lombard, Octavia, and Filbert streets.

The lagoon, which had first been sighted by the Spanish in 1776—Juan Bautista de Anza camped on its shore on March 28th that year—was a large amoeba-shaped pond that quickly found popularity as a laundry facility. Initially Indian and Mexican women set up amateur operations, but they were soon joined by burly red-shirted washmen who brought in three-legged iron kettles for boiling shirts, and who could be seen vigorously scrubbing clothes on their washboards at the water's edge. Washerwoman's Lagoon functioned well for awhile due to a creek at the Lombard side that drained effluent out to the salt marshes by the bay. But eventually pollution took its toll, so in the early 1880s the authorities used convict labor to fill in the lagoon. The chain-gang prisoners would fill their carts with sand, toss their leg balls in on top, and off they would go on their successive trips.

The name Cow Hollow was derived from what quickly became the primary occupation of the district—dairy farming. The first dairy set up shop in 1853. By the late 1860s there were 23 dairies in Cow Hollow ranging in size from those that had only a handful of cows to several that had up to 300. Activity peaked about 1880 when a total of 38 dairies dotted the region.

The area was actually unsuited to grazing, inasmuch as there was not much grass or other forage. The cows were mainly kept in corrals or pens and were fed hay and "distillery slop," which was residue from the mashed and heated grains, hops, and barley used in the making of whiskey and beer at nearby distilleries. Increasingly unsanitary conditions and diseased cows led to calls for action, so starting in 1889 city health officials led a crusade to close down the dairies. By 1897 only three were left. Dairy farming moved to sparsely settled areas in Marin, Alameda, and San Mateo counties.

The removal of the dairies in the 1890s, combined with streets being graded and paved, finally opened Cow Hollow to residential development on a broader scale, eventually turning it into one of the City's choicest neighborhoods.

*Start this walk at the entrance to Blackstone Court, on the west side of Franklin between Lombard and Greenwich streets.*

**❶ Blackstone Court** (c.1847).

This short, dead-end alley, which veers off from Franklin Street at about a 30-degree angle, is said to have been part of an old trail dating back to before the gold rush. Its roots could go back perhaps to as early as the 1830s when trails leading from Yerba Buena to the Presidio military reservation to the west passed this way. The prime attraction in this vicinity was Washerwoman's Lagoon, which was located just to the west of here. Dwellings started to go up in the area to take advantage of the lagoon's abundant fresh water.

To provide some order for the growing community, someone, perhaps City Surveyor Jasper O'Farrell, starting in 1847 laid out a 43-acre tract comprising 24 100-vara lots to the east and southeast of the lagoon. In an interesting twist, this grid was positioned at a diagonal to the main north-south, east-west grid north of Market Street that Jasper O'Farrell had just completed for downtown San Francisco. If this was done to align this plan with Market Street and the 100-vara lots south of that artery, then the surveyor's aim was off, since the base line of this grid varied a few degrees from Market Street. What seems more likely is that the surveyor set his survey to align with the shoreline, which in this area was then just a stone's throw away and ran in a fairly straight line at an angle to the northeast—just as this grid did.

In any event, although new dwellings here after 1847 were aligned on the "Lagoon Survey" grid, no streets were named or carved through the shifting sands that made up the region. Maps from the 1850s to the early 1900s show, not surprisingly, a changing scene. The location that became Blackstone Court was originally sandwiched in between a small pond to the east and the much larger Washerwoman's Lagoon, whose eastern shore was one block to the west. Interestingly, the Coast Survey Map of 1852 shows Blackstone Court right on a line with one of the Lagoon Survey's grid lines. And an 1869 map shows a trail right about here, one that connected to another trail just to the west that looped around the north end of Washerwoman's Lagoon.

The Lagoon Survey plan disappeared when the dominant grid of Jasper O'Farrell's downtown moved west as the city expanded in this direction. Starting in 1889, dwellings were moved out of the way, their property owners compensated, and Franklin, Gough, Greenwich, Filbert, and neighboring streets were cut through and graded. Only Blackstone Court remains as a last vestige of the Lagoon Survey and perhaps of a circa 1860s trail as well.

---

*Walk down Blackstone Court. The public street portion of Blackstone Court ends at the metal gate. Beyond this is private property, so please do not go beyond the gate and trespass. You can see the two buildings to be discussed next from here:*

---

**❷ 11 Blackstone Court** (c.1850s and later) **and 30 Blackstone Court** (1885).

Blackstone Court was named for Nathaniel Blackstone, a commission merchant who was a member of the Vigilance Committee of 1856. He settled here in 1853 and built a house about where the vacant lot you see behind the motel is now. It was later numbered 7 Blackstone Court, and was only torn down in the late 1930s or early 1940s.

The two-story dwelling with the porches next to the lot is 11 Blackstone Court. Originally a circa 1850s single-story cottage whose veranda had Tudor arches with Gothic Revival wood supports, it was moved to this location by 1893 — probably from somewhere close by. Between then and 1899 the building was jacked up and a new first floor was inserted underneath. The property was owned by Cherubino Favilla, a furniture store proprietor, who lived here with his family from at least 1897 to 1904. Favilla's descendants continued to own it until 1970. Sometime in the early 1960s the veranda was stripped of its Victorian decoration and the wood supports were replaced with metal. Subsequently the siding was changed and new windows were installed. In sum, very little remains of the original cottage.

Past the fence, in the back of the lot beyond the garage and just partially visible, is 30 Blackstone Court. A single-story dwelling with shingle siding and a gable roof, it was built in 1885 by Charles Abraham, a nurseryman. At his Western Nursery he grew and imported rare plants from all over the world — including the first bougainvilleas brought to California — and shared them with others, including the gardeners at Golden Gate Park. Plants thrived in this area due to the lake-enriched soil.

Abraham once owned most of the block; surrounding his home was a windmill, a water tower, and five greenhouses. He died in 1929 but his niece and heir, Anna Hechinger, continued on until 1947 when she closed the operation and sold most of the property to developers. Abraham's house was then moved from its Greenwich Street frontage, turned 90 degrees, and positioned where it stands today. A final few remnants of Abraham's nursery can be seen peeking up above the fence on the south side of the alley where some fruit-bearing and other trees remain.

---

*Return to Franklin Street and turn right. At the next block, Greenwich, cross the street, turn right and go two blocks down to Octavia. (As you reach the intersection of Greenwich and Gough on the way you will be standing right about in the center of what was Washerwoman's Lagoon.) At Octavia turn left. A few doors up on the left is:*

---

❸ **2940 Octavia Street** (1870).

There are a couple of more farm houses associated with dairymen on this tour, but according to architectural historian William Kostura this fine Italianate single-story dwelling is "the last known architecturally intact dairy farm house in all of Cow Hollow." It was erected in 1870 as the homestead of a small dairy operation that Frenchman Thomas Bareilles started on the southeast corner of Octavia and Greenwich streets. The dairy ceased operation in 1882.

---

*Continue up Octavia to Filbert and turn right. Go west on Filbert to Laguna Street and cross over. The second structure on the right is:*

---

❹ **1902 Filbert Street** (c.1857).

This modest two-story structure, recently a bed-and-breakfast, has long had a reputation as having been a roadhouse that dates from the 1850s and that fronted the old Presidio Road, which in the 19th century passed by just across the street. The building well may date from the 1850s but it did not stand at this location until the 1890s. The Sanborn fire insurance map (The Sanborn Company did detailed

maps of major U.S. cities showing buildings for fire insurance purposes) of 1893 shows this lot—and it was the only such one on this
block—as vacant. The 1899 Sanborn map does show a structure here
that fits this building's description, so it must have been moved here
from somewhere else.

---

*Continue west on Filbert to:*

---

**❺  1978, 1980, 1982 Filbert Street** (1878).

This charming and unusual three-unit ensemble was built in 1878
by a Swiss immigrant who managed a local dairy. Since the man, a Mr.
Hancke or Huneke, was a carpenter and woodworker he might have
built these himself.

---

*Continue west on Filbert to Webster Street. Cross Webster and walk down
the half a block to the corner of Pixley. On the southwest corner is:*

---

**❻  3027 Webster Street** (c.1880).

This unusual Cape-Cod style house of uncertain date might have
once been a stable and may have been moved here from Vallejo Street.
It was allegedly lived in by two spinsters who kept a few cows on the
other side of Pixley Street. Seeming to support this notion, in 1946 a
new owner of the property found a cowbell while digging in the
garden. The subtly curved bargeboard on the gable, which gives the
illusion that the roof is curved, was an ornament added in the early
20th century.

**❼  Pixley Street** (c.1860s).

This three-block-long alley is named for Frank M. Pixley (see
biography) a 19th century politician and founder and editor of the
literary newspaper *The Argonaut*. The official City map of 1869 shows
Pixley Street—as yet unnamed—as a six-block-long alley extending
from its present western end at Steiner Street down to Gough. Since
Gough Street at that point was still under the water of Washerwoman's Lagoon it may well be that the alley was then not much
more than a line on a map, at least in its eastern two or three blocks.

The name Pixley for this street shows up on maps at least by the 1880s, while Pixley was still alive. Since records show that the influential Pixley and his wife separately owned lots on both sides of the alley at one time, perhaps Pixley was able to have the street named for himself.

---

*Retrace your steps back to Filbert Street. On the southwest corner of Filbert and Webster is:*

---

### ❽ 2963 Webster Street – The Vedanta Temple (1905, 1908).

The cusped mughal arches on the arcaded third floor and the five unusual domes that form the roof make this one of the most idiosyncratic and unusual buildings in San Francisco. Originally a two-story building erected in 1905, the top floor and roof were added in 1908. Said to be the first Hindu temple in the United States, it is owned by the Vedanta Society of Northern California. Vedanta (the word itself is taken from two Sanskrit words meaning "the end of knowledge"—or put another way, the discovery of the ultimate absolute truth) is an ancient Hindu philosophy/religion that through its teachings seeks to develop a higher state of consciousness.

The Vedanta Temple, circa 1910.

Vedanta's creed that all religions are merely

different paths to the same goal is supposedly reflected in the exotic domes on the roof. The five domes allegedly represent various religions, although heavily weighted toward Indian ones: the crenellated tower on the Webster Street side symbolizes Christianity, while the other four are patterned after various temples in India, including the Taj Mahal. (The dome farthest down Filbert Street is a miniature version of the Taj's.) The domes are hollow, and in the early days served as miniature temples where offerings were made.

If you cross over the street at this point, at the doorway on the Filbert Street side you will see some green Sanskrit lettering embedded in the white tile over the door. It reads: "Salutations to Lord Ramakrishna." Ramakrishna was the Indian swami or holy man whose disciples founded this order. At the temple's dedication on January 6, 1906 the local temple spokesman, in order to play down any cult-like aspect to that statement and to make it more palatable to western ears, told the *Chronicle* reporter covering the event—who dutifully reported it in his story the next day—that what it said was "May the Absolute Bless All."

When the new Vedanta temple opened at Vallejo and Fillmore streets in 1959, many of this temple's functions were shifted there. Today this building is dark much of the time, but is used occasionally for lectures, Sunday school classes, and for memorial services. A few men live here on a monastic basis.

---

*A few doors down Filbert Street on the north side is:*

---

### ❾ 2130 Filbert Street (c.1850s?).

The previously mentioned 1902 Filbert Street may not have been a roadhouse fronting the old Presidio Road in the 19th century, but this intriguing structure may well have been. The U.S. Coast Survey map of 1857 and a similar one of 1869 both show several dwellings in this area, and were even on this spot, as far as can be determined. The simple vernacular architecture of this structure with its shingle siding, French doors, and veranda point to an early date. Verandas rarely appeared on San Francisco dwellings after the 1850s, and 2130 once had two of them. A photo taken from the roof of the Vedanta temple around 1910 shows that this building then had a veranda on the smaller top floor as well.

When the present owner purchased this property he was told that it "had been a carriage house for Ghirardelli." That's difficult to verify at this point, but the ground floor certainly has the looks of a stable. Sanborn maps, which first covered this area starting in 1893, show that a one-and-a-half story dwelling with at least one veranda stood here, slightly back from the present front lot line. A stable stood in the rear along the Pixley Street frontage. Sometime between 1905 and 1913 the stable disappeared and this building changed to a three-story structure. It would not be a stretch to conclude that the building was jacked up and that the stable was inserted underneath as a ground floor.

---

*Continue west on Filbert on the north side of the street. Cross over Fillmore and walk down three doors to:*

---

### ❿ 3119 Fillmore Street – Location of the Six Gallery
(1955–1959).

This long and narrow store, which has long been a retail emporium, was, in the 1950s, a cooperative art gallery that showcased the works of students at the San Francisco Art Institute. On Friday evening October 7, 1955 it was taken over by a bunch of local poets who came to read their work to their fellow poets and an audience of about 75 interested spectators.

The evening turned out to be a signal event in 20th century American literature since it kicked off the public debut of the Beat movement (see the North Beach walk for more on the Beats). Among the poets reading from their work that night was Allen Ginsburg (1926–1997) who gave the first public reading of his as yet unfinished and soon-to-be landmark poem *Howl*. He was probably nervous and since he was fueled by red wine, he started out a little drunk but sobered up as he got further into it. He no doubt started to feel the power of his work as he was egged on by the response of the crowd and by cheerleader-of-sorts Jack Kerouac who chanted "Go, go" in response to the intense emotion that *Howl* generated.

A few days afterward local poet and publisher Lawrence

Ferlinghetti sent Ginsburg a telegram echoing Ralph Waldo Emerson after he had read Walt Whitman's *Leaves of Grass*: "I greet you at the beginning of a great career." And he added this postscript: "When do I get the manuscript?" Ferlinghetti published *Howl*, of course, and it remains a bestseller at Ferlinghetti's bookshop, City Lights, in North Beach.

---

*Return to Filbert Street. Cross over to the south side of the street and walk down a few doors to:*

---

**⓫ 2221 Filbert Street** (1895).

This small structure was once a stable and barn. Note the old hay-loft door above, and the projecting beam that was used for winching hay into the loft.

---

*Continue down to Steiner Street and take a left. Go up most of the block toward Union Street. Across Steiner, the two-story building next to the corner is:*

---

**⓬ 3011 Steiner Street** (c.1880).

Like 2130 Filbert, this structure appears to have been jacked up and had a stable inserted underneath. The top floor was a single-story building that originally stood right next door, on the corner. It housed a saloon, whose entrance no doubt was what is now the tall window in the middle.

---

*Continue up to the corner of Steiner and Union streets.*

---

**⓭ Block bounded by Union, Steiner, Green, and Fillmore streets – Site of the Frank Pixley Mansion** (c.1856-1898).

Frank Pixley, *The Argonaut* founder and editor, was always a non-conformist and chose to live in unfashionable Cow Hollow instead of closer to downtown like most of his contemporaries. He eventually owned real estate all over the neighborhood, but for his own home he purchased this block and in the mid-1850s erected a large house here in the midst of a grove of trees. The entrance to the property was a path that led from the southwest corner of Union and Fillmore through the woods to the house. Pixley lived there until his death in 1895. His wife, Amelia, survived him by three years. In her will she specified that the house be burned. By 1905 the Pixley heirs had sold off almost the entire block, and it was subdivided into the lots that exist today.

*On the southwest corner of Union and Steiner streets is:*

### ⓮ 2325 Union Street – Episcopal Church of St. Mary the Virgin (1891).

Another Pixley-owned property was the 50-vara lot on the southwest corner of Union and Steiner. Pixley was "an agnostic with a touch of atheism," but he admired the courage of the Reverend William Bolton in approaching him for a donation, and gave Bolton part of the lot as a site for a church. This chapel, built of redwood and pine and covered with dark shingles, was erected in 1891. Planted in a garden and surrounded by a rustic wooden fence, it resembles an English country church (Bolton had emigrated from England just two years previously).

The church's spare interior resembles a New England meeting house. A plaque on the north wall near the door is dedicated to Frank Pixley and states that his ashes are interred within its walls (although another account says his cremated remains were buried at Laurel Hill cemetery). A fountain in the courtyard off the Union Street entrance is actually the last remaining uncapped spring in Cow Hollow. It drains into the city sewer system.

*Stay on the north side of Union and walk east two and a half blocks. Stop in front of:*

### ⓯ 2040 Union Street – the Cudworth House (1874).

This handsome two-story Italianate with a front yard was once the home of James W. Cudworth and his family. Cudworth, a native of Vermont and a forty-niner, settled in Cow Hollow, where in the 1850s and '60s he operated a dairy on the old Presidio Road from which he sold milk to the army garrison at the Presidio. In the 1870s he

The Cudworth House, circa 1875.

switched to the more lucrative field of real estate. Until 1897, the year before he died, he built at least 15 homes in Cow Hollow, including his own here at 2040 Union Street. A photo of the house taken not long after its completion shows that the triple bay window next to the front door and the second-story slanted bay windows both in front and around on the east side were later additions.

The alley on the west side of the house leads to the property's barn. A hole in the northeast corner is where hay was thrown down to the horses. Note the rope and pulley suspended from the projecting beam on the upper floor. A coachman slept up there as well.

The Cudworth house, now divided into shops and businesses, is right in the heart of the upscale Union Street shopping district. The transformation of Union Street from chiefly residential to a thoroughfare chock-a-block with chic boutiques with pricey merchandise started in the 1950s.

---

*Across the street is:*

---

### ⑯ 2055 Union Street – the Metro Theater (1924).

The Metro movie theater opened here in 1924 during the golden age of movie palaces. It was designed by James and Merritt Reid, whose signature work in San Francisco is the Fairmont Hotel on Nob

Hill. The theater's current look however, dates from 1941 when it was revamped by architect Timothy Pflueger. Pflueger was no doubt chosen because of earlier movie theaters he had designed such as the Castro Theater in Eureka Valley and the Paramount in Oakland. The blade sign and the marquee date from the Pflueger remodel. In 1998 the Metro's interior also was restored to its 1941 look.

The land where the Metro sits—and in fact most of the frontage on Union in this block—was owned by James Cudworth, and by his heirs after he died. They sold much of it over the years but did not dispose of the last parcel—just down from the Metro Theater on the southwest corner of Union and Buchanan—until the late 1960s. The three-story brick building there now was erected on the former Cudworth plot in 1970.

---

*Continue east one block on Union past Buchanan to:*

---

### ⑰ 1980 Union Street (c.1880).

These units with the double-peaked roofs topped by pinnacles and sharing a common porch were also built by James Cudworth. They are sometimes known as the "twin wedding houses" because they were allegedly purchased by a father as a wedding present for his twin daughters.

---

*Go east on Union for another two and half blocks to Gough Street. Cross over Union to the southwest corner of Union and Gough. The building just up Gough Street from the corner garden is:*

---

### ⑱ 2645 Gough Street – the Octagon House (1861).

The Octagon House owes its existence to a New Yorker named Orson Fowler, who in the mid-19th century spread the gospel that eight-sided houses were not only cheaper to build and were more energy efficient, but they also provided for a healthier environment since they admitted more air and light into the interior. All the rage in the 1850s and '60s, close to 700 octagon houses were built throughout the U.S. Only two remain in San Francisco (the other is on the Russian Hill walk).

**The Octagon House.**

This octagon house was built in 1861 by William C. McElroy, who worked as a boilermaker, miller, and nurseryman. During the house's restoration in the 1950s a tin-box time capsule was discovered. It contained a letter from McElroy detailing his life, and events such as the Civil War and the growth of San Francisco.

The house originally stood across Gough Street on the southeast corner of Gough and Union. From 1852 to 1859 this land was owned by Charles Gough, a milkman who later served on the commission that named streets in the Western Addition. Nearly a century later, after the Pacific Gas & Electric Company acquired the property, they offered it for sale for $1.00 to whomever would move it. In 1951 the National Society of Colonial Dames of America purchased it, and moved it here the following year. Since the Colonial Dames area of interest is furniture and decorative arts of the Colonial and Federal periods (i.e., from the 18th and 19th centuries) the house is furnished with a Chippendale mahogany sofa, a Hepplewhite sideboard, and other such pieces. Also on display here are signatures on documents of various kinds by all but two of the signers of the Declaration of Independence. All of the famous names are here—Thomas Jefferson, Benjamin Franklin, John Hancock—as well as a host of lesser ones.

**Charles Gough named Gough Street after himself and Octavia Street after his sister.**

The Octagon House is open to the public about three or four days a month. Call (415) 441-7512 for information.

---

*Continue up Gough Street to the corner of Green Street.*

---

## ⓳ Gough and Green streets – NW corner – Allyne Park (1950s).

Surrounded by a wooden fence, this tree-shaded park with a sloping green lawn was once the site of the home of Lucy and Edith Allyne, members of the Colonial Dames, who donated the north half of their property to the Octagon House. After the Allyne sisters died they willed their remaining half to the City, which turned the land into this charming park.

---

*Go west on Green Street one block to Octavia. On the southwest corner of Green and Octavia is:*

---

**② 1801 Green Street – Golden Gate Valley Library** (1917).

Part of a network of neighborhood branch libraries built in the early 20th century with money donated by financier and philanthropist Andrew Carnegie, the Golden Gate Valley branch (Spring Valley and then Golden Gate Valley were the original names for Cow Hollow) was designed by architect Ernest Coxhead (1863–1933). He modeled this U-shaped structure clad with glazed terra cotta after a Roman basilica.

Coxhead, a native of England, was a classically trained architect who was a member of the Royal Institute of British Architects. After spending a few years in southern California he settled in San Francisco in 1889, where he spent the rest of his career designing both commercial and residential buildings. He did a number of fine homes in western Pacific Heights including his own, which still stands six blocks away at 2421 Green Street.

---

*Walk west on Green one block to Laguna Street.*

---

**② Intersection of Green and Laguna – Site of the First House in Cow Hollow** (1847).

The intersection of Green and Laguna—just off the southwest corner actually, according to an early map—is the site of the Elijah Ward Pell house, the first dwelling in Cow Hollow. Pell had come to San Francisco in 1846 on the ship *Brooklyn* as part of Samuel Brannan's Mormon contingent. He was excommunicated for "licentious behavior" during the voyage, which perhaps explains why he settled here far away from the other Mormons clustered at Yerba Buena. Pell bought a 100-square-yard lot here from Thomas Larkin in 1847, where he established a home and a fenced-in garden. It was not until the early 1850s that Pell had any neighbors.

*Go down a half a block on the south side of Green Street to:*

**㉒  1950, 1958, 1960 Green Street** (c.1875).

These three row house apartments were built in the mid-1870s by Isaac Hecht, a German immigrant shoemaker who had originally settled in Baltimore before coming to San Francisco. He most likely built these as income-producing rental units. Noteworthy about this single three-story structure is that it has been turned around. The Green Street façade was originally the back of the building. The front, with the characteristic Italianate slanted bay windows, now faces toward Union Street.

*Continue west two blocks on Green Street to:*

**㉓  2160 Green Street – the Sherman House** (1876, 1901).

Leander S. Sherman (1847–1926) came to San Francisco from Boston as a 14-year old in 1861. After stints as a street sweeper and clock repairer he got a job as a clerk in a music store. He saved his money and bought out his employer—the business eventually becoming Sherman and Clay, purveyor of pianos, organs, and other musical instruments, with showrooms in a number of western U.S. cities. In 1876 he built this sprawling Italianate/French Second Empire-style mansion with a box-like mansard roof third floor. In 1901 he hired as architects the Reid Brothers to add a three-story recital hall at the west end of the house.

A supporter of the symphony and the opera, Sherman frequently hosted leading singers, musicians, and performers during their visits to San Francisco. Enrico Caruso, Lotta Crabtree, Luisa Tetrazzini, and Jan Paderewski are a few of the notables who entertained or were entertained here.

In the 1930s, a few years after Sherman's death, the house was turned into an elegant restaurant. Two decades later it became a ballet school. In 1972 it was almost torn down—a demolition permit had been applied for—since the then owner, sculptor Barbara Herbert, was finding the house too expensive to maintain. Fortunately, delays and a landmark designation, which places restrictions on what an owner can do with a property, saved it. A luxury hotel in the 1980s and '90s, the Sherman House is once again a single-family home.

---

*Go a block and a half farther west on Green Street to Steiner. On the north-west corner of Green and Steiner is:*

---

**❷❹ 2320 Green Street – St. Vincent de Paul Roman Catholic Church** (1916).

The striking feature of this church is its dramatic architecture. With its soaring tower, bracketed gambrel roof, and forceful wooden detailing, it looks like a lodge in the Swiss Alps. That is probably what inspired it. Father Ryan, the resident priest at the time, returned from a trip to Switzerland shortly before commissioning architect Frank Shea to carry out the design. Shea did a number of other churches for the Catholic Archdiocese, but none of them looked like this.

---

*Continue west on Green to Pierce Street. Cross over to the southeast corner of the intersection and head up Pierce a half a block. Stop in front of:*

---

**❷❺ 2727 Pierce Street – the Casebolt Mansion** (1866).

This grand Italianate villa, set back from the street, was built in 1866 by Henry Casebolt, a Virginia blacksmith who had come to San Francisco 15 years earlier with his wife and 11 children. He soon expanded his blacksmithing skills into a carriage-making business. He prospered, and in 1865 built a horsecar passenger line along Sutter Street that eventually extended from downtown out to Pacific Heights and Harbor View near the Presidio.

Casebolt invented the lever-operated grip used on cable cars, and the bobtail car—a coach designed especially for women passengers— complete with velvet sofas and carpets. But he is most known for his development of the "balloon car," a funny-looking horse-drawn car that resembled a carved out metallic football. Its big advantage was that it did not need a turntable to reverse direction. An operator merely removed the pin in the couple at the end of the line and moved the horse, not the car, around to the other end.

When Casebolt erected his mansion it sat alone in splendid isola-tion—this area was the country—and the one time blacksmith's house, sitting on a ridge as it does, looked like a feudal manor overlooking its lands. Indeed, two decades later, immediately across the street, Chinese laborers wearing their trademark conical hats could be seen toiling away in a large vegetable garden they had created on the still empty block.

# Frank M. Pixley

## (1825–1895)

Frank Pixley was a man who liked nothing better than a good fight. He was opinionated, outspoken, even quarrelsome. (Addressing a group of suffragettes he proclaimed that he preferred "a Florence Nightingale to a Susan B. Anthony.") During the Civil War, Pixley went back east to see the fighting first hand. Denied access to the battlefield by Secretary of War Edwin Stanton he pressed ahead anyway, meeting up with Ulysses S. Grant at Cold Harbor where the general-in-chief of the Union Army accompanied him to the front lines. A few years, later while traveling in Europe, Pixley holed up in Paris during its siege by the Germans during the Franco-Prussian War, becoming one of the few Americans to witness the action first hand.

Frank M. Pixley.

Pixley was a native of upstate New York, a forty-niner who, after a stint panning gold in the Sierra, came to San Francisco in 1851. A lawyer by trade, he served a term as City Attorney during 1851–52. He was a gifted orator with a lifelong interest in politics, and ran for office numerous times. He served a term in the California Assembly in 1858 and a few years later was elected attorney general on the ticket with Leland Stanford for governor. This elective office proved to be his last, since his abrasive attitude made him more enemies than friends. In later years he served in various appointed offices, such as park commissioner and as a regent of the University of California.

Pixley's lasting contribution was his founding of *The Argonaut,* a weekly magazine and literary journal that he began in 1877. It was published continuously until 1958, although the format changed over the years. Pixley had started his journalistic career as chief editorial writer for the *Chronicle* but his editorials were so inflammatory that he was fired. So he founded *The Argonaut*, in which his lead column, called Olla Podrida—appropriately named for a spicy stew, which his column was—allowed him to give vent to his feelings. Contrary to most newspapers of the day, Pixley went easy on the Southern Pacific Railroad—a company roundly hated because of its monopoly of transportation in the state—likely because of his friendship with Leland Stanford. But when Stanford was eased out of the SP's presidency by Collis P. Huntington, the editor went on the attack against Huntington and the railroad.

The early *Argonaut* was the *New Yorker* of its day, offering a mixture of essays, articles, reviews, and gossip. More importantly it was noted for its fine prose and poetry, featuring leading writers such as Bret Harte, Mark Twain, and Ina Coolbrith. Local novelist and author Gertrude Atherton was first published in its pages.

In the late 1880s Pixley's health started to fail and he had to give up his editorial duties to colleagues. Suffering from kidney problems, palsy, and perhaps dementia, he retreated to his Cow Hollow estate where he was looked after by his also ailing wife, Amelia. Pixley died on August 11, 1895 only two days after his niece, Fannie Morrison Weller, died of a self-administered overdose of morphine. After his death, Pixley's dark secret was revealed: his "niece" was in fact his illegitimate daughter.

Pixley Street, a three-block-long alley between Steiner and Buchanan streets just north of Filbert, is named for Frank Pixley.

# Embarcadero – The Old Waterfront

---

**Length:** 1.5 miles / 2.5 kilometers.
**Time:** 1½ hours.
**Walk Rating:** Easy.
**Hills:** None.
**Public Transit:** The Muni 42 bus line runs down Battery and up
Sansome streets. The F streetcar line runs along the Embarcadero.
**Parking:** Metered street parking is relatively easy to find on weekends,
and is free on Sunday to boot. There are several parking lots off Front
Street between Broadway and Union streets.
**Restrooms:** There is a coin-operated (25 cents) public toilet at the start
of the tour in the plaza across from the Ferry Building.

---

The Embarcadero of today, with its palm trees, light
rail system, and noontime strollers and joggers, is a far cry from
what it was in the 19$^{th}$ and much of the 20$^{th}$ centuries. It was a
noisier, smellier, dirtier place crawling with ship captains, sailors,
and longshoremen. Where you now see fine hotels and trendy restaurants once stood grimy waterfront saloons and transient sailors'
boardinghouses.

One of the more unsavory aspects of waterfront life in San Francisco from 1849 to about 1915 was shanghaiing (a term coined in San
Francisco about 1853)—the forced recruitment of sailors to serve on
ships departing the city. Being a sailor on a 19$^{th}$ century sailing ship
was nobody's idea of fun. It meant long hours of backbreaking work
for little pay in a cramped, sometimes foul and abusive environment
for months at a time at sea. Ship owners and ship captains needed live
bodies to perform the necessary shipboard tasks, and many were not
particular as to who were recruited or how they were recruited. On
shore, shanghaiers or crimps, as they were known, filled this need—
oftentimes by ruse or force. They frequently used drugged liquor
(beer and schnapps laced with opium was a favorite) to induce grog-
giness and render their victims pliable. At its peak the Embarcadero
was home to more than fifty sailors' saloons/boarding houses, many
of which were the targets of crimps.

Starting in 1849 the waterfront advanced rapidly into the bay from

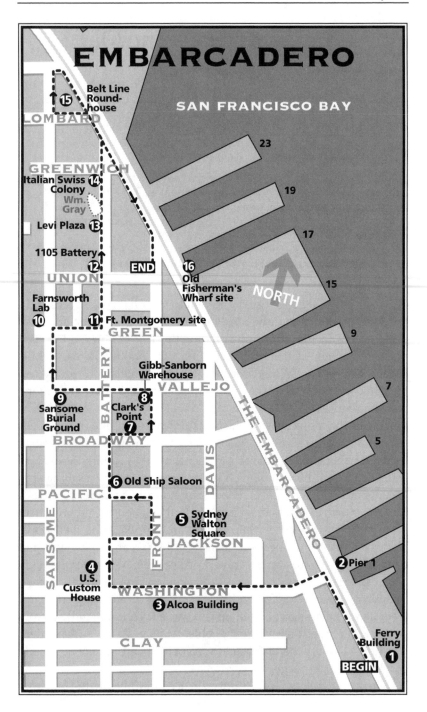

# EMBARCADERO

**SAN FRANCISCO BAY**

Belt Line Round-house ⑮

23

19

17

15

NORTH

9

7

5

⑭ Italian Swiss Colony
Wm. Gray

⑬ Levi Plaza

1105 Battery ⑫

END

⑯ Old Fisherman's Wharf site

Farnsworth Lab ⑩

⑪ Ft. Montgomery site

Gibb-Sanborn Warehouse

⑨ Sansome Burial Ground

⑧ Clark's Point ⑦

⑥ Old Ship Saloon

⑤ Sydney Walton Square

④ U.S. Custom House

③ Alcoa Building

② Pier 1

Ferry Building ①

**BEGIN**

LOMBARD
GREENWICH
UNION
GREEN
VALLEJO
BROADWAY
PACIFIC
JACKSON
WASHINGTON
CLAY
BATTERY
SANSOME
DAVIS
FRONT
THE EMBARCADERO

# EMBARCADERO

**1** **Ferry Building**

**2** **Pier 1**

**3** **One Maritime Plaza - Alcoa Building**

**4** **555 Battery Street - U.S. Custom House**

**5** **Sydney Walton Square**

**6** **298 Pacific Avenue - Old Ship Saloon**

**7** **Clark's Point**

**8** **855 Front Street - Gibb-Sanborn Warehouse**

**9** **Sansome Burial Ground**

**10** **200 Green Street - Farnsworth Lab**

**11** **100-120 Green Street - Site of Fort Montgomery**

**12** **1105 Battery Street**

**13** **Levi Plaza**

**14** **1265 Battery Street - Italian Swiss Colony**

**15** **Belt Line Roundhouse**

**16** **Embarcadero near Union Street - Site of Old Fisherman's Wharf**

the original Yerba Buena shoreline. A few decades later the new shoreline was a ragged jumble of piers that were nothing more than extensions of city streets ranging from the Telegraph Hill area to Market Street. To help stabilize the fill in Yerba Buena Cove and to better define the shoreline a seawall was constructed in 1868. But its zigzag pattern at the water's edge made connections between piers difficult and the resultant silting required constant dredging, making it impractical. Ten years later construction began near the present-day Fisherman's Wharf on the curving seawall that sits under the present Embarcadero. By 1902 it had reached the Ferry Building, and finally was completed in 1931 with the construction of the even numbered piers south of that terminal.

After more than a century of activity, San Francisco's once vibrant commercial waterfront started a decline from which it never recovered and which was hastened in the 1960s by the coming of containerization. There was a failure to modernize to accommodate the huge steel railroad car-size shipping containers that revolutionized the industry, and the bulk of the business moved to Oakland and the other west coast ports that had prepared for it. The port of San Francisco today still has commercial uses, but it is focusing more on leisure time activities and recreational use.

---

*Start this tour directly across from the Ferry Building on the sidewalk next to the southbound traffic lanes.*

---

### ❶ The Ferry Building (1898).

The Ferry Building is one of San Francisco's oldest and most notable landmarks. The present structure replaced a previous one on this same site, called the Ferry House, which was built in 1875. It was little more than a long, arcaded wooden shed with separate stalls where horse-drawn streetcars and later cable cars picked up and deposited passengers. Prior to its construction the main passenger landing spot had been the Davis Street Wharf between Broadway and Vallejo Street. But the move to the present location was a logical choice because it was the terminus for Market Street, the city's grand boulevard, and because major east-west downtown streets like California, Sacramento, and Clay led directly toward it.

The current building was designed by A. Page Brown (1859–1896) a talented young architect who had traveled in Europe and had trained with the noted New York architectural firm of McKim Mead & White. He had absorbed their penchant for classically inspired monumental architecture. Thus the long arcade, the repetitive arches (reminiscent of a Roman aqueduct), and the Corinthian columns mounted on pedestals on the façade, are all elements derived from Classical Rome. Brown modeled the tower after the Giralda bell tower of the cathedral in Seville, Spain.

The Ferry Building, circa 1900.

Only 34 when awarded the contract for the Ferry Building in September 1895, Brown was thrown from a horse while out riding less than a month later. Tragically, he never left the hospital and died in January 1896. His plans for the Ferry Building were largely complete at the time of his death, so it was left to another architect, Howard Swain, to finish up and supervise the actual construction.

The Ferry Building was dedicated in 1898 and became the showcase entrance to San Francisco. The structure survived 1906 because U.S. Navy and city fireboats under orders from General Frederick Funston, the military official leading rescue efforts, sprayed it with saltwater pumped from the bay. Saving the Ferry Building was considered vital because it offered an escape route from the burning city; it also preserved it as a gateway for supplies and relief being sent in. The quake did shake loose large chunks of the Colusa sandstone cladding from the tower. After the cleanup this was replaced by reinforced concrete.

For the better part of four decades the Ferry Building served as the City's transportation hub. But with the building of the Golden Gate and Bay bridges in the mid-1930s, ferry use started a steady

**At its peak in the 1930s, over 100,000 people a day—or almost 40 million people a year—passed through its portals, making it the second busiest transit depot in the world after London's Charing Cross Station.**

decline that terminated in 1958 when the last of the traditional ferries made its final run. In the 1970s sleek diesel-powered ferries commenced operation between Marin County and San Francisco. The Larkspur and Sausalito ferries dock directly behind the Ferry Building, thus maintaining a connection to its storied past.

At the beginning of the 21st century the ground floor of the Ferry Building was converted into an array of markets and retail shops, and the area in front of the Ferry Building was remodeled into an inviting plaza clustered with palm trees. It's a vast improvement over what had occupied this space before—the Embarcadero freeway, a two-deck traffic artery noted for its ugliness and the way it obscured the Ferry Building and effectively cut if off from Market Street and the rest of the city. The freeway, which had been erected in 1959, was severely damaged by the Loma Prieta earthquake of 1989. It was torn down in 1991, thus returning the open-air feeling to the Embarcadero and paving the way for the redesign and landscaping you see today.

Before proceeding to the next site, look at the tower one more time. An interesting thing about it is that it's not quite square with Market Street, as you might expect, it's at a slight angle. That's because the tower is aligned with the building whose arcade, in turn, is anchored to the seawall directly beneath it.

---

*Walk north along the sidewalk up to Washington Street. Cross over to the corner for a look across the Embarcadero at:*

---

❷ **Pier 1** (1931).

Pier 1 provides a good example of the changes that have occurred to the waterfront over the years. Constructed when the seawall reached this area around 1900 this pier served as a loading dock and transshipment point for refined sugar to other Bay Area locations. With its close proximity to the ferry terminal it also found use as an overflow anchorage for ferry boats. With the decline in maritime use of the port in the late 20th century it was converted to an automobile parking lot. In 2000 it was remodeled into offices for the Port of San Francisco, and an open-to-the-public pedestrian walkway surrounding the pier was added. The handsome Classical Revival bulkhead (the façade), a style typical of the piers north of the Ferry Building as you can see from its immediate neighbors Piers 3 and 5, was put on in 1931. These bulkheads give the Embarcadero a nice stylistic unity that stems from the influence of the City Beautiful movement.

*Walk up Washington Street the equivalent of four blocks to the corner of Battery Street. This section of Washington, from 1906 to the early 1960s, was part of the wholesale produce district before redevelopment led to the construction of the surrounding high rises. To your left is:*

### ❸ One Maritime Plaza – Alcoa Building (1964).

This dark, 25-story office building with the large X cross bracing is notable for two reasons. First, while many buildings in San Francisco are seismically reinforced, the cross bracing here, which performs that function, is on the outside of the building rather than inside. Second, this tower occupies and blocks off a street—Front Street.

*On the northwest corner of Washington and Battery streets is:*

### ❹ 555 Battery Street – U.S. Custom House (1911).

One of the most overlooked and underappreciated public buildings in San Francisco, this granite-faced custom house was constructed by the federal government between 1906 and 1911 (it took so long because in the wake of the 1906 disaster some building materials were in short supply.) It replaced a previous Greek Revival structure that dated from 1855 and that had been torn down just prior to 1906.

The government spared practically no expense: both the interior and the exterior are of the finest materials and reflect first rate workmanship. Some items on the façade worth noting are the lions' heads, which are carved from single blocks of granite, the oversize red brass lamps with their hand blown purple glass flanking the front door, and the ornate bronze bars covering the windows. The latter were not just decorative; large sums of money were kept here in the early days.

If you are taking this tour on a weekday during business hours take a look at the interior as well. The lobby and main floor are clad floor to ceiling in white Italian Carrara marble with insets in the floor of black Belgian marble. The office doors are all of solid oak. Also worth a look is the oblong Custom Hall on the second floor. The upper walls beneath the skylight are decorated with large hand-painted panoramas of San Francisco and the Panama Canal commemorating San Francisco's hosting of the 1915 fair. (If you want to see how things have changed in the way of federal government expenditures for their office buildings in the modern era, visit the Appraisers Building (1964)—directly behind the Custom House—and contrast its linoleum floors, metal desks, and naked neon lighting with this one.)

The Custom House is still used to appraise certain imported goods, but much of the foreign freight entering the country today is inspected at the airports or at dockside.

Across the street, on the northeast corner of Battery and Washington, is the site of the first Merchants Exchange Building (its successor stands now at California near Montgomery in the heart of the financial district). It was a classically grand three-story brick and stone structure with Corinthian columns and statuary. It was built in 1855 as was its neighbor across Battery Street, the first custom house. Both buildings were sources of pride to 1850s era San Franciscans who pointed to them as proof that a city whose streets were muddy and whose sidewalks mostly were still unplanked was on its way to becoming a grand metropolis.

---

*As you continue this walk by heading toward Jackson Street you will pass the entrance to the Golden Gateway Apartments (more on this in the next section) across Battery from the Custom House. At Jackson Street turn right, go one block to Front, and turn left. Across Front Street is:*

**The southeast corner of Battery and Jackson during the late 19th century was known as "Lime Juice Corner." It held ramshackle saloons frequented by British sailors, who were known as "limeys" because English ships carried lime juice on their voyages to combat scurvy.**

---

❺ **Sydney Walton Square (bounded by Front, Pacific, Davis, and Jackson streets).**

In the 1860s and 70s this neighborhood was the waterfront section of the Barbary Coast and was a mean, violent part of town, especially after dark. Two of the more notorious saloon/boarding houses noted for shanghaiing were located here. At 33 Pacific Street, on the other side of Sydney Walton Square just past Davis Street, stood Shanghai Kelly's saloon. Kelly, a stocky, red-haired, hot-tempered Irishman, was one of the most ingenious and feared crimps on the waterfront. He lured men to his establishment by offering free women and booze and then he and his thugs would employ drugged liquor, blackjacks, or whatever it took to render a prospective shiphand helpless enough to get him on an outbound ship.

One of Kelly's neighbors was a Miss Piggott (surprisingly, some crimps were women) who ran a saloon on Davis Street near Jackson. Her modus operandi was to position the unwary at a spot at the bar above a trapdoor. After the victim sipped her special cocktail of doctored liquor she rapped the poor fellow on the head with a bung starter (a wooden mallet), the trap door was sprung, and the newborn sailor was soon on his way out to sea through the Golden Gate.

Starting in 1873 and well into the 20th century the north half of the park before you was the site of the Colombo Market, an Italian-run cooperative wholesale vegetable market. (An alley called Clark Street once divided the block between Jackson and Pacific streets.) It was the centerpiece of a larger surrounding market area where vendors hawked poultry, eggs, and other foodstuffs. The half-block was covered by a roof that protected the stalls underneath which vended over thirty different kinds of produce—cabbages, carrots, turnips, onions, beets, etc. as well as exotic spices such as oregano, marjoram, and sweet basil.

Vendors would start arriving at 3 a.m., their horse-drawn wagons having come mostly from the southern part of the city near Mission Street where a great number of truck gardens were located. After the produce was sorted and stacked, buyers from the big retail markets, the hotels, and the larger boarding houses would appear to make their purchases. By about 9 a.m., after all the major customers had departed with their goods, housewives, Chinese peddlers, and other bargain hunters would show up and buy the leftovers at half price.

At least two major companies' roots derive from the Colombo Market. What became the Del Monte Corporation was founded by Marco J. Fontana, who started his career working for one of the produce brokers serving the market. Fontana's experiments with canning bruised fruit brought home from the market led to his founding a canning company, his building of The Cannery on the north waterfront, and the establishment of the cooperative that became Del Monte. The Bank of America's founder, A. P. Giannini, also got his start in this area working as a teenager for his stepfather's firm, Scatena & Company, a fruit broker. The produce brokers started a form of primitive banking by advancing money to farmers to help plant their crops and bring them to market. Giannini's involvement with banking did not start until after he had retired from the food brokerage business, but he never forgot his roots. Many of the Bank of America's prime customers in later years were California's major agricultural producers.

The wholesale produce district continued in this area after 1906 and up until the early 1960s, when the complex surrounding it, known as the Golden Gateway Center, was built. The first phase of the project consisted of the high-rise apartment buildings you see to the south and southeast. As originally planned, more high rises were set for the area immediately surrounding the park. But protests by the Telegraph Hill Dwellers Association and others who were outraged by the large scale of the towers and the fact they were starting to block views of the waterfront, led the developers to scale down the rest of the project. The low-rise units bordering the park on the north and east resulted from this change of plans, giving this lovely little park more breathing space and making it a lunchtime oasis for local workers. The square is named for Sydney G. Walton (1901–1960), a member of the Redevelopment Agency that planned this project.

The ivy-covered arch at the park's western edge is the only surviving remnant of the Colombo Market. This cement-faced brick structure dates from about 1907 and once served as the entryway for a lane that ran through to Davis Street and provided access to the vegetable vendors on either side.

---

*Continue up Front Street to Pacific and turn left. As you head toward the intersection of Battery Street look at the brick building on the northeast corner of Pacific and Battery. On the side near the top is the painted advertisement: "Old Ship Saloon, Henry Klee, Prop."*

---

### ❻ 298 Pacific Street – Old Ship Saloon Building (1907).

This nondescript three-story brick building is the only known structure extant in San Francisco that has a verifiable link to shanghaiing. The Old Ship Saloon's history dates back to 1849 when the ship *Arkansas* arrived in San Francisco and berthed itself here at Pacific Street—at that time still just a pier jutting into the bay. Abandoned as

**Henry Klee and the Old Ship Saloon.**

her passengers and crew joined in the rush to the gold fields, she quickly became landlocked as bay fill pushed the waterfront farther east. An enterprising soul cut a hole in the bow and turned her into a saloon. The *Arkansas* became known as "the old ship," and the tavern inside adopted the name. The ship met its end in 1857 when construction on a new hotel started. A crew of Chinese laborers was brought in and the *Arkansas* was dismantled and cut up for firewood.

Although it's not certain when the Old Ship Saloon first made its home in the building on the corner, its association with shanghaiing apparently started early. James Laflin, a noted crimp who came to San Francisco as a cabin boy on the *Arkansas,* was one of the tavern's first bartenders. After his tenure, records show that at least several others collected money here for shanghaiing men for ships.

Henry Klee, a German immigrant whose name adorns the wall on the side of the building, took over management of the saloon in 1897. The building at that time was a two-story affair with the second story serving as a sailors' boardinghouse. In 1907 following the destruction caused by the fire the year before, the present three-story building was erected. A photograph taken shortly after the reopening shows Klee, his staff, and some patrons posing outside at the front door. Klee, a barrel-chested man with a walrus mustache, looked every inch the kind of no-nonsense individual one would have to have been to operate a tough waterfront saloon on San Francisco's Barbary Coast.

During the 1940s the hotel/boardinghouse portion upstairs gained a bit of notoriety as a brothel catering to the needs of World War II servicemen. Waterfront saloon, shanghaiing depot, whorehouse—this building has seen it all. In a nice sense of coming full circle, the bar, which had been named "Bricks" (for the unfinished brick walls inside) for much of the 20$^{th}$ century, was remodeled and renamed the Old Ship Saloon in 1999. The present owners have put up a nice little model of the ship *Arkansas* on a pole over the front entrance.

---

*Go north on Battery Street one block and cross over Broadway. Go half a block down to look at the plaques on the facades of 120 and 100 Broadway.*

---

### ❼ Broadway between Battery and Front streets – Clark's Point.

This point marks the original shoreline. Before the discovery of gold in 1848 a couple of noteworthy events took place here. On July 31, 1846 the ship *Brooklyn* carrying Mormon elder Sam Brannan and over 200 of his followers arrived here instantly doubling the population of Yerba Buena (as San Francisco was still called then.) They were hoping to establish a new Mormon colony in virgin territory, but to Brannan's dismay they had arrived just weeks after the U.S. had asserted its authority and claimed California. Brannan went on to become a leading citizen of the town. His real estate investments made him California's first millionaire.

The following year William Squire Clark, another early pioneer, built San Francisco's first wharf here, extending Broadway 150 feet out into the bay. To build the wharf Clark had to go to present day Corte Madera and fell redwood, since there were no suitable trees in San Francisco. He sawed them into lumber and then ferried them across the bay. For a pile driver he used ballast pig iron.

Construction of the wharf proved to be masterful timing because it was completed in September 1847 just a few months before gold was discovered. The Broadway Wharf enabled deepwater sailing vessels to directly unload their cargo on shore; previously goods had to be brought ashore via lighterage. Clark's wharf maintained a monopoly until 1849, when wharves began extending into the bay from other downtown city streets.

---

*Walk to the corner of Front Street, turn left and go the corner of Vallejo for a look at the building on the southwest corner:*

---

### ➑ 855 Front Street – Gibb-Sanborn Warehouse (1855).

This brick warehouse is a rare survivor from San Francisco's gold rush era.

When it was built in 1855 (on landfill) the shore of San Francisco Bay was literally right across the street. Erected by Daniel Gibb, a Scotsman and 49er who became a successful merchant, it served as a warehouse for over a century — mainly for wine, seeds, and beans. In 1972 the building was converted to office use. At that time the exterior was sandblasted to remove a coating of paint, which explains why the brick has such a rough texture.

Although the upper walls tumbled in the 1906 quake and were reconstructed — look at the seams in the brick between the first and second floors particularly on the Vallejo Street side — the building looks remarkably as it did when first built. The cast iron door with the oblong pull ring at the Front Street entrance may be original. At the building's base you can see the granite sill, and below that behind the planter boxes, the exposed foundation stones, which were probably quarried from nearby Telegraph Hill. Also note the marble street name insets embedded in the brick walls on the corner of the building about half way up.

---

*Walk two blocks west on Vallejo Street to the corner of Sansome Street.*

---

### ➒ Vallejo and Sansome streets – SE corner – Sansome Burial Ground (1846).

The southeast corner of Vallejo and Sansome streets served as one of the town's earliest cemeteries. By 1846, perhaps even earlier, bodies of sailors who died at sea were brought ashore and buried here. Burials ceased after only a few years, and in the hubbub of the gold rush the wooden grave markers were probably removed and used for firewood, because the graveyard was forgotten until 1857 when a rockslide caused by an excavation nearby for ship's ballast exposed some of the graves. The bodies were removed to Yerba Buena cemetery (where the Civic Center is now); or at least most of them were, because the following year a local newspaper, the *Daily Alta,* noted that workmen had uncovered another skeleton.

---

*Walk one block north on Sansome to the intersection of Green Street. On the northwest corner is:*

---

## ⑩ 200 Green Street – Location of the Invention of Television (1927) and Site of the Gray Brothers Quarry (c.1890-1914).

The rather plain two-story industrial building before you (built in 1923) is where television was invented in 1927 by 21-year-old Philo Farnsworth. Known as "the Genius of Green Street," Farnsworth, initially with just his wife and brother-in-law as assistants, set up shop in September 1926 in a 20-foot by 30-foot space on the second floor in the back of the building. After a year of intense labor, on September 7, 1927 he gave the first successful demonstration of a machine that would become ubiquitous in homes around the world— television. After more tinkering, two years later he made the first successful transmission to another location when he broadcast an image to a receiver at the Merchants Exchange Building half a mile away. Farnsworth continued his experiments at this location until 1931, when in a deal with the Philco Radio Corporation he moved his operation to Philadelphia.

Prior to the construction of this building, this corner was the site of Gray Brothers' rock crusher and quarry. George and Harry Gray manufactured "artificial stone" (or cement as we call it today), which was used for paving city sidewalks and curbs. Crushed rock was the main ingredient, and Telegraph Hill's hard serpentine was ideal.

All throughout the 1890s and early 1900s, like beavers trying to fell a tree, the Gray brothers blasted away at the sides of Telegraph Hill with dynamite, loosening rock and, increasingly, the foundations of houses that sat upon the hill above. Angry residents time and again obtained various injunctions and restraining orders, which the Gray brothers largely ignored. During the Fourth of July celebrations in 1909, while still under a court order not to blast, the company was so brazen as to time their explosions with the firings of the Presidio's cannons. Irate residents descended on the quarrymen, driving them away.

With their underhanded tactics and nefarious dealings with sub-contractors and employees, the Gray brothers were constantly embroiled in litigation; they were the subject of at least 52 lawsuits. To delay paying their workers as long as possible they starting issuing promissory notes payable only on an irregular basis. Frustration boiled over in November 1914 when one laborer, who had repeatedly had his pay requests turned aside, shot and killed George Gray. The Gray brothers and their tactics were so reviled that when the killer, Joseph Lococo, was tried for murder he not only was acquitted but cheers went up in the courtroom when the verdict was announced. The death of George Gray and the filing for bankruptcy the following year by Harry Gray finally put an end to Gray Brothers' destruction of Telegraph Hill.

*Walk one block east on Green Street for a look at the three-story painted brick building on the northwest corner of Green and Battery:*

### ⓫ 100-120 Green Street (1904) – Site of Fort Montgomery (1840s).

This site, which was right on the waterfront prior to the gold rush, was the location of Fort Montgomery. Initially called "the battery"— from which Battery Street got its name—it was put up in July 1846 as a defensive fortification just after the American takeover of Yerba Buena. As a fort it was really not much more than a collection of logs thrown together and equipped with some barely functional cannon hauled over from the Castillo de San Joaquin, the old Spanish fort that was replaced by Fort Point. The last recorded mention of Fort Montgomery came in late 1849. It was very likely dismantled for its wood to be used as building material for other structures.

*Walk one block north on Battery to Union Street. On the northwest corner is:*

### ⓬ 1105 Battery Street – Independent Wood Company Building (1907).

This two-story brick building, occupied by offices now, was built in 1907 for the Independent Wood Company, a dealer in wooden posts, railroad ties, and the like. The ground floor was retail/office space, and the second floor was rented out to sailors. The rest of what was then a 50-vara lot was open-air storage for the wood company's products.

About 1912 the wood company left, and from then on into the 1980s this building served as a bar/restaurant operating under a variety of names and owners. One of the more charming, and perhaps provocative, names was "Selina's Bar and Champagne Parlor." A clue to the restaurants' ties to this structure can be found in the faded and partially obliterated painted beer and restaurant advertising signs on the north side of the building in the narrow alley.

---

*Walk a half a block farther north on Battery to:*

---

### ⓭ Intersection of Battery and Filbert streets – Levi Plaza (1981).

The red brick office buildings surrounding this plaza form the corporate headquarters of Levi Strauss & Co., manufacturer of the well known brand of blue jeans, "Levi's." The company's origins date to 1853 when Levi Strauss, a German immigrant, arrived in San Francisco and started a dry goods business. Included in his stock was canvas, which he quickly converted into "waist overalls" when he saw the gold miners' need for sturdy pants. The patented riveted pockets were actually the idea of another man, Jacob Davis, a Carson City, Nevada tailor who came up with the idea when miners came to him complaining that their pants pockets were ripping open under the weight of heavy ore samples. In return for financing Davis, Levi Strauss and he jointly shared the patent.

The plaza itself was created in the mid-1980s. The landscaping was done by the noted designer Lawrence Halprin. It has a nice historical echo in that the trees, the granite boulders, and the flowing water of the centerpiece fountain are meant to simulate the Sierra foothills where Levi Strauss got his start peddling his canvas waist overalls to the miners.

At the time of the gold rush this area was the waterfront. The original shoreline ran right through the middle of the main two blocks of the complex, roughly paralleling Battery between Union and Greenwich streets. The remains of at least a half a dozen ships of that era lie entombed in this immediate area. One of them is the *William Gray*, which lies 18 feet below ground in the area just east of the fountain at the northwest corner of Battery and Filbert streets. If you stand on the sidewalk there you will be standing right over it. The *William Gray* arrived in San Francisco in June 1850 after a more than six-month journey from Boston via Cape Horn. In contrast to most ships at that time the 295-ton (a good-sized ship but not huge) *Gray* arrived with only four passengers, suggesting that she was a cargo ship. Indeed, by July 1852 she had been converted to a floating storeship. By 1857 her useful life apparently was at an end because she was dismantled and her remains scuttled here.

During the early 1930s, at the depth of the Depression, this area of the waterfront was largely vacant land and was the site of scattered makeshift shelters for the destitute and the homeless. A volunteer soup kitchen doled out meals daily to long lines of down-on-their-luck unemployed men. Dorothea Lange took a famous photograph here at that time called "White Angel Bread Line," showing an older man wearing a battered white hat, leaning over a rail while waiting his turn in line, his gnarled hands clasped in front of his tin soup cup, his mouth a grim line of despair. That photograph was taken in the triangular piece of land across Levi Plaza from Battery Street. Today the area is a lovely, tree-shaded park with a man-made stream where local workers eat their lunch on nice days.

---

*If you haven't crossed over Battery Street for a look at the park, do so and then walk up Battery to the intersection of Greenwich Street for a look at the tall red brick building on the southwest corner of Battery and Greenwich.*

---

## ⓮ 1265 Battery Street – former Italian Swiss Colony Building (1903).

One of the finest looking warehouses ever to be constructed in San Francisco, this building was erected in 1903 by the Italian Swiss Colony Company, a cooperative of Italian wine growers who owned 1,500 acres of vineyards in Sonoma County. This and several other nearby buildings (now torn down) served as their city headquarters. The Classical Roman decorative motifs, such as the pilasters with Ionic capitals, the scroll keystones, and the balustrade on the roof, are a conscious reflection of the group's Italian heritage.

The high arched doorways on the ground floor were once cargo bays. Railroad tracks branching off from the Embarcadero ran right into the building on the Greenwich Street side. Horse-drawn drays backed up to the Battery Street side to pick up barrels and cases of wine for deliveries around town.

The building survived 1906 because of its sturdy construction. The upper floors had to support giant wine tanks that could hold, in the aggregate, up to 2.5 million gallons of wine. Prohibition, which started in 1919, brought the company to a halt; during the 1920s the building was occupied by the Golden Gate Milk Products Company. Today, like virtually all other warehouses in the area, it has been converted to office space (with a ground-floor restaurant.)

---

*Walk up Battery to the intersection of Lombard and the Embarcadero and turn left on Lombard. Go one block to Sansome and turn right. Once you pass the end of the concrete building on your right, turn into the open courtyard having the railroad tracks.*

**On the northwest corner of Sansome and Lombard once stood the Adams & Company warehouse, built in 1853. It was torn down in 1969 to make way for the condominium development that stands there now.**

---

### ⓯ Belt Line Railroad Roundhouse (1914) and Sandhouse (1918).

This building served as a carbarn and turntable for the Belt Line Railroad, which operated trains along San Francisco's Embarcadero. Fifty miles of track once ran along the waterfront and nearby streets from the Presidio to Hunters Point. Tracks extended right into the piers, where boxcars were loaded with freight. Then state-owned locomotives pushed or pulled the cars along the Embarcadero either to waterfront warehouses or to the Southern Pacific yards south of Market, where they would be attached to freight trains bound for such destinations as Mexico or the East Coast.

The line started operation in 1891. It saw its peak usage in the early 1940s when, during the war it not only hauled goods and cargo but also troop trains carrying GIs to the Presidio and to the army transport docks at Fort Mason—sometimes at night under the cover of a blackout. Rail traffic along the waterfront pretty much ceased by the mid-1980s as industrial maritime activity dwindled and was increasingly displaced by tourism and commercial and residential real estate activity. In 1991, a century after it started, the Belt Line Railroad ceased operations; most of the tracks were torn up or paved over.

This roundhouse has been preserved as a last remnant. The bays still have their original numbers of 1 to 5; the rails leading from them are some of the very few still left. The building was remodeled into offices in 1984.

In the courtyard behind the Roundhouse along the Embarcadero side, a water tank-type fountain provides a reminder of the steam locomotives (diesel engines only started replacing steam here in 1943) that once powered the trains here. Directly behind this fountain, alongside the Embarcadero, is a small one-story structure, the Sandhouse (now office space as well). On damp or rainy days when the rails became slick, sand would be spread on them to help give the trains traction. The Sandhouse not only served as a sand repository but also held a tumbler so that wet sand could be gathered up, dried out, and used again.

The concrete building behind the Roundhouse, Two Roundhouse Plaza, which faces Greenwich Street, is modern construction and is not historic. A blacksmith shop, a water tank, and other train-yard related structures once stood on this site. Right about this spot, by the way, which was the water's edge then, is where most of the storied clipper ships docked during the 1850s after their runs from Atlantic ports to San Francisco via Cape Horn.

---

*Walk south along the Embarcadero past the Fog City Diner and the back side of Levi Plaza Park to the intersection of Union Street. (Follow the little winding, tree-shaded path as you get toward Union).*

---

### ⓰ Embarcadero at Union Street – Site of Old Fisherman's Wharf (1880s–1900).

In the late 19<sup>th</sup> century two narrow piers positioned on the Embarcadero between Union and Filbert streets served as the original Fisherman's Wharf. That wharf was strictly for fisherman and definitely was not a tourist attraction. When not out catching fish, the Italian fishermen, who dominated the industry, could be seen on the planked

# Philo T. Farnsworth

## (1906–1971)

Of all major American inventors Philo Farnsworth, the inventor of television, is surely the least heralded. Samuel B. Morse with the telegraph, Alexander Graham Bell with the telephone, and Thomas Edison with the electric light bulb to their credits, are names well known in the annals of invention. But ask anyone who invented television and the reaction will most likely be a blank stare or a scratch of the head.

Philo Farnsworth, a Mormon farm boy, was an inveterate tinkerer fascinated by electricity. As a precocious sixteen-year-old growing up in rural Utah in 1922 he presented his science teacher with a sketch of his idea for an electronic television. After finishing school, and being single minded about his quest to prove that his idea would work, Farnsworth set up shop in a nondescript building at the foot of San Francisco's Telegraph Hill. Like most inventors his methods included trial and error, but he had an unerring instinct for where he was going.

**Philo Farnsworth with an early television set.**

After a year's effort, during which he even made his own glass tubes for his experiments, on September 7, 1927 he gave a demonstration of the world's first all electronic TV picture. (Other TV systems were in development at the same time as Farnsworth's but they were all mechanical, based on spinning disks to project an image; Farnsworth's was the first all-electrical system.)

The first transmission was simply a black line on a bluish screen. But by playing around with it Farnsworth and his assistants discovered that they could project moving images as well—cigarette smoke blown into the transmitter, for example, showed up on the screen. Soon after his successful showing Farnsworth invited his financial backers to the lab for a presentation. One asked when they would see some dollars from his invention. Farnsworth was ready. In reply to the question, a $ quickly appeared on the screen.

Farnsworth's invention brought him much acclaim and attention. Scientists from U.C. Berkeley, Stanford University, and other local colleges came to call, as did reigning Hollywood movie stars such as Douglas Fairbanks and Mary Pickford. After a few more years at his Green Street lab, Farnsworth moved his operation to Philadelphia, where for some years afterward he was embroiled in litigation against giant RCA Corporation as to who had actually invented television. It was a David vs. Goliath matchup, but Farnsworth eventually prevailed and RCA ended up having to pay him royalties on his patents.

In the 1940s Farnsworth sold his company to the International Telephone and Telegraph Corporation. He spent the remainder of his life working for ITT, mainly in the areas of mathematics and nuclear fusion. In 1968 Farnsworth returned to his Green Street lab one last time as part of a documentary that was being filmed about his life. He spent his last few years in his native state of Utah where he died in 1971 at age 64. Even with the addition of color, digitalization, and many other improvements, Farnworth's inventions and patents remain the basis of all TV and video technology today.

# Financial District

**Length:** 1.2 miles / 1.9 kilometers.
**Time:** 1½ hours.
**Walk Rating:** Easy.
**Hills:** None.
**Public Transit:** Muni bus line 15 runs along Kearny and Sansome streets. The 42 line also runs on Sansome. The Montgomery BART station is located on Market Street at the foot of Montgomery Street.
**Parking:** Parking in Financial District garages is prohibitively expensive on weekdays. On weekends, free parking is available underneath the Embarcadero Center buildings, which are located between Clay and Sacramento and Battery and Drumm streets. You can also look for street parking on weekends – mornings are the best times. Parking meters are in effect on Saturdays but are free on Sundays. Check curbside street signs, since some thoroughfares, such as Montgomery Street, are tow away zones at certain hours.
**Restrooms:** There are no public restrooms along the route.

The history of San Francisco's financial district stretches back over a century and a half to the days of the gold rush, when people from all over the world arrived here to make their fortunes. The skyscrapers of today occupy the site of Yerba Buena Cove where the ships bearing the Argonauts dropped anchor. Since San Francisco was founded this area has been the center of action.

Montgomery Street—sometimes called "Wall Street West" because it is home to the city's leading banks, brokerages, and insurance companies—is the district's main artery. In the 19th century the financial district was largely centered around the northern end of Montgomery Street, that is from California to Washington streets. This is where the majority of the banking, express, steamship, and stagecoach lines were located. The southern portion of the street, from California to Market Street, was mostly given over to retail establishments and large hotels. One 19th century French visitor described this stretch of Montgomery as equivalent to "the rue de la Paix in Paris, the Piccadilly of London, and the Broadway of New York." After the 1906 fire leveled the district (a few survivors such as the Kohl and Mills buildings remained standing), the hotels were not replaced and the area became exclusively office buildings.

# FINANCIAL DISTRICT

**❶** One Montgomery Street - Wells Fargo Bank

**❷** Montgomery Street - East side between Post and Sutter

**❸** 130 Sutter Street - Hallidie Building

**❹** 111 Sutter Street - Hunter-Dulin Building

**❺** Site of Occidental Hotel

**❻** 235 Montgomery Street - Russ Building

**❼** 220 Montgomery Street - Mills Building

**❽** 130 Pine Street - Pacific Coast Stock Exchange

**❾** Site of Nevada Bank

**❿** 345 Montgomery Street - Bank of America

**⓫** Site of Duncan's Bank

**⓬** 465 California Street - Merchants Exchange

**⓭** Leidesdorff Street

**⓮** 400 California Street - Bank of California

**⓯** Site of Leidesdorff Warehouse

**⓰** Site of "Cast Iron" Building

**⓱** Site of Parrott Building

**⓲** 400 Montgomery Street - Kohl Building

**⓳** 420 Montgomery Street - Wells Fargo Museum

**⓴** Site of Indian Sweat House

**㉑** Site of Hudson's Bay trading post

**㉒** Site of Armory Hall

**㉓** Site of What Cheer House

**㉔** 343 Sansome Street - Site of Howison's Pier

**㉕** Site of Hoff Store

**㉖** Site of "Fort Gunnybags"

**㉗** 400 Sansome Street - Old Federal Reserve Bank

**㉘** Leidesdorff and Commercial streets - Site of Long Wharf

**㉙** 608 Commercial Street - Sub-Treasury Building

**㉚** Site of Daily Morning Call newspaper

**㉛** Site of Emperor Norton lodging house

This tour will mainly traverse Montgomery Street—which skirted the original shoreline—with side trips down adjoining streets.

---

*Start this tour on the northeast corner of Montgomery and Post/Market streets. Across Montgomery Street on the northwest corner of the intersection is:*

---

### ❶ One Montgomery Street - Wells Fargo/First National Bank (1908) / Site of Masonic Lodge (1860–1906).

Currently the location of the One Montgomery Street branch of Wells Fargo Bank, this fine banking temple with the colonnaded corner entrance was designed by Willis Polk to house the First National Bank. Originally it was a 13-story building that extended only two arcades down the Montgomery Street side. But a few changes have been made since then. In 1921 the Montgomery side was extended down to its current end point in the middle of the block, the design being copied by another architect to match Polk's original. The other major change came in the early 1980s when the top ten stories were removed and replaced

**The spacious interior of this building with its elaborate coffered ceiling, fluted columns, and its carved griffin marble writing stands make this perhaps the most sumptuous banking hall in the city.**

by the setback office tower that now looms over the old structure. (First National, the building's original namesake, later merged with Crocker Bank which in turn was taken over by Wells Fargo in 1986.)

The building on this site prior to the current one was the home of the Masonic Lodge, an edifice that was the epitome of Gothic Revival. The three-story building with Gothic arches and triform windows could, from a distance, have been mistaken for a church. It stood here from 1860 until it burned in 1906. The Masons built a new lodge for themselves in 1911 at Market Street and Van Ness Avenue. In 1958 they moved to their present grand temple on Nob Hill.

### ❷ Montgomery Street – East side between Post and Sutter streets.

Prior to 1906, this side of Montgomery Street—now crowded with soaring non-descript high-rise office towers—was representative of much of what downtown San Francisco's business district looked like in the 19th century. Along this block then were mostly two- and three-story Victorian structures, with retail on the ground floor and office space above. The one exception was the 1894 eight-story Union Trust Building on the Market Street end, which housed the headquarters of the Southern Pacific Railroad. But the other half dozen buildings contained the offices of real estate brokers, train ticket agents, wine and liquor dealers, even a detective agency. And about in the middle of the block was the street-level Johnson's Restaurant, which billed itself as "The Modern Down-Town Ladies' Restaurant. Service and Quality First-Class without Fee or Tip."

---

*Walk up Montgomery one block to the corner of Sutter Street, turn left and go up half the block for a look across the street at:*

---

### ❸ 130 Sutter Street - Hallidie Building (1917).

Another structure by the prolific Willis Polk, the Hallidie Building is one of the architect's more distinctive and famous works. Named for cable car inventor Andrew Hallidie and commissioned by the Regents of the University of California—hence the blue and gold paint job (the school's colors)—the Hallidie Building is noted for its exterior glass curtain wall, said to be the first use of such a glass façade. It extends a full foot beyond the concrete shell of the building itself and almost seems to be suspended in air. The glass curtain wall was more than just an inspired decorative element, however. The first use of the building was as a garment factory: admitting exterior light was one of the design's objectives.

---

*Walk back to the corner of Montgomery and Sutter and cross the intersection to the northeast corner. Look back at the building on the southwest corner:*

---

### ❹ 111 Sutter Street - Hunter-Dulin Building (1926) / Site of Lick House Hotel (1862–1906).

Few people take the time to look up at high-rises these days, but this is one well worth the effort. This corner is a good place to take in the entirety of this fine building. Called the Hunter-Dulin Building after the Los Angeles based investment company that paid for its construction, it was designed by the New York architectural firm of Schultze and Weaver, who also did the Waldorf-Astoria and the Sherry-Netherland hotels in Manhattan. Covered with glazed terra cotta and topped by a mansard roof with copper cresting, the distinctive feature is the Romanesque/French Chateau-style ornamentation. The detailing on the roof in particular would make this building a standout anywhere, but it is especially notable here in San Francisco where virtually all other high-rise rooflines terminate in Victorian/Edwardian-style cornices or, more typically, in featureless Modernist slab endings.

**Dashiell Hammett fans have determined, from close readings of *The Maltese Falcon*, that this is the building where private detective Sam Spade had his office.**

Prior to 1906 this corner (actually much of the block) was the site of the Lick House, which from the time of its construction in 1861–62 until the Palace Hotel opened in 1875, was the city's finest hotel. It was built by James Lick (1796–1876), a native of Pennsylvania who settled in Peru in the 1830s. He arrived in San Francisco from Lima just a few weeks before gold was discovered in January 1848. With masterful timing, and flush with $30,000 in gold from selling his piano-manufacturing business, Lick bought lots all over the downtown area, including most of the block bounded by Post, Montgomery, Sutter, and Kearny streets—for which he paid $275 in February 1848. (The gold discovery did not become public until April.) Prior to that, this area had been a sandy wasteland, which had been used initially as a cattle pound and then as a circus arena.

Lick, a perfectionist and a man who appreciated fine craftsmanship, spared no expense on his hotel. The three-story edifice had a bar, billiard rooms, a reading room, and its own barbershop. But the centerpiece was its palatial dining room. The word palatial is no exaggeration; it was modeled after the dining hall in the Palace of Versailles, which Lick had visited as a young man on a trip to Paris. The huge room, finished with a mosaic parquetry floor made up of nearly 88,000 pieces of exotic woods, could seat 400. Its 32 foot high walls were covered with large scenes of Yosemite, the Golden Gate, and other California scenes by the noted landscape painter Thomas Hill. In between the paintings, double Corinthian columns lined the room. Twenty feet off the floor an eight-foot-wide viewing gallery extended the length of the room; it was used by guests not invited to banquets so that they could watch the gustatory proceedings below.

After suffering a series of strokes in the last few years of his life, the taciturn and sometimes quarrelsome Lick died at age 80 in his second-floor suite overlooking the intersection of Montgomery and Sutter streets. The Lick House was bought by Bonanza King James Fair who made the hotel his home until he in turn died in 1894. The property was inherited by his daughters who sold it to the Hunter-Dulin Company.

**❺ East side of Montgomery Street between Sutter and Bush streets – Site of Occidental Hotel** (1862–1906).

The Occidental Hotel in 1874.

Before 1906 this side of Montgomery between Sutter and Bush streets was the location of the Occidental Hotel, another of San Francisco's first class hostelries, although it was not quite as opulent as the Lick House. It was a four-story affair that was built in three stages between 1862 and 1870, and eventually became a four-sided structure surrounding a central courtyard. It was popular with army and navy officers in transit (who were given a preferred rate), with local speculators and capitalists, retired merchants, and with rich widows. Ladies in fact had their own entrance. It was carpeted, had a doorman, and was free of the cuspidors placed elsewhere in the hotel.

Standards of hygiene were lower in those days. One resident of the hotel in the late 1890s recalled the large rats that ranged freely throughout the place. They had grown so fat and tame scrounging the hotel restaurant's food they would take bread from the hands of visitors who approached them in the hallways. At night they could be heard running through the crawl space above the ceilings in the rooms.

*Walk one block farther north on Montgomery to the northeast corner of Bush Street. Occupying the block on the west side of the street is:*

❻ **235 Montgomery Street – Russ Building** (1927) / **Site of Russ House** (1862–1906).

When the block-long Russ Building was completed in 1927 it dominated Montgomery Street. It was the tallest building in San Francisco, at 31 stories, and remained so until 1964. It was designed by architect George Kelham, who three years later, would execute a similar but even more engaging variation of a setback office tower when he did the Shell Building (see Market Street walk). The Russ Building was the first high rise in San Francisco to have a garage for automobiles.

The ornamentation is that of Gothic Revival, probably chosen because Gothic arches lend themselves to a heightened sense of verticality, which the Russ Building certainly has. The lobby with groin vaults and the front entryway with niches for saints on each side bring to mind a cathedral. Perhaps the illusion was intentional: it is a cathedral of commerce.

The building gets its name from pioneer Emanuel Charles Christian Russ (1785–1857) who came to San Francisco in March 1847 with his wife and nine children. Within a few days of his arrival he purchased this site—which at the time was little more than shifting sand hills—for $75 and erected a ramshackle home made from wooden boards salvaged from the ship he had arrived on. Russ, a German immigrant of Polish descent, was a silversmith by trade, and in the wake of the gold rush he prospered as a jeweler and assayer. In 1862 his heirs erected on this site a three-story brick Italianate structure, the Russ House, a hotel that catered to farmers, merchants, and miners. It charged $2 to $2.50 a night for a room, whereas its more upscale neighbors, the Lick and the Occidental, cost $3 to $5 a night.

Like most everything else on Montgomery Street the Russ House burned in 1906. It was replaced by a three-story office building, which in turn was demolished to make way for the present 1927 Russ Building.

*On the northeast corner of Montgomery and Bush is:*

## ❼ 220 Montgomery Street – Mills Building (1891) / Site of Platt's Hall (1860–1890).

Just as its cross-street neighbor the Russ Building was the tallest of its time, so was the Mills Building when it was erected over three decades earlier. Ten stories high, it was also one of the earliest steel frame and masonry buildings in the city. It was designed by the noted Chicago firm of Burnham and Root, and stands as the City's best example of what was known as the Chicago School of Architecture and the works of its leading practitioner, Louis Sullivan. The Romanesque arch of the main entrance decorated with leaves and other symmetrical designs carved from white marble are highly characteristic of this style of architecture, which prevailed in the late 19$^{th}$ and early 20$^{th}$ centuries.

The Mills Building was gutted by the 1906 fire, but much of the exterior remained standing, making it one of the few structures in the downtown area to survive the catastrophe. It was reconstructed in 1908 and enlarged in 1914 and 1918. In 1931 the 21-story Mills Tower at the rear of the building on Bush Street was added.

The Mills Building is named for Darius Ogden Mills (1825–1910), a forty-niner who was cofounder and president of the Bank of California. In later years he devoted his life to philanthropy, building hotels with affordable rates for the working class. Millbrae, down the peninsula, where Mills had an estate, is named for him.

Before the Mills Building was erected, this corner was the site of Platt's Hall, a three-story brick building that opened in 1860. The hall itself was a large square auditorium that served as the city's central gathering place for events. Lectures, concerts, political rallies, school graduation ceremonies, boxing matches, and other events attracting large crowds were held here. Visiting celebrities who spoke here included Henry Ward Beecher, Susan B. Anthony, the midget Tom Thumb, and Irish playwright Oscar Wilde who read poetry here in April 1882 while on a U.S. lecture tour. His performance was widely panned, since Wilde spoke in a dull, low monotone that nearly put the audience to sleep.

---

*Continue up Montgomery to the corner of Pine Street and turn right.*

*Go down Pine to the end of the block, where on the southwest corner
of the intersection with Sansome is:*

### ❽ 130 Pine Street – Pacific Coast
### Stock Exchange Building (1915).

Like most parcels of land in downtown San Francisco this lot on
the corner of Pine and Sansome has had a succession of owners and
uses. It had a number of relatively anonymous owners starting with
the original grantee in 1847 until 1875, when Bonanza King James C.
Flood bought the property. Flood conveyed it to his partner James
Fair in 1877 who, two years later, erected a five-story brick and
cast-iron building, which was inherited by his youngest daughter
Virginia (who married into the Vanderbilt family) after his death in
1894. Fair's building was destroyed by the 1906 calamity, and in 1909
Virginia Vanderbilt sold the vacant lot to the U.S. Government. In
1915 the government erected the granite Tuscan-colonnaded building standing here now for use as a subtreasury building. But with the
creation of the Federal Reserve System in 1913 the massive vaults of
the subtreasury became superfluous and the building was converted
to storage.

By the late 1920s the San Francisco Stock Exchange—whose origins go back to 1882 when it began as the Stock and Bond
Exchange—was looking for more space because of the increase in
trading volume in the Roaring Twenties. The SFSE bought the building in 1928 and hired architect Timothy Pflueger, who refashioned
the interior and designed the adjoining 12-story Office Exchange
Tower (155 Sansome) behind it, erected in 1930.

To add a decorative element to the Pine Street façade, Pflueger
hired sculptor Ralph Stackpole (1885–1973). Between 1929 and 1932,
when they were unveiled, Stackpole created the two giant granite
pylons flanking the colonnade. These massive pylons with their
almost androgynous figures resemble the monumental heroic sculpture of Stalinist Russia. Indeed, that may have been where Stackpole's
sympathies lay in that turbulent era: the little boy on the pylon west
of the front door is raising his fist in what seems to be a socialist
salute. Stackpole went on to do one of the Coit Tower murals the following year, and in 1939 he created the keynote sculpture *Pacifica* for
the Treasure Island World's Fair.

The stock and options traders moved out of the building a few years ago; the space has been converted to other commercial uses.

*Cross Pine Street and go back to the intersection of Montgomery.*

### ❾ Pine and Montgomery streets – NW corner – Site of Nevada Bank (1875–1906).

At this corner prior to 1906 stood the Nevada Bank of San Francisco. It was the bank of the four partners known as the Silver or Bonanza Kings: James C. Flood, James Fair, John Mackay, and William O'Brien. The four had become fabulously wealthy as the owners of the richest silver mine of the Comstock Lode in western Nevada. To help manage their millions, to increase their prestige, and not incidentally to thumb their noses at their biggest competitor, William Ralston and the Bank of California, they established their own bank. In 1875 they erected on this corner a handsome four-story masonry building called, not surprisingly, the Nevada Block.

O'Brien died in 1879, and as time passed the other partners lost interest in their bank. The resulting lack of supervision left an opening for their head cashier, who nearly bankrupted the firm and the partners in the late 1880s with an ill-conceived attempt to corner the market on wheat by pledging the bank's assets for huge loans to buy the grain. The bank survived but in weakened condition. In 1905 it was taken over by Wells Fargo.

The 1906 earthquake and fire destroyed the building but its vaults remained intact. Guards were posted round the clock, and when the ashes had cooled enough to open them, several days later, the $3 million in gold and silver they held was retrieved.

*Walk down one block to the southeast corner of Montgomery and California streets. Across Montgomery on the southwest corner of the intersection is:*

### ❿ 345 Montgomery Street – Bank of America (1968) / Site of William A. Leidesdorff residence (1846-1847).

The banking hall on the corner here is the main San Francisco office of the Bank of America, which was founded in the City as the Bank of Italy in 1904 by A.P. Giannini (1870–1949). Giannini, in an age when the old adage of banks only lending money to those who didn't need it was never truer, got his bank started by catering to the "little guy"—immigrants, farmers, and small merchants. He was an innovator who pioneered the concept of branch banking, who made loans to "risky" agricultural enterprises, and who helped the fledgling movie industry get started by financing hundreds of motion pictures, including such classics as *It's a Wonderful Life* and *Gone With the Wind.* The Bank of America also came to the rescue of the Golden Gate Bridge by buying bonds to fund its construction during the darkest days of the Depression in the early 1930s.

Giannini lived to see his bank become the largest in the U.S. but he died before the construction of this banking hall and the towering headquarters building behind it, which was completed in 1971. The design of the office tower generated controversy because of its massive scale, dark coloration, and the sterile windswept plaza in front. Before the bank purchased the site in the 1960s this block held nearly a dozen small buildings that housed mainly retailers and a hotel.

The first building to occupy this corner was put up in the early 1840s by Robert Ridley, a Cockney clerk for the Hudson's Bay Company. It was a single-story adobe house catty-corner to what is now the intersection of Montgomery and California streets. It stood only a stone's throw from the water's edge, which was then beyond where Leidesdorff Street crosses California, a half block away. The house had a veranda and boasted the only flower garden in Yerba Buena.

In 1846 Ridley sold the house to civic leader William Leidesdorff who made it into a center of the town's social life. In October of that year Leidesdorff hosted a reception and ball in honor of Commodore Robert F. Stockton, the commander of U.S. Naval forces. (The U.S. had taken possession of California in July.) Spirits were high, there was plenty to eat and drink, and "the assembled female beauty of Yerba Buena were gathered." Stockton "kissed the pretty ones," and "shook hands with the old and ugly ones…" noted a guest who wrote an account of the affair.

### ⓫ Montgomery and California streets – SE corner – Site of "Duncan's Bank" (1875–1906).

One of San Francisco's more colorful, if lesser known, figures was Joseph C. Duncan (1818–1898). A bit of a rogue, he was a charming philanderer who had successive and sometimes overlapping careers as an auctioneer, publisher, art dealer, real estate speculator, and banker. He auctioned goods for courtesan Lola Montez, employed author Henry George (*Progress and Poverty*) for a time as a printer, and was the lover of poet Ina Coolbrith. He also was the father, by his third wife, of the noted dancer Isadora Duncan (1877–1927).

By 1875 he had turned his attentions to banking, and in that year he erected a four-story iron and stone building on this corner to house several financial institutions he had stakes in, including The Safe Deposit Company of San Francisco. The latter was noted for its huge vault in the basement of the building. It was 30 x 35', was 11' high and was made of thirty bands of iron and steel bolted and welded together. Surrounding it for effect were 12 bronze statues of spear-carrying conquistadors; real uniformed armed guards patrolled its perimeter day and night. Lloyds of London deemed it "burglar proof." It had such notoriety that it was a veritable tourist attraction.

Despite the solidity of his vault, Duncan's bank was undercapitalized and when financial difficulties arose it went bankrupt in 1877 after only two years in business. Criminal charges of fraud and forgery were filed and angry depositors called for his scalp. Duncan went underground and managed to avoid arrest for five months by disguising himself as a woman. Captured and jailed, he was tried four times over his bank's failure, but in the end managed to wangle an acquittal. The one-time banker drowned in 1898 when he boarded a British steamship bound for New York from London that sank shortly after leaving port. Duncan's body washed ashore the next day still dressed in a dancing costume he was wearing from a party held on board the night before.

**The Safe Deposit Building, "Duncan's Bank."**

---

*Turn right on Montgomery Street. A few steps down on the right is:*

---

## ⑫ 465 California Street – Merchants Exchange Building (1903) / Site of Dr. John Townsend House (1847).

Designed by the ubiquitous Willis Polk, the Merchants Exchange Building was, along with the Mills and Kohl buildings, one of the few office buildings whose exterior walls survived the 1906 disaster. This structure was the third Merchants Exchange; it grew from a need during the gold rush for merchants and traders of various kinds to have a central place to congregate.

This building also served a practical function. The belvedere on the roof—which can only be seen from a distance—was used to receive signals from incoming ships, which were then relayed to merchants in the great hall in the lobby so that members could have first crack at the cargoes when the ships docked at the Embarcadero. If you are on this tour during weekday business hours go into the marble-clad entrance and back to the great hall, which is now a bank. In the bays on the walls are large and beautiful paintings by artist William Coulter of maritime scenes set on San Francisco Bay and elsewhere in the Pacific Rim.

Two generations before this building was erected, Dr. John Townsend in 1847 put up the first structure on this site, a combination house and physician's office. Townsend had come overland in 1844 and was one of the town's leading citizens in the late 1840s. Townsend Street south of Market is named for him.

---

*The little alley bordering the Merchants Exchange on the east is Leidesdorff Street.*

---

## ⑬ Leidesdorff Street (c.1850).

This block of Leidesdorff Street (named for William Leidesdorff, this thoroughfare will be discussed more fully toward the end of this walk) between California and Pine was known as "Pauper Alley" in the late 19th century. Accounts differ as to whether the name came from losses generated by stock speculators dealing with curbstone brokers nearby, or whether from bets on horse races made in the poolrooms that once stood on this block. Either way, the name was surely justly deserved.

*Walk the half block down to Sansome Street. Across California
on the northwest corner of the intersection is:*

**⑭ 400 California Street – Bank of California** (1908)
**/ Site of the Bank of California** (1866–1905)
**/ Site of the Tehama House Hotel** (1851–1864).

With its grand multi-story Corinthian columns this is the epitome
of what a banking temple should be. It was built in 1908 to replace the
previous headquarters of the Bank of California (now Union Bank of
California), which had been torn down just prior to the earthquake of
1906. That building, although lacking the overt grandeur of this structure, was a two-story gem erected in 1866. Sheathed in blue sandstone, it was modeled after the Renaissance-influenced Library of St.
Mark in Venice. Both stories were comprised of alternating classical
columns and arcaded windows. The perimeter of the roof was lined
with a balustrade surmounted with finial-topped orbs. The interior,
with nineteen foot ceilings, black marble, Spanish mahogany, and
other polished woods, was equally impressive.

The bank building and the bank itself were largely the creation of
San Francisco's leading financier of the time, William C. Ralston
(1826–1875). Ralston had started modestly in the early 1850s, but
being ambitious and strong-willed he formed a partnership with
Darius Ogden Mills, the City's leading banker. It was a good match—
the cautious, conservative Mills served to temper the aggressive,
almost reckless Ralston. Ralston however got the upper hand and he
used the bank's money to make heavy bets on the Comstock silver
mines, which in the 1860s were experiencing a drop-off in production.
It proved only temporary, for in the early 1870s huge new veins of ore
were discovered; the bank's coffers filled and Ralston became rich.

Giddy with his newfound wealth, Ralston soon became overex-
tended in various expensive and unproductive enterprises, and
within a few years a crisis arose. On August 26, 1875 a run started on
the Bank of California. Panicky depositors clustered on California
Street in front of the bank, trying to gain access to their money. The
bank closed its doors early that day, its reserves of gold and silver
dangerously low. At the bank board's request Ralston submitted his
resignation. The following day, during his customary swim at

Aquatic Park near Fisherman's Wharf, he died suddenly of an apparent stroke. The popular Ralston, who was only 49, was given the grandest funeral San Francisco had ever witnessed.

Before the Bank of California purchased this site in 1864 this was the location of the Tehama House (erected 1851), one of early San Francisco's finest hotels. The three-story wood-frame structure was favored by the city's elite of the time, including Joshua Norton who was merely a prosperous merchant before he later morphed into Norton I, Emperor of the United States and Protector of Mexico (there is more on Norton at the end of the walk). When the Bank of California purchased the property, the old hotel, instead of being demolished, was sawed in half and carted to different locations—where eventually the portions became lost to history.

If you are on this tour during weekday business hours be sure to visit the Museum of Money of the American West, located in the basement of the Bank of California. It's a small room but it houses a rich display of artifacts related to San Francisco history, including nuggets and coins from the gold rush era, the original assay pellets that confirmed the richness of the Comstock silver mines, and the elegant dueling pistols from the Broderick-Terry duel of 1859 in which former Chief Justice of the California Supreme Court David Terry killed U.S. Senator and San Francisco resident David C. Broderick.

---

*Cross California Street if you haven't already done so and walk west a half a block back to Leidesdorff Street.*

---

### ⓰ California and Leidesdorff streets – NE corner – Site of Leidesdorff warehouse (1840s).

This corner was originally occupied by a simple one-story edifice that served as a hide warehouse for the previously mentioned William Leidesdorff. The warehouse was built in the mid-1840s on what was then the shore of Yerba Buena Cove. It was placed right at the water's edge so that at high tide shallow-draft boats could come right along side and unload cowhides collected from the various local cattle ranches. There they would be stored until ships from Boston and other East Coast ports arrived to trade goods for them.

## ⓖ California and Leidesdorff streets – NW corner
## – Site of "Cast Iron" Building (1873–1960).

Three decades later, and long after Leidesdorff's warehouse was gone, the waterfront had been pushed half a dozen blocks farther east as Yerba Buena Cove was filled in to create more level land, and this locale became the heart of the financial district. In 1873, just across Leidesdorff Street, a large three-story building with a cast iron façade weighing 200 tons was built to house the Bank of London and San Francisco. In fire-conscious San Francisco iron was considered fireproof. While this proved a mixed blessing in the fires of the 1850s—smaller buildings especially buckled and warped in the heat (and trapped their inhabitants inside, literally roasting them to death)—during the 1906 holocaust the interior of the London Bank building was gutted but the sturdy cast-iron walls held firm. The building was refurbished and went through a succession of owners, mostly banks, and survived until as late as 1960 when the then occupant, American Trust Company, was merged into Wells Fargo, who dismantled it to make way for the present nondescript high rise.

The only survivor from that building, and indeed from that era, is the iron stanchion with the acorn finial on the sidewalk near the corner. This cast-iron cylinder is a hitching post that has miraculously survived in this location (although not in this exact spot) since 1873. The compartment doors held feed bags: bank patrons arriving in their carriages could keep their horses happily munching away while they conducted their business in the bank.

---

*Continue up to the southeast corner of California and Montgomery streets.*

---

## ⓗ California and Montgomery streets – NW corner
## – Site of second Custom House (1850–1851)
## / the Parrott Building (1852–1926).

When the first custom house—located in the old adobe at Portsmouth Square—outgrew its space in 1850, it moved to this corner where it leased a four-story red brick building that had been erected in 1849 by pioneer William Heath Davis (for whom Davis Street is named). The building had an unusual dual wooden staircase leading to all floors from its Montgomery Street entrance, an element that likely only served to hasten its demise; the building was des-troyed in the last major fire of the early days, the one of June 22, 1851.

The following year a new structure, the Parrott Building—named for its owner John Parrott—was erected. Parrott was determined that his building would be indestructible. Granite cubes, numbered and pre-cut, were imported from China along with a crew of Chinese la-borers who fitted them together like a giant Lego block. Iron shutters were bolted to the windows of the three-story building as a fire safety measure.

The building did indeed prove its worth. In 1866 when a worker attempted to open a package that contained nitroglycerine there was a huge explosion that killed at least nine people; the building was left virtually unscathed. The 1906 earthquake did it no harm either. As the flames advanced, army fire brigades attempted to dynamite the structure in hopes of creating a firebreak. They failed and the Parrott Building remained standing. It survived until 1926 when it was de-molished to make way for the present 15-story structure. Called the Financial Center, this served as an office building until the until the 1980s. A decade later it was gutted in preparation for it being con-verted into the Omni Hotel, which opened in 2002.

### ⑱ 400 Montgomery Street – Kohl Building (1901) / Site of the Express Building (1853).

The Kohl Building, on the northeast corner of this intersection, is yet another of Willis Polk's efforts. This handsome building is clad in greenish-gray Colusa sandstone and shows Polk's love of decorative detail, especially above the two-story doorway on Montgomery Street and in the upper stories with their Baroque/Renaissance-style columns. The building was erected in 1901 for Alvinza Hayward, a former associate of William Ralston's. The structure is designed in an "H" shape allegedly because the client wanted it to serve as an em-blem for his last name.

Probably Polk's greatest success with this building is that it was "fireproof" or nearly so. Because of design features such as the use of metal reinforcing on the ceilings and around the doors and windows, the fire failed to penetrate above the fourth floor. It thus became the only structure downtown not to have suffered any earthquake dam-age and also not to have been totally gutted. As a result, the fire department was able to use the building as a command post during the 1906 conflagration.

Not long before the 1906 earthquake and fire the building was purchased by C. Frederick Kohl of Burlingame and renamed. Kohl, a man of leisure who employed his time supervising the estate left to him by his retired sea-captain father, who had made a fortune in Alaska fisheries, suffered a tragic series of events a few years later. In 1909 a French maid he had employed assaulted several people at a dinner party he was giving. After Kohl had her taken into custody she sued for false arrest. At the trial two years later Kohl won the case, but as he emerged from an elevator

The Kohl Building, circa 1907.

to leave the courthouse the maid, Marie Verges, shot him in the chest at close range with a Derringer. Kohl was seriously wounded but survived. Verges, after spending time in a mental institution in her native France, was released and spent the next few years alternately in France and Canada bombarding Kohl with threatening notes. The strain of it all, combined with the lingering effects of his chest wound, apparently proved too much for Kohl. In November 1921 in his room at the Del Monte Lodge in Carmel he put a gun to his head and ended his life.

In his will Kohl, who was separated from his wife, left most of his $4 million estate to his mistress, Marion L. Lord, who lived in a San Francisco hotel and who was the ex-wife of Alfred P. Lord of the East Coast Lord & Taylor retail chain. After the usual litigation to break the terms of the will by the aggrieved widow and assorted relatives, Marion Lord prevailed and received most of it as intended—including the Kohl Building.

Going back to the early days, in 1854 this corner was the site of Sam Brannan's Express Building, a four-story edifice with a stone façade and New Orleans-style iron balconies around the windows on the upper floors. Samuel Brannan (1819–1889), one of the dominant figures of San Francisco in the 1840s and 1850s, had arrived in 1846 as head of a large group of Mormons looking to establish a new colony of Latter Day Saints in the Far West. The discovery of gold quickly changed the landscape however, and Brannan, armed with large profits from selling supplies to miners from a hardware store in Sacramento and apparently aided by tithes he had collected from his fellow Mormons, bought prime real estate all over town and quickly became a millionaire. His early good fortune did not last. Alcoholism got the better of him; he died a pauper in San Diego.

*Walk a few steps north on Montgomery Street. At mid-block is:*

### ⑲ 420 Montgomery Street – Wells Fargo History Museum.

Wells Fargo, a name long associated with the history of the West, got its start in San Francisco in a modest two-story brick building just about where their museum stands today. The company was founded to provide express, mail, and banking services to merchants and miners in the wake of the gold rush. By the 1860s Wells Fargo stagecoaches carrying their trademark strongboxes were familiar sights on roads throughout the western U.S.

If you are on this walk during weekday business hours this two-floor museum is well worth a look. The showcase artifact on the main floor is an original Wells Fargo stagecoach, more than a century old. You can't get inside or even touch this one, but upstairs is a mockup of a stagecoach that you can board. Sit inside, and while the coach rocks back and forth on its creaking leather supports a recording gives a narration of an actual stagecoach journey taken by a young man in 1859 from St. Louis to San Francisco. It provides a graphic re-creation of just how uncomfortable such a trip must have been.

Other items of interest here are samples of gold from all the major Mother Lode rivers, postmarked letters to San Franciscans from mining towns, some of which no longer exist, and artifacts from the 1906 earthquake and fire including two small cylinders of dimes that were fused together by the heat. Also worth a look, on the second floor, is the story of the infamous stagecoach robber Black Bart, who held up

28 Wells Fargo stages before he was arrested and sent to San Quentin prison.

---

*Continue on Montgomery to the corner of Sacramento Street.*

---

### ⑳ Montgomery and Sacramento streets – SW corner – Site of Indian sweat house (early 1840s).

Located near this spot until about 1842 was an Indian temescal or sweat house, which was used by the local native Americans as a combination hot-air bath and place of spiritual purification. It consisted of a hole in the ground about six to eight feet deep, which was tightly covered with brush and had a hole in the center to let smoke out from the fire within. A narrow stream then ran down Sacramento Street and formed a small freshwater pool known as Laguna Dulce ("sweet water") just east of the temescal. After about half an hour, or when they were dripping with sweat, the Indians would refresh themselves by plunging into this pool.

### ㉑ Montgomery and Sacramento streets – NW corner – Site of Jacob Leese warehouse (1838–1841) / Hudson's Bay trading post (1841–1846).

Where the highrise office tower 505 Montgomery Street now stands was the site of the earliest commercial building on Montgomery Street, a large frame structure put up in 1838 by Jacob P. Leese. Leese, the second resident of Yerba Buena (after William A. Richardson), constructed it near the shoreline to store goods, mainly hides, that could be traded with the ships that were increasingly anchoring in the cove.

Three years later Leese sold his building to the Hudson's Bay Company, the big British trading firm, and moved to Sonoma. The company held on for five years, but with a declining fur catch, the increasing presence of the Americans, and the suicide of William Glen Rae, their alcoholic agent-in-charge, they closed their operation and sold the building to two local residents, Henry Mellus and William D. M. Howard. As the gold rush frenzy transformed San Francisco, the structure was soon replaced by more solid buildings, including—on the southwest corner of Montgomery and Commercial streets—the banking house of James King of William. King's murder in 1856 was to lead to the formation of the Second Vigilance Committee (see the Portsmouth Square walk).

### ⓴ Montgomery and Sacramento streets – NE corner – Site of "Armory Hall" (1853).

Across Sacramento Street on the northeast corner stood another piece of Sam Brannan's real estate empire, a 60-foot-square four-story brick building put up in 1853. It got the name Armory Hall from the local volunteer militias that used its fourth floor as a drill room.

---

*Walk east on Sacramento Street to the intersection of Leidesdorff. A plaque on the east side of the building on the southwest corner identifies this as the location of the What Cheer House.*

---

### ㉓ Sacramento and Leidesdorff streets – SW corner – Site of What Cheer House (1852–1906).

One of San Francisco's earliest hostelries, the What Cheer House was distinctive for several reasons: it was a temperance hotel in a hard drinking town; it was the first and for a while the only hotel to offer meals a la carte as well as table d'hote; it had a library with 2,000 books; and it also featured a small museum filled with an eclectic mix of items including Indian artifacts, seashells, assorted reptiles pickled in alcohol-filled

What Cheer House, 1865.

jars, and a collection of over 700 stuffed birds from all over the world.

Its most famous guest, Ulysses S. Grant, checked in in August 1854. Grant, virtually unknown at the time, had arrived in town by boat from Eureka where he had been stationed as an army captain at Fort Humboldt. But he had had a falling out with his commanding officer, felt his prospects for advancement were limited, and he missed his wife and children, so he resigned his commission and came to San Francisco to await a ship to take him back east to rejoin his family.

At low ebb, Grant spent a quiet hiatus in the City bunking in his 50-cent-a-day room (which included three meals) and reading books on military history in the hotel's library. He roamed the town, occasionally taking his ease in a chair in the lobby of the nearby Montgomery Block where his rumpled and unprepossessing presence drew little notice. Grant of course rejoined the army at the start of the Civil War. When he returned to San Francisco in 1879 he stayed at the Palace Hotel, where the war hero and former president of the United States was feted royally and lionized as a native son.

---

*Across the alley attached to the side of the building on the southeast corner of the intersection is a plaque, complete with an embossed portrait, honoring William A. Leidesdorff for whom the street is named. Continue down Sacramento to Sansome Street and turn right.*

---

### ㉔ 343 Sansome Street (1908) – Site of Howison's Pier (1850–1851).

The core of this building dates from 1908. It was designed by noted architect John Galen Howard, founder of the U.C. Berkeley School of Architecture. In 1929 what was originally an eight-story brick and terra cotta structure had five floors added and was remodeled in the prevailing art deco style of the time. The lobby in particular provides good examples of the art deco style, with Italian and Belgian marble, etched-glass wall sconces, and the gilt-enameled elevator doors.

Development on this site goes back to as early as 1850 when this part of Sacramento Street was a pier, called Howison's Wharf, extending into the bay. Stores and other commercial establishments were erected alongside the wharf to facilitate trade with the ships arriving in Yerba Buena Cove. One such unnamed store stood here at the southwest corner of Sacramento and Sansome streets. During excavations in 1989 to make way for the new corner addition to 343 Sansome, artifacts from this establishment were recovered.

Some of them are on display in the lobby to the right of the entrance by the original art deco elevator doors. On shelves on the wall are intact bottles of various kinds: green glass liquor bottles, condiment and preserve bottles, glazed ceramic cider and mineral water bottles, and a really fine "blob-top" mineral water bottle made of cobalt blue glass. A glass case in the center of this small room holds other artifacts, including parts of clay pipes, a ceramic cold cream jar, a polished bone and brass shaving brush, and two items that serve as vivid reminders that San Francisco at the time was still very much a frontier town—a branding iron, and a large broadaxe with a partially burned handle.

---

*Continue down Sacramento Street one block to Battery Street.*

---

### ㉕ Sacramento and Battery streets – SW corner – Site of Hoff Store (1851).

Like 343 Sansome, this corner too was the site of a commercial establishment connected to Howison's Pier. In this case we know the name of it—the Hoff store. William C. Hoff was a forty-niner from Jamestown, New York who by the spring of 1850 had built a two-story wood-frame building here attached to Howison's Pier. It served as a combination ship chandlery and store. Of all the fires that ravaged early San Francisco the one of May 3–4, 1851 caused the most wide-spread destruction. Flames from the blaze could be seen 85 miles away in Monterey. Hoff's store burned in that fire and its contents dropped into the bay mud below and were covered over as the city expanded into the cove.

In 1986 during excavation for the present office high rise on this spot the remains of the Hoff store were discovered by local archeologist Allen Pastron, who found a wealth of artifacts covered with mud and ash 15 feet below street level. Among the objects retrieved were hundreds of bottles of French champagne, intact clear glass jars of imported olives with their lids still sealed, dozens of large ceramic crocks filled with butter, the rusted remains of U.S. Army carbines, lead shot, nails, work boots, shovels, Chinese porcelains, and patent

medicines such as "Mrs. Winslow's Soothing Syrup." It was a rare ar-
cheological find in that by contrast to most digs, which uncover artifacts spread over a long period of time—centuries or more in some
cases—this one revealed deposits of a one-day event and provided a
snapshot of a San Francisco store as it was on May 3, 1851.

---

*Walk two blocks down Sacramento to Davis Street. As you pass the build-
ing on the southeast corner of Sacramento and Front, look at the plaque
about Fort Gunnybags on the east wall. At Davis Street, cross to the other
side of Sacramento.*

---

**㉖ Sacramento Street – East side between Davis and Front
streets – Site of "Fort Gunnybags"** (1856).

About mid-block, but closer to Davis Street, was the site in 1856 of
a two-story liquor warehouse that served as the command post for
the Second Committee of Vigilance. The event that led to the formation of this vigilante group—composed of the leading businessmen
in town—was the killing of James King of William, a newspaper publisher who had been gunned down by James Casey, a former convict
who had resented King's publishing that fact in his paper (see the
Portsmouth Square walk for more details). The Committee's headquarters, located here, was Fort Vigilance, more commonly known as
"Fort Gunnybags," for the protective ring of sandbags placed in front
of the building.

When King died of his gunshot wound on May 22, 1856 the Committee lost no time in exacting justice. After a hurried trial that same
day, Casey and another man they had earlier taken into custody, a
gambler named Charles Cora who had killed a U.S. marshal, were
marched out onto planks extending from the windows on the second
floor. Casey, after giving a rambling farewell speech in which he
prayed for his mother, nearly fainted when the noose was wrapped
around his neck. Cora, with a gambler's practiced nonchalance, faced
the end with an air of calm. While close to 3,000 committee members
and spectators looked on, the cords attached to the ends of the planks
were released and the two men dropped to their deaths. Both were
buried at the Mission Dolores cemetery, where their grave markers
can still be seen.

The Second Committee of Vigilance stayed in business a few more months and closed out its reign with two more executions. These occurred in the middle of Davis Street between Sacramento and Commercial, or just about midway between where the Gap and Banana Republic stores are today. Instead of makeshift planks, the Committee erected a real gallows this time. On July 29, 1856 Joseph Hetherington, who had shot and killed a doctor, and Philander Brace, who had a long criminal history despite being only 21 years old, were led up the scaffold and had nooses placed around their necks. Hetherington proclaimed his innocence while Brace shouted out obscenities. As spectators perched on nearby buildings and committee members lined up in neat rows as soldiers at arms, the trap doors were sprung, writing an end to a turbulent period in San Francisco history.

---

*Walk back up Sacramento Street two blocks. On the north side between Battery and Sansome streets is:*

---

## ㉗ 400 Sansome Street – Old Federal Reserve Bank (1923).

Architect George Kelham, who designed the Old Main Library and the Russ and Shell Buildings among others, designed this rectangular temple as the Federal Reserve's western U.S. headquarters during 1917–18. Due to World War I however, the building wasn't completed until 1923. With its multi-story Ionic columns topped by free-standing eagles, this edifice presents a monumental appearance; prior to about World War II government buildings were consciously meant to impress.

During a 1925 excavation for an armored car entrance on Battery Street the remains of the storied gold-rush ship *Apollo* were discovered. The ship itself was beyond saving but dozens of artifacts were recovered. They are now on display at the Maritime Museum across from Ghirardelli Square.

The Federal Reserve occupied this building until 1983 when it moved into its new headquarters at 101 Market Street (see the Market Street walk).

---

*Walk two blocks up Sacramento to Leidesdorff Street. Turn right and go one block to Commercial Street. Look back south down Leidesdorff Street.*

---

## ㉘ Leidesdorff Street (c.1850) and Commercial Street – Site of Long Wharf (1849).

Leidesdorff is one of the oddest streets in San Francisco. It runs three blocks from Pine to Clay streets. Not only is each of the three blocks a different width, but in two of them the width of the street changes in the middle of the block. And the block between Sacramento and Clay varies further in that if you look south from the intersection of Leidesdorff and Commercial Street you will see that this block jogs about three feet to the west of the other two.

Why these oddities? The answer will never be known for sure since the records were lost in 1906, but one salient fact is that Leidesdorff Street—at least the two northernmost blocks from California to Clay streets—closely parallel the original shoreline of Yerba Buena Cove. It could be that Leidesdorff was a trail along the water's edge, perhaps even an old Indian trail which simply through use became a thoroughfare that was eventually paved over.

The intersection of Commercial and Leidesdorff streets was where construction on the Commercial or Central or Long Wharf, as it was commonly known, began in May 1849. It quickly became the city's premier wharf, and soon extended far enough into the bay so that ships could dock alongside and be able to unload cargo without having to use lighters to get goods ashore. Commercial structures built on piles arose on either side, and a few old ships were roped to it to serve as rooms for rent or as storage.

Long Wharf was a microcosm of San Francisco in the year 1849. Steamboats, barks, schooners, and sailing vessels of all kinds tied up against the wharf in the process of transporting people and goods to destinations as close as Oakland or as far away as China. Drays, handcarts, and sometimes fine carriages rattled up and down its plank boards as a polyglot mix of people from countries all over the globe, wearing a variety of dress and speaking a veritable Babel of languages, came to do their business. Gamblers, monte dealers, and shell-game con men set up temporary stands and took money from the gullible. Thieves and pickpockets worked the crowd; fights and robberies were not uncommon.

*Walk a little more than a block west on Commercial Street (be careful crossing Montgomery Street). On the north side, the one-story brick and stone building is:*

## ㉙ 608 Commercial Street – Former Sub-Treasury Building (1877).

Dating from 1877, the Sub-Treasury building is the oldest survivor in the downtown area outside of Jackson Square. It stands on the site of the first San Francisco branch mint (1854–74) and was built to serve the federal government as a branch of the treasury after a larger mint had been constructed at Fifth and Mission streets in 1874. The sub-treasury's function was to handle transactions between the government and private individuals, and to store coin and bullion used in those transactions. This building was originally four stories high, but the top three floors did not survive the earthquake and fire of 1906. The main floor and the basement vault containing $13 million of gold and silver were saved. The Sub-Treasury continued its operations here until 1915, when its replacement was built at 301 Pine Street (which became the Pacific Coast Stock Exchange).

The building now houses the Pacific Heritage Museum. Although it primarily features changing exhibits related to Pacific Basin culture, there is a permanent display on the history of the Sub-Treasury Building. The vault contains replica strong boxes and coin bags.

## ㉚ 632 Commercial Street – Site of *Daily Morning Call* newspaper (1860s).

Adjoining the U.S. Mint were the offices of the *Daily Morning Call.* There were lots of newspapers in San Francisco then, but in 1864 this one employed a young reporter named Mark Twain (1835–1910). Twain had arrived in the City after a couple of years working for the *Territorial Enterprise* newspaper in Virginia City, Nevada. Bret Harte, who was already somewhat established as a writer, and who had a day job at the mint as secretary to the superintendent, took the young reporter under his wing and helped him polish his prose.

Twain, who had started writing the kind of humorous pieces at the *Enterprise* that would soon make him famous, found straight reporting at the *Call* a struggle, calling it "...awful drudgery for a lazy man." When he wrote an indignant account about a gang of Irish hoodlums who stoned a Chinese laundryman for fun while a policeman tolerantly looked on and did nothing, the paper's owner/editor refused to run it saying he didn't want to offend his mostly Irish working-class readership — they hated the Chinese. Not surprisingly, Twain was fired after only a few months.

He soon returned to the style he favored with articles for other local newspapers and periodicals, and started on the road to fame when his short story *The Celebrated Jumping Frog of Calaveras County* was published in 1865. Twain soon left San Francisco for good, and went on to write such classics of American literature as *The Adventures of Huckleberry Finn*. But it was San Francisco where he really got his start and learned his craft.

## ㉛ Empire Park – Commercial Street – Site of Emperor Norton's lodging house (1870s).

About where tiny Empire Park is today was once the site of the modest lodging house where Joshua Norton (1819–1880), better known as Norton I, Emperor of the United States and Protector of Mexico, bedded down after a full day amongst his subjects.

San Francisco's most colorful 19th century eccentric, Norton was a forty-niner who had made a fortune in wholesale food brokerage then lost it all in a scheme to corner the rice market. In 1859 he persuaded a local newspaper to print an item in which he proclaimed himself emperor of the United States. Whether this transformation was simply a shrewd career move in light of his reduced circumstances or whether he was mentally ill is hard to say. Studio photographs of him suggest the latter. Whatever the case, San Francisco's mad emperor soon became a civic joke enjoyed by all. As he strolled about town in his military uniform (donated by a general at the Presidio) his subjects bowed as he passed. He dined free at local restaurants that solicited his patronage and put signs in their windows reading "The Emperor Norton eats here." Newspapers printed his fanciful proclamations, and local capitalists submitted to the small tithes he assessed them.

Yet out of the public spotlight he lived simply for an emperor, retiring here and paying his landlord 50 cents in cash each night for a six-by-ten-foot room with a cot, a chair, and a washstand. He hung his uniform on a nail on the wall. When he died suddenly in January 1880 there was genuine sorrow. He was buried at Masonic Cemetery in Laurel Heights, and when the bodies were relocated to Colma in 1934 his skeleton, still wearing its uniform, was reburied at Woodlawn Cemetery.

# William A. Leidesdorff
## (1810–1848)

William Leidesdorff was one of early San Francisco's leading citizens. His life began in a rather unpromising fashion: he was born illegitimate on the island of St. Croix in the West Indies, the son of a Danish sailor and native mulatto mother. As a young man he migrated to New Orleans, determined to make something of himself. Despite his African American heritage he was apparently able to pass as white, for he apprenticed to a successful cotton broker. Before long, however, he switched careers and soon became a skilled ship captain.

In 1841 he piloted a vessel through the Strait of Magellan, and up the west coast of the Americas, and landed at the tiny Mexican pueblo of Yerba Buena on the shore of San Francisco Bay, where he decided to settle down. He quickly established himself as a waterfront trader—and sometime smuggler—who prospered in the sparsely populated town. He became a Mexican citizen—which entitled him to own property—and he quickly took advantage, receiving a 35,000 acre land grant on the American River near Sacramento. In San Francisco, as Yerba Buena was renamed in January 1847, he purchased a number of city lots, built a waterfront warehouse, and the City Hotel, the town's premier pre-gold rush hostelry.

Active in municipal affairs, he became a member of the town council and the school board; he also served as the city's first treasurer. Thomas O. Larkin, the Monterey-based American consul to the ruling Mexican government thought

William A. Leidesdorff.

enough of him to make him Vice-Consul and kept him in place in Yerba Buena. Leidesdorff was well connected; he knew and had dealings with all of the leading lights of early San Francisco: Captain John B. Montgomery, Washington A. Bartlett, Thomas O. Larkin, Joseph Folsom, Commodore Robert F. Stockton, all of whom, like Leidesdorff himself, had city streets named after them.

Befitting his position, Leidesdorff was hospitable in the Spanish/Mexican tradition. He lived with his common-law wife, a Russian-Alaskan woman from Sitka, in a bungalow-style adobe home on the corner of Montgomery and California streets, and entertained frequently. Although he apparently got along well with most people he was described as having a temper. He was once arrested because of an altercation with another man after an argument over a bet on a horse race.

In April 1848, shortly after the discovery of gold had become public, John Sutter notified Leidesdorff that placer miners were ranging over his land in the Sacramento area foraging for gold. It was a glimmer of what might have been, but tragically Leidesdorff suddenly became ill and died of "brain fever"—perhaps encephalitis or typhus—on May 18, 1848. The whole town mourned his passing. He was given a grand funeral, and a solemn procession accompanied his body to Mission Dolores where he was buried under the chapel.

Leidesdorff never married, had no children, and left no will. He was about $50,000 in debt when he died, largely due to unrepaid loans he had made to the American forces fighting in California during the war with Mexico. Since he died intestate his holdings became embroiled in litigation. The discovery of gold and the resulting boom in real estate values quickly increased the value of his properties to nearly $1 million within a couple of years of his death. Joseph Folsom, who himself was soon to die prematurely, ended up with most of his estate.

# Haight-Ashbury

**Length:** 1.7 miles / 2.7 kilometers.
**Time:** 2 hours.
**Walk Rating:** Moderate to Strenuous.
**Hills:** Lyon Street from Oak to Page is a moderate uphill. Buena Vista West on the way to stop 9 and continuing to stop 11 on Piedmont Street is a moderate to strenuous three-block-long uphill climb. It is downhill from there until you reach the corner of Haight and Ashbury on the way to stop 15. The walk is on level ground the rest of the way.
**Public Transit:** Muni bus lines 6, 7, and 71 run the length of Haight Street from Market.
**Parking:** No public garages or parking lots. Street parking is usually not too difficult to find on Oak Street next to the Panhandle.
**Restrooms:** There is a coin-operated (25 cents) public toilet near the end of the tour at Stanyan and Waller streets just inside Golden Gate Park.

The name Haight-Ashbury today is known world-wide as the epicenter of the youthful rebellion of the 1960s. But its history stretches back more than a century prior to that notable time. It was late to develop as a residential neighborhood, primarily because it was part of the "Outside Lands," which was the area past Divisadero Street, the western border of the city in the 1850s. Initially it was much like the rest of the city, with the ubiquitous sand dunes. But it did offer enough in the way of arable land, clumps of oak trees, and clear springs to attract a few ranchers and dairy farmers, who claimed spreads starting in the 1850s and '60s.

Real interest in the area didn't develop until 1870 when work started on Golden Gate Park. The park had originally been planned to start at Divisadero Street, but squatters and land speculators who had claimed parcels from there to what became Stanyan Street, ten blocks to the west, proved difficult to dislodge. So a compromise was reached whereby in return for clear title to their other holdings, the squatters would give up their claims to a narrow strip of land leading into the main body of the park. What was to be the eastern portion of the park was thus narrowed to the block-wide strip now known as the Panhandle. The grid pattern of streets was extended south to become the nucleus of what became Haight-Ashbury.

Despite the attraction of the park, residential and other develop-

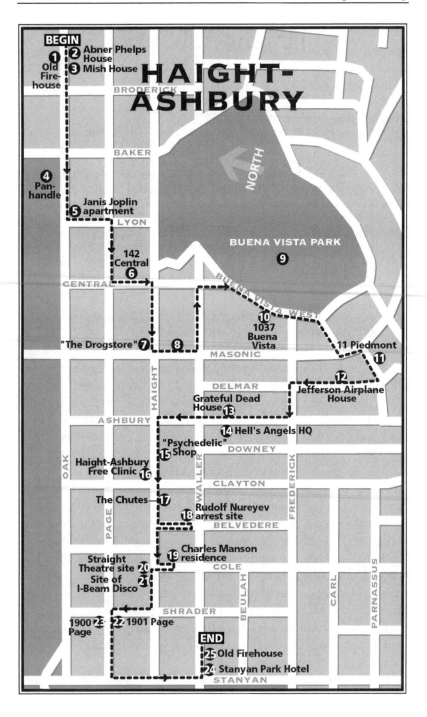

**BEGIN**

**1** Old Fire-house

**2** Abner Phelps House

**3** Mish House

# HAIGHT-ASHBURY

BRODERICK

BAKER

**4** Pan-handle

**5** Janis Joplin apartment

LYON

**6** 142 Central

CENTRAL

NORTH

BUENA VISTA PARK

**9**

BUENA VISTA WEST

**7** "The Drogstore"

**8**

**10** 1037 Buena Vista

**11** 11 Piedmont

MASONIC

**12**

DELMAR

Jefferson Airplane House

HAIGHT

Grateful Dead House **13**

ASHBURY

**14** Hell's Angels HQ

OAK

**15** "Psychedelic" Shop

DOWNEY

FREDERICK

Haight-Ashbury Free Clinic **16**

WALLER

CLAYTON

The Chutes **17**

PAGE

**18** Rudolf Nureyev arrest site

BELVEDERE

**19** Charles Manson residence

Straight Theatre site **20**

COLE

BEULAH

CARL

PARNASSUS

Site of I-Beam Disco **21**

SHRADER

1900 Page **23**   **22** 1901 Page

**END**

**25** Old Firehouse

**24** Stanyan Park Hotel

STANYAN

# HAIGHT-ASHBURY

**1** 1152 Oak Street - Old Firehouse

**2** 1111 Oak Street - Abner Phelps House

**3** 1153 Oak Street - Mish House

**4** Golden Gate Park Panhandle

**5** 122 Lyon Street - Location of Janis Joplin apartment

**6** 142 Central Avenue

**7** 1398 Haight Street - Location of "The Drogstore"

**8** 1200 Block of Masonic

**9** Buena Vista Park

**10** 737 Buena Vista West

**11** 11 Piedmont Street

**12** 130 Delmar Street - Location of Jefferson Airplane House

**13** 710 Ashbury Street - Location of Grateful Dead House

**14** 715 Ashbury Street - Location of Hell's Angels HQ

**15** 1535 Haight Street - Location of Psychedelic Shop

**16** 558 Clayton Street - Haight-Ashbury Free Clinic

**17** Site of The Chutes

**18** 42 Belvedere Street - Location of Rudolph Nureyev arrest

**19** 636 Cole Street - Location of Charles Manson residence

**20** 1700 Haight Street - Site of Straight Theater

**21** 1748 Haight Street - Old Masonic Hall

**22** 1901 Page Street

**23** 1900 Page Street

**24** 750 Stanyan Street - Stanyan Park Hotel

**25** 1757 Waller Street - Old Firehouse

ment didn't get started until a cable-car line was put through on Haight Street to Stanyan in 1883. Houses first went up along both sides of the Panhandle and in the Ashbury Heights area to the south. The wealthy built second homes—typically on the bigger and more prestigious corner lots—and the middle parts of the blocks filled in with more modest flats and single-family homes. Both sides of Haight Street (now the main commercial artery) from Masonic to Shrader, and the cross streets nearby, remained vacant for decades, however. That land was owned by John H. Baird, a forty-niner, whose widow, Veronica, didn't start releasing most of those parcels for sale until after 1902.

As Golden Gate Park became a popular weekend destination the west end of Haight-Ashbury developed into a resort area. A baseball field and an amusement park were built in the 1880s and 1890s respectively. Stanyan Street was the commercial hub then, with saloons, hotels, and a number of bicycle shops—cycling was all the rage in the 1890s. The Haight still has more than its share of bicycle shops today—a legacy of that craze.

The 1906 earthquake proved a disaster for most of San Francisco but not for Haight-Ashbury: migrants in need of housing and services poured into the undamaged district. Prosperity continued into the 1920s, although by then the novelty of the area had worn off for the elite; the district became solidly middle class. The 1930s proved a tough time not only because of the Great Depression but also because the Twin Peaks and Sunset public transit tunnels (built in 1917 and 1928 respectively) opened up the western area of the city for development. Those factors, combined with the mobility the automobile offered, led to a migration out of the neighborhood. After World War II things changed again as African Americans became more of a presence in the district, especially in the 1960s after redevelopment forced them out of the nearby Fillmore.

By the mid-1960s the first ferment of that turbulent decade was starting to make itself known as the baby-boom generation began to come of age. Haight-Ashbury, with its cheap rents, college students from nearby USF and San Francisco State, and castoff Beats from North Beach, soon became ground zero for hippies. The era peaked in 1967 with the now famous Summer of Love. An era of innocence and good feeling initially prevailed as seminal rock bands such as the

Grateful Dead, the Jefferson Airplane, and Janis Joplin and Big Brother and the Holding company gave free concerts in Golden Gate Park and the Panhandle.

But the easily available drugs and sex proved too much of a lure and a coarser element soon invaded. Hells Angels, criminals, and opportunists of all kinds (including Charles Manson) arrived, and by late that summer the scene had turned ugly. Harder drugs such as methamphetamine, or "speed," and heroin replaced the more benign (and legal until October 1966) LSD. Things deteriorated quickly, and over the next few years the Haight, as Haight-Ashbury is more commonly called today, became a dangerous slum. By the early 1970s about a third of Haight Street's shops were abandoned and boarded up.

Starting about the mid-1970s, however, escalating real estate prices led to a renaissance that still continues. Gentrification has touched the Haight just as it has much of San Francisco, but despite that the district still manages to retain much of its anti-establishment and hippie flavor, particularly along Haight Street itself.

---

*Start this tour on the sidewalk in front of 1111 Oak Street (the white house with the two balconies and front yard) which is between Divisadero and Broderick streets. The first house on this tour is the building with the tall square tower, across the street:*

---

### ❶ 1152 Oak Street – Old Firehouse – Engine Company #21 (1893).

Built in 1893—the date can still clearly be seen in a circle on the gable—this is the oldest city firehouse still under the ownership of the San Francisco Fire Department. It was built in response to a fire that had occurred a few blocks away at Page and Lyon streets several months earlier. The nearest station at that time was at Laguna and McAllister streets, over a mile away; something closer to the developing neighborhood was needed.

Although it is no longer an active firehouse—it recently served as a gym for firefighters—the interior still has its original brass firepole and cast-iron spiral staircase leading to the sleeping quarters on the second floor. The iron staircase is likely just one of two such remaining in city firehouses. The front façade of the building has changed a

**1152 Oak Street–Engine Company #21.**

bit over the years. Originally the rectangular front door and window flanking the double doors had arched tops, and the first floor was rusticated to make it look like stone.

From the time the SFFD was organized, in 1866, until as late as 1922, fire engines and equipment were horse-driven. (At this station automotive power replaced horses in 1915.) Horses were stabled here, as at other firehouses, and at the sound of the alarm they were positioned under harnesses suspended from the ceiling and then cinched up. Meanwhile, the boilers of the steam-operated fire engines would be fired up, and when the pressure reached the requisite level the horses were attached and off they would go. Once back at the station house the hoses would be spread on the sidewalk and cleaned and then hung in the drying tower, which is the tower atop the west corner of the building with the alternating fish-scale and diamond-shaped shingles. When dry, the hoses would be loaded onto the fire truck, ready for fresh use.

Engine Company #21 fought both the famous Baldwin Hotel fire in 1898 (see the Market Street walk) and, of course, the 1906 conflagration. During the latter, the company was on duty for over 50 hours straight before returning to the firehouse exhausted late on the morning of April 20.

> Nineteenth-century firehouses had spiral staircases because horses, which were stabled on the ground floor, could walk up straight stairways.

### ❷ 1111 Oak Street – Abner Phelps House (c.1851).

The origin and date of construction of this house—which all sources agree is one of the oldest, if not the oldest house in San

Francisco—is a bit murky. With its double verandas, dormer windows, and above-ground basement, this Gothic Revival structure resembles a southern riverfront cottage. One of original owner Abner Phelps' descendants claims it was built in New Orleans (his wife's hometown) in 1827 and was brought around the Horn to make her feel more at ease in San Francisco. During a 1976 restoration however, it was discovered that the house is made of redwood, which would make it of local construction since redwood is not native to the South.

Abner Phelps (1804–1873) was actually a native of Vermont but he had spent most of his adult life in the South, including time in New Orleans, prior to emigrating to San Francisco in 1849. A lawyer by trade, he had his office downtown and rode his horse to work every day over the mostly rough ground to his offices in the Montgomery Block 2½ miles away. Phelps and his wife had seven children, six of whom survived to adulthood. Five of them never married, and four of them—two sons and two daughters—continued to live in this house until the last one died in 1940.

When the house was put up in the early 1850s as part of a 160-acre plot that was then outside the city boundaries, the property had a stables, barn, and a windmill. The house stood then closer to the corner of Oak and Divisadero. But as the grid pattern of streets advanced this way in the early 1890s the house was repositioned to face Divisadero. Its address was, in fact, for many years 329 Divisadero. In 1904 it was moved back from the street so that commercial storefronts could be built along Divisadero and Oak streets. It remained in that position until 1978, when it was moved one last time so that its main façade with the two verandas faced Oak Street. The stores on Oak Street were torn down and the formal garden now in place was added. Today the building is zoned commercial, and houses offices.

*Next door is:*

## ❸ 1153 Oak Street – Mish House (c.1885)

In a city with a lot of elaborately detailed Victorians this one still manages to stand out. The ornate cornice with its fanciful brackets and grooved dentils is certainly noteworthy but the use of Ionic-topped collonettes as part of the decorative treatment of the windows gives the house a further baroque cast. Yet these elements manage to showcase it without being ostentatious. The mansard roof that originally crowned the building would have put these decorative elements in better perspective. To gain a grasp of the pure decorative nature of these adornments, go around to the back of the house and contrast the totally plain back wall with that of the more visible front and side.

The house takes its name from the original owners, Phenes and Sarah Mish. After her husband died, in 1895, Mrs. Mish, who had a millinery and dress-making business downtown, continued living here until her death, in 1916. In the 1920s the house was rented to lodgers until the Mish heirs sold it in 1928. It was then converted into apartments. In the early 1930s a dance school operated out of it. Since the 1960s it has been occupied by a private social welfare firm.

---

*Walk west on Oak Street two and a half blocks to the corner of Lyon Street. The greensward off to your right is:*

---

### ❹ The Golden Gate Park Panhandle (1870).

This pleasant blade of parkland with its green lawn and mature trees is marred only by the steady thrum of automobile traffic going up Fell Street on one side and down Oak Street on the other. It must have had a different feel to it in the 19th century when the major noise consisted of the clip-clop of horses pulling the carriages that promenaded here. At that time a long thoroughfare called The Avenue ran down the middle of the Panhandle, and here the city's elite showed off. One account in the 1880s noted Leland Stanford's rig with his "gold-mounted harness and perfectly appointed servants" making its way through the crowd.

The area maintained its allure for at least another generation. Early in the 20th century, Mayor James Duval Phelan promoted a plan that would have extended the Panhandle all the way to Market Street. He envisioned it becoming another Champs-Elyseées, complete with grand buildings lining both sides instead of the commonplace bay-windowed Victorians. But nothing came of the idea.

In 1906 the Panhandle served as a safe-haven camp for refugees fleeing the city's destroyed downtown. Tents, and later simple wooden cottages, went up to provide for their housing needs. Visitors of a different sort—hippies—made this strip of land a favored hangout in the 1960s. Jimi Hendrix and bands such as the Grateful Dead and Big Brother and the Holding Company gave well-attended free concerts on the Panhandle in 1966 and 1967.

---

*Walk up Lyon Street a short distance and stop in front of #122.*

---

**❺ 122 Lyon Street, #1 – Residence of Janis Joplin** (1967–68).

Rock star Janis Joplin lived in apartment #1 of this remodeled, and now nondescript, Victorian for a little over a year during 1967-68.

The hard driving rocker was living here when she gained real fame, first with her appearance at the Monterey Pop Festival and then when she recorded her first album, "Cheap Thrills." (She had wanted to call it "Sex, Drugs, and Cheap Thrills" but that was vetoed.) Joplin used to walk her half-collie dog George down the hill in the Panhandle, but when her landlord discovered that she had a pet she was evicted.

---

*Walk up to the intersection of Lyon and Page. Noteworthy here from an architectural point of view are the fine large Queen Anne Victorians on each corner. Three of them have corner towers, but they vary: one is a standard "witch's cap," another is bell-shaped, and the third is a pyramidal octagon. Walk west one block on Page Street to Central and take a left. Halfway up the block is:*

---

**❻ 142 Central Avenue** (1899).

In the 1960s and '70s the basement of this rounded bay Victorian served as a recording studio for local bands such as Big Brother and the Holding Company, and Steve Miller, who did the vocals for his hit song "Fly Like an Eagle" here. According to Joel Selvin in his book *The Musical History Tour* this was also the scene in 1976 of a gruesome crime. A handyman employed by band manager David Leahy went berserk one night. He stabbed Leahy's secretary to death and attacked Leahy and his wife with an axe while they were sleeping.

*Continue up Central to Haight Street, take a right and go one block*
*to Masonic. On the northeast corner of the intersection is:*

**❼ 1398 Haight Street – Site of "The Drogstore"** (1967).

The ground floor of this building, in 1967, housed a popular café and hippie hangout called "The Drogstore." The owners had wanted to call it "The Drugstore Café" to associate the name with the good-times drug culture that was still prevalent, but the police found the name too suggestive and forced the change. The site now houses a restaurant that has changed names and owners several times since then.

*Cross Haight Street and walk south on Masonic into the next block.*

**❽ 1200 Block of Masonic Street** (1896).

All of the Queen Anne houses here on the east side of Masonic up to Waller Street, with the exception of #1200 and #1244, were built by the firm of Cranston and Keenan in 1896. Robert Dickie Cranston (1849–1916) was a native of Canada who migrated west shortly after the completion of the transcontinental railroad in 1869 opened the way for easier travel to California. Cranston initially worked as a carpenter on the Sutro Tunnel in Virginia City, Nevada before moving on to San Francisco. He became a carpenter/builder/architect, and in 1889, as residential development reached the Haight, started putting up homes here. For a time in the 1890s he partnered with Hugh Keenan, and later with his two sons Robert A. and William (the latter was the father of U.S. Senator Alan Cranston).

Cranston also did most of the east side of the 1300 block of Masonic as well as several blocks of Page, Cole, and Ashbury streets elsewhere in the district. Most of his houses still stand, although some have been altered. This prolific builder did not just choose this part of town as one of opportunity or convenience. He liked it enough to live here with his family in several of the homes he himself erected, living variously at two locations on Page Street and then at 635 Ashbury, which was where he was living when he died. His name still sometimes surfaces today when current homeowners occasionally tell of finding his business card in their newel posts during remodeling. It was the builder's equivalent of an artist signing his picture.

---

*Walk up to Waller Street, cross over, and then take a left. Go to the end of the block where Waller meets Buena Vista West Drive. The green covered hill in front of you is:*

---

**❾ Buena Vista Park** (1867).

This 36-acre park, which rises to a height of 569 feet, was originally called Hill Park and was largely barren, except for a few native oaks, when reserved as a park in 1867 as part of the City's deal with squatters that set aside Golden Gate Park for public use. It was officially dedicated and renamed Buena Vista Park in 1894. John McLaren, the superintendent of Golden Gate Park, supervised the planting of seedlings that were provided by Mayor Adolph Sutro every Arbor Day during the late 1890s.

During the 1906 fire the hill's slopes and summit provided spectators with a great vantage point from which to watch the city burn. In the 1910s new stairways, paths, and a few tennis courts were added. Further improvements came in the 1930s when laborers hired by the Works Progress Administration constructed new retaining walls and drainage ditches. The latter were largely composed of shards of marble and granite headstones from the nearby recently dismantled Lone Mountain Cemetery. Most of the engraved pieces were turned face down to the ground, but in a few places they are face up and reveal a bit of inscription here and there.

The hippie invasion of the Haight during the 1960s led to a decline of the park since transients camping out used the trees and bushes as cover for drug dealing and casual sex. Some of these unsavory aspects continued into the 1980s when gays made it a favorite spot for anonymous sexual encounters. In recent years, however, the park has been cleaned up and become safer as local neighborhood associations have been more watchful and have lobbied for improvements.

You can access the park from the trail across the street that leads off to the left or there are good entry points from farther up the hill. From the park's summit there is a nice view through the trees of the northern part of San Francisco and the stretch of the bay from the Marin headlands to Russian Hill.

*Go right on Buena Vista West until you come to the large house with the gated driveway:*

**⑩  737 Buena Vista West** (1897).

This stately house, a mixture of Beaux-Arts Classicism and Colonial Revival, was built in 1897, apparently for Richard Spreckels, a nephew of sugar magnate Claus Spreckels. It is said to have had its share of noted residents, including journalist Ambrose Bierce and writer Jack London—the latter allegedly wrote one of his better known stories, *White Fang*, here. In the 1960s a small recording studio was installed. Both Quicksilver Messenger Service and the Steve Miller band recorded here and during the 1970s vocalist Graham Nash of Crosby, Stills and Nash lived here. After Nash's residence, the house briefly became a bed-and-breakfast. It is now once again a private residence.

*Continue up the hill past Frederick Street to Java and turn right. (If you want to go directly to the summit of Buena Vista Park, continue up Buena Vista West a short distance. A paved path will take you right to the summit.) Turn left on Masonic up the hill, go a short distance, and then turn right on Piedmont. A few houses down on the left is:*

**⑪  11 Piedmont Street** (c.1860s).

This simple Greek Revival/Victorian cottage, which looks a little out of place here tucked in between more modern houses, is a rare survivor from the days when Haight-Ashbury was still dotted with dairy farms. Its history is a little murky. What is certain is that it was once owned by a German immigrant named F. W. M. Lange and that this farmhouse, which was once the main building of a dairy farm, was moved here from another location.

Lange came to San Francisco in 1864 and started a dairy ranch on Sutter Street between Broderick and Divisadero. In 1870 he purchased nine acres in what became the four blocks bounded by Stanyan, Carl, Cole, and Grattan streets. San Franciscans of the time distrusted paper money, and the story goes that when Lange went to pay owner Peter Schadt with currency he was told to come back with the purchase price in gold coin, which he did.

In 1888 the house was moved here from somewhere nearby. It could have been from the above location; other accounts mention the corner of Frederick and Ashbury, and another says a site near the Panhandle. Accounts also differ as to why it was moved. One says a Lange daughter wanted the house moved uphill to avoid the fleas that infested the sand dunes below; another version is that it was moved to be closer to a well. There is support for the latter theory in that water department records show that a water hookup was not effected here until the early 1900s, suggesting that the family was indeed relying on well water until then.

---

*Continue on Piedmont the short half block to Delmar Street and take a right. Walk down to 130 Delmar, and as you do note the great variety of architectural styles on both sides of the street. Besides a few Queen Anne Victorians there are examples of Beaux-Arts Classicism, Tudor Revival, and Mission Revival. There is even one resembling a New England shingle-style farmhouse.*

---

### ⑫ 130 Delmar Street (1890) – Jefferson Airplane House (1967–68).

This sprawling Victorian cottage was occupied by the Jefferson Airplane during the Summer of Love in 1967. They lived a quiet existence compared to their neighbors, the Grateful Dead, a block away (see next entry), but they made up for it later. The band moved in May 1968 to a mansion at 2400 Fulton Street on the other side of Golden Gate Park, where they had some raucous parties, including a memorable New Years Eve party in 1979 with John Belushi and the Blues Brothers after the latter's farewell performance at Winterland.

---

*Continue down Delmar to Frederick Street, cross over, and turn left. Go the one block to Ashbury. Turn right, go down most of the block, and stop in front of:*

---

### ⑬ 710 Ashbury Street (c.1890) – Grateful Dead House (1966–68).

This Queen Anne, part of a grouping of six built by Robert Dickie Cranston, was the home and headquarters from the fall of 1966 to

March 1968 of the band most iden-
tified with the Haight and its culture, the Grateful Dead. (The name
Grateful Dead came from an Egyp-
tian tomb inscription.)

On October 2, 1967 California
state agents and San Francisco police raided "the Dead's way-out 13-
room pad" as the *Chronicle* called
the house in a front-page story the
next day, and confiscated close to a
pound of marijuana and hashish.
Band members Bob Weir and Ron
("Pig Pen") McKernan—ironically
the only two of the group not into
drugs—were arrested, along with
several staffers and a half dozen
young women who were described

**710 Ashbury Street.**

as "friends" or "visitors." As the first arrestee came out in handcuffs
"one long-haired girl yelled out a familiar 12-letter epithet at the
officers." At the trial eight months later Weir and McKernan were
convicted of the misdemeanor of being in a place where marijuana
was used, and paid fines of $100 each. The others paid similar fines.

---

*Across the street is:*

---

**⓮ 715 Ashbury Street** (c.1895) **– Hell's Angels
Headquarters** (late 1960s).

It is hard to imagine today, but this pleasant, well-maintained
Victorian was, in the late 1960s, the San Francisco headquarters of the
Hell's Angels. The bad-boy motorcycle group had a number of run-
ins with San Francisco police in the Haight in those days, the most
notorious of which occurred right in front of this house on September
9, 1969. At 12:30 a.m. a young man, Cassel Brenner, who lived next
door at 709 Ashbury, came home to find the gang's motorcycles
cluttering the sidewalk. When he innocently asked several members
sitting on the porch what was going on one of them threw a can of

beer at Brenner's car, shattering his windshield. Thirsting for action, about a dozen Angels with chains and tire irons converged on the vehicle, battered it, and then pushed it down toward Waller Street where it came to a stop in a driveway.

Two beat cops showed up in response to the commotion and when they saw that they were outnumbered they radioed for help. Two dozen reinforcements quickly arrived, and after a struggle and several injuries the police hauled 37 Angels and their girlfriends off to jail. They also confiscated four handguns, eight bullwhips, ten machetes, twelve daggers, and a quantity of marijuana and pills.

---

*Walk down Ashbury a block and a half to Haight Street and turn left. Halfway down the block on the left side is:*

---

### ⓯ 1535 Haight Street – Site of the Psychedelic Shop (1966–67).

Virtually all of the head shops and other businesses peculiar to the 1960s have long since been converted to other uses. A prime example is this one. Where a pizza parlor now stands was once the Haight's first psychedelic shop. It opened in January 1966 and sold records, posters, incense, books, and tickets to rock concerts. The place quickly became a favorite local hangout.

In October 1967, the San Francisco police, ever vigilant, raided the shop and confiscated copies of a book called *The Love Book* being sold there. The book, which had only sold about 50 copies prior to the bust, quickly saw sales skyrocket. The author, grateful for the publicity, announced that she would donate one percent of her profits to the police retirement fund.

---

*Continue on Haight Street and cross over Clayton Street to the southwest corner of that intersection. Look over at the building on the northeast corner.*

---

### ⓰ 558 Clayton Street – Haight-Ashbury Free Clinic
(since 1967).

About the only survivor from the days of the Summer of Love is the landmark Haight-Ashbury Free Clinic. It was founded at this location in June 1967 by Dr. David Smith, a young M.D. who had studied pharmacology, with a special interest in LSD, at the nearby campus of the University of California at San Francisco.

Smith's timing was perfect. The Summer of Love was peaking and drug use and overdoses were reaching a critical point. When the clinic opened on June 6, even with no advertising or publicity, there was a line around the block. A receptive clientele did not guarantee success, however. Funding was such a chronic problem in the early days that the clinic was forced to close briefly several times. To keep things going, impresario Bill Graham staged benefit concerts featuring local bands to raise money.

Today, supported by government grants and private donations, the clinic treats much more than just drug problems and makes its services available to all who need them. It is a special boon to those who need them the most—the down-and-out and the uninsured. Now in operation for over 30 years, the Haight-Ashbury Free Clinic has served as a model for the more than 300 such clinics that now operate in the U.S.

## ⑰ The Block bounded by Clayton, Haight, Cole, and Waller streets – Site of "The Chutes" amusement park (1895-1902).

This entire block (you are standing on the northeast corner) was occupied in the late 19th century by "The Chutes," an amusement park that featured a giant water slide. Flat bottom boats holding up to eight people would be cranked up to a platform and then released down a chute. The boats would reach a top speed of 60 miles per hour—far faster than any automobile of the time could go—before pancaking into a pool of water.

The water slide was the first and foremost draw, but other attractions were quickly added: a camera obscura, a vaudeville house said to be the largest west of Chicago, and a scenic railway that ran around the park's perimeter. There also was a zoo, which had an elephant, a grizzly bear, a variety of monkeys, and what was billed as the only family of orangutans in America. For visitors' enjoyment the latter were seated at a table and dressed in human clothes, the father complete with a pipe in his mouth. Crowd pleasers such as lions, tigers, leopards, and jaguars were also on view. At night, after the park was closed, the big cats could be heard roaring in the darkness, something that must have been unsettling to nearby residents.

Shooting galleries were very popular at the time, and The Chutes had its own variation. Racial sensitivity was virtually nonexistent then. The one here consisted of "two female

"The Chutes."

negroes . . . scrubbing at washboards, . . ." in which players would try to shoot clay pipes out of their mouths. The Chutes' promotional brochure assured visitors that "the figures are so realistic that many persons looking upon them believe that they are human beings actually engaged in doing laundry work."

The Chutes stayed at this location for only seven years, until 1902, and then due to the pressures of development moved over to Fulton Street north of Golden Gate Park. It subsequently moved to Fillmore Street in the Western Addition before closing permanently in 1911. After the closure here in 1902, this block was quickly sold to developers and subdivided mostly into 25-foot-wide lots. Belvedere Street was also extended through from Waller Street, further subdividing this block.

---

*Continue west on Haight Street the short distance to Belvedere and turn left. The better part of the way up the block toward Waller is:*

---

### ⑱ 42 Belvedere Street – Site of Rudolph Nureyev arrest (1967).

On July 11, 1967 San Francisco police, responding to complaints by neighbors about a noisy party being held in the third floor flat at 42 Belvedere, discovered marijuana on the premises as guests climbed over the back fence and scampered onto the roof of the building in an attempt to avoid capture. Eighteen people were arrested, including ballet stars Rudolph Nureyev and Margot Fonteyn. They had performed in San Francisco earlier in the evening and, after dining at Trader Vic's, had decided to check out the Haight. Police found both on the roof. Fonteyn was found wrapped in a "magnificent white mink coat" crouching near a parapet, while Nureyev was discovered lying face down near the edge of the roof.

After four hours in custody on charges of disturbing the peace and being present in a place where marijuana was being kept, the pair posted bail of $330 each. The district attorney, apparently afraid of negative publicity, declined to prosecute. Fonteyn took her arrest with relative good cheer, but the unsmiling Nureyev was not amused. "You're all children," he snapped at reporters as he left the Hall of Justice. One of the three roommates who lived at 42 Belvedere had the last word on the matter. The luckless young man, Kirk Terrill, had the misfortune to come home just a few minutes before the police came barging in early that morning and got swept up in the arrest. The rueful Terrill saw a silver lining in the matter: "At least I got busted with class," he said.

---

*Retrace your steps and cross Belvedere Street. Go down the south side of Haight to the next street, Cole. Turn left on Cole and go down to:*

---

## ⑲ 636 Cole Street – Charles Manson residence (1967).

This otherwise unremarkable Edwardian flat was, for a brief time during the Summer of Love, the home of the notorious mass murderer Charles Manson. Released from prison in March 1967, and still a relatively petty criminal, Manson arrived in San Francisco that month and quickly discovered the Haight and its freely available drugs and sex. A man with hypnotic powers, he assembled a coterie of mostly young women who formed the nucleus of his "family," the one that would soon do his deadly bidding.

Manson and his disciples lived here from about April through July 1967. They then left San Francisco for good, traveling up and down the West Coast and around the southwest in an old school bus before ending up in southern California. In August 1969 Manson's followers carried out, at his direction, the gruesome murders of actress Sharon

Tate and her friends at her home in Beverly Hills. The murders and the subsequent trial riveted the nation. Manson remains in prison.

---

*Retrace your steps to the southeast corner of Haight and Cole streets. Across Haight Street on the opposite corner is:*

---

## ⑳ 1700 Haight Street – Site of the Haight/Straight Theater (1910–1979).

The building with the Goodwill store on the ground floor was the site for many years of the Haight Theater. Built in 1910 as a nickel-odeon, it was turned into a general features movie theater in 1915, which it continued to be until the 1950s when it converted to showing gay films. A little later it became an Assembly of God Church.

In May 1966 the by-then vacant building was leased by a local trio who began work on converting it to a dance hall. Its backers thought it would be a real moneymaker. Both the Avalon Ballroom and Bill Graham's The Fillmore were doing land-office business booking rock groups. But those venues were several miles away; the Haight Theater was right in the heart of the action. Opposition to their efforts soon surfaced from neighbors concerned about noise and increased traffic—and city authorities looked none too favorably on the plan either. Their delaying tactics in approving the necessary permits pushed the opening date back more than a year, to July 1967. And that permit only allowed plays, not dances, to be presented at the newly renamed Straight Theater.

Two months later the Straight's backers discovered that while a dance hall needed a permit, a school of dance did not. Within days the place opened with Grateful Dead band members Jerome Garcia and "Dr. P. Pen," (the group's drummer) listed as "dance instructors." "Student body cards" were sold and the Straight Theater was finally in business as originally envisioned. It had a short-lived run, however. The Summer of Love was already over. The theater closed in 1969 and sat vacant for a decade before being demolished.

---

*The long four-story building next door is:*

**㉑ 1738 Haight Street – Site of the I-Beam Disco** (1970s-1990s).

This new construction four-story retail/residential building replaces the two-story Park Masonic Lodge #449, erected in 1914. The Masons, faced with declining membership, sold the building and moved out in the 1950s. In the 1970s, with the "Saturday Night Fever" craze, the upper floor was converted to a gay disco called the I-Beam. In the early 1980s the club switched to a New Wave format. Some of the top bands of that era, such as the Red Hot Chili Peppers and the Counting Crows, played there. The club closed in the early 1990s; the building remained vacant for a decade before being demolished.

---

*Cross Haight Street to the north side and go down to Shrader Street. At Shrader, turn right, go one block to Page Street and cross over to the southwest corner of Page and Shrader. On that corner is:*

---

**㉒ 1901 Page Street** (1896).

A rarity in this neighborhood, 1901 Page Street is a free-standing home with two side yards and a back yard. Architecturally the 19-room house is a mixture of Beaux-Arts Classicism with its enriched cornice and rinceau frieze, Greek Revival with its Ionic columned supported portico, and Colonial Revival with its glass-paned front door and single-light sash windows. Not surprisingly, it strongly resembles 737 Buena Vista West (which was built a year later) since both houses were designed by the same architect, Edward J. Vogel.

In an unusual design feature, the house has three porthole windows banded by wreaths flanking the large double window on the eastern façade. Symmetry is the norm with such traditional architectural styles, so one would usually expect to find four windows rather than three in such a design. Also odd is the way the small window with the ornate frame impinges upon the porthole window on the upper right. The window looks like an afterthought, and may have been added only after the original blueprints had been drawn up.

The house was built in 1896, allegedly by a sea captain. The next owner was Kathleen Thompson Norris, a best-selling novelist and one-time reporter for the *Call* and society editor for the *Evening Bulletin*. After marrying Charles Norris she moved to New York, and the house stood vacant for two decades. In the 1940s it served as a workshop for the Catholic Church. The house returned to single-family ownership in the early 1950s.

---

*Across the street on the northwest corner of the intersection is:*

---

**㉓ 1900 Page Street** (c.1896).

One of the handsomest apartment buildings in the Haight, this solid-looking three-story structure with a fourth floor cupola has Richardson Romanesque-style arched doorways resting on double columns. As with 1901 Page Street, the entrance stairway here is of marble. Note also the rounded edges to the steps. Care and expense was taken with both of these buildings.

---

*Walk west on the final block of Page Street to Stanyan. Take a left on Stanyan and go two blocks to Waller. On the southeast corner of that intersection is:*

---

**㉔ Stanyan Park Hotel** (1905).

As Golden Gate Park grew and developed in the late 19th and early 20th centuries, Stanyan Street, at its eastern border, became the Haight's vibrant commercial strip, home to hotels, saloons, and bicycle shops, among other businesses. The Stanyan Park Hotel is the last survivor of what was once a cluster of seven hotels on this street. (Two other structures that were once apartment hotels remain as apartment buildings only—the "Frederick" on the southwest corner of Frederick and Stanyan and the "Bon Air" at Stanyan and Oak streets.) The hotel was built in 1904–5 by Henry Heagerty, a saloon-keeper who managed a tavern on this site for two decades before the hotel was built.

The Stanyan Park, to distinguish itself from its competitors, was designed by the respected firm of Martens and Coffey which gave the building a kind of understated, classical elegance designed to attract an upscale clientele. Originally called the Park View Hotel, it has gone through several name changes over the years; for its longest stretch, from 1930 to 1975, it was known as the Stadium Hotel in a nod to Kezar Stadium, the sports arena across the street in Golden Gate Park. This noble building, now a registered National Historic Landmark, survived 1906, the hippie invasion, and the 1989 Loma Prieta earthquake.

Prior to the construction of the hotel, this corner, and indeed the whole block bounded by Stanyan, Waller, Shrader, and Frederick streets, was the site of the California League Base Ball Grounds, which opened here in 1887. Home plate, and the main grandstand behind it—with Heagerty's saloon underneath—were situated on the Stanyan/Waller corner. Baseball games were played here until 1893, and attracted as many as 7,000 people per game. In 1897, with the organization of the Pacific Coast League, the teams that played here moved to a new stadium at Eighth and Harrison streets. This block was then developed for other uses, including the Stanyan Park Hotel.

---

*A few doors down Waller on the south side of the street is:*

---

### ㉕ 1757 Waller Street – Old Firehouse – Engine Company #30 (1896).

One of the other buildings that went up here after the ballpark was demolished in 1894 or 1895 was this firehouse. This was one of the larger city firehouses: it was manned by three officers, a captain and two lieutenants, and 24 firemen. The building housed Engine Company #30 from 1896 to 1917, and Truck Company #12 and Chemical Tank Wagon #5 from 1917 to 1956. The emblems from the latter's occupancy are still clearly visible on the façade of this restored building.

In the early 1950s a study of all the city's firehouses recommended that some be closed. This was one of them, so it was declared surplus and sold at public auction in 1959 for $12,500. The building has since been in private hands and has served a number of uses including as architects' offices and as a furniture showroom. In November 1966 the Haight Independent Proprietors (HIP), an organization of local merchants catering to the hippie trade (head shops and such), held a press conference here to herald the formation of their organization and to denounce the fact that the local merchants organization wouldn't admit them as members. Today the building houses a nonprofit social services organization.

# Janis Joplin
## (1943-1970)

Of all the rock stars of the 1960s, none had a more meteoric rise and fall than Janis Joplin. A struggling singer and virtually unknown in 1966, she created a sensation at the Monterey pop and jazz festivals in 1967. In 1969, after several hit albums, she graced the cover of Newsweek. But even so, Rolling Stone magazine was already pointing to her deterioration, labeling her "The Judy Garland of Rock." A year later she was dead.

She was born in Port Arthur, Texas in 1943, the eldest daughter of a Texaco engineer and a college admissions officer. Bright and ambitious and a good student, but deeply insecure, she constantly required reassurance and affection. Part of that stemmed from her looks: she was plain, even homely looking, and had bad skin. In high school she was treated as "one of the guys." She was also bisexual, a factor no doubt in her lifelong pose as a nonconformist and outcast.

Janis Joplin at the Avalon Ballroom, August 1968.

After a brief stint at the University of Texas in Austin she was cruelly voted "the ugliest man on campus." Not surprisingly, she quickly left her home state, and migrated to San Francisco in January 1963 where she found greater acceptance in a city known for its tolerance. She quickly landed singing gigs in several coffee houses in North Beach, mixing her blues vocals with the prevailing folk music of the day. When not performing, she could be found in the local saloons drinking and shooting pool.

Always peripatetic, over the next few years she shifted between Texas, where she visited family and friends, and the Bay Area, where she settled permanently starting in 1966. (She lived in the Haight during 1967-68.) She became the vocalist with a local band that year, Big Brother and the Holding Company, and drew notice for her raw, whiskey-gravelled voice and her high voltage performances, which had the power to bring audiences stomping to their feet.

After rave notices at Monterey and the 1968 release of her first album, "Cheap Thrills," her status as a rock icon was assured. But the demands of stardom, combined with a chronic dependence on alcohol and added to an addiction to heroin, soon proved to be too much. On October 4, 1970 while in Los Angeles recording a new album, she dropped dead of a drug overdose at the age of 27. While her death was ruled accidental—and it was in the sense that she did not shoot up the night of her death with the intention of doing herself in—she was a desperately unhappy woman who had talked of suicide with intimates.

More than 30 years after her death her raspy-voiced vocals on such hits as "Me and Bobby McGee" and "Mercedes Benz" still get a lot of play on rock music stations today.

# Jackson Square
# and the Barbary Coast

**Length:** 0.4 mile / 0.65 kilometers.
**Time:** ¾ hour.
**Walk Rating:** Easy.
**Hills:** None.
**Public Transit:** The 15 bus runs along Columbus Avenue, the 42 on Sansome Street.
**Parking:** The closest garage is the one under Portsmouth Square, just to the west at Washington and Kearny streets. Street parking – metered spaces only – can be hard to find. Sunday morning is the best time to take this tour as there are no crowds and street parking is not only free but relatively easy to find.
**Restrooms:** The public restroom at Portsmouth Square is the closest.

Huddled in the shadows of downtown's skyscrapers stand the city's oldest commercial buildings. Jackson Square holds the key to understanding San Francisco, for its early roots are found here. Its reputation as a hard drinking, whore-mongering, everything-goes-city are found in these few blocks. Mainly because of the cluster of buildings surviving from the 1850s and 1860s, Jackson Square in 1972 was designated San Francisco's first historic district. (Unlike Portsmouth Square or Washington Square, Jackson Square is not a park. It's merely a name applied to this area.) Nearly two dozen buildings are city landmarks.

This walk divides into two parts. The first, covering Montgomery and Jackson streets, encompasses the city's brick and stone commercial buildings from the 1850s and 1860s. The second, which covers the two blocks of Pacific Avenue between Sansome and Kearny, was the heart of the post-1906 Barbary Coast. The buildings here are less significant historically and architecturally, but they housed some of San Francisco's more notorious saloons and dance halls.

This whole area was originally hard by the shore of the bay. Some of the buildings on Jackson Street, particularly the ones on the south side of the 400 block, are built mainly on landfill. The shoreline came up almost to Montgomery Street; at high tide, water sluiced into a bulbous-shaped lagoon halfway up the next block of Jackson Street

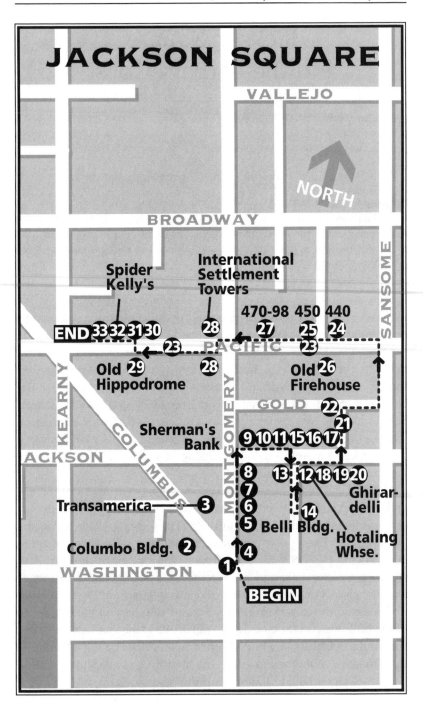

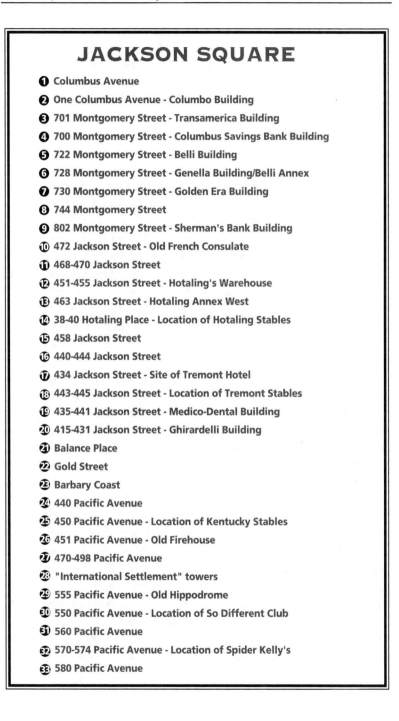

# JACKSON SQUARE

**❶** Columbus Avenue

**❷** One Columbus Avenue - Columbo Building

**❸** 701 Montgomery Street - Transamerica Building

**❹** 700 Montgomery Street - Columbus Savings Bank Building

**❺** 722 Montgomery Street - Belli Building

**❻** 728 Montgomery Street - Genella Building/Belli Annex

**❼** 730 Montgomery Street - Golden Era Building

**❽** 744 Montgomery Street

**❾** 802 Montgomery Street - Sherman's Bank Building

**❿** 472 Jackson Street - Old French Consulate

**⓫** 468-470 Jackson Street

**⓬** 451-455 Jackson Street - Hotaling's Warehouse

**⓭** 463 Jackson Street - Hotaling Annex West

**⓮** 38-40 Hotaling Place - Location of Hotaling Stables

**⓯** 458 Jackson Street

**⓰** 440-444 Jackson Street

**⓱** 434 Jackson Street - Site of Tremont Hotel

**⓲** 443-445 Jackson Street - Location of Tremont Stables

**⓳** 435-441 Jackson Street - Medico-Dental Building

**⓴** 415-431 Jackson Street - Ghirardelli Building

**㉑** Balance Place

**㉒** Gold Street

**㉓** Barbary Coast

**㉔** 440 Pacific Avenue

**㉕** 450 Pacific Avenue - Location of Kentucky Stables

**㉖** 451 Pacific Avenue - Old Firehouse

**㉗** 470-498 Pacific Avenue

**㉘** "International Settlement" towers

**㉙** 555 Pacific Avenue - Old Hippodrome

**㉚** 550 Pacific Avenue - Location of So Different Club

**㉛** 560 Pacific Avenue

**㉜** 570-574 Pacific Avenue - Location of Spider Kelly's

**㉝** 580 Pacific Avenue

west of Montgomery. In 1844, residents of Yerba Buena (as San Francisco was then called) even built a wooden footbridge over the narrow neck of the lagoon at Jackson and Montgomery to make it easier to follow the shoreline of Yerba Buena Cove.

With land at a premium during the first few years after the discovery of gold, the immediate shoreline area was quickly filled in and buildings went up helter skelter. These initial flimsy structures were mostly of canvas and wood. But after a half a dozen fires devastated the city between 1849 and 1851, sturdier buildings of brick and iron replaced them. The Jackson Square area, so close to the waterfront, was prime commercial real estate and in the 1850s and 1860s handsome brick and stone buildings of mostly two to four stories were erected. They housed merchants, banks, and consulates of foreign nations. Some of the town's leading businessmen had offices here.

Starting about 1870, however, this location started to decline in prestige as the center of commerce moved south and east toward Market Street and the ferry depot. During the latter part of the 19th century this area became more industrial. Many of the buildings, especially in the 400 block of Jackson, were used as liquor warehouses at one time or another.

In 1906 this area became noteworthy because it was virtually the only section of downtown San Francisco to escape destruction by fire. A U.S. Navy crew operating on the northern waterfront at North Beach amazingly ran a fire hose all the way over Telegraph Hill, and by pumping water from the bay doused the approaching flames. When the fire threatened these blocks a second time, area merchants managed to save their businesses once again.

Although the buildings were saved, the first half of the 20th century was not kind to Jackson Square: it suffered a progressive decline that culminated in the Great Depression of the 1930s. Finally in the early 1950s the district underwent a renewal led by wholesale interior decorators and antique dealers, who moved in and rehabilitated these fine old buildings. Many of these tenants still remain, but in recent years lawyers, architects, ad agencies, and other professionals, along with restaurants, have opened shop here.

Jackson Square, with its splendid low-rise, historic, and visually interesting buildings, is one of San Francisco's most appealing areas in which to stroll.

*Start this tour on the southeast corner of Washington and Montgomery streets at the foot of Columbus Avenue. Forming a nice gateway to North Beach and Jackson Square as you look north are three buildings with classical ornamentation. After a brief history of Columbus Avenue these three will be the first, from left to right, that will be discussed on this tour.*

**❶ Columbus Avenue** (1874).

Columbus Avenue is virtually the only street in downtown San Francisco that attempts to follow the natural lay of the land. It was cut through the existing grid pattern of streets between May 1873 and September 1874 to provide a better connection between the north waterfront and downtown. It was originally called Montgomery Avenue, but in 1909 a lot of city streets were renamed and since the boulevard cuts through the heart of North Beach with its large Italian population, it was renamed to honor Christopher Columbus. Columbus Avenue roughly parallels the old trail to the Presidio, which started a block away on Kearny Street just off Portsmouth Square.

**❷ One Columbus Avenue – Columbo Building** (1913).

The Columbo Building occupies a notable site since this was the original location of the Bank of Italy, which later grew into the mighty Bank of America. The Bank of Italy was founded by Amadeo P. Giannini and opened in a former saloon on this site in 1904. The fledgling bank faced a literal trial by fire when the earthquake hit on April 18, 1906. As the fire headed his way, Giannini loaded a horse- drawn cart with all of the bank's assets, including $80,000 in gold, and drove to his home in San Mateo. To disguise his valuables Giannini covered them with crates of fruits and vegetables. He said later that for the next few weeks the bank's money smelled of orange juice. It was a good thing for Giannini that he acted quickly, because unlike his neighbors on the east side of Montgomery Street, which survived the blaze, the fire caught up to his building and reduced it to ashes.

Recently threatened with demolition to be replaced by a high rise, the Columbo Building may be converted into the Chinatown campus of City College. The architects were the Reid Brothers, who also designed the Fairmont Hotel. With its modest classical detailing this building is not as flamboyant as its neighbors across Columbus

Avenue, but combined with them makes for a nice visual unity at this important intersection. If given the okay, the college will add a modern third story to the building.

**❸ 701 Montgomery Street – Transamerica Building** (1909).

As his banking empire grew, A. P. Giannini in 1929 formed the Transamerica Corporation as a holding company for his various banks. In 1938 he moved the headquarters for Transamerica into this fine wedding-cake slice of a building in glazed white terra cotta. Transamerica is now headquartered in the modern pyramidal building just a block away and is no longer associated with the Bank of America, but this building is still called the Transamerica Building and the name is still emblazoned along the Columbus Avenue side.

The elaborate cornice above the second floor is indicative of the fact that this was once a two-story building. A wonderfully ornate cupola with an eagle perched on top was removed when the third floor was added in 1916. Note the main entrance right at the gore corner. (A gore lot is triangular in shape.) Corner entrances like this—and not just on gore lots—were common features of commercial buildings in the City in the 19th and early 20th centuries. This one and the one on the Columbus Savings Bank Building across Montgomery Street are among the few that are left.

**❹ 700 Montgomery Street – Columbus Savings Bank** (1905).

John Fugazi established the first bank in San Francisco designed specifically to serve the local Italian-American community. Fugazi, whose primary enterprise was the White Star shipping line, became a banker in an almost casual way—customers used the large safe in his North Beach office to store gold for remittances home to the old country and for other transactions. From those beginnings it was an easy transition to banking. So in 1893 he founded the Columbus Savings and Loan Society.

The company's first offices were located in the same building across Columbus Avenue where A. P. Giannini started the Bank of Italy in 1904. Giannini, in fact, had gotten his start in banking when his father-in-law died in 1902 and he inherited a directorship on the board of Fugazi's bank. Columbus Savings was a very conservative institution however, lending only to established business owners and blue-chip customers. Giannini, sensing a large, untapped market—the individual with little credit or collateral but with big potential for future growth—fell out with Fugazi and left to start his own bank, the aforementioned Bank of Italy. Giannini not only set up shop next door, but he soon obtained Fugazi's lease, becoming his landlord. This was intolerable to Fugazi so he moved across the street, where in 1905 he built this handsome building. Giannini's bank grew into an empire and in 1927 he absorbed the Fugazi bank into his operation.

---

*Cross Washington Street and go half a block up Montgomery Street to the building with the red brick façade at the address of 722-728 Montgomery. This structure and the one to its left (as you face it), which is 728, were merged into one at the time that famed lawyer Melvin Belli bought them in 1959. Since each has its own rich history they will be discussed separately.*

---

These buildings and many of the ones immediately following here and around the corner on Jackson Street are difficult to date with precision. Construction took place along this section of Montgomery Street as early as 1849. None of the current buildings dates from earlier than 1851 however, because on June 22 of that year the sixth and last of the major fires to devastate early San Francisco wiped out this part of town.

### ❺ 722 Montgomery Street – Langerman's / Belli Building (c.1853).

The apparent first owner of 722 Montgomery was William Langerman, who used it as a tobacco and sugar warehouse. Langerman was a prominent merchant and a member of the Vigilance Committee of 1851. In December 1857 the building was turned into a theater; Lotta Crabtree is known to have performed here. In the 1860s it became the offices of a commission merchant and auctioneer. In the 1870s and 1880s it served as a bathhouse, first Turkish-style, then changing to hydrotherapy. The building, like the others in this block, survived 1906.

After the Great Depression of the 1930s and Jackson Square's subsequent revival in the early 1950s, flamboyant attorney Melvin

Belli (1907–1996), who represented such celebrity clients as Errol Flynn, Lenny Bruce, and Jack Ruby, bought the building. He renovated it and added a few extra decorative elements, such as the wrought iron gate, which came from New Orleans, and the painted wooden window boxes. Up until

**722–728 Montgomery Street.**

the building was rendered unsafe by the 1989 earthquake, Belli could be seen behind his desk in his ground floor one-of-a-kind office stuffed as it was with a riot of unusual and arresting objects including old roll-top desks, a barber chair, and "Elmer," the full-length skeleton that he used in court in medical malpractice cases.

**❻ 728 Montgomery Street – Genella Building / Belli Annex** (c.1851).

Like its neighbor, the just discussed 722 Montgomery, this building has seen a number of different tenants over the years: Joseph Genella established a china and glassware business here in 1853; the Odd Fellows used it as a meeting place for many years starting in 1854; H. and W. Pierce Company, a commission merchant and loan broker, had offices here in the 19th century; and a one-man puppet theater operated out of a room on an upper floor from the 1920s to the 1940s. But the main residents from about 1880 to 1959 when Melvin Belli bought the building were artists who maintained studios here. Some of the more notable ones were Arthur Mathews, Maynard Dixon, and Ralph Stackpole. The building received its Bohemian stamp of approval early on. In April 1882 Oscar Wilde was the guest of honor at a party here. Wilde was in town speaking at Platt's Hall a few blocks down Montgomery Street as part of a U.S. lecture tour.

**❼ 730 Montgomery Street – Golden Era Building** (c.1852).

This building gets its name from the *Golden Era*, a weekly newspaper that began here and occupied a second floor office for over two years beginning in December 1852. Although it is typically thought of as a literary newspaper because it published works by Mark Twain, Ina Coolbrith, and Bret Harte (Harte's first work ever published, a poem, appeared in a March 1857 issue), the *Golden Era* billed itself as a "family newspaper," covering "Literature, Agriculture, the Mining Interest, Local and Foreign News, Commerce, Education, Morals, and Amusements." It continued publication for almost 40 years.

The cast-iron pillars on the front of this building are of note because at the bases on the ones on each end is given not just the name of the manufacturer, Vulcan Iron Works (a San Francisco firm whose foundry was located south of Market Street), but also the date—1892. Since the original structure dates from the early 1850s, these pillars must have been put in as part of a remodel.

### ❽ 744 Montgomery Street / 499 Jackson Street (1965).

At the end of this block stands a modern building erected in 1965 to replace an 1850s-era three-story brick building that stood here for over a hundred years before being torn down in 1964. The building it replaced housed Pioche & Bayerque, an important pioneer bank that provided financing for some of the state's first railroads as well as for local gas and water works.

The old building had a plaque on it identifying it as the location of the town of Yerba Buena's first public improvement, a wooden foot-bridge that crossed the neck of the lagoon that used to exist here. The town's residents were so proud of their new bridge that when it was put up in 1844, 30 inhabitants—almost the entire population—gathered to admire it. They jumped up and down on it to test its strength.

---

*Cross over Jackson Street to the northeast corner of Montgomery and Jackson.*

---

### ❾ 802 Montgomery Street / 498 Jackson Street – Sherman's Bank (1854).

This building, which has seen a variety of tenants in its more than 150 year history, was built as a bank. Its first manager was William Tecumseh Sherman. Sherman, of course, is best known as the Union general who laid Georgia and much of the South to waste during the Civil War. But prior to that he established and managed this branch of what was officially known as the Bank of Lucas, Turner & Company, a St. Louis-based bank. Sherman arrived in California in 1847 as a young Army officer, but with no wars to fight and other opportunities abounding he resigned his commission in 1853 and stayed on in gold-rush San Francisco.

At the behest of his employers, in late 1853 he purchased a 60' by 60' lot on the northeast corner of Jackson and Montgomery from James Lick for $31,000. (Lick, with masterful timing, had purchased a 50-vara parcel with an adobe house on it on this corner in early February 1848 for $3,000 just before the discovery of gold became known. Less than six years later he sold less than a quarter of that land for $31,000.) Sherman spent another $53,000 erecting this building, which was completed in July 1854. Proud as a papa of a newborn, he wrote to the owners in St. Louis: "It has grown out of the mud a beauty. It is the handsomest building in this town...I enjoy it as much as an artist does a fine picture."

Sherman had good business sense and was a fine manager, and initially the bank prospered. By early 1855 however, business conditions had soured and in February of that year panicky depositors descended on all of the city's banks and demanded their money. Several of the town's largest banks failed as a result of the run, but the Bank of Lucas, Turner & Company (thanks to Sherman's prudence it was better capitalized than most) weathered the storm.

The bank lasted only a couple of more years: Sherman's public opposition to the Vigilance Committee of 1856—most of whose members were the town's leading merchants—had led to an informal boycott of his bank. Business declined, the bank ceased operations in 1857, and Sherman left San Francisco for New York to manage a Lucas, Turner branch there.

The bank building underwent a variety of uses in the ensuing years. At the time of the 1906 earthquake it was a French restaurant called The Eiffel Tower. By the late 1920s, as unlikely as it may seem, it was a sausage factory. Following that it was a soy sauce factory. Today the area is no longer industrial in character and, like many of its neighbors, is home to retail space and professional offices.

The building's appearance has changed somewhat since Sherman's day. The major change is that it no longer has a third story. It was removed after the 1906 earthquake as a safety measure. The second-story windows, which are now unadorned, were once capped by handsome triangular pediments. The Jackson Street side with its bricked up windows—done sometime in the 19th century—was originally covered with mastic, a stucco/plaster-like finish. Exposed brick walls are considered chic today but in the Victorian era they were not, and prestige buildings were finished with stone or facings and decorations meant to look like stone. The Montgomery Street side is of stone, and this handsome original granite façade is what still invests this building with some of the grandeur that initially made Sherman so proud. Interestingly, this kind of granite is not found locally. It may have come around the Horn from the East Coast, or perhaps was imported from China.

---

*Walk two doors east on the north side of Jackson Street to:*

---

### ❿ 472 Jackson Street – Old French Consulate (c.1851).

Number 472 Jackson is a fine and well-preserved example of the rather plain two-story brick buildings with iron shutters that went up in towns all over northern California during the 1850s. A fair number are still to be found in old gold-rush towns in the Mother Lode, but this is virtually the only one left in San Francisco. It likely dates from 1851, and is probably built on the foundation of an earlier building.

Iron shutters—these are the originals—were hailed as a fire safety innovation when they came into wide use in San Francisco in the 1850s. They did a good job in preventing flames from reaching inside a building, but a major drawback was that the iron expanded in the heat and thus prevented them from being opened. Some poor souls perished in subsequent fires due to the intense radiant heat generated after they had shut themselves up in such buildings and couldn't escape.

The building was erected for a French wine and liquor dealer, and that was its primary use at least through the 1870s. From 1865 to 1876 it also housed the office of the French consul in San Francisco, and it is that association from which it takes its name as the Old French Consulate.

**⓫ 468–470 Jackson Street** (c.1852).

This three-story brick building has a history similar to its previously discussed next door neighbor at 472. It was built by an Italian, not French, food and liquor merchant, but it too served as a consulate—in this case for Spain in the 1850s, for Chile from 1856 to 1857, and for France starting in 1861 until the consulate moved its office next door to 472 Jackson in 1865. But it primarily served as office space and storage for wine importers and liquor dealers until early in the 20$^{th}$ century.

On the sidewalk just to the right of the doorway to 468 note what appears to be a small portion of the original granite gutter, which must have diverted rainwater into the street.

**⓬ 451–455 Jackson Street – Hotaling's Warehouse** (1866).

The striking four-story, three-floor Italianate edifice across the street on the southeast corner of Jackson and Hotaling is the building known as Hotaling's Warehouse. Anson P. Hotaling was a pioneer liquor dealer who erected this beautiful building in 1866 as the office and warehouse for his wholesale liquor business. It remained the center of the Hotaling company's operations until 1943.

The building survived the 1906 holocaust unscathed. When a local minister claimed that God had punished the City for its wicked ways a local wit named Charles K. Field penned in reply the often repeated ditty:

> "If, as one says, God spanked the town
>    For being overfrisky
> Why did He burn the churches down
>    And save Hotaling's whisky?"

When Field wrote the last line it originally read "The Old Kirk Whisky." (Old Kirk was a local brand bottled and distributed by the firm.) Hotaling, who knew a good promotional opportunity when he saw one, substituted Hotaling for Old Kirk and publicized it, and that version is the one that has come down to posterity. What is noteworthy about this is the kernel of truth embedded in the rhyme since even though the city's churches and almost everything else in the fire's path burned, a remarkable number of saloons and liquor emporiums escaped unharmed. Not just the Hotaling Warehouse but at least two other structures not far from here—Wagner's Beer Hall in North Beach and the Audiffred Building on the Embarcadero, which had a saloon on the ground floor—also remained standing. Stories abound that firefighters were bribed with liquor from these establishments' stocks if only they would save the buildings. That may well have been the case. In this instance, to save his company's stock, Hotaling's manager, when he heard that soldiers were planning to dynamite the warehouse, corralled some men from the waterfront and had them roll heavy kegs of whiskey out of the building and down the street

**451–455 Jackson Street – Hotaling's Warehouse.**

away from the fire zone. The men were paid the rich sum of $1.00 an hour, and were also given bottles of imported ale and stout to keep them motivated during their labors.

Architecturally this building presents a grand appearance with its rich effusion of ornament. It is a brick building but the scored plaster facing along with the immoderate use of quoins give the illusion of stone. The alternating arched and triangular pediments over the second- and third-story windows provide the extra classical ornamentation that makes this building stand out from its neighbors. As with the Old French Consulate building across the street, the iron shutters here are original.

### ⓮ 463 Jackson Street – Hotaling Annex West (c.1860).

Across Hotaling Alley is another fine commercial Italianate—the Hotaling Annex. The Annex, built about 1860, is not quite as grand as the Hotaling Warehouse. It resembles it quite a bit however, and since it was built before its cross-alley neighbor it's quite possible it influenced the latter's design. Sometime before 1890, A. P. Hotaling purchased this building and incorporated it into his expanding business.

During the 1930s, after Hotaling's use of the building lessened, some of the office space here served as the headquarters for the Depression-era Federal Artists and Writers Project wherein local talent was employed by the government to work on Coit Tower and other such projects. Some stayed on after the Depression and maintained studios and workspaces here, turning it into a mini Bohemia. In the early 1950s both this building and the Hotaling Warehouse gained a new life as showrooms for the interior design trade, initiating the revival of Jackson Square.

---

*Cross over Jackson Street and walk into Hotaling Alley. This one-block thoroughfare marks the approximate location of a pre-gold rush trail along the original shoreline leading to the little wooden bridge over the Jackson Street lagoon—called Laguna Salada.*

---

### ⓴ 38–40 Hotaling Place – Hotaling Stables (c.1860s).

This looks like one building and now is, but originally it was two separate structures. The wooden strip extending down from the cornice about two-thirds of the way along marks the dividing line. The two buildings were combined into one before 1894.

The north building (adjoining the Hotaling Warehouse) was originally a stable and served the growing Hotaling empire. The paired windows on the second and third floor were no doubt once the hayloft doors. The south building was originally a back-alley warehouse for the H. & W. Pierce Company at 728 Montgomery Street. The rear of that building faces this one. A tunnel, now bricked up, runs under Hotaling Alley and connects the basements of these two buildings.

---

*Walk back to Jackson Street and turn right to stand in front of the Hotaling Warehouse at 451–455. Across the street, left to right, are the next three buildings on this walk.*

---

### ⓯ 458 Jackson Street (early 1850s).

This simple one-story painted brick building was purchased by a French sea captain as an investment property on a visit to San Francisco, probably during the 1850s, and today is still owned by his descendants. Like so many others in this block, for much of the 19<sup>th</sup> century its tenants were wholesale wine and liquor merchants. A seed company occupied the building from the 1930s to the 1950s.

### ⓰ 440–444 Jackson Street (1891).

Starting in 1883 this site was the location of the Presidio and Ferries Railroad Car Barn. The initial structure was replaced by the current one, which dates from 1891. It was mainly a horsecar line at that time (the horses pulled the cars up Jackson Street and Columbus Avenue to Washington Square from where cable cars took passengers the rest of the way to the Presidio), and this building was used as a stable for the horses. After the 1906 disaster the city's streetcar lines were electrified and the stable was converted to a carbarn and repair shop until after 1912, when the city-owned Municipal Railway took over this line and others.

The building originally had a second floor, which was removed in 1907. The façade underwent a major remodeling in 1955.

### ⓱ 434 Jackson Street (1907) – Site of the Tremont Hotel (1855–1870).

Although this handsome building looks as if it dates from the 1850s, it was built in 1907, after the fire. It replaced an earlier building on this site, the Tremont Hotel, a four-story structure that was erected in 1855. The Tremont stayed in business until 1870 when, as the area became less fashionable, it reopened as a more downmarket hostelry, the White House Hotel, and operated under that name until 1886.

During the 1860s and 1870s several retail establishments operated out of this location, one of which—the Pioneer Marble Steam Works— sold granite and marble mantles and other decorative pieces. In the 20<sup>th</sup> century the ground floor housed a retail liquor and tobacco store. There also was a wire works on the premises. The top floor was used as lodgings.

The handsome ground-floor arcade of the current building echoes its predecessor. The doorways of the original building most likely would have had cast-iron shutters.

---

*Back across the street and next to the Hotaling Warehouse is:*

---

## ⑱ 443–445 Jackson Street – Hotaling Annex East / Tremont Stables (c.1860).

**443–445 Jackson Street.**

From 1871 to 1883 this small two-story building was used as a stable for the hotel across the street. It was known as the Tremont Stables, although the hotel ceased using the name Tremont in 1870. A. P. Hotaling eventually bought the building and incorporated it into his liquor business. Since little money was usually spent on decorating stables, he probably altered the façade after purchasing it so that it would conform to his building next door.

In later years the building housed a flour factory and perhaps a cigar manufacturing operation. In the decade prior to its renovation in the early 1950s into a wholesale home furnishings showroom it was occupied by a printing firm.

## ⑲ 435–441 Jackson Street – Medico-Dental Building (1861).

Said to be built on a foundation of two gold-rush-era ships, this building has long been referred to as the Medico-Dental Building because of the decorative *caducei* over four of the iron pilasters on the façade. The *caduceus*, a winged staff entwined with serpents, has served as a symbol of the medical profession since the early 1800s. The only difficulty with its association here however is that this building has no known link with medical use or practitioners. A more fitting explanation for its appearance here is that the *caduceus* is also the symbol for Mercury, the ancient Roman god of commerce. Interestingly, the previously mentioned Transamerica Building also is adorned with *caducei*. They are located in the center of the decorative bronze balconies on the second floor.

The building's primary use in the 19th century was as a wine and liquor warehouse and later for tobacco storage. Following that, coffee, and then paint and varnishes took their turn. In the 1920s, Chinese merchants operated out of here, but by the 1930s it was a paper company's warehouse. And like most of its neighbors, in the 1950s it became a designer's showroom.

**⓴ 415–431 Jackson Street – Ghirardelli Building** (1853).

For almost four decades this building served as the main office and manufacturing plant of the Ghirardelli Chocolate Company. Founder Domingo Ghirardelli arrived in San Francisco in 1849; he operated out of a number of locations before consolidating his business here about 1856. Initially he sold coffee, spices, and others foodstuffs, including wine and liquor for a brief time, before deciding to concentrate exclusively on chocolate. It was here in the 1860s that he discovered, by accident, his greatest product. One warm day a bag of chocolate was left suspended from a rafter. The cocoa butter drained out; the remaining chocolate was pulverized into a powder called *broma*. By the 1940s, Ghirardelli & Company was selling millions of pounds annually of this ground chocolate.

The Ghirardelli plant remained at this location until Domingo Ghirardelli's death in 1894. His sons, who carried on the business and wanted to expand, then moved the manufacturing operation the following year to a two-and-a-half acre plot on North Point Street. That area, which included the Pioneer Woolen Mills Building, is now called Ghirardelli Square.

About 1880, Domingo Ghirardelli purchased the building next door, 407 Jackson Street, and incorporated it into his business. Number 407 Jackson was built in 1860. The remodeling of the façade surrounding the two upper stories of this building has robbed it of its character.

---

*Cross over Jackson Street to the little alley called Balance.*

---

**⓴ Balance Place** (c.1849).

One of the shortest streets (if you can call it a street) in the city, if not the shortest, this street first appears on a San Francisco map dated 1849–1850. The name Balance has an unusual history behind it. If a reporter's story in the *Alta California* in May 1882 is correct, the *Balance* was an ancient ship that was built in Calcutta in 1741.

In the early 1800s she was sailing under the British flag, but when captured by the Americans during the War of 1812 she was renamed the *Balance* by her new American skipper to balance a ship he had earlier lost to the British.

The *Balance* arrived in San Francisco in November 1849 carrying 47 passengers from New York. Her last recorded location was at Jackson and Front streets where she was used a storeship. Some time probably not long after, as fill pushed the shoreline farther out into the bay, her life as a storeship came to end and she was salvaged and scuttled. So with her last known location being at Jackson and Front, over two blocks from the tiny street bearing her name, it seems unlikely that she lies directly below the pavement here. It could be that she initially docked here on her arrival at what was then the Jackson Street Wharf, or perhaps because she must have had a reputation as the grand old lady of gold-rush ships and did end up nearby, she was so honored.

---

*Walk through Balance Place to the alley that connects to it:*

---

## ㉒ Gold Street (c.1849).

Gold Street is another curious little street. Like Balance it was not part of Jasper O'Farrell's original street plan of 1847. Just wide enough to accommodate a horse-drawn cart, it was apparently put through to provide greater ease of access for what was becoming a densely packed part of town. But why here, and not, say, in the middle of the block? Furthermore, why lay it out so that starting from Sansome Street it would dead-end two-thirds of the way up to James Lick's property, which is exactly what an 1852 map of San Francisco shows it did? An answer might be found in an 1848 map, which shows that the original shoreline ran east to west in the one block stretch just a shade to the south of where Gold Street is now. It's speculation of course, but perhaps what became Gold Street was the continuation of the trail that threaded around the shoreline from roughly Hotaling Place, across the wooden footbridge at Jackson near Montgomery, and then continued past here on the way to Clark's

Point at Broadway and Battery—the site of the town's first wharf. Existing trails sometimes have a way of prevailing even when formal designs are overlaid upon them. The old Indian trail that became Broadway in Manhattan which threads its way down the island through the grid pattern of streets, is a classic example.

As for the name Gold Street? It would be odd indeed if there were not a street in San Francisco named Gold, but why this location? Some sources claim that it was due to assay offices being located here, but there is no such supporting evidence. One possible explanation is that James Lick, after he purchased his 50-vara lot and adobe up at the other end of Gold Street, buried his remaining stash of gold coins in the cellar of his house. So in the late 1840s and early 1850s there was gold buried under Gold Street or at least very close by.

---

*Turn right at Gold Street, go the short distance to Sansome, then turn left and walk to the northwest corner of Pacific and Sansome. Before you walk the final two blocks of this tour, a little more background on the Barbary Coast might be useful.*

---

## ㉓ The Barbary Coast.

After the gold rush, and the earthquake and fire of 1906, the Barbary Coast, which was named after the pirate-infested North African coastline, is probably San Francisco's most storied phenomenon. It was called "a wild carnival of crime" and it certainly contained elements of both. Streets in this area were lined with dance halls, concert saloons, brothels, and the appropriately named deadfalls (low life bars that served watery beer and cheap wine).

These streets are quiet today, but noise was the hallmark then. Many places provided musical entertainment ranging from solo piano players to small orchestras. The idea was to draw the customer in. Once inside, every effort was directed toward separating the mark from his money, and the quicker the better. In the roughest of places those who didn't spend freely enough were sometimes physically intimidated, drugged, or just plain knocked cold and robbed.

The most sordid and blatantly criminal days of the Barbary Coast were from the 1860s to the 1880s. The Coast at that time also stretched farther west on Pacific and Jackson streets into what is now Chinatown. The 1906 earthquake and fire destroyed the district along with

Pacific Street – the Barbary Coast, circa 1912.

much of the rest of the city, and what was rebuilt was a smaller and tamer (if the word tame can be used in conjunction with the Barbary Coast) quarter. But the old times didn't return for very long. In 1914 the state legislature passed the Red Light Abatement Act which was upheld by the courts in 1917 and when Prohibition soon followed, the once raucous Barbary Coast pretty much came to an end.

In the 1930s and 1940s the one-block section of Pacific between Montgomery and Kearny had a brief revival as what was called the "International Settlement." The music and the bright lights returned attracting servicemen during and after World War II, but by the early 1950s the lights dimmed and the area began its gentle descent into the quiet thoroughfare it is today. This part of the tour will cover mainly the post-1906 Barbary Coast, since a number of buildings still remain from that era.

---

*Walk west on Pacific Street. Five doors up on the north side of the street is:*

### ❷❹ 440 Pacific Avenue (1911).

This fine-looking two-story-and-a-basement edifice was very likely erected as a brothel. After the decline of the Barbary Coast it was converted to lodgings for transients. The building has been restored in recent years. It is interesting to note that most of the bricks between the first-floor window sill and the sidewalk have been scorched by fire. It could well be that these were remainders from the 1906 fire and were in good enough condition to be salvaged.

### ❷❺ 450 Pacific Avenue – Kentucky Stables Building (c.1905).

Just across the little alley of Osgood Place is a four-story brick building that was erected just before the earthquake of 1906 and survived it virtually unscathed. The wide ground floor doors give evidence that this was originally a carriage house and livery stable. The windows around on the Osgood side were where bundles of hay and grain for the horses were taken in. The upper floor was once home to a Chinese-run cigar factory.

---

*Right across the street from Osgood Place is:*

---

### ㉖ 451 Pacific Avenue – Old Fire House – Engine Company #1 (1908).

This former firehouse with Tuscan columns on the upper story looks very much as if it dates from the 19th century, but was in fact built in 1908. It replaced an 1872 firehouse that stood here and it probably strongly resembles its predecessor. On the crest near the roofline you can see the letters "SFFD" still visible on the escutcheon but it is hard to see with the two trees in front. "Engine No. 1" is chiseled over what was the fire engine doorway.

---

*Continue on up the north side of Pacific to the corner of Montgomery Street. On your right, the long two-story building is:*

---

### ㉗ 470–490 Pacific Avenue (1907 and c.1910).

The ground floor of these two-story buildings was originally a Barbary Coast saloon and dance hall. The upper floor served as transient lodgings. The western portion of the building, on the corner with Montgomery Street, was built in 1907; the longer, eastern half was put up about three years later. Melvin Belli used this space as his law office after the Belli Building on Montgomery Street was damaged in the 1989 Loma Prieta earthquake.

---

*Cross over the intersection to the southwest corner of Pacific and Montgomery streets.*

---

### ㉘ "International Settlement" towers (1930s).

This block of Pacific, between Montgomery and Kearny streets, was the heart of the post-1906 Barbary Coast. It was known as "Terrific Street" and was shoulder-to-shoulder bars, cafes, dance halls, and nightclubs of one stripe or another. On busy nights it was difficult for cars to drive through because of the crowds. During the 1930s and 1940s the area underwent a revival after Prohibition was repealed, and during the war years it was called "International Settlement" (to give it an exotic flavor) and was especially popular with servicemen. Bar brawls between soldiers and sailors sometimes spilled out into the street. The steel tower you see on this corner and on the northwest corner as well once held a sign between them over the street that said International Settlement. There were two identical towers and a sign at the Kearny Street end of this block as well.

---

*Walk down the south side of the street. Stop in front of:*

---

### ㉙  555 Pacific Avenue – Old Hippodrome (1907).

This former saloon and dance hall with its carnival-like bulb lighting and plaster casts of naked maidens is virtually the only building left that still retains some of the flavor of the post-1906 Barbary Coast. This building is a 1907 reconstruction along the same outlines of a dance hall that stood here previously.

From about 1910 until the mid-1930s the Hippodrome actually was located across the street at 560 Pacific. The dance hall here operated under various names, including the Red Mill. Later, in an apparent attempt to give it more class, the French equivalent was used — Moulin Rouge. Some remodeling was done in 1937 including the removal of plaster relief panels at each end of the recessed foyer that depicted a lusty satyr chasing a naked nymph. At some point similar panels — the ones you see now — were put up again, but the satyr was converted to another woman. These lack the vivacity of the originals. It was perhaps also in the 1930s that what was once a continuous line of double swinging doors at the entrance was cut back to just two.

By the late 1930s the Hippodrome must have moved here to 555 Pacific, because its former location across the street was soon occupied by the Monaco Theatre Restaurant.

---

*Across the street are the last four buildings on this tour.*
*From right to left they are:*

## ❸⓿ 550 Pacific Avenue – So Different Club(1906).

This modest three-story brick building was one of the first to go up in this area after the 1906 fire. It housed the So Different Club (sometimes called Purcell's), a music saloon which was started by Lew Purcell and Sam King, two ex-Pullman porters. Although owned by African Americans it catered to all races.

The So Different Club in its layout and in its operation was typical of many of the Barbary Coast saloons. As one entered, the bar was on the left, a small stand for the musicians stood at the rear, and on the right sat "the girls." A patron would buy little copper dance chits that cost 20 cents apiece. He would give one to the girl (she would get 10 cents of it, the house the other half), the band would strike up, and they would dance—briefly. Up to 30 dances would be crammed into an hour. All the while a floor manager/bouncer would circulate taking drink orders. Some of the girls lived on the two upper floors, and when they had a live one they would repair upstairs where they could nicely supplement their income.

Also somewhat typical was violence. One night a soldier who thought a sailor had stolen his girl pulled a gun and fired six shots in the crowded room. Miraculously no one was hit. He returned a few night later, and when he found the girl and the sailor in a room upstairs he shot and killed them both.

Although the So Different Club attracted the same kind of clientele as its neighbors it was a cut above the other Barbary Coast joints in that it attracted some of the most innovative musicians of its day. Jelly Roll Morton, King Oliver, and other ragtime and jazz greats of the 1910s played here. And the So Different Jazz Band was said to be the first group to use jazz in their name. The club was also where some of the hottest dance crazes of the early 20th century got their starts. The Turkey Trot and the Texas Tommy (tommy was slang for a prostitute) are said to have originated here.

## ❸❶ 564 Pacific Avenue (1910).

As noted, from about 1910 to the 1930s this was the site of the Hippodrome dance hall. The main entrance was flanked by two tall columns. When the Hippodrome moved back across the street the building was remodeled and the Monaco Theatre Restaurant, offering three dinner shows a night, moved in. Like the rest of its brethren along this block the Monaco lasted into the early 1950s. In 1966 the building was remodeled using the brick facing you see today.

---

*To see the last two buildings on this tour it would be best to cross the street.*

---

## ❷ 570–574 Pacific Avenue – Location of Spider Kelly's Saloon (1911–1913).

This four-story building originally housed a hotel on the upper floors variously called the Pacific, the Nottingham, and the Seattle. But its most famous tenant was the ground floor saloon, Spider Kelly's, the name Spider coming from the proprietor's former career as a lightweight boxer. The place was a favorite of sailors and had an especially sleazy reputation. A police captain visiting from Chicago called it "the worst dive in the world."

## ❸ 580 Pacific Avenue (1907).

This tiny tan brick structure dating from 1907 once housed a saloon called Diana's. It is chiefly of interest because the façade with its double swinging doors with brass bar handles and beveled glass windows is relatively unchanged. The exterior strongly evokes the image of the no-frills saloon that this used to be.

---

*Walk to the corner of Kearny Street.*

---

The block just concluded was the heart of the post-1906 Barbary Coast. The pre-1906 Coast was just to the west of here. The next two blocks of Pacific, now part of Chinatown, harbored some of the most sordid and crime-ridden saloons. Just around the corner, the block of Kearny Street between Pacific and Broadway was, in the 19th century, called "Battle Row." It was a mixture of low-class dance halls, deadfalls, and brothels. The prostitution was so blatant that shades were not drawn—passersby could watch the activity within.

# Japantown / The Fillmore

**Length:** 1.2 miles / 1.9 kilometers.
**Time:** 1½ hours.
**Walk Rating:** Easy.
**Hills:** Buchanan Street between Pine and Bush is a moderate downhill.
**Public Transit:** The 38 bus line runs frequently along Geary Boulevard. The 2, 3, and 4 bus lines run along Sutter Street (and east on Post from Laguna Street).
**Parking:** There are city-owned parking garages under the Kintetsu Mall (entrances are on Post Street off Webster and on Geary Boulevard east of Webster) and under the Kabuki cineplex (entrance on Fillmore between Geary and Post). Unmetered street parking can sometimes be found, particularly along Bush and Pine streets.
**Restrooms:** There are two sets of public restrooms in Japantown's Kintetsu Mall. One is located on your right shortly after you enter the mall from the plaza, and the other is in the Kinokuniya Building on the ground floor to your right after you come down the stairs before exiting the building.

No San Francisco neighborhood has undergone more upheaval and change than Japantown and the Fillmore. It was an area that was slow in developing due to its distance from the core downtown area. Throughout the 1850s and '60s it was nothing more than a vast space of shifting sand and sparse vegetation populated by rabbits and quail. The only dwellings consisted of a few rude structures on Bush Street, which at first was nothing more that a dirt trail, and then a rude planked roadway that led to Lone Mountain Cemetery (whose eastern boundary was where Presidio Avenue is today.)

Formal housing only started in the 1870s when developers like The Real Estate Associates built Victorian tract homes here. Construction continued at a steady but slow pace for the rest of the century. The 1906 earthquake and fire brought much change and development as thousands of residents moved into the unaffected district from the destroyed downtown. Fillmore Street quickly became the City's prime retail avenue. Once the city was rebuilt, major stores moved back downtown but many of the residents stayed. The district became one of the more ethnically diverse, with a mixture of Chinese, Jews of various nationalities, Russians, African Americans, and Japanese.

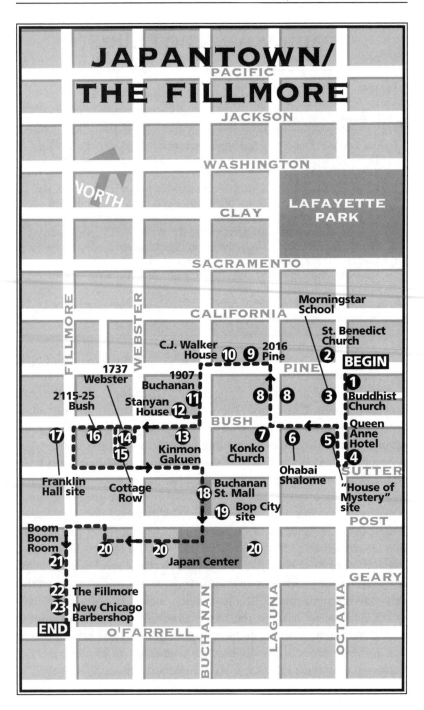

# JAPANTOWN/
# THE FILLMORE

PACIFIC

JACKSON

WASHINGTON

NORTH

CLAY

**LAFAYETTE PARK**

SACRAMENTO

FILLMORE

WEBSTER

CALIFORNIA

Morningstar School

C.J. Walker House **10** **9** 2016 Pine

St. Benedict Church

**2**

**BEGIN**

PINE

**1**

1737 Webster

1907 Buchanan

**3**

Buddhist Church

2115-25 Bush

Stanyan House **12**

**11**

**8** **8**

Queen Anne Hotel

BUSH

**17** **16** **14**

**13**

**7** **6** **5**

**4**

**15**

Kinmon Gakuen

Konko Church

Ohabai Shalome

SUTTER

Franklin Hall site

Cottage Row

**18** Buchanan St. Mall

"House of Mystery" site

**19** Bop City site

POST

Boom Boom Room

**20** **20**

**20**

**21**

**Japan Center**

GEARY

**22** The Fillmore

**23** New Chicago Barbershop

LAGUNA

OCTAVIA

**END**

O'FARRELL

BUCHANAN

# JAPANTOWN/ THE FILLMORE

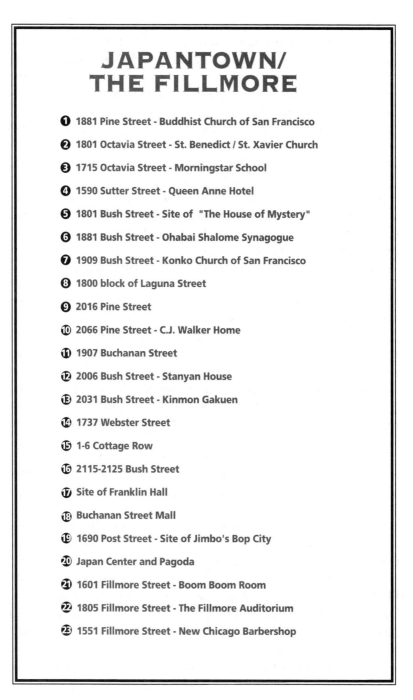

❶ 1881 Pine Street - Buddhist Church of San Francisco

❷ 1801 Octavia Street - St. Benedict / St. Xavier Church

❸ 1715 Octavia Street - Morningstar School

❹ 1590 Sutter Street - Queen Anne Hotel

❺ 1801 Bush Street - Site of "The House of Mystery"

❻ 1881 Bush Street - Ohabai Shalome Synagogue

❼ 1909 Bush Street - Konko Church of San Francisco

❽ 1800 block of Laguna Street

❾ 2016 Pine Street

❿ 2066 Pine Street - C.J. Walker Home

⓫ 1907 Buchanan Street

⓬ 2006 Bush Street - Stanyan House

⓭ 2031 Bush Street - Kinmon Gakuen

⓮ 1737 Webster Street

⓯ 1-6 Cottage Row

⓰ 2115-2125 Bush Street

⓱ Site of Franklin Hall

⓲ Buchanan Street Mall

⓳ 1690 Post Street - Site of Jimbo's Bop City

⓴ Japan Center and Pagoda

㉑ 1601 Fillmore Street - Boom Boom Room

㉒ 1805 Fillmore Street - The Fillmore Auditorium

㉓ 1551 Fillmore Street - New Chicago Barbershop

The Japanese eventually made the area their prime enclave, but they only settled here in large numbers after 1906. Prior to the earthquake and fire they had mainly settled in Chinatown, chiefly along Grant Avenue between Sutter and Sacramento streets. By 1940 the Japanese population numbered about 7,000 in the 24-block area between California, Octavia, O'Farrell, and Fillmore streets.

Japantown—or Japanese Town as residents preferred to call it—was changed forever by the attack on Pearl Harbor on December 7, 1941. Racist sentiment and fear boiled to the fore. In the spring of 1942 President Franklin D. Roosevelt signed Executive Order 9066 authorizing the removal of all ethnic Japanese on the West Coast, including those who were American citizens (which about two-thirds were). Japantown's residents were rounded up and sent to desolate relocation camps throughout the western U.S.

The Japanese disappeared from their enclave almost overnight. Immediately afterward, African Americans, who had come mainly from the deep South to work in Bay Area shipyards and defense plants, moved in—they weren't welcome in other neighborhoods—and occupied the vacant homes and businesses. By the end of World War II the Fillmore was a thriving black community of some 30,000 people. The good wages that the war workers made—along with the need for entertainment—led to a lively neighborhood club scene. The good times continued into the 1950s. All of the greats of the jazz era from Louis Armstrong on down came to town to play. The Fillmore became known as "Harlem West."

But change was brewing. After the war, whites increasingly moved to new housing in the suburbs, leaving minorities in the older housing stock. With fewer economic opportunities for blacks after the war's end the Fillmore started to decline. It became a prime target for "slum clearance." Starting in the late 1950s and lasting for about a decade, the mostly African American residents of the Fillmore were forced from their homes, and their properties were condemned and torn down. Whole city blocks of Victorians fell to the wreckers ball. Black residents started calling the Fillmore the "No More." New housing belatedly went up, and as a sop to the Japanese, a modern Japan Center was built with neighboring buildings featuring traditional Japanese architecture.

The old Japantown and the old Fillmore are gone forever, but like a tree that has been severely pruned only to sprout new shoots, both communities, now smaller in scope, have come back. Japantown celebrates its culture with several street fairs each year, including the Nihonmachi and Cherry Blossom Festivals. And in the Fillmore, jazz is experiencing a revival as several new clubs have opened in recent years.

---

*Start this tour on the southeast corner of Pine and Octavia streets.*

---

### ❶ 1881 Pine Street – Buddhist Church of San Francisco (1937).

Founded in 1898, when two priests came from Kyoto, Japan to establish a mission in the U.S., the Buddhist Church has occupied this location since 1914. The present building, which is surprisingly similar in architectural design to Protestant churches, was erected in 1937. The spur to its construction was the donation to this congregation, in 1935, of holy relics of the Buddha—believed to be the only ones in America—from the King of Siam. The sacred relics are encased in the stupa, which is the donut-stacked dome on the roof of the building. (You may want to cross to the other side of Pine Street for a better look at the stupa.)

Just to the right of the church's entrance on Pine Street, partially obscured by the evergreen tree, is the building's cornerstone. It's a bit startling to see the prominent swastika embedded in it. The four "Ls" that compose it symbolize the four loves of Buddhism—the love of one's parents, of one's community, of one's country, and the love of teachings. During World War II the swastika came to symbolize hate, not love. The words "Butsu Shari Hoto" placed around the swastika mean that the stupa on the roof contains a bone from the Buddha. Inside the cornerstone is a box containing 20,000 paper lotus petals. Each is inscribed with the name of a member who contributed 15 cents or more to the church's construction.

In 1942 the Japanese parishioners were shipped off to Topaz, Utah, an abandoned Mormon agricultural community that was turned into a relocation camp, or prison, where they spent the remainder of the war. Local white residents looked after the church and the goods of the departed members while they were gone.

*Look to the northwest corner of Pine and Octavia, where you will see:*

## ❷ 1801 Octavia Street – St. Benedict Parish / St. Francis Xavier Church (1939).

St. Francis Xavier Church (named for the Spanish missionary who introduced Catholicism to Japan in 1549) was founded in San Francisco in 1913 for the small group of Japanese Catholics then resident in the City. Originally located on Pine Street a few blocks away, and

then on Buchanan, the congregation moved to this site in 1939. A grand Victorian mansion, probably dating from the late 1870s, was purchased by the church and greatly remodeled. From an old photograph of the original structure and from a look at the interior it appears that the front two-thirds of the Victorian was demolished and replaced by the current Asian temple façade.

1801 Octavia Street– then.

The back third, which now houses the church offices, was saved, but had its exterior completely stripped and plastered over with stucco.

The congregation had barely settled into its new building when, as happened to its neighbor the Buddhist Church, its parishioners were herded off to the Topaz, Utah relocation camp in 1942. Father William Stoecke, the local priest, went to Topaz with his flock, staying with them until they all returned when the war was over. The church reopened and continued serving the Japanese Catholic community until 1994, when the name St. Benedict was added and it was largely converted to serving the deaf of all races. Japanese Catholics, most of them elderly, now just have religious services one Sunday a month.

1801 Octavia Street – now.

*Walk south on Octavia Street a short distance to get a better look at the three-story Asian-style building on the other side of the street.*

### ❸ 1715 Octavia Street – Morning Star School (1930).

This formidable structure with its massive green-glazed tile eave over the first floor was constructed during 1929–30, replacing a Victorian mansion. It was erected by St. Francis Xavier Church to serve as the grade school for children of its parishioners. It remained a parochial school until 1985 when dwindling attendance forced its closure. It served as a Montessori school for awhile, and then after remodeling and the addition of the new building next to it on the corner, it reopened in 2001 as a boys' high school as part of the Catholic Schools of the Sacred Heart.

*Continue south on Octavia. Cross over Bush Street and walk one block to Sutter. To get a better look at the grand Victorian building on the northeast corner of Octavia and Sutter, cross over Octavia to the northwest corner of the intersection.*

### ❹ 1590 Sutter Street – Queen Anne Hotel (1890).

This imposing Queen Anne Victorian was built during 1889–90 by James G. Fair, one of the Comstock "Silver Kings." Its first tenant was Miss Mary Lake's School for Young Ladies, where the daughters of the well-to-do took instruction in music, math, art, and other subjects. When Fair died in 1894 his daughter Virginia inherited the property. In 1896 the school moved out and she leased it to the Cosmos Club, a men's social club composed of the city's elite. James L. Flood, Governor George Pardee, and many others were some of the movers and shakers who were members. When Virginia Fair Vanderbilt sold the property in 1909 the Cosmos Club departed.

The structure subsequently became a boarding house, and then in 1926 it was purchased by the Episcopal Church which opened it as the Girls' Friendly Society Lodge, "a home for working women." In 1950 it became a guest house called The Lodge. When that closed in 1975 the building was boarded up. After refurbishing, it reopened in 1981 as a boutique hostelry, the present Queen Anne Hotel.

*Walk north on the west side of Octavia most of the block. Just past all but the last of the huge eucalyptus trees at the curb you will see a large, round, glazed terra cotta medallion embedded in the concrete between the sidewalk and the curb. It is a tribute to Mary Ellen Pleasant, an African American pioneer who once lived in a house here where the modern L-shaped office building stands today.*

### ❺ 1801 Bush Street – Site of 1661 Octavia – The "House of Mystery" (1879–1927).

In the late 19$^{th}$ century this lot was the site of what the press called "The House of Mystery," because it was the scene of the sudden death of Thomas Bell, Mary Ellen Pleasant's friend and apparent business associate. The house that stood here was a gray, three-story frame Victorian with a mansard roof, whose $100,000 cost was paid by Mary Pleasant. It was erected in 1879, perhaps as a wedding present for

Octavia Street – The "House of Mystery," garden, and stable.

Thomas and Teresa Bell because they moved in as soon as they were married that year. Teresa was a protégée of Mary Ellen and the latter had apparently arranged the match with Thomas Bell. The three of them lived together under the same roof, but what the exact nature of this ménage à trois was will never be known. Mary Ellen not only ran the household including all of the financial aspects but, as Thomas and Teresa seem to have had a parting of the ways at some point, she also acted as intermediary between the two.

On the night of October 15, 1892, after everyone had gone to bed, Thomas Bell, who had been ill, was heard to call out "Where am I?" He then crashed with a thud to the hard basement floor from a second-story landing. He died the next day. His death was ruled accidental, and at the time there were no questions raised about foul play. But after Mary Ellen and Teresa had a bitter falling out seven years later, which ended with Mary Ellen being ejected from the house she had built, rumors started that Thomas Bell's death had been no accident and that the "Voodoo Queen" had had something to do with it. Hence the press's love of playing up "The House of Mystery" tag.

**The only physical remnant left of "The House of Mystery," which was torn down in 1927, are the large eucalyptus trees near the curb that were planted by Mary Ellen Pleasant in the 1880s.**

In the 19<sup>th</sup> century the Pleasant/Bell property occupied the whole frontage of Octavia Street from Bush to Sutter. The southern half had a formal garden and a stable at the rear, about where the end of the parking lot at mid-block is today.

---

*At the corner of Octavia and Bush turn left to the west and go down most of the block toward Laguna to:*

---

### ❻ 1881 Bush Street – Ohabai Shalome Synagogue (1895).

This now thoroughly refurbished building was once a Jewish synagogue for Congregation Ohabai Shalome ("Lovers of Peace"). Its roots go back to 1863 when its founding members, concerned that Temple Emanu-El's practices were becoming too liberal, split off from them and founded their own congregation. In 1895 they moved from downtown to the Western Addition and built this temple. Interestingly, in terms of architectural design, this building strongly resembles the grand Temple Emanu-El synagogue that once stood at 450 Sutter Street. Its exotic second story Venetian-style arcade is modeled after the Doge's palace in Venice. The two rounded, capped towers once supported distinctive minaret-like spires, but they were removed after being damaged by a storm in 1915.

In 1934, with the congregation's membership dwindling Ohabai Shalome sold the building to Teruro Kasuga who turned it into a Zen

Buddhist mission. Like its Japanese brethren at St. Xavier and the Buddhist Church of San Francisco, its parishioners were herded off to detention camps at the start of World War II. A Christian group occupied it during the war years. The Buddhists then reclaimed it, but by 1975 the building had been abandoned and was taken over by the San Francisco Redevelopment Agency.

The structure suffered progressive deterioration for almost three decades before a consortium of local churches purchased it with the aim of converting it and the lot on the corner into low-cost assisted living senior housing. Most of the housing units are in the new building on the corner, while the old temple has the dining hall, a library, and offices.

---

*Continue west on Bush Street. Cross over Laguna and stop in front of the church on the southwest corner of the intersection.*

---

### ❼ 1909 Bush Street – Konko Church of San Francisco (1973).

Konko—named for its 19$^{th}$-century founder, Ikagami Konko Daijin—is a sect of Shintoism, an ancient Japanese religion that emphasizes nature and ancestor worship. The San Francisco branch started in 1930 in a Victorian house two blocks away on Pine Street. It later moved to this location where it occupied an Italianate Victorian which was torn down in 1971. That was replaced in 1973 with the present structure, which was built to a traditional Japanese design using old-fashioned carpentry techniques. The simple, unadorned interior, furnished in blond wood, features an altar with offerings of flowers, food, and rice wine.

---

*Cross Bush Street to the northwest corner of the intersection. Walk up this block of Laguna Street to Pine and note the Victorians on both sides of the street as you do.*

---

### ❽ 1800 block of Laguna Street (east side 1877, west side 1889).

The two sides of this street comprise one of the more intact blocks of Victorian tract housing left in the City. The east side of the street was put up in 1877 in the prevailing Italianate style by The Real Estate Associates (TREA), a housing developer that during the 1870s built over 1,000 homes on speculation in a number of San Francisco neighborhoods. (Several more of their houses will be mentioned a few stops ahead. See also the Mission District walk for more on TREA.) Except for some modern-day remodeling, note how little variation there is the design and decoration of these houses. This was standard housing of the time, targeted at middle-class buyers.

The houses on the west side of the street were constructed a little over a decade later, when the Stick style was in vogue, by William Hinkel, a prolific builder of the time. He too used a standard house plan but he varied the decorative details a bit, especially the roof lines, to give his houses a little more individuality. One thing worth noting about the houses on both sides of the street is that there is space between them. They do not stand shoulder-to-shoulder as so many Victorians in the City do. This no doubt was a selling feature and no doubt was reflected in the price.

As you walk up Laguna on the west side of the street look at 1825–29 Laguna. A plaque affixed to the façade gives a brief history of this dwelling. It was originally built by a riverboat captain. A Japanese family owned it in the 1930s and, in an all too familiar story, they were sent to a camp during the war. When the Japanese moved out, prostitutes moved in and the place became a brothel.

Just before you reach Pine Street note also the last Victorian on this side of the street. The address is now 1855 Laguna, but if you look at the stained-glass transom you will see the original address which was 1819. It was not uncommon for houses to be renumbered, especially after 1906.

---

*At Pine Street cross over to the north side. A few doors to the west is:*

---

### ❾ 2016 Pine Street (c.1870–1893).

Architecturally, this has to be one of the strangest houses in San Francisco. The three main floors were all constructed during different decades, infusing the house with decorative elements from the Italianate, Stick, and Queen Anne periods. The building apparently started as a one-story cottage in the 1860s or 1870s. That is now the second story, done in the Italianate style. In the 1880s, the first floor, with the rectangular corner bay window typical of the Stick style, was inserted under the original floor. And in 1893 the Queen Anne style roof with its Palladian window and garlands on the frieze was added. A curious footnote to the latter addition is that the contract for that work was signed by Mary Ellen Pleasant. The house was owned by a Rebecca Gordon, who may have been one of Mary Ellen's protégée's. Ms. Gordon married a Charles H. Boone about 1894, so maybe this was an alliance created by the majordomo of the House of Mystery.

In 1928, after the death of one of the subsequent owners, the house was sold to the current owner and tenant, the Nichiren Buddhist Church of America. They added the nondescript addition on the east side of the building (perhaps to house members returning from the camps after the war) as well as the basement, and in doing so they likely moved the whole structure slightly to the left. This may explain why the steps through the sidewalk wall don't line up with the entrance to the house.

---

*Continue west on Pine Street a few doors to:*

---

**❿ 2066 Pine Street** (1876) **- Madame C.J. Walker Home for Girls and Women** (1921–1972).

Named for one of the country's first black woman millionaires, the C. J. Walker Home for Girls and Women was established in this house in 1921 to aid young African American women who were new to the City. Supported financially by the Third Baptist Church, the Home helped the newcomers find jobs and affordable housing. It added a social hall in the basement in 1926, which provided a place for recreation as well. The house proved an important focal point during World War II when the black population of the neighborhood increased greatly. The C. J. Walker Home ended more than 50 years at this location when it moved to Hayes Street in 1972. The house then reverted to private ownership. Stucco that had been applied to the façade in the 1940s was removed and the building's original Italianate details were restored.

---

*Continue to the intersection of Buchanan Street. Cross to the southeast corner and walk down the west side of Buchanan most of the block to:*

---

## ⑪ 1907 Buchanan Street (c.1860s).

This small one-story frame cottage, which was probably built before 1868, was moved to this location in 1877 by its owner, Charles Stanyan (more on him on the next stop on this walk). It originally stood on the northeast corner of Bush and Hyde streets, where St. Francis Memorial Hospital is today. Interestingly, writer Bret Harte is known to have lived at that corner in 1866, but whether he lived in this house hasn't been documented.

*Go to the corner of Bush Street and turn right. The second house up is:*

## ⑫ 2006 Bush Street – Charles Stanyan House (c.1860).

One of the first homes built in this area, this cottage-like structure with a rare front porch was a real pioneer, because when it was put up here among sand dunes it was an inconvenient mile and a half from downtown. Bush was the first street extended out this far, but it was nothing more that a plank roadway that led to Lone Mountain and other cemeteries that sprang up west of Presidio Avenue in the 1850s and '60s.

The first known owner and occupant was Charles H. Stanyan (1830–1889) who at various times was a miner, teamster, and real estate investor. He served on the Board of Supervisors from 1865 to 1869 and was appointed chairman of the board's Outside Lands Committee, which was largely responsible for setting aside the acreage that became Golden Gate Park. Stanyan Street, at the park's eastern border, is named for him.

Stanyan's Bush Street house—he also had a home near Polk and Sacramento streets—originally was the only structure on the fifty-vara lot that makes up the southeast corner of this block. An old photograph shows the home surrounded by a large lawn and garden. As previously noted, he moved the house now numbered 1907 Buchanan Street to this property in 1877, and then in 1885 he built the matching Stick- style flats that now stand on both sides of the Stanyan House.

*Go back to the corner and cross to the other side of Bush. Walk west about*
*half way down the block to:*

### ⓭ 2031 Bush Street (1926) – **Kinmon Gakuen.**

Kinmon Gakuen ("Golden Gate School") was founded on this site
in 1911 as a Japanese-language school. Its intent was to keep Japanese
language and culture alive for new immigrants to the U.S. The present structure dates from 1926 and replaced an Italianate Victorian.

The institute closed in 1942 with the advent of the war, and the
building was used as a collection point for Japantown residents, who
were tagged with numbers like so many pieces of luggage before
being loaded onto buses and taken to the Tanforan race track in San
Mateo. They were held there—where some were made to bed down
in horse stalls—for several months before being shipped to the detention camp at Topaz, Utah.

During the war the building became the Booker T. Washington
Center. Today it is the Nihonmachi Little Friends School, a Japanese
preschool.

*Continue west on Bush to Webster. Cross Webster and turn left.*
*The second house down on the right side is:*

### ⓮ 1737 Webster Street (1885).

This tall, two-flat Stick Victorian was designed by the Newsom
Brothers, who did residences in a number of San Francisco neighborhoods but whose signature work is the grand Carson House in
Eureka. Their love of decorative detail, sometimes just for its own
sake, is shown here especially in the totally unnecessary use of the
pipe-stem colonnettes that frame the windows.

This house was moved here in 1974 from its original location on
Turk Street near Franklin, a block that was cleared to make way for
Opera Plaza. It was built in 1885 as a residence for German immigrant
John J. Vollmer and his family. Vollmer operated a grocery store at the
corner of Turk and Franklin streets for many years. The house was
still owned by Vollmer's descendants when it was condemned and
purchased by the Redevelopment Agency in 1967 as part of the urban
renewal effort in the Western Addition.

If you look closely at the innermost Corinthian capital on the north side of the portico you can see that it has been shaved a bit. The building virtually had to be shoehorned into this space between its two neighbors. The only way to make it fit was to cut off that piece.

---

*Retrace your steps to the corner of Bush and turn left. Down a few doors, just past 2109 Bush Street (the dark shingled Victorian), is:*

---

### ⓯ 1–6 Cottage Row (1882).

This narrow, brick-paved walkway, which is lined with bushes and small trees and cuts through to Sutter Street, contains six small two-story frame cottages with gable roofs that are part of a historic district known as Cottage Row. Although they vary in appearance today, they once were identical. They were built for Charles L. Taylor, a real estate investor who had business interests in shipping, lumber, and marine insurance. He also served a two-year term as a member of the Board of Supervisors just prior to building these six units in 1882. He spent only $5,000 for their construction; they were intended as rental income property. They share common walls and only measure 20' x 23' in size, so they must have been strictly for those on a budget.

They are individually owned today and are quite desirable, located as they are away from busy Bush Street and across from a mini park. During the 1930s, Cottage Row was informally known as "Japan Street," since most of the residents then were Japanese-Americans. In their tiny, five-foot-deep backyards they grew vegetables that they sold in an open-air market held on the Row on Saturdays.

---

*Retrace your steps on Cottage Row, return to Bush Street, and turn left. The next six houses down toward Fillmore Street are:*

---

### ⓰ 2115–2125 Bush Street (1875).

Despite the continuous whirr of one-way automobile traffic down Bush Street today these six two-story Italianate row houses, set back from the street as they are, with their lush front yard gardens and their lack of garages, still manage to evoke a less hurried era, a time when people sat on their front steps and perhaps waved to the driver of the horse-car line that passed this way in the 19<sup>th</sup> century.

They were constructed during 1874-75 by The Real Estate Associates, who did the aforementioned Italianate side of the 1800 block of Laguna Street. The Bush Street houses, and others that once stood on Fillmore and behind on Sutter Street as part of the same development, were marketed to upper-middle-class businessmen and professionals, and sold for between $4,200 and $6,600. These houses, interestingly, have 1870s slanted bay windows, but they are located on the façades on the back, not on the front as was much more common.

---

*Continue to the corner of Fillmore Street. Across the street once stood:*

---

**⓱  Bush and Fillmore streets – SW corner – Site of Franklin Hall** (1895–1941).

On this corner, now occupied by a Walgreens pharmacy, once stood Franklin Hall, a four-story wooden building that served as an auditorium and Gay Nineties dance hall. The leading attraction of its early years was "Professor" Bothwell Brown, who billed himself as "California's Greatest Female Impersonator." When the 1906 earthquake struck and the City's leaders were forced from the Fairmont Hotel, where they had taken temporary refuge after City Hall had largely been destroyed, they moved into Franklin Hall. Out went "California's Greatest Female Impersonator" and in came the mayor, the police chief, and other top officials. They stayed here for a year and a half before moving to the Whitcomb Hotel on Market Street, where they remained until 1916 when the new city hall was completed.

Franklin Hall was used in later years as a meeting hall for various groups and for political rallies, but by the 1930s it was derelict. It was torn down in 1941 to make way for a gas station.

---

*Walk down Fillmore to Sutter Street and turn left.*

*Cross over Webster Street—this part of it was widened when the Redevelopment Agency's bulldozers came through here in the 1970s—and continue up Sutter to Buchanan Street.*

*At Buchanan Street walk the one block south to Post on this pedestrian mall.*

---

### ⑱ Buchanan Street between Sutter and Post streets – Buchanan Street Mall (1976).

After the construction of the Japan Center (two stops ahead on this walk) in the 1960s, developers turned their attention to the blocks just north. This block of Buchanan Street was turned into a pedestrian-only mall with shops and restaurants on both sides and was completed in 1976. The Japanese-styled buildings are meant to represent a mountain village in Japan. The cobblestone paving winding down the center symbolizes a brook.

The mall's highlights are the two Origami Fountains by local sculptor Ruth Asawa. (Origami is the Japanese art of paper folding.) The original fountains were made of steel. When they were turned off during a drought they rusted, and were removed in 1995. In 1999 Ruth Asawa replaced them with two bronze fountains nearly identical to the originals, and the water was turned back on.

---

*Just next door to Soko Hardware (Soko is the Japanese word for San Francisco) on the northeast corner of Buchanan and Post streets once stood:*

### ⑲ 1690 Post Street – Site of Jimbo's Bop City(1950–1965).

In the heyday of the Fillmore, before the Redevelopment Agency moved in, the district was packed with jazz clubs. Probably the most renowned—"Known the World Over" was its claim—was Bop City, which opened in 1950 in the back of a Victorian that once stood just off the northeast corner of Post and Buchanan.

Operated by Jimbo Edwards, a black former automobile salesman, the place started as a breakfast spot and waffle shop. It did away with the waffles and switched to selling fried chicken after Lenny Bruce came in one day and made a mess by pouring syrup not only on his waffles but seemingly on everything else as well. Edwards built a small stage for musicians in the back of his restaurant which quickly became the scene of a hot after-hours jazz club called "Bop City." (It was named for a New York City jazz club that had recently closed.) All of the jazz greats of the day came to the club at one time or another: Duke Ellington, Count Basie, Dizzy Gillespie, Billie Holiday, John Coltrane, Miles Davis. One night, about 1952, Louis Armstrong came in after performing at another club nearby and listened to saxophonist Charlie "Yardbird" Parker play. It was the only known time that these two jazz greats were together under the same roof.

Bop City closed in 1965. When the construction began on the Buchanan Street Mall, Bop City's Victorian was moved two blocks down to Fillmore Street where it stands today as 1712 Fillmore, the home to Marcus Books. The famous back room where Bop City ruled did not seem to make the transition, however.

---

*Cross Post Street and go into the open plaza.*

---

## ⑳ Japan Center and Japantown Peace Plaza (1968).

This plaza, which was remodeled with new lighting and flagstone paving in the year 2000, is the heart of the Japan Center, a three-block-long shopping arcade of contemporary design that houses a multitude of Japanese restaurants and shops. It is anchored on the east end at Laguna Street by the Kabuki Hotel and on the west end at Fillmore by the Sundance Cinemas multiplex.

Construction began on the complex in 1960 after the land was cleared of the Victorian-era housing that stood here, and was finally completed in 1968. The architect (except for the Peace Plaza and Peace Pagoda) was Minoru Yamasaki, who did a number of large commercial projects around the U.S. including the World Trade Center in New York, which was destroyed on September 11, 2001.

The five-tiered, 100-foot-high concrete pagoda in the southwest corner of the plaza was a gift to the people of San Francisco from the people of Japan. It is modeled after 9th century miniature pagodas that were dedicated to peace in Nara, the ancient capital of Japan. The Peace Pagoda was erected in March 1968 when the Japan Center opened.

---

*To see some of the complex on the way to the next stop on this tour, walk west through the doors leading into the Kintetsu Mall. After passing by various restaurants and shops you will walk through the enclosed Webster Street bridge into the next building. When you get to the Kinokuniya Bookstore (which carries some English language titles too), on your left, take the stairway (or the elevator) down to the first floor and exit on Sutter Street. Take a left to Fillmore Street, cross over to the west side and go to Geary*

*Boulevard. Stop in front of the bar/nightclub on the northwest corner of the intersection of Geary and Fillmore.*

**㉑ 1601 Fillmore Street – John Lee Hooker's Boom Boom Room – Location of Jack's Bar** (1982–1997).

This nightclub and bar, now named for the late blues legend John Lee Hooker, has roots that go back to 1933 when Jack's Bar opened on Sutter Street between Fillmore and Webster. It was the first bar in the area to cater to African Americans. It stood at 1931 Sutter for four decades, until it moved north up Fillmore Street to make way for the current housing development on the site. After relocating a couple of times, it ended up on this corner in 1982. Jack's became the Boom Boom Room in 1997. The current venue represents part of the revival of live music in the neighborhood, although the acts tend more toward rhythm and blues than the jazz that dominated the Fillmore in its heyday. Inside, the walls are lined with photos of John Lee Hooker and other blues and jazz musicians.

*Cross Geary Boulevard. The buff brick commercial building on the southwest corner of Geary and Fillmore is:*

**㉒ 1805 Geary Boulevard** (1912) **– Fillmore Auditorium**

Now the home of the famous Fillmore Auditorium, this building dates from 1912. The second-floor auditorium/dance floor was first known as the Majestic Ball Room, which it remained until the mid-1930s. It took on various other names and uses until it picked up its present moniker in 1957. From the 1940s until the early 1960s it featured popular black performers of the day, such as Billie Holliday, Ray Charles, James Brown, The Temptations, and Little Richard, as musical tastes changed in a progression from jazz and rhythm and blues to soul to rock.

But the Fillmore Auditorium, more commonly called "The Fillmore," which is synonymous today with the burgeoning rock music scene of the 1960s, had its heyday starting in January 1966 when impresario Bill Graham began presenting all of the great bands of that era: Jefferson Airplane, the Grateful Dead, Big Brother and the

Holding Company with Janis Joplin, Santana, Creedence Clearwater Revival, The Who, Led Zeppelin, Pink Floyd, and many others. The glory days here were surprisingly short—Graham closed it down in July 1968 when he moved his operation to the Fillmore West on Market Street.

Graham returned in the late 1980s, but his run then was relatively brief since the 1989 Loma Prieta earthquake shuttered the building for repairs. The legendary promoter died in a helicopter crash in 1991. When the auditorium reopened three years later after seismic upgrading was completed, it was under the aegis of his organization, Bill Graham Presents, which still operates the hall today.

*Continue down Fillmore Street on the west side a few doors to:*

### ❷❸ 1551 Fillmore Street – New Chicago Barbershop (since 1968).

The New Chicago Barbershop is one of the few black-owned businesses that still gives a taste of the old Fillmore as it was in its heyday. It has been at this location since 1968 but has been in business since 1952, having moved here from Ellis Street. According to manager Reggie Pettus, this space, prior to New Chicago moving in, was used by the creators of the famous psychedelic posters that advertised the Fillmore's concerts. The City Directory for the mid-1960s shows this address as being vacant, so if that indeed is true they must have been working here on an unofficial and ad hoc basis.

# Mary Ellen "Mammy" Pleasant
## (1814-1904)

No figure in San Francisco history is more shrouded in myth and mystery than African American pioneer Mary Ellen "Mammy" Pleasant. Charges that she murdered her employer and business partner Thomas Bell, owned brothels, and practiced voodoo, have sullied her reputation. Probably none of them is true, yet it is true that she led an eventful and colorful life.

She was said to have been born a slave somewhere in the South, but by her own account she was born a free black in Philadelphia in 1814. As a child she was sent to Nantucket, where she displayed such a talent as a clerk in a retail shop that she never was allowed time off to go to school. As a teenager she moved back to Philadelphia, where she married a black carpenter and contractor who, when

**Mary Ellen Pleasant.**

he died, left her a good sum of money. (She later married a John James Plaissance or Pleasant, hence the last name by which she was later known.)

With the money left her by her first husband, Mary Ellen became a financial supporter of the Abolitionist cause. She took an active role in the Underground Railroad—helping runaway slaves make their way north to freedom. In the early 1850s she made her way to San Francisco, and for the next decade she continued her anti-slavery efforts, sheltering slaves who had made it to California. In 1858 she even made a trip to Canada to meet with Abolitionist leader John Brown. She gave him $500 in gold to help with the cause. She also fought discrimination locally. When she was thrown off a San Francisco omnibus in 1868 because of her race, she sued. She was awarded $500 in damages, but the judgment was later overturned on appeal.

An excellent cook and an attractive woman, Mary Ellen had no trouble finding work as a boardinghouse keeper when she first arrived in the largely bachelor society that was San Francisco. By the late 1860s she was able to open several boardinghouses of her own, one of which, at 920 Washington Street, became one of the more fashionable in town, attracting leading politicians and businessmen of the day. D. O. Mills, William C. Ralston, and William Sharon are a few of the notables of the day who dined there. Through rubbing shoulders with the City's elite and eavesdropping on their dinner table conversations, Pleasant gleaned profitable stock tips that she funneled through Thomas Bell, a financier who in essence became her partner, and some say her lover. She further reveled in her power as a matchmaker, arranging introductions between the well-to-do bachelors who frequented her establishments and her female employees and protégées.

Mary Ellen Pleasant lived to be 89 years old, and until the final few years of her life enjoyed much in the way of good fortune. Perhaps because she was a black woman with "piercing eyes that looked right through you," who was bright, outspoken, and who exuded power, she inspired a certain amount of fear. The *San Francisco Chronicle* in an 1899 feature article called her "The Queen of the Voodoo," a charge unsupported by any real evidence. She had a bitter feud with the widow of Thomas Bell after his death, and died in poverty in 1904. It was a sad end for a woman who had listed her occupation in the 1890 census as "Capitalist." She is buried in Napa, where her headstone reads simply "She Was a Friend of John Brown."

# Market Street

**Length:** 1 mile / 1.6 kilometers.

**Time:** 1¼ hours (add ½ hour or so if you visit the Federal Reserve exhibit).

**Walk Rating:** Easy.

**Hills:** None.

**Public Transit:** The F streetcar runs the length of Market Street and numerous bus lines travel portions of it. BART stations are located near the foot of Market Street, at Montgomery Street, and near Powell Street. The California Street cable car line terminus is where this tour begins, next to the Hyatt Regency Hotel.

**Parking:** Parking is not allowed on Market Street itself at any time. Since garages in the vicinity are expensive, it would be best to take public transit. On Sundays, however, parking on adjoining streets is relatively easy to find and free as well.

**Restrooms:** There are coin-operated (25 cents) public toilets at the beginning of this tour just down Market Street from the cable car terminus and near the end of the tour at the Powell Street cable car turnaround.

Market Street is San Francisco's grand boulevard —its parade ground, if you will. All of San Francisco's major parades go up Market Street. Many start from the Ferry Building at its foot and end at City Hall. Spanish American War veterans, to World War I doughboys, to World War II GIs, to St. Patrick's Day celebrants, to labor union workers, to heroes from the city's sports teams such as the baseball Giants and football Forty-Niners, to gays and lesbians, have all marched up Market Street.

It is doubtful that Jasper O'Farrell, the surveyor who planned Market Street, foresaw that a Gay-Lesbian Freedom Day parade would one day ride and strut along his broad boulevard, but when he laid out this extra wide street in 1847 (at 120 feet it was twice the width of the town's other streets) he surely intended it to be a showcase location and focal point for the city. Market Street was likely named after Philadelphia's Market Street; the name was probably suggested by George Hyde, a Philadelphian who had arrived in San Francisco the previous year. But in 1847 O'Farrell's Market Street was no more than a line on a map. Sand dunes as high as 80 feet blocked passage in many parts. It was not until 1859–60 in fact that lower

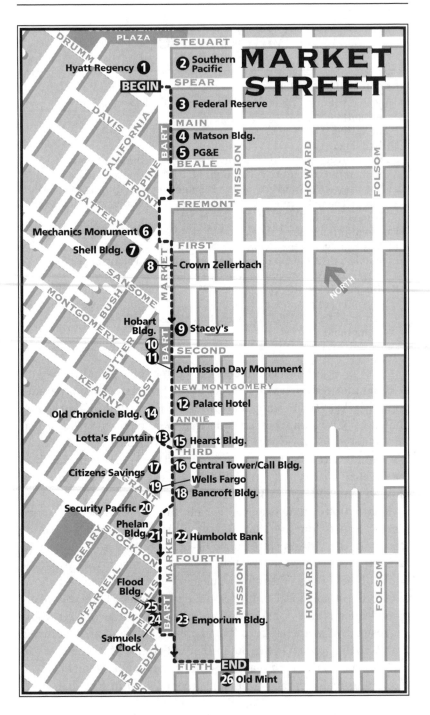

# MARKET STREET

❶ Five Embarcadero Center - Hyatt Regency Hotel

❷ One Market Street - Southern Pacific Building

❸ 101 Market Street - Federal Reserve Building

❹ 215 Market Street - Matson Building

❺ 245 Market Street - PG&E Building

❻ Mechanics Monument

❼ 100 Bush Street - Shell Building

❽ One Bush Street - Crown Zellerbach Building

❾ 581 Market Street - Stacey's Bookstore

❿ 582 Market Street - Hobart Building

⓫ Admission Day Monument

⓬ 50 New Montgomery Street - Palace Hotel

⓭ Lotta's Fountain

⓮ 690 Market Street - Chronicle Building

⓯ 5 Third Street - Hearst Building

⓰ 703 Market Street - Central Tower - Old Call Building

⓱ 704 Market Street - Citizens Savings Building

⓲ 721 Market Street - Bancroft Building

⓳ 2 Grant Avenue - Wells Fargo Bank

⓴ One Grant Avenue - former Security Pacific Bank Building

㉑ 760 Market Street - Phelan Building

㉒ 785 Market Street - Humboldt Bank Building

㉓ 835 Market Street - former Emporium store

㉔ Albert Samuels Clock

㉕ 870 Market Street - Flood Building

㉖ Old Mint

Market Street was finally graded and wooden plank sidewalks were laid down.

The leveling of the sand hills opened up the street to transportation. Horse-drawn streetcars were the first mode of public conveyance, starting in the 1860s. When the first ferry building was erected at the foot of Market Street in 1875, the boulevard's destiny as a major transportation artery was assured. Cable cars first appeared there in the late 1870s. After the earthquake of 1906, electric streetcars replaced the cable cars, and with only intermittent interruptions have run there ever since. With the building of the two bridges in the late 1930s and the subsequent drastic reduction in ferry service, Market Street as a public traffic artery has declined in importance. But San Francisco can claim today to be the only major American city with streetcars still running on its main street.

Builders and architects gravitated toward this broad showplace boulevard. The seven-story Palace Hotel, erected in 1875 at Market and New Montgomery, was the City's tallest building for over a decade. By the 1890s, with advances in construction technologies, taller buildings went up, with Market Street being their prime location. San Francisco's first "skyscraper," the ten-story plus clock tower Chronicle Building at Market and Kearny, went up in 1889. Others quickly followed, transforming the once Victorian city of predominately two-and three-story commercial structures into the high-rise metropolis it is today.

---

*Start this tour at the cable car terminus at California and Market streets. The large building with the driveway in front is:*

---

### ❶ Five Embarcadero Center – Hyatt Regency Hotel (1972).

Designed by Atlanta-based architect John Portman, the 17-story Hyatt Regency boasts the most dramatic hotel lobby in San Francisco. The soaring interior space leads the eye up a series of terraced walkways festooned with hanging plants. The Hyatt Regency replaced a previous hostelry on the site, the Hotel Terminal, a modest six-story affair that dated from 1908. Photographs from that era show painted billboards on the side of the building advertising rooms for "$1.00 night, $1.50 with bath."

*Across the street, occupying the block of Market between Steuart and Spear streets, is:*

## ❷ One Market Street – Southern Pacific Building (1916).

This handsome brick and stone building designed by Bliss and Faville until recently housed the headquarters of the once mighty Southern Pacific Company. The SP (initially known as the Central Pacific), built the western half of the transcontinental railroad, and through generous land grants and transportation monopolies built an economic powerhouse that held California in a virtual stranglehold in the 19th century. The SP's power was on the wane by the time this edifice was constructed, but the company still wielded considerable economic clout up until recently. The name Southern Pacific officially disappeared from the corporate world in 1996 when the company merged with Union Pacific, a railroad rival. The new combined company maintained offices here until 1998.

*Cross Market Street to see the building occupying the block between Spear and Main streets:*

## ❸ 101 Market Street – Federal Reserve Building (1983).

The Federal Reserve moved into this new building in 1983 after occupying a Neo-Classical banking temple on Sansome Street in the heart of the financial district for almost sixty years. This structure replaced a collection of small office buildings and hotels put up after the 1906 earthquake.

The west end of the lobby houses exhibits that explore the history and workings of the Federal Reserve System. Many are interactive, which make them appealing to children as well as adults. One of them, called "Dollar Detectives," shows how, by pressing buttons that illuminate $20 bills, you can tell a counterfeit from a genuine one.

Also be sure to see the currency room, which has a fine selection of American currency from Colonial times to the present, including many rare examples. Of relevance to local history are $10 and $20 notes from the First National Gold Bank of San Francisco, an institution founded at 316 Montgomery Street in 1870. Gold was much preferred to paper money in 19th-century San Francisco and throughout the West. Because of this, Congress allowed a few banks, such as the First National Gold Bank, to issue currency backed by gold. The Gold Bank was a direct predecessor of Crocker Bank, which in 1986 merged with Wells Fargo Bank.

The lobby exhibits are open to guided tours only. See their website, www. frbsf.org/tours, for days and hours.

---

*Cross over Main Street to see the building on the*
*southwest corner of Market and Main:*

---

### ❹ Market and Main streets – SW corner – Matson Building (1924).

This imposing building was once the headquarters of Matson Navigation, a company founded in 1882 by William Matson (1849–1917), a Swedish immigrant, who started by trading goods between San Francisco and the Hawaiian Islands. From a single three-masted schooner he built a company into what became the largest privately held shipping line on the West Coast. At its peak in the 1950s Matson Navigation had dozens of cargo ships and several of the most luxurious passenger ocean liners afloat, including the *Lurline,* which ferried Hollywood movie stars and other well-heeled patrons to Hawaii and back. By 1970 however, the company had fallen on hard times. With the ascendancy of airlines, ocean-based passenger travel was no longer profitable, and the *Lurline* and other ships had to be sold. Crippling waterfront strikes in the early 1970s further hurt the company; in 1972 Matson Navigation sold its building to its next-door neighbor, PG&E. Matson eventually moved its offices to leased space at 333 Market Street. Ironically, it was just steps away from 327 Market Street where William Matson had his headquarters when the company was incorporated in 1901.

Captain Matson didn't live to see his new headquarters building constructed in 1924 but he surely would have approved. Like the Southern Pacific Building two blocks away, the Matson Building was also designed by Bliss and Faville. But this Italian Renaissance-style structure with its top-story arcaded windows and its skin of polychrome glazed terra cotta has a finer cast to it. Decorative nautical touches such as ships anchors, dolphins, and shells abound in keeping with the company's business.

Terra cotta scored and painted to look like rope also adds a nice touch, as can be seen in the capitals of the Ionic columns and in the "M" on the escutcheon over the main doorway. Another company marker can be seen in the lobby: the brass elevator doors are scored with a map of the Hawaiian Islands.

---

*Next door is:*

---

### ❺ 245 Market Street – Pacific Gas & Electric (1925).

Built almost simultaneously with its neighbor the Matson Building, the PG&E headquarters is a handsome complement to it, resembling it in style. The architects were Bakewell & Brown, who most notably designed City Hall. Here also the architects have added decorative elements to the façade symbolic of the company's business and origins. Above the arched doorway the dam with the water spewing through the gates is obvious. The stone carved California mountain goats over the first-floor windows represent the high Sierra, which is where PG&E gets the water that is the source of its hydroelectric power. Another touch, although one hard to see, are the flames atop the urns on the sixteenth floor, which naturally allude to the "G" or gas portion of PG&E.

---

*Walk up Market to Fremont Street and cross over to the north side of the street. Walk up to Battery Street for a look at:*

---

### ❻ In the plaza at Bush and Market streets
### - Mechanics Monument (1899).

This fine bronze sculpture is unusual in that although dedicated to a specific man, it is not a bust or full-length statue of that man. It is a memorial from James Donahue to his father, Peter Donahue (1822–1885). The elder Donahue was an Irish immigrant and forty-niner who, after a brief, unsuccessful fling at gold mining, established a blacksmith shop at Montgomery and Jackson streets. This small business grew into a giant enterprise—the Union Iron Works—a foundry and metalworks that eventually expanded into ship building.

The sculpture celebrates the kind of hard, manual labor that was prevalent in 19th-century San Francisco (especially south of Market) but that workers sitting in front of their computers in the surrounding steel-and-glass high-rise office buildings would find utterly foreign today. It depicts five men struggling to poke a hole through a metal plate with a punch press. The near total nudity of the men stirred controversy. There was even talk of adding pants to the figures.

The sculptor was Douglas Tilden (1860–1935). Tilden was born in Chico and suffered an early setback when he became deaf and mute at age four as a result of an attack of scarlet fever. His first career was as a teacher of the deaf. At age 23

**The Mechanics Monument, 1905.**

he discovered that he had a natural talent for sculpture, but with formal study in Paris his career blossomed, earning him a number of commissions after his return to the Bay Area. Although he was married for a number of years before divorcing, the homoerotic nature of some of Tilden's work, including the scantily-clad young males in this sculpture, has led to some speculation that Tilden was gay. In his later years the sculptor's output declined and he died an impoverished recluse.

A few steps to the northwest, embedded in the sidewalk, is a bronze plaque marking this as the original shoreline at the time gold was discovered in 1848. Everything from here to the Ferry Building is filled land.

*Cross over Market to the southeast corner of First Street. From here you can get a good look at:*

## ❼ 100 Bush Street (at Battery) – Shell Building (1930).

Built as the western U.S. regional headquarters for the Shell Oil Company, this handsome office tower clad in a sepia-toned glazed terra cotta was designed by architect George Kelham, who also did the Russ Building and the Old Main Library. The design was inspired by an influential entry in the Chicago Tribune Tower competition of 1922, which featured a stepped-back tower (as this one does).

Today the Shell Building is one high rise among many, but at the time of its construction its 28 stories overshadowed its neighbors, most of which ranged from three to ten stories in height. It must have initially generated admiring glances, perhaps even awe. The fact that it also dwarfed the nearby Ferry Building tower, which for many years had been the tallest building in San Francisco, was heavily symbolic for gasoline-powered automobiles, and the bridges across the bay they spawned would soon reduce ferries and the Ferry Building to minor status in the world of transportation.

---

*Cross First Street. Near the corner is another bronze plaque in the sidewalk marking the original shoreline. Start walking up Market for a look across the street at:*

---

## ❽ One Bush Street – Crown Zellerbach Building (1959).

Comparable to New York's Lever House, this green-glass high-rise office tower and the adjoining one-story circular structure with a carousel roof is San Francisco's finest example of the International Style. The design was derived from the ideas of architect Le Corbusier and others in which cities of the future were envisioned as clusters of free-standing towers surrounded by breathing room. While such a utopian vision if created whole could lead to a socialist kind of sterility, this one building, as an isolated example, works beautifully here because the plaza creates an airy open space in the middle of a high-density district. If a traditional building had consumed the whole triangular block it likely would have perpetuated the high sheer wall monolithic look of most of the rest of Market Street—to its detriment. It's highly unlikely that a building like this— that is not built to the lot lines and that consumes so little of the available footprint—would be built today. Land in San Francisco is simply too expensive not to be developed for maximum economic return.

The name Crown Zellerbach derives from the paper company whose headquarters this was when the building was erected. Anthony Zellerbach (1832–1911) helped build an international paper business out of a small stationery store that he opened nearby in 1870.

---

*Continue up Market Street most of the way of this long block to:*

---

### ❾ 581 Market Street – Stacey's Bookstore.

Stacey's, one of San Francisco's premier bookstores, is also one of its oldest. It was started by John Stacey who, in 1923, opened a small medical book shop in an office in the Flood Building farther up Market. In 1947, having outgrown its original space, it moved to 551 Market Street—next door to where it is now. But when Standard Oil purchased that building and erected the Chevron Building in 1959, Stacey's moved next door to its present location. Both the interior and exterior of this building have been remodeled several times since then, most recently in 1996. The building itself is notable not just for its handsome new façade but because, at only two stories, it is one of the few low-rise buildings remaining on mostly skyscraper downtown Market Street. The store today has expanded far beyond its roots in medical and technical books to a full-line bookstore with over 120,000 titles.

---

*Walk up to Second Street and look across the street at:*

---

### ❿ 582 Market Street – Hobart Building (1914).

One of the finest looking office buildings on Market Street, and indeed in San Francisco, the Hobart Building today is unfortunately overlooked because it is dwarfed by the steel-and-glass high rises surrounding it. The tower, with its just right proportions and its encrusted glazed terra cotta detailing, is what makes this building such a visual treat. The building was designed by Willis Polk and is one of his finest. It was also one of his favorite designs.

It was erected by the estate of Walter Scott Hobart (1840–1892). Hobart came to California in 1858 while still a teenager, determined to strike it rich mining gold. He failed at prospecting as an individual, but after saving his money earned as a $4-a-day ore-cart pusher at the Gould & Curry mine in Virginia City, Nevada he made winning investments in various mines, eventually becoming a partner in one of the biggest gold producers in California's Mother Lode. By the time of his death he had branched out into utilities and real estate, leaving a behind an estate estimated at close to $5 million.

Polk's design replaced an earlier Hobart Building on the site that had been built in 1888 (it was destroyed in 1906) and that was a rather ordinary six-story polychromatic brick-and-stone Victorian structure. Hobart had chosen this mid-block site (corner locations are more desirable) because it faced Second Street, a prestigious thoroughfare at the time since it led to Rincon Hill, San Francisco's first enclave for the wealthy. The present Hobart Building does the site even more justice.

---

*Cross Second Street and walk a short distance to where across the street you will see a bronze sculpture of a man atop a granite base:*

---

## ⓫ Market, Post, and Montgomery streets – Admission Day (or Native Sons) Monument (1897).

This sculpture, a $25,000 gift to the City from Mayor James Duval Phelan was, like the Mechanics Monument, done by Douglas Tilden. It commemorates California's admission to the Union on September 9, 1850, and depicts a white male forty-niner in a heroic pose: gun in his holster, pickax over his shoulder, waving an American flag. The bronze angel atop the granite shaft holds a book inscribed with the date September IX.

**At the dedication on September 5, 1897, sculptor Tilden was introduced. The crowd called for a speech but the mute Tilden was literally speechless.**

This monument originally stood at the intersection of Market, Mason, and Turk streets but was removed to Golden Gate Park in 1948 because it was considered to be a traffic hazard. In 1977 it was installed here.

---

*Continue on Market and cross New Montgomery Street.*

---

### ⑫ 50 New Montgomery Street – The Palace Hotel (1909).

The Palace Hotel is one of the most storied buildings in San Francisco. This is the second one to occupy the site. The first, built in 1875, was destroyed by the 1906 fire. The site's history goes back further than that, of course. Like much of the rest of San Francisco at the time of the gold rush this area was blanketed with sand hills and held little in the way of promise.

The land here was originally owned by an early Irish pioneer named Doyle. In the early 1850s Mr. Doyle, in a magnanimous gesture, donated this parcel to the Catholic Church, which then built a church and orphanage. (Amazingly the church, which dates from 1854, still exists and stands today on Eddy Street near Divisadero.) In making the donation, however, Doyle failed to include a reversionary clause which would have prevented the Church from selling the property for financial gain. In the early 1870s, that is exactly what happened—financier William Ralston came along and paid the Church a six-figure sum for the property.

The first Palace Hotel was the pet project of flamboyant William Ralston, who had made a fortune from the Comstock silver mines through his part ownership of the Bank of California. Ralston wanted a truly world-class hotel, one that would make a statement about San Francisco's coming of age, and after spending $5 million he got it. When completed in October 1875 the seven-story, 120 foot high hotel with 800 rooms—each with its own marble fireplace—not only towered over the rest of San Francisco but was the largest hotel in the U.S. The exterior was painted pure white with the exception of the bolt heads of the iron reinforcing rods threaded through the building. These were painted gold. This grand edifice, set among the muddy streets, plank sidewalks, and mostly ramshackle two- and three-story structures that were its neighbors must have shimmered like a vision. It truly looked like a palace.

Inside the hotel, the seven floors, each with its own gallery and promenade, looked down upon a central marble-paved courtyard and carriage turnaround surrounded by potted plants and trees. Directly above, an elaborate domed ceiling of amber-colored glass bathed the hotel in a soft, natural light. The rooms, which could receive messages via pneumatic tube and which also received filtered air from a primitive air-conditioning system, were furnished with hand-carved and polished mahogany, teak, ebony, and rosewood.

To protect all this opulence against fire, a 630,000 gallon cistern was installed in the basement (it's still there today). But to no avail. For in 1906 the hotel was gutted by the massive fire that swept the city in the aftermath of the earthquake. The exterior walls, supported by extra deep foundations and iron reinforcing bolts, withstood the quake. But the owners, the Sharon family, decided to pull them down and start anew. In 1909, the new Palace Hotel arose on the site of the old. It looks similar to the first one, the most notable difference being that it lacks its predecessor's Victorian bay windows.

The Palace, particularly in its early years, was *the* place to stay. Many leading figures have slept here, including Oscar Wilde, J. P. Morgan, Civil War general William Tecumseh Sherman, and U.S. Presidents Ulysses S. Grant and Theodore Roosevelt. King David Kalahaua of Hawaii died here (January 20, 1891) as did President Warren G. Harding (August 2, 1923). Famed tenor Enrico Caruso was staying here when the earthquake struck on April 18, 1906. He emerged from the building shaken and wearing a towel around his throat to protect his golden voice, vowing never to return to San Francisco. He never did.

The Palace Hotel today still evokes an aura of 19th-century graciousness lacking in most other hotels, even those with roots in the Victorian/Edwardian era. The interior is well worth a look. If you enter from the Market Street entrance not far from the corner of Market and New Montgomery turn right shortly after you enter and take a peek at the Pied Piper bar. It is named for the vivid mural over the bar painted by artist Maxfield Parrish in 1909. Continue down the hallway. On the right is a glass case containing some historic hotel artifacts: selections of holiday menus from various years pre-and post-fire; strands of crystals from the hotel's original chandeliers; a letter from hotel owner F. W. Sharon to Maxfield Parrish dated May 8, 1909 commissioning the Pied Piper Pied mural at a cost of $6,000. Finally, continue on a little father for a look at the Garden Court. This was the location of the first Palace's marble-flagged carriage turnaround which in the early twentieth century was converted into a lounge. Today it houses the sumptuous Garden Court restaurant. With its potted palms and decorative glass skylight it is a great place to enjoy a leisurely Sunday brunch, and to imagine what the Palace was like in the golden years of the Victorian age.

---

*Continue up Market Street past Annie Alley, and at the intersection cross Market Street to the Geary and Kearny island for a look at the tall monument:*

---

**⓮ Lotta's Fountain** (1875).

This charming throwback is the oldest public monument in San Francisco. A drinking fountain (now dry), it was a gift to the City by Lotta Crabtree (1847–1924), a popular singer and actress who launched her career in San Francisco. The pretty, talented Lotta started performing as a child and appeared in all of the City's major theaters in the late 1850s and early 1860s. She left in 1864 to tour the rest of the country, rarely returning, but she never forgot the city that gave her her start. She donated this custom-made fountain—which was modeled after a lighthouse in one of her plays—and dedicated it to San Francisco's citizens.

At the dedication on September 9, 1875— the 25th anniversary of California's admission to the Union—noisy celebrants, who had been drinking something stronger than water, became so boisterous that two squads of soldiers had to be called in to quell what nearly turned into a riot.

Lotta's Fountain, now a National Historic Landmark, has always served as a focal point and rendezvous. After the 1906 disaster the fountain became a rallying point for those searching for missing relatives. On Christmas Eve 1910, famed opera singer Luisa Tetrazzini gave a free concert here to a huge throng. And on November 6, 1915 Lotta Crabtree herself, having returned to San Francisco for Lotta Crabtree Day at the Panama Pacific Exposition, appeared at the fountain in a ceremony honoring her. In 1999 the cast-iron fountain was restored and repainted a bronze color believed to be close to the original. Every April 18 since 1924 the fountain has been the scene of a ceremony commemorating the anniversary of the 1906 earthquake and fire.

On the east side of the fountain you can see the original bronze medallion from Lotta Crabtree dedicating it to "the citizens of San Francisco." Above it, at the base of the shaft, is a low-relief bronze plaque commemorating Luisa Tetrazzini's 1910 appearance when she "sang to the people of San Francisco." What is interesting about these phrases is the change from "citizens" to "people." The use of "citizens" on the 1875 plaque suggests a San Francisco small enough where everyone could gather at a central meeting point (such as Lotta's Fountain). By 1910, thirty-five years later, the use of the more encompassing "people" suggests a different city, which it certainly was after the 1906 disaster, having been rebuilt into a new and grander metropolis.

The intersection of Market, Kearny, and Third streets was known, in the late 19th and early 20th centuries, as "Newspaper Angle," because it was here that the City's major newspapers, the *Chronicle,* the *Examiner,* and the *Call* built showplace headquarters office buildings. This location was no doubt chosen because at the time it was the city's busiest intersection—Market Street was the main boulevard, Kearny Street was the main retail shopping street (Union Square only superceded it later), and Third Street was the main traffic artery leading into the city from the Peninsula. Newspapers like to be close to where the action is—that is where there is "news." All three papers' buildings still stand although none houses newspaper offices today.

---

*Directly behind Lotta's Fountain is the first of these buildings:*

---

## ⑭ 690 Market Street – De Young/Chronicle Building (1889).

Until recently covered by a rather nondescript façade, which was added during a remodeling in 1962, the De Young Building (named for *Chronicle* co-founder M. H. de Young) is one of San Francisco's more historic high rises. Originally a ten-story building with a clock tower, it boasted a steel frame that allowed it to reach such a lofty height. It was the City's first "skyscraper" and the tallest building west of the Mississippi when it was erected in 1889. An advertising broadsheet of the time bragged that the building was thoroughly fireproof, it had the largest clock in the world, and that it was entirely lighted by electricity.

It was designed by the prestigious Chicago-based architectural firm of Burnham and Root who crafted it in the latest style of the time, Richardson Romanesque. The 1962 remodeling, which obscured the façade, was removed in 2005. That remodeling also resulted in the removal of the clock tower (not replaced) that once crowned the building. The *Chronicle* moved out of the building in 1923 to its current location at Fifth and Mission streets.

---

*Cross back over Market Street to the corner of Third for a look at:*

---

**⓭ 5 Third Street – Hearst Building** (1910).

Until 1965 this building housed the offices of the *San Francisco Examiner*, the flagship paper of legendary newspaper tycoon William Randolph Hearst (1863–1951). Hearst, who received the paper as a gift from his father, Senator George Hearst, in 1887, moved to this location in 1890. He tore down the building already there, the Nucleus Hotel, which when constructed in 1853 had been Market Street's first brick building. Initially he planned to erect a Richardson Romanesque skyscraper designed by Willis Polk. But that never came to pass, and Hearst instead had a lesser known architect design a seven-story Mission Revival-style building with a loggia and Spanish tile roof that received much favorable comment because it was quite a departure from most commercial architecture of the time. It did not survive the 1906 fire.

Its destruction gave Hearst the opportunity to start over on the site. This time, no doubt wishing to eclipse his rivals and neighbors the *Chronicle* and the *Call*, he decided on a 26-story edifice with a clock tower. A height limit of 12 stories had been imposed on Market Street by this time, so Hearst had to settle for the current building—which somewhat resembles its predecessor. Until his death in 1951 Hearst maintained a suite in the 12$^{th}$ floor penthouse.

---

*From this corner you can get a look at the next building on this tour:*

---

**⓮ 703 Market Street – Central Tower – Old Call Building** (1898).

The last of the three great newspaper towers at this intersection, the Call Building—now known at the Central Tower—once housed the offices of the *San Francisco Call*. The *Call* was owned by Claus Spreckels, a once penniless German immigrant who, after forty years in this country, had amassed a $35 million fortune based on sugar refining, utilities, banking, and real estate. Like most self-made millionaires of the time he was competitive to his core. He chose this site for his paper's headquarters in large measure because he wanted his building to outshine those of his rivals, the *Chronicle* and the *Examiner*.

To that end he had the architects, the Reid Brothers (soon to design the Fairmont Hotel), build what became for a time the tallest building west of Chicago, an 18-story steel-frame skyscraper having a circular crown covered with elaborate terra cotta decoration. It fulfilled all of his wishes: he got a prestige building taller and handsomer than the Chronicle Building, and in the afternoon when the sun moved around to the west his new tower literally overshadowed the Hearst Building. It also boasted San Francisco's first rooftop restaurant open to the public.

The landmark building always drew stares—none more so than during the April 1906 fire when it burned in spectacular fashion. The

The Call Building.

fire first breached it on the third floor, but rather than burning upward as you might expect, it burned from the top down. The building's elevators acted like giant flues and sucked the third floor flames up to the top. San Franciscans watched in fascinated horror as spontaneous combustion blew out the top-floor windows and the flames advanced downward floor by floor. Although the interior was thoroughly gutted, the steel frame held the exterior intact and it was totally refurbished within two years after the fire.

In 1938 however, in a nod toward modernization, the exterior was substantially remodeled and the building was renamed the Central

Tower. The distinctive dome was removed and refashioned into a stepped-back six-story tower extension to create more floor space, and the building was stripped of all of its ornamentation. Shorn of its distinctive top it soon became just another office tower.

A few remnants of the old Call Building can be found inside where many of the office doors still have the original brass handles monogrammed with an elaborate intertwined "CS," for Claus Spreckels.

The *Call* moved its offices to Mission Street near Fourth in the 1920s. The paper merged with several other dailies in the ensuing decades before finally folding as the *News-Call Bulletin* in 1965.

---

*Across Market Street from the Central Tower is:*

---

### ❶ 700 Market Street – Citizens Savings Building (1902).

Rich with Renaissance detailing, this fine building is visually appealing to those entering the city from the Third Street corridor. The handsome mansard roof with its copper cresting and dormer windows give it almost more of a residential look than a commercial one. Erected in 1902 as the Mutual Savings Bank Building, it was only slightly damaged in 1906, but was subsequently remodeled. The addition to the right (1964), at the corner, with its blank wall fortunately doesn't detract from the main building's façade.

---

*From the Central Tower walk down three buildings to:*

---

### ❶ 731 Market Street – Site of the Bancroft Building (1869–1886).

This modern day structure is named for the more famous 19th century building that once stood here. Hubert Howe Bancroft (1832–1918) came to San Francisco in 1852, and like so many others tried his hand unsuccessfully at gold mining. In 1856, after stints as a teamster and clerk, he opened a bookstore on Montgomery Street. From an initial one man operation he built up a bookstore/publishing/printing/stationery business employing over 200 people.

In 1869, to accommodate his growing company, he erected a five-story brick building with an iron façade at this location. (The address was 721–723 Market Street.) Since even at that date most of San

Francisco's commercial businesses were still congregated on Montgomery, Kearny, and Sansome streets north of Bush, Bancroft's move was considered a little foolish. His friends joked that he was moving to the country. But with the coming of the Palace and Baldwin hotels just a few years later, commercial traffic soon made its way up Market Street and Bancroft continued to prosper.

In later years Bancroft turned the day-to-day operations of the business over to his brother Albert so that he could concentrate on his passion for collecting rare books on Californiana and related subjects and on producing a series of multi-volume histories of the West, works that remain his chief legacy. Luckily for Bancroft, when his Market Street building was destroyed by fire in 1886, his valuable library was at his Valencia Street home. In 1905 he sold his unsurpassed collection for $300,000 to the University of California at Berkeley, where it forms the nucleus of what has become the Bancroft Library.

---

*Across the street at the foot of Grant Avenue are two bank buildings of note. The first is:*

---

### ⑲  2 Grant Avenue – Wells Fargo Bank (1910).

Formerly Union Trust (which merged with Wells Fargo in 1923), this notable Classical Revival bank makes for a nice variation from a traditional banking temple. One distinctive feature that sets it apart from other such banks is its rooftop balustrade in place of a pediment. A special touch is the way the building curves in on its Market Street side to connect with the Grant Avenue façade, thus making for a smooth transition between both streets. The architect was Clinton Day, who also designed the much-loved City of Paris Building on Union Square. That structure was torn down to make way for Neiman Marcus.

---

*The second bank building is:*

---

### ⑳  One Grant Avenue – former Security Pacific Bank Building (1910).

Originally the Savings Union Bank, later Security Pacific (before merging with Bank of America), and now converted to retail space, this classical temple typifies a Classical Revival-style bank. It was modeled after the Pantheon in Rome and designed by Walter D. Bliss and William Faville, who had apprenticed under the famed New York architectural firm of McKim, Mead & White, a firm that looked to ancient Rome for much of its inspiration. This building, together with the Wells Fargo Bank across the street, make for a fine visual gateway to Grant Avenue.

---

*To your left on the north side of Market across from O'Farrell Street is a magnificent 10-story flatiron building:*

---

**㉑ 760–784 Market Street – Phelan Building** (1908).

The most elegant flatiron in San Francisco, the Phelan (pronounced Feelan) Building, which is clad in a glazed cream terra cotta, stands like a giant slice of a Baroque wedding cake on this prominent gore lot. The architect was William Curlett, who did the previously mentioned Citizens Savings Building with the fine mansard roof.

It was built by James Duval Phelan (1861–1930) who was mayor of San Francisco (1897–1902) and U.S. Senator from California (1915–1921). It replaced a previous Phelan Building, a five-story bay-windowed Victorian with a mansard roof topped by iron cresting, erected by his father, James Phelan (1821–1892), which burned in 1906. The current building's lobby contains a bronze bust of the elder Phelan.

---

*Cross over Market to the Phelan Building and look back across the street at the tall tower with the dome:*

---

**㉒ 785 Market Street – Humboldt Bank Building** (1906).

The original Humboldt Bank Building was a ten-story, steel-frame structure with load-bearing brick walls that was under construction at the time the 1906 earthquake struck. Because it was largely destroyed by the quake, in rebuilding it, steel cross-bracing was added. The height was increased to the current 18 stories.

The distinctive feature is the dome on top, which was inspired by the influential Call Building, its neighbor down the street. This dome is only about half the size of what that one was and is not nearly as elaborate. Nevertheless, this slender tower with its decorative Baroque-style dome adds visual appeal to a city skyline largely given over to anonymous steel-and-glass highrises. The ground floor originally housed the Humboldt Savings Bank.

A 1919 promotional brochure for the Humboldt Bank trumpeted that thrifty depositors could open a savings account for $1.00 or more with interest compounded semiannually.

---

*Walk down to the middle of the next block for a look at:*

---

**❷❸ 835 Market Street – former Emporium Store** (1896) / **Site of St. Ignatius College** (1855–1880).

"A hole surrounded by sand hills" is how one Jesuit priest described this site at the time the first rickety wooden building of the new St. Ignatius College was put up here in 1855. It wasn't a promising location for San Francisco's first institution of higher learning, but the sand hills were eventually leveled, and what later was renamed the University of San Francisco grew and developed here until 1880 when it moved to a grand new building on the southwest corner of Van Ness Avenue and Grove Street (where Davies Symphony Hall is now).

This 1896 structure, built for the John Parrott estate, was for most of the 20th century home to the Emporium, for many years San Francisco's premier department store. The earthquake and fire of 1906 gutted the interior but the stately Renaissance/Baroque façade was saved and the store was rebuilt behind it. When the Emporium-Capwell chain was bought by Federated Department Stores in 1998 the store closed and its century-long history at this site came to an end. (The building is now part of the Westfield Centre.)

---

*Walk to 856 Market and look at the large street clock on the sidewalk near the curb.*

---

**❷❹ Albert Samuels Clock** (1915).

Until the advent of inexpensive wristwatches made personal timepieces readily available, many people relied on street clocks such as these to keep track of time. Prominent landmarks such as the Ferry

Building and the Chronicle Building had large clocks built right into their structures, but smaller businesses, especially jewelers, sometimes put up street clocks to be of public service and, not incidentally, as advertising vehicles for their own wares.

One such clock is the Albert Samuels Clock which, if you look at the plaque adorning it, modestly bills itself as "One of the finest street clocks in America." Brightly painted and made of iron, with clocks on all four sides, this one was made by the Albert Samuels Jewelers Company and was installed on Market Street in February 1915 to coincide with the opening of the Panama Pacific International Exposition, being held that year along San Francisco's northern waterfront. At that time the Samuels store was located across the street, on the southeast corner of Market and Fifth. But in 1943 the store moved to 856 Market Street and the clock was placed in front of it, where it still stands today. Albert Samuels died in 1973; his heirs sold to new owners in 1976. The name lasted until 1990, when the jewelry store at this location was closed and a new retail business moved in.

If you look closely at the plaque on the clock you will see oval brass medallions with the word "Lucky" encircled within. One might speculate whether this may be a reference to Lucky Baldwin who owned the Baldwin Hotel, which stood just steps away, where the Flood Building is now (see next entry).

---

*For more on the Baldwin Hotel and the Flood Building, walk down to the corner of Market and Fifth for a better look at it this grandiose flatiron.*

---

### ❷❺ 870 Market Street – Flood Building (1905)
### – Site of the Baldwin Hotel (1877–1898).

Before the massive Flood Building was erected there stood on this site one of San Francisco's grand 19th century hotels, the Baldwin. It was the pet project of Comstock millionaire Elias J. "Lucky" Baldwin. Baldwin spared no expense during several years of construction, ordering furniture and drapery from Europe, silverware from Tiffany, and a grandiose clock from the latter firm that humorist Mark Twain once joked "not only tells the hours and minutes and seconds, but the turn of the tides, the phases of the moon, the price of eggs and who's got your umbrella."

When it was completed, in 1877, Baldwin had a gargantuan French Renaissance-style pile topped with a mansard roof surmounted by a tall central cupola. Inside, the hotel was decorated with the kind of rococo lavishness favored in Victorian times—lots of red plush, crystal chandeliers, and overstuffed leather chairs. Baldwin's timing, so good when it came to stock trading, failed him with his hotel, because it opened just as the Comstock silver mines were becoming depleted. The ensuing unfavorable economic climate, high overhead, and competition from the Palace Hotel down the street kept his hotel in the red for most of its existence. It hung on until 1898, when it was destroyed by fire. Baldwin had not insured it and could not rebuild. He sold the property to James L. Flood, son of Comstock millionaire James Clair Flood, for $1.2 million to pay off a remaining mortgage of $900,000.

In 1905 Flood erected this monumental 12-story office building. At the time it was the largest structure in San Francisco (in terms of square footage). The architect was Albert Pissis, who also designed the Emporium Building across Market Street. It is surely no accident that these buildings resemble those lining Paris's grand boulevards, because Pissis had attended Paris's Ecole des Beaux Arts. He was influenced not only by the school's emphasis on classical design but no doubt by his environment as well. These two build-

The Baldwin Hotel, 1878.

ings, clad in gray Colusa sandstone, give a kind of Parisian imperial grandeur to this key retail shopping area.

Through the years the Flood Building has weathered numerous events that have threatened its integrity and even its existence. Its interior was gutted by the 1906 fire, but the frame was structurally sound and it was completely refurbished. In 1951 the owners planned to tear it down, since the Walgreens drugstore chain had made an offer to buy it and replace it with its own building. The Korean War intervened however and the U.S. military commandeered the building, citing a need for office space for the war effort. The war interval ended talk of selling the building. The ground-floor retail spaces have undergone a number of remodelings over the years, but above the second floor the exterior looks much the same as it did in 1905.

On the floor in the entryway to the Market Street lobby there is an elaborate entwined monogram "JCF," a reference to James Clair Flood, the family patriarch to whom the building is dedicated. In the lobby is a bronze bust of the son, the man who built it, James L. Flood. Fans of mystery writer Dashiell Hammett (creator of *The Maltese Falcon* and detective Sam Spade) might be interested to know that Hammett, in the early 1920s, worked as an operative for the Pinkerton Detective Agency here in the Flood Building in room 314.

---

*Go to Fifth Street and head south a half block toward Mission Street for a look at:*

---

### ❷❻ Fifth and Mission streets – NW corner – the Old Mint
(1874).

This beautiful Greek Revival edifice, constructed between 1869 and 1874, is the only federal building of that era on the West Coast. It was once the busiest mint in the country, churning out the silver dollars and gold coins needed as a medium of exchange for the growing economy. It also served to store gold bullion, and in fact once held one-third of the nation's gold reserves. The building was one of the few in the downtown area to survive the 1906 fire. Although the fire's intense heat melted its windows, the mint was saved by a dedicated crew who tapped the cisterns in the basement to keep the roof and exterior walls wet.

This mint continued in operation until 1937, when it was superceded by the New Mint on Hermann Street near Duboce Triangle. For the following three-plus decades the Old Mint served as office space for various federal government agencies. Closed since 1994, after two decades of service as a museum, it will once again serve that purpose after much-needed refurbishing.

# Lucky Baldwin
## (1828–1909)

Elias J. "Lucky" Baldwin was the image incarnate of the pioneer from humble beginnings who came west in the wake of the gold rush and who went on to fame and fortune. He was a man's man as it was defined at the time: a crack shot who had fought Indians on the plains and hunted big game in India; a shrewd stock speculator who made millions of dollars trading volatile Comstock mining shares; a horse breeder and racing enthusiast; and a Lothario whose romantic entanglements with much younger women always kept him in the news.

"Lucky" Baldwin.

Born and raised in the Midwest, Baldwin came overland with a wagon train to California in 1853. After an arduous journey he arrived bedraggled and barefoot in the Sierra mining town of Hangtown (now Placerville). He quickly moved to San Francisco where at first he gave little hint of the financial mogul he was to become, working variously at running a livery stable and a brick manufactory.

When the Comstock silver mines started producing their great wealth in the 1860s however, Baldwin saw opportunity. Spending time in Virginia City, Nevada, the source of the treasure, he carefully investigated the lode's potential. Taking advantage of the extreme volatility in the trading of mining shares he developed a talent for buying in when prices were at their lows and selling out when they peaked.

He allegedly was branded with the name "Lucky" when he

left on a hunting trip to India and gave instructions to his broker to sell some stock when it reached a certain price. But Baldwin had forgotten to leave behind the key to his safe where the certificates were held. When he returned he found that his shares had rocketed in price more than 1,000 percent, earning him another fortune. All told, Baldwin earned $7.5 million from his stock trading, a huge sum in those days. It was the basis of a fortune that later encompassed a real estate empire that gave him land holdings of 8,000 acres at Lake Tahoe, 56,000 acres in southern California east of Los Angeles, and several prime properties in San Francisco including his showplace Baldwin Hotel on Market Street at Powell.

Baldwin always claimed to have hated the tag "Lucky" saying that his success was due to hard work not luck. But he can't have objected too strenuously because the name (and his money) drew people, especially pretty, young women, to him. He was married four times and had numerous affairs, many of which were chronicled in the newspapers. He was also the target of gunfire on at least two occasions arising from these entanglements. Once, as a defendant in a courtroom breach-of-promise suit, a sister of the alleged paramour approached him from behind and at point blank range pointed a revolver at his head. But in pulling the trigger she jerked the gun, sending the bullet whizzing over Baldwin's head and into the courtroom wall. Perhaps he was really "Lucky" after all.

In his later years Baldwin became increasingly penurious, holding onto cash at all costs, forcing his creditors to sue him to collect their money. It was a reputation he delighted in; the multimillionaire didn't want to be seen as a soft touch. Despite his strong presence in San Francisco in the second half of the 19th century he is today virtually forgotten in northern California. His legacy lives on in southern California however, in the names Baldwin Park, Baldwin Hills, and especially in the pride and joy of the final years of his life: the Santa Anita racetrack, which he developed as the centerpiece of his huge ranch there.

# Mission District

**Length:** 2 miles / 3.2 kilometers.

**Time:** 2 hours (add ½ hour or so if you tour Mission Dolores).

**Walk Rating:** Easy.

**Hills:** As you get toward the end of the tour, the half block of Guerrero Street between 20$^{th}$ and Liberty is a mild to moderate uphill. Liberty Street is a gentle downhill. Twenty-first Street is a moderate uphill. Hill Street is a gentle downhill.

**Public Transit:** Muni bus line 26 runs the length of Valencia Street and the 22 line runs along 16$^{th}$ Street. Nearby, the J streetcar goes along Church Street and there is a BART station at 16$^{th}$ and Mission streets.

**Parking:** No garages or parking lots. Street parking is metered only on the major commercial streets such as Valencia and the nearby portions of its major cross streets.

**Restrooms:** If you visit Mission Dolores (small charge for admission) at the start of this tour, you may use the restrooms there.

The Mission District is San Francisco's oldest neighborhood. Named for Mission Dolores, the church founded by the Spanish in 1776, this area was chosen for settlement because it lay in a sheltered valley where the soil and climate were better than in most other parts of what was to become San Francisco. There also was abundant freshwater provided by a stream-fed lagoon—the Laguna de los Dolores—so named because the exploring party of 1776 came across it on the Friday before Palm Sunday, the Friday of Sorrows.

The mission complex prospered initially but started to decline in the early 1800s. Mexico's independence from Spain in 1821 cut off financial support, and secularization in the 1830s led to the mission's abandonment by the religious authorities. Mission Dolores and its surrounding structures were then neglected until the 1840s when Mormon settlers moved into some of the vacant buildings. The Mormons were quickly followed by others in the wake of the gold rush. In 1851 a planked toll road was opened from downtown for several miles along Mission Street, and settlement thus soon broadened beyond the original mission area. A good many of these initial settlers were squatters. Because land title issues were only resolved in the late 1860s, it was only then that the area was finally opened for formal development. With its good weather, flat land, and abundant open

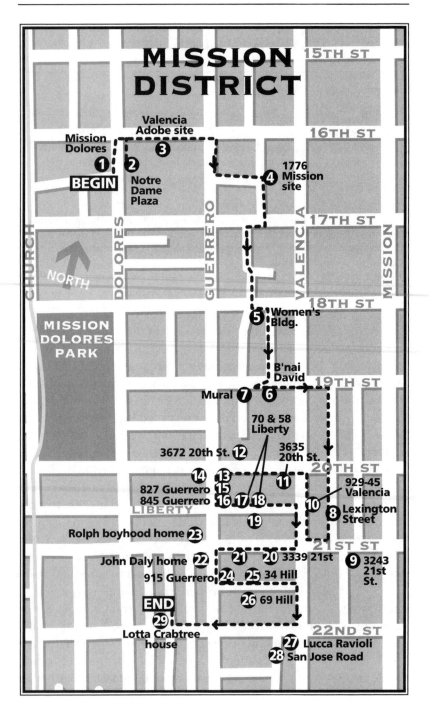

# MISSION DISTRICT

15TH ST

16TH ST

Valencia
Adobe site

Mission
Dolores

**1**

**BEGIN**

**2**

**3**

Notre
Dame
Plaza

1776
Mission
site

**4**

GUERRERO

VALENCIA

MISSION

DOLORES

CHURCH

NORTH

MISSION
DOLORES
PARK

17TH ST

18TH ST

**5** Women's
Bldg.

B'nai
David

Mural **7** **6**

19TH ST

70 & 58
Liberty

3672 20th St. **12**

3635
20th St.

**14** **13**

827 Guerrero **15**
845 Guerrero **16** **17** **18**

**11**

20TH ST

929-45
Valencia

**10**

**19**

**8** Lexington
Street

LIBERTY

Rolph boyhood home **23**

21ST ST

**21**     **20** 3339 21st

John Daly home **22**

915 Guerrero **24** **25** 34 Hill

**9** 3243
21st
St.

**END**

**26** 69 Hill

**29**

Lotta Crabtree
house

22ND ST

**27** Lucca Ravioli
**28** San Jose Road

# MISSION DISTRICT

❶ Mission Dolores

❷ 347 Dolores Street - Notre Dame Plaza

❸ Site of Valencia Adobe

❹ Camp and Albion streets - Site of 1776 Mission

❺ 3543 18th Street - Women's Building

❻ 3535 19th Street - former B'nai David Synagogue

❼ Mission Playground Mural - "New World Tree"

❽ Lexington Street

❾ 3243 21st Street

❿ 929 to 945 Valencia Street

⓫ 3635 20th Street

⓬ 3672 20th Street

⓭ 801 Guerrero Street

⓮ 3701 20th Street

⓯ 827 Guerrero Street

⓰ 845 Guerrero Street

⓱ 70 Liberty Street

⓲ 58 Liberty Street

⓳ 45 and 49 Liberty Street

⓴ 3339 21st Street

㉑ 3367-75 21st Street

㉒ 900 Guerrero Street - John Daly home

㉓ 3416 21st Street - Mayor Rolph boyhood home

㉔ 915 Guerrero Street

㉕ 34 Hill Street

㉖ 69 Hill Street

㉗ 1100 Valencia Street - Lucca Ravioli Company

㉘ San Jose Avenue - Old San Jose Road

㉙ 90 Fair Oaks Street - Lotta Crabtree property

space the Mission District in the late 19$^{th}$ century became a choice area of settlement for middle-class professionals.

The 1906 fire carved deep into the Mission before being stopped at its western edge at Dolores Street and at its southern at 20$^{th}$ Street. Italian refugees from burned-out North Beach and Irish ones from South of Market came here in the wake of the fire, and many of them ended up staying. Latinos first came as agricultural workers as early as the 1920s, but they only started immigrating in large numbers from Mexico and Central America in the 1950s and '60s. That trend has continued over the past few decades; today the Mission District's population is more than 50 percent Latino. Their heritage and traditions are evident today in the many colorful murals that decorate buildings throughout the district.

---

*Start this tour at Mission Dolores (west side of Dolores between 16$^{th}$ and 17$^{th}$ streets).*

---

### ❶ Mission Dolores (1791).

Constructed between 1788 and 1791 by mostly Indian labor, Mission Dolores is the oldest building in San Francisco and the only one left that dates from the days of the Spanish explorers. (The first church of 1776 was located on Camp Street – see Stop #4 on this walk.) Made up of more than thirty-six thousand large adobe bricks, with walls over four feet thick, the church has a solid, almost stocky appearance. Despite that it is well proportioned, even graceful. The mission's bells, in the three niches on the façade, were brought from Mexico in the 1820s.

The chapel survived the 1906 earthquake—and the one of 1989— virtually unscathed, but the larger parish church next door, which was constructed in 1876, collapsed during the 1906 quake. It was replaced by the present basilica, which dates from 1913—although its façade was substantially remodeled in the 1920s.

The chapel's interior boasts simple wooden pews that are offset by a hand-carved altar and figurines made in Mexico about 1800. The painted ceiling and beams replicate Indian-designed patterns, the colors of which were originally made from vegetable dyes. The roof still has the original timbers, which at one time were fastened together with wooden manzanita pegs and rawhide thongs. In 1918, as an earthquake-proofing measure, the beams were strengthened with steel reinforcing ties. Also at that time clapboard siding on the church's exterior walls was taken down, revealing the whitewashed adobe walls once again. Buried beneath the chapel floor are William Leidesdorff (see Financial District walk) and Lt. José Moraga, a leader of the Spanish settlement party of 1776.

There is a small museum in back of the nave (reached via the door marked "To Museum") where relics from the mission's early days are on display. Among the items are replicas of sacred artifacts donated by Father Junipero Serra and various secular objects reflecting everyday life at the mission. There is also a cutaway section of a wall showing the rough adobe bricks behind the white plaster finish.

Beyond the museum is the oldest cemetery in San Francisco. The mission's burial ground was originally four times larger and extended back to Church Street. Burials occurred soon after the mission was established, but none of the very early grave markers, which were made of wood, has survived. One of the earliest remaining headstones is that of Luís Argüello, the first Mexican governor of Alta California (1822–1825), who died in 1830. Several other Spanish-Mexican notables who have San Francisco streets named after them, such as Francisco Guerrero and possibly José Noe, are buried here. (Noé's family is buried here but it's not certain he is.) Also interred here are James Casey and Charles Cora, who were hanged by the Vigilance Committee of 1856.

The cemetery reflects the international character of San Francisco. Beside the tombstones of the Hispanic founders are ones marking the graves of early French, Italian, Irish, Scottish, and Australian residents. A statue of an Indian maiden commemorates the as many as five thousand Native Americans who were buried on the mission grounds. Some of these nameless dead are likely still buried under nearby streets and buildings.

---

*After you leave Mission Dolores, walk up to the corner of 16<sup>th</sup> Street. Cross Dolores to the southeast corner of the intersection. The long building with the acorn-shaped cupola down the street is Notre Dame Plaza. It is not open to the public, but walk down Dolores Street for a closer look:*

## ❷ 347 Dolores Street – Notre Dame Plaza – Site of a Bull Ring (c.1840s-c.1853).

Directly across the street from Mission Dolores, with its appeal to heaven and the better angels of our nature, once stood a structure that appealed to mankind's baser instincts and that featured pure blood lust—a bull ring. Here bull versus bear fights were held, with the animals engaged in a bloody fight to the death before cheering crowds gathered around the wooden ring.

A visitor from Switzerland, who witnessed such a contest here in 1852, told how a grizzly bear was released from a cage into the ring and then was expertly lassoed by vaqueros who chained a rear foot to a post in the center of the ring. The bull was then brought in, and to get him fighting mad some bandilleras (darts) were shot into his hide. Enraged, he charged the bear, who initially rolled himself into a ball on the ground as a defensive measure. After a bloody struggle the bear won by biting into the nape of the bull's neck. The sound of the bull's vertebrae cracking could be heard as the bear clamped down with his powerful jaws.

The stock-market terms bull and bear markets possibly derive from bull-versus-bear fights. A bull tosses his horns in the air, so a bull market goes up; a bear falls to the ground, thus a bear market goes down.

Sometimes the players varied in these contests, and an Indian, made drunk especially for the purpose, would be pushed into the ring to be gored by a bull.

The bull ring, which was about 100 feet in diameter, stood a short distance back from Dolores Street; its center was right about where the exit driveway for Notre Dame Plaza is today. The ring was dismantled by 1854; outcries over the brutality of such events led to their banishment.

In 1866 the Sisters of Notre Dame de Namur built a convent and school here for young women seeking a Christian education. In the mid-1870s the school was chartered as a college as well and was allowed to confer degrees. The rather plain structure that housed the school was enlarged and remodeled in 1894, complete with a grand columned portico. In 1906, as the flames from the great fire advanced this way, the building was dynamited to create a firebreak. The effort was successful—the fire was stopped at Dolores Street.

The school was quickly rebuilt on the foundations of the old—the concrete wall fronting the property and the dual front staircase are from the earlier building—and from its reopening in 1907 until 1981 it served as Notre Dame High School. In 1997, after the interior was thoroughly remodeled, it became Notre Dame Plaza, a low-income senior housing facility. In back of the building a landscaped, courtyard/garden with benches has been added. The residents who take their leisure there on sunny days likely have no idea that a corner of their tranquil garden was once part of a bullfighting ring where violent and bloody spectacles were once held.

---

*Walk back to the corner of Dolores and 16<sup>th</sup> and turn right on 16<sup>th</sup> Street. About halfway down the block toward Guerrero Street is:*

---

### ❸ 16<sup>th</sup> Street between Dolores and Guerrero streets – Site of the Candelario Valencia Adobe (1840s).

About midway down this block and occupying about half the block of the 16<sup>th</sup> Street frontage was the home of Candelario Valencia. (The building actually extended out into what is now 16<sup>th</sup> Street.) Valencia, who had been a soldier at the Presidio from 1823 to 1833, lived here with his wife and six children in the 1840s, and perhaps earlier, in an adobe structure that measured more than 200 feet in length and was over 20 feet wide. Nearby Valencia Street is likely named for him, although it's possible that it was named for his father, José Manuel Valencia, who had been a soldier with de Anza's company. The younger Valencia seems the better bet because he lived near the street bearing his name and he lived closer to the time when the streets were laid out.

Parts of the Valencia adobe may have lasted until the 1880s, since the Sanborn fire insurance map of 1887 shows a few remnants of structures in this area labeled as "Ruins." Across the street on the same map are "shanties" that were in actuality part of the Indian rancheria that was once part of the Mission complex.

---

*Continue down 16<sup>th</sup> Street to Guerrero. Cross Guerrero Street and turn right. Go half a block to Camp Street. Turn left and go to the end where it intersects with Albion Street. In front of the triple-door garage is a bronze plaque on a stand marking:*

---

## ❹ Camp and Albion streets – Site of the Original Mission Dolores (1776).

This intersection marks what was the northwest shore of the Laguna de los Dolores and it was here that Juan Bautista de Anza and his party camped on June 27, 1776 after riding over from the Presidio to establish a location for the mission. Two days later the group celebrated a mass under a makeshift brush shelter they had built. They soon built a sturdier structure. The official dedication of their new church was held on October 9 when a cross was erected atop their chapel. After the ceremony the celebrants enjoyed a barbecue and feast. The Indians, perhaps anticipating what the future would bring, appeared less than enthusiastic, as Father Palou, the founding priest, noted in his diary that day: "The day has been a joyful one for all. Only the savages did not enjoy themselves on this happy day."

The mission did not stay on this site for long. It was moved, likely to free up this land—so close to fresh water—for agricultural use. The mission and its retinue relocated several times nearby before settling at the present location on Dolores Street in 1783.

---

*Go south half a block down Albion Street to 17<sup>th</sup> Street. For the sake of safety it is best to go to the intersection of either Valencia or Guerrero to cross over 17<sup>th</sup>, but once on the south side of the latter, walk down Dearborn Street, an alley in the middle of the block, until you reach its end where it intersects with 18<sup>th</sup> Street. Directly across Dearborn from 18<sup>th</sup> is:*

---

## ❺ 3543 18<sup>th</sup> Street – The Women's Building (1910).

One of the more visible manifestations of the Mission District's Latino heritage is the abundance of murals (inspired by the great Mexican muralists of the 1920s and '30s, such as Diego Rivera and Jose Clemente Orozco) that adorn buildings and alleys throughout the district. One of the most dramatic is found here. Straight across 18<sup>th</sup> Street from Dearborn Alley is the Women's Building, which is covered with a virtual tattoo of mural artwork.

Completed in 1994 after two years of labor by a team of seven women artists, the murals—the Lapidge Street side is even more embellished—provide portraits of both famous and archetypal women and designs of various ethnic groups, all done in vibrant

**The Women's Building.**

whorls of color. On the 18^th Street façade the figure on top in the center represents the Goddess of Light. Flanking her on the sides are an African American and Ohlone Indian woman. Below them are swirls of color representing fabrics and quilt designs from around the world. Embedded in the swirls are the names of notable women: Maya Angelou, Rachel Carson, Emma Goldman, and many others. The Lapidge Street façade, around the corner, is topped by a portrait of Nobel Prize-winning activist Rigoberta Menchu. Below her are representations of goddesses from cultures around the world.

The Women's Building got started in 1979 after a parent organization purchased it from the previous owner, the Sons of Norway. Today the building functions as a community center for women and for relevant women's issues such as child care, sexual assault, gay/lesbian, and other concerns.

*Go down Lapidge Alley to 19^th Street. Directly across from the end of Lapidge is:*

### ❻ 3535 19^th Street – former B'nai David Synagogue (1908).

The Jewish population in San Francisco in the wake of the gold rush was mainly Reform (such as the Temple Emanu-El and Temple Sherith Israel congregations) and came from many different countries. From about 1880 to 1910 a new wave of Jewish immigrants came to San Francisco from eastern Europe, most of them from Russia, Poland, and Romania. They tended to be Orthodox. They established their own congregation—B'nai David—in the Mission District. Originally located near 16^th and Mission streets, they built this unassuming temple here after the 1906 fire. Stucco and tile over a wood frame, the building typifies what has been called "recessive protective architecture." In other words, it was designed to not call attention to itself, bespeaking an attitude born of centuries of persecution.

Part of the building's historic significance—it is a City Landmark—and what set it apart from other Jewish temples, was its mikvah, or ritual bath, which was used for purification purposes. This mikvah was the first one in northern California. Orthodox Jews came from as far as Nevada to use it.

The B'nai David congregation flourished initially but started to decline in the 1930s and '40s as the members dispersed. Some moved to the Jewish community around McAllister Street in the Fillmore. By about 1960 regular synagogue services had ceased here, and during the early 1970s the celebration of high holy days stopped as well and the temple closed. The mikvah was moved over to Menorah Square, a Jewish retirement home in Pacific Heights. The building was sold, the interior was revamped, and in 1981 it was converted to apartments.

*A few doors farther west on 19^th Street toward Guerrero is:*

### ❼ Mission Playground Mural – "New World Tree" (1987).

This Mission District mural depicts a naked man and woman whose raised arms jointly hold a baby backlit by a burst of light. Entitled "New World Tree," it was painted in 1987 by four artists as a collaborative effort. The fanciful artwork with its flowing stream below and tree limbs above gives this building a nice harmony with the park in front of it.

---

*Turn around and head back east on 19th Street. At Valencia, cross over and go one-third of a block to Lexington Street. Walk this one block of Lexington up to 20th Street and as you do so note that all of the buildings here are Edwardian in style, not Victorian. That is because the 1906 fire was not finally stopped until it reached 20th Street. This block burned while the next section of Lexington, between 20th and 21st, was spared. Cross 20th Street and walk up Lexington toward 21st Street.*

---

## ❽ Lexington Street between 20th and 21st streets (1875).

Starting in the 1860s, as development spread beyond the downtown area, what became known as "homestead associations" sprang up to fill the growing need for housing. These organizations consisted of dues-paying members who pooled their money to purchase blocks of land that they then subdivided into lots, upon which the members then built their homes. The Mission District was a prime target for these groups.

In the 1870s a corporation called The Real Estate Associates (TREA) took this idea one step further by not only buying land but by building houses on speculation on the acquired property. TREA eventually built over 1,000 homes in San Francisco, more than 100 of which were in the Mission District's Liberty-Hill area. In 1875 they purchased the whole block bounded by Mission, Valencia, 20th, and 21st streets and subdivided it further by putting through two small thoroughfares, Lexington and San Carlos (the alley just east of here). Over the next two years they built and sold most of the houses that they had erected on the 120 lots in this block.

Lexington Street—which was originally called Stevenson Street—is possibly the most intact street of 19th century speculative-built housing left in San Francisco. These particular houses were the least expensive of this TREA development. The lots here are slightly smaller at 22 feet x 75 feet compared to a normal lot size of 25 feet x 100 feet; they and the houses on them sold for an average of $3,350, versus $5,000 or more for their neighbors on the major streets. The houses are a mix of mass-produced wood-frame Italianates, both flat-front and slanted-bay styles. Virtually all of the Lexington Street houses date from 1876. Their buyers were craftsmen, foremen, teachers, and small business owners. About half of the homes' facades have been remodeled, most with stucco. Several have their original iron fences in front and a handful do not have driveways—their small front yards are still intact. Despite the changes over the years there is still enough unchanged here to convey what this street must have been like in the 19th century when these houses were new.

---

*At Lexington and 21st Street stop for a moment and look across the street to your left. On the southeast corner of 21st and Bartlett Street is:*

---

**❾ 3243 21st Street** (1883).

This large two-story home, surrounded by a white picket fence, and two similar houses next door, give a good idea of what this entire neighborhood looked like in the late 19th century. It was a middle class residential area populated by moderately prosperous shopkeepers, laborers, and tradesmen. This corner house and its two neighbors are good examples of the Stick-style architecture that was in vogue in the 1880s. The façades of all three of the these houses—once single family homes, now converted to flats—are relatively unaltered. Even the wooden steps leading up to them appear to be the originals.

---

*Go west on 21st Street to Valencia Street. Turn right at Valencia. About halfway up the block on the east side of Valencia are:*

---

**❿ 929 to 945 Valencia Street** (1876).

These well maintained (and in some cases restored) Italianate bay window row houses were part of The Real Estate Associates development that encompassed the block bounded by 20th, and 21st, Mission, and Valencia streets. Note that because the houses are on a major traffic artery they are much grander than the cottage-like dwellings on Lexington Street. Of these four, 933 Valencia—the house second to the left—still has a front garden and no driveway, an increasing rarity these days.

---

*Continue north on Valencia to 20<sup>th</sup> Street. At 20<sup>th</sup> cross Valencia on the south side and go up 20<sup>th</sup> Street a few doors to:*

---

## ⓫ 3635 20<sup>th</sup> Street (1886).

The handsomest home on this block is this tall two-story-with-basement Victorian. It still has its original iron fence and is the only house on the block with a separate side yard. The addition of a garage in place of the front yard/garden illustrates for the umpteenth time how the automobile has changed a 19<sup>th</sup> century street scene.

---

*Walk about two-thirds of the way up 20<sup>th</sup> Street, and as you do recall that this was where the 1906 fire was stopped: all the buildings on the north side of the street are post-1906 Edwardians, while those on the south side are mostly 19<sup>th</sup> century Victorians. Across the street is:*

---

## ⓬ 3672 20<sup>th</sup> Street (c.1875).

This otherwise unremarkable two-story Victorian is notable simply because it is a Victorian on the side of the street that burned in 1906. The explanation for its presence in this location is that it was moved here after the fire. The façade was stripped of its decoration and stuccoed over at some point, but the west side of the building was left untouched—it still has its original ornamentation. In what appears to be an attempt to make a transition between the two, a bracketed cornice has been reapplied to the façade, but note that the brackets are much simpler than the incised scrolls on the side.

---

*Continue up 20<sup>th</sup> Street to the southeast corner of 20<sup>th</sup> and Guerrero streets.*

---

## ⓭ 801 Guerrero Street (1871).

This two-story residence with quoins and other 19<sup>th</sup> century decorative elements once again points up the difference between the typically exuberant Victorian flourishes, as seen on the south side of 20<sup>th</sup> Street, and the more restrained ornamentation characteristic of the 20<sup>th</sup> century buildings on the north side. This house—now divided into three units—has an unusual one-two-one bay window on the front.

**801 Guerrero Street.**

*Across the street on the southwest corner of this intersection is:*

**⑭ 3701 20ᵗʰ Street** (1868).

This rather plain Victorian is notable because there has been a corner grocery store on the ground floor here ever since this building was constructed in 1868. A local resident in an interview recalled that in the 1920s there was a dance hall upstairs where residential units are now.

---

*Walk south on Guerrero Street up the incline and stop in front of:*

---

**⑮ 827 Guerrero Street** (1881, 1890).

This City Landmark, a house of unusual design, might best be described as "Eclectic Queen Anne." It was built in 1881, probably as a rather standard Italianate, but it was enlarged and totally remodeled in 1890 by the Newsom Brothers. Architects Samuel and J. C. Newsom designed a number of dwellings in San Francisco and elsewhere, but are best noted for their Carson House mansion in Eureka, California. Here they have taken a number of traditional Queen Anne embellishments and given them enough of a twist to make this house unique: the gable is clipped rather than pointed; the witch's cap crowning the tower is bell-shaped rather than conical; and the double door-entry is framed by a horseshoe arch rather than a standard columned portico. Several individual decorative touches have also been added. Of special interest are the three hand-carved faces at each end of the arch.

The original owner of the house was John McMullen, who was first the manager and then the president of the San Francisco Bridge Company, a contractor that specialized in maritime construction. The firm pioneered a number of dredging techniques. S. F. Bridge engaged in projects worldwide, but locally they dredged the Oakland Harbor, built part of the San Francisco seawall, and constructed docks at Fort Mason and Hunters Point.

McMullen and his wife sold the house in early 1908 to John Young, a druggist. Young and his descendants lived here until 1937. In the mid-1950s the house was converted to a licensed board and care home. It recently returned to private ownership.

### ⓰ 845 Guerrero Street (1871).

Another City Landmark, and one of the oldest houses in the neighborhood, is 845 Guerrero, built in 1871 for Marsden Kershaw, co-owner of a coal yard. The beauty of this flat-front Italianate is its simplicity. In contrast to most Victorian-era houses, where the embellishments almost seem to overwhelm the house itself, here the decorative elements are so understated and so nicely integrated with the structure that they seem part of an organic whole. The lovely garden surrounding the property further enhances the beauty of the setting. A single-car garage was tastefully and unobtrusively added on Liberty Street behind the house in 1976.

---

*Turn the corner and walk down Liberty Street to:*

---

### ⓱ 70 Liberty Street (1876).

Liberty Street and Hill Street, two blocks to the south, are part of a City historic district. These two streets and other buildings in the neighborhood were included because the Victorian homes here provide a good example of middle-class residential housing in the late 19th century. The Mission District was one of San Francisco's first "suburbs," and the houses here, set back from the street and with their front and rear gardens, enhance the suburban feel.

The large three-story dwelling at 70 Liberty Street near the top of the grade dominates the block. It was originally only two stories, but the U.S. Coast Guard took over the building during World War II and added the third story because they needed more space. They replicated the Victorian style almost perfectly. The only clue that the top floor was an addition is the wooden rail that runs around the siding between the second and third stories. The cornice may well be original; it seems logical that it would have been removed and then placed back on top of the new construction.

**⓲ 58 Liberty Street** (c.1876).

The lot this house occupies was purchased in 1869 by two partners as part of a parcel that included the previously mentioned 70 Liberty Street. They apparently built this house on speculation, and in 1876 sold it to a David T. Bagley, a commission merchant and former mining secretary.

Unusual architectural features here are the porthole windows in what appears to be a half-story on the top floor above the second-floor window gables. (They are best seen from across the street.) Like most homes on this street, this once single-family home has been converted into apartments.

---

*Cross the street for a look at:*

---

**⓳ 45 and 49 Liberty Street** (1867, c.1870s).

Forty-five Liberty Street is perhaps the oldest house extant in the area. It was built by Marshall Doane, a hay-press manufacturer. Sometime in the 1870s Doane erected the duplex next door, 49 Liberty Street, as income property. Rather than being free-standing, the two buildings share a common wall. Doane and his descendants occupied #45 until 1903. The three units continued as single-family housing until 1913, when they were converted into six apartments. A driveway to the east of the Doane house leads to the rear of the rear of the property, where there likely was a carriage house in the 19th century.

---

*Continue to Valencia Street. At the intersection of Liberty and Valencia you will have a good view of the previously mentioned grouping at 929–945*

*Valencia Street. Turn right on Valencia, cross 21ˢᵗ Street, and walk up the south side of 21ˢᵗ. You will pass by a mix of Victorians on your way to:*

### ⓴ 3339 21ˢᵗ Street (1876, 1890).

Part of a nice collection of Italianate and Stick Victorians on this side of the street, this house was initially an Italianate but was remodeled in 1890 by James Kavanaugh, the Irish carpenter and builder of "Postcard Row" on Alamo Square. This house is the only one along this stretch that still has its original iron fence.

### ㉑ 3367–3375 21ˢᵗ Street (1885).

The architectural firm that designed this group of three Stick-style houses was Pissis and Moore. Albert Pissis was one of San Francisco's leading architects at the turn of the 20ᵗʰ century. He designed the Flood Building, the Emporium, and the fine Hibernia Bank Building (see Market Street and Civic Center walks). But those came later. Like many professionals he started at a more modest level with residential projects such as this one. The most noteworthy feature of these units is that the porch columns and engaged columns by the door frames are designs derived from the furniture of Charles Eastlake, whose last name is sometimes attached to the Stick—or Stick-Eastlake—style of design that prevailed in the 1880s.

*Continue up 21ˢᵗ Street and stop on the southeast corner of Guerrero Street.*

### ㉒ 900 Guerrero Street – John Daly home (1895).

The grand house with the decorative paint job across Guerrero on the southwest corner of the intersection was built for dairyman John Daly in 1895. Daly must have been a man of great inner strength and resolve, for in 1854 his mother died as the two of them were crossing the Isthmus of Panama on their way from Boston to California; the 13-year-old boy continued on alone to San Francisco. As an adult he established a successful dairy farm in San Mateo County, and did well enough to build one of the finest homes still extant in the Mission District. After the 1906 disaster, Daly subdivided his 250-acre San Mateo farm and sold the parcels to refugees displaced by the fire. In

**900 Guerrero Street.**

1911 that area, now called Daly City, was incorporated and named in his honor.

---

*Head south on Guerrero Street, but go only about ten steps from the corner and stop about where the driveway of 911 is. This is where you will get the best view—off to your right—of the two-story Italianate bay-window house with quoins up the hill across 21st Street from the Daly home. It is the first house up the hill from the three-story apartment building on the corner.*

---

### ㉓ 3416 21st Street (c.1875) – "Sunny Jim" Rolph boyhood home (1870s–1880s).

This modest dwelling was the boyhood home of James ("Sunny Jim") Rolph Jr. (1869–1934), who was mayor of San Francisco from 1912 to 1931—by far the longest term of anyone in that office. He was then governor of California from 1931 until his death in 1934. The good-natured and flamboyant Rolph, who wore his trademark cowboy boots even with a tuxedo, grew up in this house in the 1870s and 1880s. The area at that time was still mostly undeveloped; the dirt streets became rivers of mud during the rainy season. The oldest of seven children, Rolph kept a chicken coop in the backyard. The mayor inherited the property when his father died in 1918, and he must have had a soft spot for the home because he still owned it (although he lived elsewhere) when he died of a sudden heart attack in 1934. Like many Victorian houses this one had its façade stripped and "modernized" with stucco, but it has recently been restored to its original appearance.

### ㉔ 915 Guerrero Street (1879, 1890s).

Of interest here is the unusual Islamic-arch entryway and the handrail on the left adorned with a Chinese dragon with bared teeth and protruding tongue. The house was built in 1879 in the Italianate style, and was remodeled—probably in the 1890s, with these extras. The house immediately to the right—919 Guerrero—now completely altered and covered with sprayed-on stucco, was once a twin of 915 (the 1879 version).

*Continue on Guerrero for half a block and turn left on Hill Street.*

### ㉕ 34 Hill Street (1880).

Hill Street, like Liberty, has an open feeling because the houses are set back from the street, allowing for front yards and/or gardens. The sense of spaciousness is even more pronounced here because the street trees are shorter than the ones on Liberty.

Thirty-four Hill Street is one of the larger homes on the block. It is also one of the few that had its own stable/carriage house (with servants living quarters above) in back. Since this was a middle-class neighborhood in the 19th century, most families could not afford their own stable; they used the commercial ones on Valencia Street. One of the early owners of 34 Hill was Dr. John Graves, a physician and long-time police surgeon, who lived here from 1905 until about 1915. A single-family home until well into the 20th century, the house later was divided into five units. In 1999 it once again became a one-family residence.

*Across the street is:*

### ㉖ 69 Hill Street (1887).

This large Stick-style house was remodeled in 1920 into a four-family home. The original front door was on the right of the façade where the window with the planter box is today. The entrance was moved to the side of the house by simply cutting away the main floor's square bay window. Since then an extra apartment has been squeezed in; it's now a five-unit building.

*Go down Hill Street past the remaining Victorians on both sides of the block and turn right on Valencia Street. On the southwest corner of Valencia and 22nd Street is:*

### ㉗ 1100 Valencia Street – Lucca Ravioli Company (1917).

Lucca Ravioli, with its house-made pastas, is a Mission District institution. At a time when the majority of the Mission's population is Latino, it serves as one of the few reminders of the area's earlier

Italian heritage. The business was founded in 1917 when this building was erected. The original owners—an Italian family, of course—ran Lucca until 1925, when they sold to other Italians whose descendants still run it today. To get the full flavor of Lucca, go in and check out the long deli counter staffed by the cadre of white males wearing aprons. You could easily imagine yourself in North Beach in the 1930s.

---

*Walk west on 22$^{nd}$ Street a short distance to the intersection of San Jose Avenue.*

---

### ❷ San Jose Avenue (1770s?).

This easily overlooked street, which winds at irregular angles south from here through the uniform grid pattern of streets, is a vestigial remnant of the San Jose Road, once the eastern boundary of José de Jesus Noé's Rancho San Miguel. Noé, for whom Noe Street and Noe Valley are named, was the last Mexican alcalde of Yerba Buena, in 1846, and his land grant that year was one of the last issued under Mexican rule. His 4,443 acre property extended west to Junipero Serra Boulevard and encompassed mostly hills, including the present day Mt. Sutro, Twin Peaks, Diamond Heights, and Mt. Davidson.

The winding San Jose Road was set as the eastern boundary of his grant because it was an existing landmark bordering other already established ranchos to the east. How long San Jose Road had been there prior to Noé's claim is an open question, but intriguingly, where it ends here at 22$^{nd}$ Street, points north directly to where the Laguna de los Dolores and the first mission of 1776 were. It might well be the original El Camino Real which connected Mission Dolores to Mission Santa Clara (founded in 1777) and its other neighbor missions to the south. And since travelers in a new land always take the path of least resistance, it's possible that the San Jose Road could have originally been an Indian trail leading to the freshwater lagoon.

---

*Continue west on 22$^{nd}$ Street to the second street past Guerrero, Fair Oaks. In the first block of Fair Oaks on the left side of the street, one house up, is:*

---

## ❷❾ 90 Fair Oaks Street (1886) – Lotta Crabtree Property.

A purchase contract still exists showing that actress Lotta Crabtree (1847–1924) sold this property to a C. W. Eckstein on December 9, 1885 for $1,300 in gold coin. It likely was a vacant lot that she had purchased as an investment property. Water Department records show that water service was first established here on May 24, 1886 for Eckstein, indicating that he built a home here after the purchase of the lot. The buyer was no doubt Cassius W. Eckstein, a policeman, who in the 1887 City Directory, was shown as living at 104 Fair Oaks. He may have built the house at 90 Fair Oaks as an income property, and lived nearby to keep an eye on his tenants.

At the time she sold the Fair Oaks parcel, Lotta Crabtree was near retirement and living in New York. The leading stage comedienne of her day, she got her start as a child performer—first in Mother Lode gold-rush towns and then in San Francisco in the 1850s. She went on to perform in major cities all over the U.S. and Europe, but returned to San Francisco from time to time. In 1875 she donated to the City the landmark that is known as Lotta's Fountain (see the Market Street walk). Due to her popularity during a long career, and wise invest-ments made along the way—evidently including this one—she was worth $4 million when she died.

The house itself was remodeled sometime during the 20th century with asbestos shingling, but that was removed and it was changed to its present vaguely Stick appearance in the early 1970s. It's not known what the house looked like originally.

# Nob Hill

**Length:** 0.5 miles / .80 kilometers.
**Time:** ¾ hour.
**Walk Rating:** Easy to Moderate.
**Hills:** The first block of the tour, Washington Street from Mason to Taylor, is a moderate to steep uphill. The last block, from California to Pine Street, is a moderate downhill.
**Public Transit:** The cable car runs both directions along California Street and along Powell Street as well. It runs east – downhill – on Washington Street past the cable car barn. The 1 bus line goes east on Clay Street toward downtown and west on Sacramento on its return journey.
**Parking:** There is a parking garage on the south side of California Street between Mason and Taylor, across from the Flood Mansion, and another one a block farther to the west underneath the Masonic Temple. Both are expensive. Street parking is tough to find.
**Restrooms:** There is a public restroom in Huntington Park.

Of all of San Francisco's forty-odd hills, Nob Hill is the most famous. In the late 19th century, Robert Louis Stevenson called it the "Hill of Palaces"—because on its crest stood the extravagant mansions of the City's moneyed elite. It was originally called Fern Hill, then Clay Street Hill, and then Knob Hill because it was a rocky knob until the summit was scraped flat to make it more habitable. The "K" in Knob was soon dropped.

Nob Hill was anything but the "Hill of Palaces" for the City's first two decades. It was a desolate outcropping covered by gnarly oaks and bushes and afflicted by blowing sand. Early residents were squatters who put up shacks and flimsy wood frame buildings, behind which they kept a few fenced-in chickens and goats. Here and there, cattle roamed the slopes.

The lower slope of the hill above Yerba Buena Cove, primarily Stockton and Powell streets west and north of Portsmouth Square, became a choice residential area starting in the 1850s. Their cross streets were not so steep as to inhibit access by horse-drawn vehicles—the main obstacle to developing the higher elevations. In the 1860s, residential development did start to reach higher up the slope. Taylor Street from Sacramento to Pacific became the residential nexus

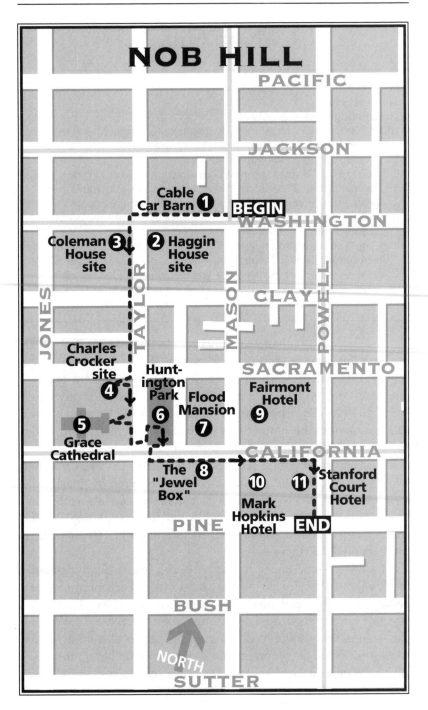

# NOB HILL

**❶** Cable Car Barn

**❷** Site of James Ben Ali Haggin House

**❸** Site of William T. Coleman House

**❹** Site of Charles Crocker estate

**❺** Grace Cathedral

**❻** Huntington Park

**❼** Flood Mansion

**❽** 1021 California Street - the "Jewel Box"

**❾** Fairmont Hotel

**❿** Mark Hopkins Hotel

**⓫** Stanford Court Hotel

of the elite and the start of the association of wealth with Nob Hill. What made this section of Taylor Street attractive was that it offered commanding views of the downtown and the bay and it was protected from the westerly winds by the higher ridge of Jones Street one block behind it. Lloyd Tevis, a leading lawyer and businessman, moved here from Rincon Hill at least by the mid-1860s. He was followed by his brother-in-law, James Ben Ali Haggin, in the early 1870s.

What really removed the impediment to developing the hill was the invention of the cable car. In 1873, Andrew Hallidie, the cable car's inventor, built the first line—along Clay Street from Kearny at Portsmouth Square to Jones Street at the top of Nob Hill. In 1878 Leland Stanford and several partners established the California Street line. The upper slopes of the hill developed rapidly thereafter, and the mansions of San Francisco's wealthiest citizens rose around the summit at California, Mason, and Sacramento streets.

The best known of the City's ruling class were the quartet known as the "Big Four"—Leland Stanford, Mark Hopkins, Charles Crocker, and Collis Huntington. They had started modestly as merchandisers of hardware and other goods in Sacramento, but a speculative investment they made in a railroad that was intended to cross the Sierra foothills to the mines—a prospect that seemed dubious at the time due to the difficult terrain that would have to be crossed—led to the start of a railroad empire and transportation monopoly that would make them rich beyond their wildest dreams. They reaped multimillion-dollar fortunes and they indulged themselves by building gargantuan homes that dominated the hill and the city.

Nob Hill also drew the attention of two of the four men who were known as the "Bonanza Kings"—James C. Flood and James Fair. They, along with two partners, had been the majority stockholders of a Virginia City, Nevada mine that turned out to be the richest silver mine ever developed. They ended up even wealthier than the Big Four yet their names are less known to history. Only Flood, in fact, built a mansion on the hill. It is the only one of all of the homes that once stood here that survived the fire of 1906.

*Start this tour at the northwest corner of Washington and Mason streets.*

## ❶ 1201 Mason Street – Cable Car Barn and Museum
(1887, 1909).

The invention of the cable car proved a boon to San Francisco's transportation and development. In the late 19th century a dozen lines extended for a total of 112 miles, serving much of the city. Today just three lines remain, covering 10.5 miles, all in the northeast corner of town. Many cities once had cable car systems, but when Seattle discontinued its lines in 1940, San Francisco's system became the sole survivor. This cable car barn is the last such in the world.

Although the lettering on the south side of the building says "Ferries and Cliff House Railway – 1887" much of the building is a 1909 reconstruction of the 1887 original. The chimney at the rear did survive the 1906 disaster with the loss of only a few bricks from its crown. Until 1911 the cable machinery was powered by steam from giant boilers; the steam was vented through this chimney.

The building now serves to house the cable cars at night after they finish their service around 1:00 a.m. During the day it's open to the public as a free museum. Andrew Hallidie's original cable car of 1873 is here. Although most of the City's cars were consumed by fire in 1906, this one survived because it was in Baltimore at an exhibition at the time. Also on display are a couple of other antique cars that date from 1876, as well as scale models of other cable cars that have appeared on city streets in years past. Other featured items are several of the giant grips that clamp on the steel cables that move underneath the streets, and various related machinery and tools. From both the museum deck and from a room in the basement you can watch the steel cables for all three lines come winding in and out of the building—truly a one-of-a-kind attraction.

---

*Walk up Washington Street one block to the southeast corner of Taylor Street.*

---

## ❷ Taylor and Washington streets – SE corner – Site of James Ben Ali Haggin House (1874–1906).

Taylor Street was once described as "the most aristocratic street in San Francisco." It was the first part of Nob Hill to be densely settled. Many of its initial residents were from the "southern aristocracy" that formed part of the residential elite who had earlier inhabited Rincon Hill and South Park.

One of these was James Ben Ali Haggin, a native of Kentucky. He purchased the upper half of the block on Taylor Street between Washington and Clay, and in 1874 he erected a huge house on the southeast corner of Taylor and Washington. On the Taylor Street main entrance, marble steps led up to a Corinthian-pillared portico. The house behind it had 50 rooms and 9 baths. It stood 50 feet high and had a mansard roof topped by a square, tapered cupola that afforded a commanding view of downtown and the bay. In back of the house stood a luxurious stable that could accommodate 40 horses.

James Ben Ali Haggin Mansion.

Haggin and his family (he and his wife Jennie had five children) were known for their hospitality. They made the society columns for their frequent parties, balls, and receptions, although Jennie Haggin must have been the more social of the two since James Haggin was described—at least in his business dealings—as rather on the dour side.

Despite their social life the couple appear to have been separated by the time of Mrs. Haggin's death in 1894. A newspaper account of the time tells of her children being present at her deathbed; her husband's name was conspicuously absent. James Haggin, who had been spending a lot of time on the East Coast, moved to Fifth Avenue in New York that year. The house apparently remained vacant until it burned in 1906. In 1909 the land where the house stood was auctioned off and divided into 16 lots. The flats and apartment buildings on this block today were erected soon after.

### ❸ Taylor and Washington streets – SW corner
### – Site of William T. Coleman House (1850s–1906).

Directly across the street from the Haggin residence at that time was the home of another leading figure of 19<sup>th</sup> century San Francisco, William T. Coleman (1824–1893). Coleman, a forty-niner who became a prominent merchant, served on the executive committees of both the 1851 and 1856 Vigilance Committees. A natural born leader, looked to by others in times of trouble, he also served as president of the Committee for Public Safety in 1877 when anti-Chinese violence erupted. He organized a pickax-handle brigade composed of other leading citizens, which in the space of a few days in July of that year helped quell disturbances caused by rabble-rouser Denis Kearney and his followers.

In 1872 Coleman bought an existing house on this site; it dated from the 1850s, one of the first large homes on the hill. Both Coleman and the previous owners enlarged it; by the time of Coleman's residency the house boasted a music room, a billiard room, a library, and a conservatory with ferns and other plants.

One evening in early August 1877 while Coleman and his wife and two sons were out, arsonists tried to burn down the house. A servant managed to douse the flames before much damage was done. Police found two buckets of tar that apparently had been used as an incendiary device, and they also discovered that the nearest fire-alarm box, at Clay and Taylor streets, had been disabled. The attack was apparently one of revenge by Denis Kearney's followers.

Coleman suffered financial reverses in the late 1880s and had to declare bankruptcy. It seems that he had to sell his house, since he moved to the Occidental Hotel on Montgomery Street in 1889. A man of great integrity, he swore that he would pay his creditors in full— and he managed to do so shortly before he died in 1893. His former residence on Nob Hill burned in 1906.

*Walk south on Taylor two blocks and stop on the southwest corner of Sacramento and Taylor streets.*

### ❹ Taylor Street between Sacramento and California streets – Site of the Charles Crocker Estate (1877–1906).

Charles Crocker, the construction chief of the Big Four during the building of the transcontinental railroad, once owned the entire block (with the exception of one small parcel) bounded by Taylor, Sacramento, Jones, and California streets. In 1877 he built a built a huge, Second Empire-style mansion facing California Street near the corner of Taylor. Eleven years later he built a mansion on the northeast corner of California and Jones streets as a wedding present for his son William.

One of the more storied episodes of San Francisco history involves the small parcel of land on Sacramento Street behind his residence, which he was not able to purchase. On it stood a modest Victorian house owned and occupied by a German undertaker, Nicholas Yung. Peeved at Yung's refusal to sell him his property, Crocker got more than even by building a forty-foot-high wooden "spite fence" around the three sides of the poor man's house, shutting off its natural light and views save for those on Sacramento Street. Yung did exact a measure of revenge. On the roof of his house he erected a ten-foot-high coffin, adorned it with a skull and crossbones, and pointed it toward the Crocker mansion. After a couple of years Yung moved his house off his lot to another part of town, but Crocker left the fence standing. It was only after the death of both men that the dispute was settled, with Yung's heirs selling the land to the Crocker family.

*To see the location of the Yung house, walk up Sacramento Street on the south side to where markers still exist to show its location. Look for the six-inch-wide granite stones laid from the fence to the curb. One extends from each of the granite pillars between the corner and the entrance to the parking lot— which was the carriage entrance to the Crocker grounds. Return to the corner of Taylor and Sacramento.*

Although the Crocker mansions burned in 1906 along with the rest of Nob Hill, a few things still remain from the estate. Most notable is the black-painted iron fence and stone retaining wall, a part of which still exists along Taylor and Sacramento streets. The black patina of the wall, and the flecks and chips missing from it, were caused by the smoke and heat of the 1906 fire.

Another item of note at this corner is the stamp embossed in the sidewalk panel next to the corner pillar on the Taylor Street side. If you look closely you can see some faint, hard-to-read letters etched into the concrete. It is the sidewalk manufacturer's mark, and it reads:

CALIFORNIA ASP CO.
SCHILLINGER PATENT
Pat July 19<sup>th</sup> 1870
Reissue May 2<sup>nd</sup> 1871

ASP stands for Artificial Stone Paving, the name of the local company that paved the sidewalk. This historic panel was saved when the Taylor Street sidewalk was redone in the late 1990s. You can see, by comparing it to the Sacramento Street side, where most of the sidewalk has been preserved, that at least some of this pavement is still original. It was laid down in the late 1870s while the Crocker mansion was being completed.

---

*Walk south on Taylor to the corner of California Street.*

---

### ❺ Grace Cathedral – Taylor and California streets – NW corner.

After the 1906 fire and the destruction of their homes the Crocker family donated the entire block to the Episcopal Church, which uses the land for the church, their administrative offices, and a boys school. Grace Cathedral itself stands on the site of the mansions of Charles and William Crocker. The cathedral's cornerstone was laid in 1910, but due to a change in the design and other problems, construction on the present structure did not begin until 1928. Work on it went on in fits and starts as funds became available; it was not completely finished until 1964. It was designed by architect Lewis Hobart and was modeled after various French Gothic and Spanish Gothic cathedrals.

Grace Cathedral's most distinctive feature is the bronze Ghiberti Doors, located in the center of the Taylor Street entrance. Designed by Renaissance sculptor Lorenzo Ghiberti, they are one of only two duplicates of the originals, which adorn the Baptistry of Florence Cathedral. The Grace copy was crafted from molds made from the originals, which were removed for safekeeping by the Florentines during World War II when the Nazis were looting Europe of its treasures. These doors were originally targeted to be installed in a war memorial in Honolulu—of all places—but a Grace Cathedral architect managed to snag them and they were installed shortly before the cathedral's dedication in 1964.

*Walk up the broad steps of the cathedral for a look at the Ghiberti doors. The panels depict scenes from the Old Testament. Notice in particular the finely detailed heads spaced around the border. They are so distinctive and so individual that Ghiberti must have modeled them after real people of his time. Return to Taylor Street, cross over and enter the park.*

❻ **Huntington Park** (1915).

Huntington Park is named after Collis P. Huntington (1821–1900), one of the Big Four and the man who was the real brains of the group. While his colleague, the vain Leland Stanford, basked in the public limelight, Huntington worked behind the scenes, greasing palms and lobbying legislators for more favorable treatment for the Southern Pacific Railroad and other companies that he and his partners controlled. He was a hard-eyed, humorless, penurious, and sometimes dishonest man. When someone once asked Adolph Sutro (mayor of San Francisco 1895–97) if he thought Huntington was trustworthy, he replied with the ringing endorsement that Huntington had "never been known to steal a red-hot stove."

This park was the site of Huntington's house, a two-story, neoclassical edifice that was relatively tasteful and restrained for the times. Modeled after an Italian palace but made of wood painted white in imitation of the marble original, it had been built in the early 1870s by David Colton. Colton, the financial manager for the Big Four, died at the age of 47 in 1878, apparently from a fall from a horse. But inasmuch as he was viewed with suspicion by several of the quartet, especially by Mark Hopkins, for his constant attempts to ingratiate himself with the partners, rumors spread that Colton had been murdered. After Colton's death the four railroad barons strong-armed Colton's widow into turning her husband's railroad stock over to them. Ellen Colton was turned out of the mansion. Huntington moved in and lived there until his death in 1900, but he rarely was home since he spent much of his time in Washington, D.C. lobbying (and bribing) congressmen.

The faux-marble Huntington mansion burned in the 1906 fire. The property sat vacant until 1915, when Huntington's widow donated the land to the City—which turned it into a public park. In the park's center, surrounded by benches, is a copy of a fountain in Rome that dates from 1585: Fontana delle Tartarughe, "the Fountain of the

Tortoises." The marble and bronze fountain was purchased by William Crocker in 1924 and was kept at his Hillsborough estate until 1955, when his family donated it to the park.

---

*After a closer look at the fountain in Huntington Park, cross California Street to the south side and walk east past the Huntington Hotel. The big brownstone mansion across the street as you approach Mason Street is:*

---

### ❼ 1000 California Street – Flood Mansion (1886) – Pacific-Union Club.

James C. Flood (1825–1889) was the only one of the so called "Bonanza Kings" to build a mansion on Nob Hill. Flood, a former saloon-keeper turned stockbroker who had had the good luck to hook up with Comstock miners James Fair and John Mackay, was the last of all of the nabobs to build here, and his is the only survivor of the once grand houses that adorned Nob Hill in the late 19th century. The house was gutted in the 1906 fire but the walls, made of Connecticut sandstone, proved sound and were saved.

Flood purchased this lot in 1882. It was an undesirable block because at the time it was still a big, craggy sand hill almost as high as the present structure. It spilled over into Mason Street, which had not yet been cut through. Flood had the hill leveled, and during 1885–1886 erected this Italianate brownstone. That Flood chose a New York-style brownstone over the prevailing wooden High Victorian designs of his neighbors likely stems from his desire to imitate New York's Fifth Avenue aristocrats. Cornelius Vanderbilt and others had constructed magnificent brownstone mansions just prior to this.

Among the Flood mansion's forty-two rooms were a Louis XV drawing room and a Moorish smoking room with a domed skylight. Surrounding the house was a bronze fence, which still stands. Amid Flood's platoon of servants was one grounds keeper whose sole task was to keep this rail polished and shiny. The rail-polisher is long gone, and the lace-patterned fence has been allowed to corrode to a soothing green.

After the 1906 holocaust the Pacific-Union Club, an exclusive men's club whose membership has always included the city's elite, purchased the property, and local architect and P-U member Willis Polk restored and remodeled the building. He made a few unobtrusive changes, such as installing a third floor between the second floor and the roof (notice the windows in what looks like a half story), and he lowered the original central tower about ten feet to meet the roofline. And he made one big change—he added the two semicircular wings. The west wing houses the dining room and the east wing the reading room.

The Pacific-Union Club's roots go back to the City's earliest days. The Pacific Club, founded in 1852, and the Union Club, founded in 1854, merged in the 1880s. Contrary to popular belief, the club's rules do not prohibit women from joining. The reason why is that when the club's rules were drawn up in the 19$^{th}$ century the idea of women becoming members was something that wouldn't have even crossed the founders' minds. Despite the lack of a formal barrier to entry by women, the club still remains all male. Membership is fixed at 750, so only upon the death of a current member—the club's flag flies at half staff when that occurs—can a new member be admitted. The building is not open to the public.

---

*Continue on ahead to:*

---

**❽ 1021 California Street – the "Jewel Box"** (c.1910).

This easily overlooked little house, known as "the Jewel Box," was built for Herbert Law, a patent-medicine and real-estate millionaire. Law, along with his brother Hartland, owned the Fairmont Hotel for a brief period (see the next section).

**❾ 950 Mason Street – Fairmont Hotel** (1906).

The Fairmont Hotel is named for James G. Fair (1831–1894), a partner of James C. Flood and one of the Bonanza Kings who made huge fortunes from the silver mines of Nevada. Fair was easily the most detested of the group. Self-aggrandizing, with a huge ego, he thought of himself as the brains of the outfit, looked at his partners mostly with contempt, and loved gloating about how he took advantage of others in business deals. He used his Comstock millions to purchase San Francisco real estate. At his peak he was worth $45 million, was estimated to own some 60 acres of prime downtown commercial property, and had a reputation as a slumlord because he failed to pay for upkeep on any of his properties—lease agreements shifted the burden of maintenance to his tenants.

Fair owned the entire block where the Fairmont now stands, and had planned to build a grand mansion of his own that surely would have rivaled or exceeded any of the other homes that already adorned the hill, but when he died in 1894 he had only erected a fence around the property. His oldest daughter, Tessie, inherited the land, and in 1902 she started construction on the present hotel. After slow going, in which she found the costs of construction more than she had anticipated, in early 1906 she sold the unfinished terra cotta-clad granite structure to the aforementioned Law Brothers.

The building was essentially finished and was just weeks away from opening when the earthquake struck on April 18, 1906. As the fire consumed the downtown area below, city officials retreated up the hill and made the Fairmont their headquarters. Mayor Eugene Schmitz, General Frederick Funston, and others plotted strategy as they sat on unopened crates of furniture in the lobby, but not for long: the flames swept over Nob Hill the following day, driving them farther west. The hotel's exterior walls survived unscathed but the interior was gutted. After a year of restoration, the hotel officially opened on April 18, 1907, one year to the day after the fire. It was the first hotel built on Nob Hill.

In 1908 the Law Brothers sold the Fairmont back to Tessie Fair Oelrichs. She retained ownership until the 1920s. In 1945 Benjamin Swig, the owner most associated with the hotel, bought a controlling interest. His family continued its ownership until the 1990s, when corporate interests took control. Over the years the Fairmont, one of San Francisco's signature hotels, has played host to presidents of the United States, foreign heads of state, and celebrities of every kind. The hotel also has served as a bit player in history. In 1945 the U.N. Charter was drafted in its Garden Room on the main floor just off the lobby.

---

*If you have time, go into the Fairmont to see its elegant, recently refurbished lobby. The tall Corinthian columns evoke the grandeur of an earlier era. Continue this walking tour on the southeast corner of Mason and California streets. On the corner is:*

---

## ⑩ Mark Hopkins Hotel (1926) – Site of Mark Hopkins Mansion (1878–1906).

Mark Hopkins (1813–1878) had the soul of a bookkeeper, which he was—he kept the accounts for the Central (later Southern) Pacific Railroad and his Big Four partners Stanford, Huntington, and Crocker. Unlike the others he was quiet, unassuming, and frugal. Too frugal for his wife, Mary. While Hopkins was content to live in a modest, rented house on Sutter Street, his wife had grander ambitions. Not satisfied with being a dutiful Victorian housewife, content to be seen and not heard, she goaded her parsimonious husband into building a hilltop mansion worthy of his station. She was a voracious reader of historical romances, and envisioned a fairy-tale-like edifice equal to those inhabited by her fictional heroines. And when construction was completed that is what she got—a carved redwood castle of towers, Gothic spires, and ornamentation run riot. Local novelist Gertrude Atherton, never at a loss for an acid quip, remarked

The Mark Hopkins Mansion.

that the house "looked as if several architects had been employed and they had fought one another to a finish!"

Mark Hopkins died in 1878 shortly before the house was completed. Widow Mary moved into the $3 million home, but only a few years later decamped for the East Coast where she was building other mansions. She married Edward Searles, her interior designer, and when she died in 1891 Searles inherited the Nob Hill mansion, which he donated to the San Francisco Art Association. The art group occupied the grand manse until it was swept away in the 1906 fire. Only the granite retaining wall surrounding the property survived.

The Art Association built a much more modest structure as a replacement after the fire, and relocated to Russian Hill (where they are known today as the San Francisco Art Institute) in 1925 when mining engineer George D. Smith bought the property. In 1926 he erected the present hotel. (During construction a large underground reservoir was discovered. If its existence had been known at the time of the 1906 fire perhaps the Hopkins house and others on the hill could have been saved.) The signature Top-of-the-Mark cocktail lounge was created in 1939 out of what was an eleven room penthouse suite. Smith maintained ownership of the hotel until 1962 when he sold it to financier Louis Lurie. Lurie's descendants own it today, although it is managed by the Inter-Continental hotel chain under a long-term contract.

---

*Walk down California Street to the Stanford Court Hotel next door.*

---

### ⑪ Stanford Court Hotel (1912) – Site of the Leland Stanford Mansion (1876–1906).

Leland Stanford (1824–1893), nominal head of the Big Four, was described as a man with "the ambition of an emperor with the spite of a peanut vendor." He loved the limelight, and although a ponderous speaker he was elected governor of California for a two-year term during the Civil War. Two decades later he served a term as U.S. Senator, one effectively purchased through judicious "donations" to state legislators who, until the direct election of senators by popular vote was established in 1913, were responsible for sending senators to Congress. A prodigious spender of his great wealth, Stanford lavished money on various projects including a mansion in Sacramento, a 55,000-acre ranch north of that city, and his Palo Alto horse farm (which, after the premature death of his 15-year-old son, became the site of Leland Stanford Jr. University).

Leland Stanford was the first of the Big Four to build on Nob Hill. In 1876 he erected an elaborate Italianate villa on this site. The interior of the Stanford mansion was a showplace that boasted the largest private dining room in the West. In the center of the house a two-story rotunda was supported by giant red granite pillars. Overhead was a roof of amber glass. Other rooms on the main floor included an East Indian parlor, a Pompeiian drawing room, and an art gallery whose decorative plants were strewn with brightly colored mechanical birds that chirped to life at the press of a button.

Even before his house was completed Stanford embarked on a business venture that he would be able to keep his eye on literally from his front doorstep. The invention of the cable car had sparked his interest, so he decided it would be a benefit to have a line that came up California Street to Nob Hill. He rounded up a group of the City's leading citizens as backers and formed the California Street Cable Railroad Company. Stanford himself purchased most of the shares of the new company, since several of his colleagues were dubious about getting their money back in an enterprise that generated its revenues in the form of five-cent fares. Investor Mark Hopkins in particular was skeptical. He was quoted as saying: "It is just as likely to pay a dividend as the 'Hotel de Hopkins,'" a reference to his mansion then being constructed next door to Stanford's. In an irony he never envisioned, a hotel, as was noted, was eventually erected on the site of his house—and it has paid dividends for its owners ever since.

With typical spare-no-expense gusto, Stanford, after securing his franchise, plunged ahead with construction, determined to make his cable-car line the best appointed and best run one in the City. Always competitive, part of Stanford's motivation was to outdo cable car inventor Andrew Hallidie and his Clay Street line. Hallidie, on hearing of Stanford's plans, had offered his services to help construct the California Street route.

Determined to do it his own way even if it meant paying Hallidie for appropriating his patented technologies, Stanford spurned the inventor's offer of technical assistance but eventually had to pay Hallidie $30,000 in royalties, something that forever after rankled the railroad mogul. To get a measure of revenge, Stanford, after the successful completion of his line, sent Hallidie a letter inviting him to take a free ride on it so he could see how a great cable car line operated. He needled Hallidie further by suggesting that in doing so he might pick up enough pointers to make his Clay Street line a first rate operation "within a hundred years or so."

The California Street cable-car line proved popular and profitable. Stanford sold his interest in the company in 1884 for a hefty gain. In the aftermath of the 1906 disaster both the Clay Street line (1873) and the Sutter Street line (1876) were not rebuilt, leaving the California Street line as the oldest surviving cable-car line in the world.

Like all the other grand homes on the hill save the Flood mansion, the Stanford residence burned in 1906. The site was purchased after the fire from the Stanford estate (Leland's wife, Jane, having died in 1905) by Lucian H. Sly, a real-estate investor, who in 1912 erected the present building, which originally served as luxury rentals, the Stanford Court Apartments. It remained such until 1969. After a major renovation in which the 90 suites of from five to 12 rooms each (including maids' chambers) were converted into 393 guest rooms, the building reopened in 1972 as the Stanford Court Hotel.

Diagonally across the intersection of California and Powell on the northeast corner where the red-brick University Club stands is where Leland Stanford's stable used to be. The interior was more elegantly furnished than many San Francisco homes of the time.

---

*To see a few last remnants of the Nob Hill of Leland Stanford and Mark Hopkins continue to the corner of California and Powell streets and then walk down Powell Street one block to the corner of Pine Street.*

---

The basalt and granite retaining walls still remaining on the Powell Street and Pine Street sides were constructed by railroad laborers in Stanford's employ. The work crews used stone from the same quarry at Rocklin, near Sacramento, to build these walls that the Southern Pacific used to build its train tunnels and bridges. The walls survived the 1906 quake virtually undamaged.

A final item of note is the decorative medieval turret that can be

# James Ben Ali Haggin

## (1820s–1914)

James Ben Ali Haggin is probably the least known of the Nob Hill plutocrats, but he was no less rich and, like the better-known Leland Stanford, Mark Hopkins, and others, he too had a grand mansion on the crest of the hill. He was born into a prominent family in Kentucky (various accounts give the date as 1821, 1822, and 1827) the son of an Irish immigrant father and a mother who was the daughter of a Turkish physician—hence the exotic sounding middle name Ben Ali. He studied law and practiced in Kentucky, Mississippi, and New Orleans before the siren song of gold drew him to California. He arrived in San Francisco in 1850.

James Ben Ali Haggin.

He seemed to know all the right people, and he quickly established partnerships with Milton Latham, soon to be a U.S. senator, Lloyd Tevis, a future president of Wells Fargo who became his brother-in-law (they married sisters), and later, Senator George Hearst (father of newspaper magnate William Randolph Hearst). He initially established a law partnership with Tevis. The two dealt in mining claims, a specialty that quickly evolved into a business partnership that bought controlling interests in mines all over the western U.S.

Using his contacts, sound judgment, and good business sense,

Haggin became very wealthy in almost effortless fashion. At his peak he is said to have had ownership stakes in over 100 mines, including the fabulous Homestake gold mine in Lead, South Dakota and the Anaconda copper mine in Montana. From there he branched out into investments in banks, utilities, and farmland. He purchased huge chunks of land in the interior valley in central California, including a 100,000-acre spread in Kern County.

He diverted the Kern River into irrigation canals to water crops, which brought him into conflict with Henry Miller and other cattlemen who wanted the water largely kept where it was to water their herds. The matter went before the courts. The cattle ranchers argued that under English common law "water ought to flow as it has been accustomed to flow" and thus irrigation was unconstitutional. The courts ruled otherwise, finding that irrigation to grow crops was a necessary public benefit. Haggin went on to develop his vast tracts; at one time he was the largest grower of hops in the U.S.

Haggin's leisure hours were devoted to horse breeding and horse racing. He had a large stable behind his Nob Hill house and he was often seen racing his four-in-hand coach along the Point Lobos Avenue straightaway near the Cliff House. And befitting his Kentucky roots he established a major horse breeding enterprise in his home state. In 1886 his horse Ben Ali won the Kentucky Derby. In later years he gave up horses, saying that it promoted "the worst habit of the American people—gambling." In its stead he turned his energies and his Kentucky land over to another bad habit, smoking, and grew tobacco instead.

Haggin, who was described by contemporaries as direct spoken, dignified, and impassive, died at his villa in Newport, Rhode Island in 1914. The little known multimillionaire (his estate was valued at nearly $22 million when finally probated in 1921) was survived by his second wife who was fifty-odd years his junior and who lived until 1965.

# North Beach

**Length:** 1 mile / 1.6 kilometers.
**Time:** 1½ hours.
**Walk Rating:** Easy.
**Hills:** Stockton Street between Francisco and Chestnut, at the beginning of the walk, is a moderate uphill grade.
**Public Transit:** Muni bus lines 15, 30, and 41 run along Columbus Avenue. (The 41 line runs peak hours only.) Bus line 12 traverses Broadway in the North Beach area.
**Parking:** There is a city-owned parking garage on Vallejo Street between Stockton and Powell streets above the Central Police Station. There are two small parking lots on Broadway between Kearny and Montgomery streets. Street parking, both metered and non-metered, can be difficult to find in this congested and popular part of town.
**Restrooms:** There is a coin-operated (25 cents) public toilet on the south side of Washington Square.

Despite its proximity to downtown, North Beach was slow to develop. Its first resident appears to have been Juana Briones, a Mexican woman who had a small dairy ranch near present-day Washington Square at least by 1844 and perhaps earlier. But she remained relatively isolated until into the 1860s, when Broadway between Kearny and Montgomery streets (still at that time the southern slope of Telegraph Hill) was graded and was lowered between sixty and seventy feet to its present level. That opened Broadway as a direct route to North Beach from the waterfront, and offered travelers a way to the area that avoided the sordidness of the Barbary Coast just to the south.

North Beach got its name because there actually was a beach on its original northern boundary, about where Francisco Street is today. But in the 1870s, as construction was begun on a seawall near present-day Fisherman's Wharf, the area was filled in and the beach disappeared. That decade also brought a development that really opened up North Beach to greater growth—the laying out of Montgomery Avenue in 1873–74 (the name was changed to Columbus Avenue in 1909). This broad street, cut at a diagonal across the inflexible grid pattern of streets laid out by Jasper O' Farrell in 1847, offered a more direct route to the northern waterfront from downtown. It provided

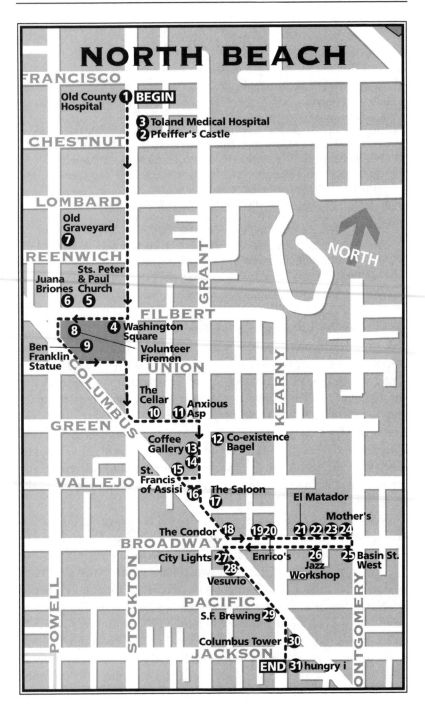

# NORTH BEACH

FRANCISCO

**Old County Hospital** ❶ BEGIN

❸ **Toland Medical Hospital**
❷ **Pfeiffer's Castle**

CHESTNUT

LOMBARD

**Old Graveyard** ❼

REENWICH

**Juana Briones** ❻    **Sts. Peter & Paul Church** ❺

FILBERT

❹ **Washington Square**

❽

**Ben Franklin Statue**    ❾    **Volunteer Firemen**

UNION

**The Cellar** ❿    ⓫ **Anxious Asp**

GREEN

**Coffee Gallery** ⓭    ⓬ **Co-existence Bagel**

⓮
⓯
**St. Francis of Assisi**

VALLEJO

⓰    **The Saloon**
⓱

**El Matador**

**Mother's**

**The Condor** ⓲    ⓳⓴    ㉑㉒㉓㉔

BROADWAY

**City Lights** ㉗    **Enrico's**    ㉖    ㉕ **Basin St. West**
㉘                      **Jazz Workshop**

**Vesuvio**

PACIFIC

**S.F. Brewing** ㉙

**Columbus Tower** ㉚

JACKSON

END ㉛ **hungry i**

GRANT

KEARNY

COLUMBUS

POWELL

STOCKTON

ONTGOMERY

NORTH

# NORTH BEACH

**❶** Site of Old County Hospital and "Old Peoples Home"

**❷** Site of "Pfeiffer's Castle"

**❸** Site of Toland Medical College

**❹** Washington Square

**❺** Saints Peter and Paul Church

**❻** Site of Juana Briones adobe

**❼** Site of Old Graveyard

**❽** Volunteer Firemen Memorial

**❾** Benjamin Franklin statue

**❿** 570 Green Street - Location of The Cellar

**⓫** 528 Green Street - Location of The Anxious Asp

**⓬** 1398 Grant Avenue - Location of the Co-Existence Bagel Shop

**⓭** 1353 Grant Avenue - Location of the Coffee Gallery

**⓮** 1339 Grant Avenue - Location of Coffee and Confusion

**⓯** St. Francis of Assisi Church

**⓰** Caffe Trieste

**⓱** The Saloon - Location of Wagner's Beer Hall

**⓲** The Condor

**⓳** 534 Broadway - site of Old Broadway Jail

**⓴** Enrico's Cafe

**㉑** 492 Broadway - Location of El Matador Nightclub

**㉒** 440 Broadway - Location of Ann's Nightclub

**㉓** 430 Broadway - Location of Mother's Nightclub

**㉔** 412 Broadway - Location of The Stone

**㉕** 401 Broadway - Location of Basin Street West

**㉖** 473 Broadway - Location of The Jazz Workshop

**㉗** City Lights Bookstore

**㉘** Vesuvio Cafe

**㉙** 155 Columbus Avenue - San Francisco Brewing

**㉚** Columbus Tower

**㉛** Site of the hungry i

an additional benefit in that the gore-shaped blocks it created proved ideal for new, small-scale commercial storefronts for barbers, tailors, and other such small businesses. Saloons in particular liked the triangular corners because they could attract customers coming from more than one direction.

North Beach has long had a reputation as San Francisco's "Little Italy." Italians, like many other nationalities, first came to San Francisco in the wake of the gold rush, but the peak period for Italian immigration to the City didn't occur until the 1890s to the 1910s. The earliest arrivals settled on Telegraph Hill because it reminded many of them of the hill towns in their native Italy and, since many earned their living as fishermen, it offered the advantage of being within walking distance of the waterfront. Once Columbus Avenue opened up North Beach for further development, the Italian Telegraph Hill dwellers started migrating down the slope into the area. Although Italians established enclaves elsewhere in the city, especially after about 1920, North Beach, with its strong sense of community, became the de facto headquarters of the community.

After World War II, the Italians of North Beach, like so many others, migrated to the suburbs—Marin County, down the peninsula, or to tonier districts of the City such as the Marina. As the Italians departed, the Chinese moved north across Broadway into the neighborhood. Although North Beach today still has an Italian flavor due to its concentration of Italian restaurants, cafes, delis, and other shops, much of the real estate there now is owned by Chinese Americans.

North Beach is also renowned today for its association with the Beats of the 1950s. The excitement lasted only a few years in the mid-to-late 1950s, when the area—primarily the few blocks centered around the intersection of Grant Avenue and Green Street—became home to coffeehouses and bars that hosted poetry readings and jazz sessions. Allen Ginsburg, Gary Snyder, Lawrence Ferlinghetti, and others formed the nucleus of the poetry renaissance. After the active Beat scene faded, about 1960, Ferlinghetti kept the literary portion alive through his City Lights bookshop.

Starting in the 1950s and '60s, North Beach, particularly along Broadway and Columbus, became the entertainment center of San Francisco. Jazz continued strong into the 1960s but was soon displaced by rock-and-roll and the topless craze, which brought North Beach headlines during that decade. Clubs such as the hungry i and the Purple Onion featured new talent—Woody Allen, Barbara Streisand, Lenny Bruce, the Kingston Trio. The scene changed in the 1970s and '80s as rock, punk rock, and heavy metal pushed most other types of performance art into the background. Today, legitimate entertainment in the area has largely disappeared, having moved on to larger venues. Broadway, in particular, which was once lined with theaters and clubs, is now mostly given over to bars, restaurants, and strip joints.

---

*Start this tour at the southwest corner of Stockton and Francisco streets.*

---

### ❶ Stockton and Francisco streets – SW corner – Site of the Old County Hospital (1857–1872) / Site of the "Old Peoples Home" (1874–1891).

It is hard to picture today, but this one block of Stockton up the hill to Chestnut Street was once the City's "hospital zone." Medical facilities of various kinds were found on both sides of the street. Occupying this corner—now a playground and basketball court for Francisco Middle School—was the County Hospital, the predecessor of today's San Francisco General.

With the closure of the State Marine Hospital in 1855, the state of California left it to the counties to bear the cost of providing medical care for the indigent sick and the insane. After first using the old facility, farther up Stockton Street, in 1857 the City and County of San Francisco purchased an 1854 three-story brick schoolhouse on this site and converted it into a hospital. At the time, this property sat virtually on the shore of the bay: the waterline was only a half a block away, just south of Bay Street.

Because this was the hospital of last resort, so to speak, conditions were less than deluxe. Overcrowding was a common occurrence, staff was in short supply—sometimes necessitating that patients help each other—and clean towels were provided only sporadically. Basic implements such as knives and forks were frequently unavailable and the food was terrible: one patient who had been a prisoner in the notorious Andersonville prison during the Civil War claimed that the food had been better there. If all these indignities were not enough, surgeons, not having separate operating rooms, performed surgeries on tables in the middle of the wards. Since anesthesia was practically non-existent, the surrounding patients not only had to endure the sight of blood as the patient was carved up in their midst but the screams of the poor victim as well.

Of course, surgery was not required for all cases. A hospital report from 1862 shows that the most common ailment treated at the hospital was secondary and tertiary syphilis, followed by rheumatism. In 1872, with no room left for expansion, the hospital moved over to Potrero Avenue where, greatly enlarged, it remains today.

Two years after the hospital moved to Potrero Avenue, the "Old Peoples Home" established itself just to the west of the old main hospital building, perhaps inhabiting one of its added-on structures. The organization was spared destruction by the 1906 calamity, since it moved in 1891 to the southwest corner of Pine and Pierce where it became known as the Crocker Old Peoples Home.

---

*Walk halfway up the west side of Stockton toward Chestnut until you are across from Pfeiffer Alley, which is on the other side of the street. Look up and toward the southeast at the four-story building on the corner of Chestnut.*

---

### ❷ Stockton and Chestnut streets – NE corner – Site of Pfeiffer's Castle (1859–c.1906).

This corner was once the site of a grand house called Pfeiffer's Castle. It was built in 1859 by William Pfeiffer, a German immigrant who had moved to San Francisco from Sacramento with his wife and children. Because of the danger of fire, he built a solid-looking, four-story brick and mortar home that somewhat resembled a castle on the Rhine in his native Germany. Pfeiffer spent so much money building his dream house, however, that it bankrupted him. Evicted from his home less than two years later, he and his family built a rude shack literally in the shadow of his mansion – in the 30 foot wide strip now called Pfeiffer's Alley. When he had been feeling more flush he had deeded this strip of land to the City for use as a city street. But he recalled that although he had signed the deed of transference his wife had not; he therefore concluded that the deed was invalid. To add to his misfortune, the City disagreed: Pfeiffer and his family were re-moved for obstructing a public street.

In 1862 Pfeiffer's Castle was converted into the Home for the Care of the Inebriate, which, given young San Francisco's plethora of saloons serving liquor at all hours, probably had a large clientele. The Home continued in business on this site until the late 1890s, when it was absorbed into St. Marks Hospital.

---

*On the lot just to the north of Pfeiffer's Castle was:*

---

❸ **Stockton and Pfeiffer streets – SE corner – Site of Toland Medical College** (1864–1898).

Constructed here in 1864 was a three-story building, surmounted by a cupola, that housed Toland Medical College. Dr. Hugh Toland was a native of South Carolina who had come to San Francisco in 1852. After a brief stab at mining he established what became a very lucrative medical practice in the City. Part of his success came from filling prescriptions by mail for patients in Mother Lode mining towns. He established a medical school bearing his name after an earlier school under the auspices of the University of the Pacific closed.

In 1870 Toland Medical College became the medical school of the University of California. In 1898, having outgrown its location here, it moved to Parnassus Heights on 20 acres of land donated by Adolph Sutro. It remains there today as the prestigious University of California, San Francisco Medical Center.

---

*Walk three and a half blocks south on Stockton and cross Filbert to the southwest corner of that intersection. Go a few steps into the park.*

---

❹ **Washington Square** (1849).

The concrete bench with the bronze plaque just a short distance into the park commemorates Juana Briones, the first settler of North Beach (more on her a few stops later on this walk). She had a dairy ranch nearby, and in what was the first use of what became Washington Square Park, she grew potatoes and vegetables here. She likely chose this spot because it lay in a valley that was watered by drainage from Telegraph and Russian hills. As the land was more suited for growing produce than for building upon, that is probably what led to its being reserved as a common area.

Washington Square became a city park or "public square" in 1849 when surveyor William Eddy drew up a new official map of San Francisco, one that expanded upon Jasper O'Farrell's plan of only two years earlier. With the discovery of gold in January 1848 things changed dramatically, so this block was set aside to preserve some open space in a city that was rapidly expanding in an uncontrolled manner.

This public square (really a rectangle) was slow to develop into anything resembling a park. Throughout the 1850s Washington Square was a sorry, muddy mess that was mostly used as a dump for the discarded bodies of dead cats and dogs and other refuse. Things improved a bit in 1860 when the local sheriff brought a chain gang over from the Broadway jail to grade the land and water the feeble grass that was starting to sprout. The attention paid Washington Square still didn't suit the Board of Supervisors, however, because in 1869 they ordered that improvements be made. So in the 1870s, trees were planted and a white picket fence was put up around the perimeter to prevent horseback riders from trampling the grass and other vegetation.

After the 1906 earthquake and fire, Washington Square, like all the other city parks, served as a camp for those burned out of their homes. "Refugee cottages"—one-room wooden shacks—were put up here and stood cheek-to-jowl, occupying virtually all of the park. (A couple of refugee shacks similar to the ones used here have been preserved behind the old Presidio Army Museum in the Presidio. They have displays inside and are open to the public.)

Washington Square as it looks today dates mainly from the late 1950s, when noted landscape architect Lawrence Halprin was brought in to carry out a renovation. The traditional cross-hatched diagonal layout of paths, which had prevailed for almost a century, was changed to the more appealing curves that now wind around the edges of the park. In 1966 the Board of Supervisors approved a proposal for an underground parking garage beneath the square, but fortunately it was vetoed by the mayor. A garage would have greatly altered the casual and relaxed ambience that makes Washington Square one of the more delightful parks in San Francisco today.

---

*Walk west on Filbert Street a half a block and stop across from Saints. Peter and Paul Church.*

---

### ❺ 666 Filbert Street – Saints Peter and Paul Church (1924).

Saints Peter and Paul Church.

Called "the marzipan church" by Lawrence Ferlinghetti because of its wedding cake façade, Saints Peter and Paul Church was dedicated in 1924 after more than a decade of construction. Decorative work on the façade continued until 1940. The motto in Italian across the front is the opening line from Dante's *Paradise* and reads: "The glory of Him who moves all things penetrates and glows throughout the universe." The current structure replaces an earlier church that had been erected on the southwest corner of Filbert and Dupont Street (now Grant Avenue) in 1884, and was destroyed in 1906.

In 1923, while the present church was under construction, Cecil B. DeMille used it as a backdrop for his classic movie *The Ten Commandments*. The scenes that were shot here revolved around a crooked building contractor who was cheating on the materials he was using. When the contractor's mother comes to see the work her son was doing, a shoddily constructed wall falls on her and kills her. More excitement surrounded the church shortly after it opened. During 1926–27 there were four separate dynamite bombings or attempted bombings of the church. Several suspects were arrested, but the attacks only came to a halt when police on a stakeout shot and killed a man who tried to flee after leaving sticks of dynamite under a window. The motive for the attacks was never determined.

Saints Peter and Paul for many years served as the touchstone for North Beach's Italian community. Parades for blessing the fleet at Fisherman's Wharf and for Columbus Day always kicked off in front of the church. While these traditions still continue, the reduced Italian presence in North Beach has made such events more symbolic than substantive. Today, only about one quarter of the congregation is of Italian extraction, and the vast majority of those are elderly. About a third of the congregation is now Chinese.

One of Saints Peter and Paul's most famous early parishioners was Joe DiMaggio. The late, great Yankee baseball player grew up in the neighborhood and learned to play ball on the North Beach playground—recently renamed Joe DiMaggio Playground—just a block to the northwest. DiMaggio married his first wife, Dorothy Arnold, in the church in 1939. (His second wife, Marilyn Monroe, he married at San Francisco's City Hall in 1951.) In 1999 his funeral was held here as well.

---

*Continue on Filbert down to the corner of Powell Street. Across the street is:*

---

## ❻ Filbert and Powell streets – NE corner – Site of Juana Briones adobe (c.1844–c.1870s).

The previously mentioned Juana Briones (1802–1889) is credited with being the first resident of North Beach. She and her husband Apollinario (who died in 1845) built an adobe house for themselves and their children close to the intersection of Filbert and Powell streets. One account places it on the northeast corner, or about where the fenced-in church parking lot is today. The adobe was the nucleus of a dairy ranch and farm that provided milk, vegetables, beef and other supplies to sailors ashore from visiting ships. It is even said that Juana sometimes took pity on sailors who deserted and sheltered them from the authorities.

Briones lived here until about 1847. She sold the property in 1858 and moved, perhaps to another ranch she owned in Santa Clara. Her adobe home here may have lasted until as late as the 1870s before being torn down.

---

*Although not directly on the route of this tour, just one block behind the Briones adobe was:*

---

**❼ Powell Street between Greenwich and Lombard – East side – Site of the Old Graveyard** (1847–1850s).

One of the City's early graveyards was established in this location (this was far from downtown at the time) in July 1847 when a soldier from Colonel Stevenson's regiment became the first to be interred here. Others soon followed: by early 1850, when the cemetery closed, about 900 burials had taken place here. Most were buried with little pomp and were laid to rest under simple wooden crosses painted white with black lettering.

The dead got little rest here—numerous indignities were soon visited upon them. In early 1851 Henry Meiggs, who was building his wharf on the north shore, graded this portion of Powell Street at his own expense to smooth the way for traffic wanting to reach his facility. In doing so his workmen exposed some of the graves. Not long after this a portion of the graveyard was converted to a sheep pen. The unkindest cut of all came in 1853 when the City had the bodies removed to the new Yerba Buena Cemetery—where the Civic Center is today. The contractor hired to do the job cared so little for the niceties that coffins were broken into pieces and the human remains were unceremoniously tossed into carts before being hauled away. And he didn't even get all of them: several years later there were still reports of skeletons being unearthed.

---

*Round the corner of the park and head up Columbus, but only go about 10 yards. To your left inside the park is the first of two public monuments.*

---

**❽ Volunteer Firemen Memorial** (1933).

This large bronze sculpture, done in heroic style by local sculptor Haig Patigian, commemorates the volunteer firemen of San Francisco who organized and ran their own fire fighting companies from 1849 until 1866, when a paid, professional, city-run operation came into being. It was a bequest of Lillie Hitchcock Coit (see Telegraph Hill walk) who earmarked $50,000 for it in her will. There was some talk of placing the statue on Telegraph Hill near Coit Tower but it ended up here instead.

---

*Walk a few steps farther up the sidewalk on Columbus. Framed by the two big trees here you will see in the center of the lawn partly encircled by half a dozen Lombardy poplar trees a statue of Ben Franklin atop a granite base. Go across the lawn for a closer look at the statue and the inscriptions on the sides of the base.*

---

### ❾ Benjamin Franklin statue (1879).

This statue, which once served as a drinking fountain, was donated to the City in 1879 by Henry D. Cogswell, a prosperous dentist and temperance advocate. Cogswell pledged to erect one statue/fountain for every 100 saloons in the City. He never made good on that boast, but his sanctimoniousness combined with the fact that most of his statues were of himself, arms extended with a temperance pledge in one hand and a glass of water in the other, did not sit well with San Franciscans or with those in most other cities and towns across the U.S. where he had them erected. Most of the statues were dismantled in short order: this may be the last one left in the country.

The granite base of the statue has several inscriptions. The most noteworthy are the two referring to time capsules: one was opened in 1979 and the other is to be unlocked in 2079. On the statue's 100th anniversary the original time capsule was opened in a festive ceremony attended by then Mayor Dianne Feinstein and other local dignitaries. Some of the items found inside the metal box in the granite shaft were parts of 18 newspapers, gold police buttons, an illustrated souvenir book of San Francisco, and a manual for streetcar conductors with such rules of conduct as "Be civil and attentive, as becomes a gentleman. . . ." A most curious object was also discovered—a tooth allegedly extracted from the French revolutionary Robespierre.

When the monument was put back together a new time capsule was inserted. Some of the items placed in it are two signed poems by Lawrence Ferlinghetti, a pair of Levi's jeans, menus from various restaurants, predictions about the future from local columnists and others and, in the ultimate slap at temperance advocate Cogswell, a bottle of cabernet sauvignon wine.

This monument originally stood at the gore corner of Kearny Street and Columbus Avenue, in front of where the Columbus Tower is today. It was moved here in 1904. The statue of Benjamin Franklin is made of ordinary pot metal (equal parts tin, lead, and zinc), not bronze. Cogswell was a philanthropist but apparently not the "spare no expense" kind. Before moving on to the next stop look at the back side of the granite shaft where its benefactor left this cheery inscription: "Presented by H.D. Cogswell to Our Boys and Girls Who Will Soon Take Our Place and Pass On."

---

*Walk south out of the park to the corner of Columbus and Union streets. Head east on Union Street on the rim of the park. One or two locations along the way will afford fine views of Saints Peter and Paul Church across the park. At Stockton Street, cross Union and go up one block to Green Street and turn left. A few doors up on the left hand side is:*

---

**⑩ 570 Green Street – Location of The Cellar** (1956–c.1962).

A 1958 guidebook to bohemian San Francisco declared "If you're looking for the `beat generation' you'll find it here." Located in the basement of 570 Green Street (the address then was 576 Green and the entrance was through the doors to the left of Caffé Sport) was a jazz club called The Cellar. In February 1957, Lawrence Ferlinghetti and Kenneth Rexroth gave a poetry reading here while a jazz quintet played behind them. This simultaneous melding of two loves of the Beat generation—poetry and jazz—captured the attention of the national media: *Time* and *Life* magazines both did stories on it. This marrying of poetry to jazz was an attempt to reach a wider audience for poetry. Although it was an interesting experiment it did not last long. Ferlinghetti liked the extra exposure it was bringing to poetry, but the jazz background proved distracting. "You ended up sounding like you were hawking fish on the street corner trying to be heard above the din," he said.

---

*A few doors farther down Green Street is:*

---

### ⓫ 528 Green Street – Site of the Anxious Asp (1956-1967).

This cubby hole of a place, lately a retail store, was once a café and bar and was another favored hangout of the Beats. Jack Kerouac and others read their poetry here. A notable attraction was the restroom—the wallpaper consisted of pages of the Kinsey Report, the ground-breaking book on sexuality that had recently been published. Janis Joplin hung out here in the 1960s, drinking and playing pool.

*Walk up to the corner of Grant Avenue. On the southwest corner of the intersection during that time was:*

### ⓬ 1398 Grant Avenue – Location of the Co-Existence Bagel Shop (1957–1960).

**This stretch of Grant— from Filbert Street, two blocks to the north, to Vallejo Street, one block farther south, was the heart of "Beat" San Francisco. One writer of the time called it "an open-air mental hospital three blocks long."**

One of the prime haunts of the Beats was a delicatessen/beer bar located here that was called the Co-Existence Bagel Shop. Oddly, it didn't serve bagels, but it was open until 4 a.m. on weekends, which made it a popular late night spot. The walls were covered with art from local talent and its jukebox stocked only progressive jazz records.

Political and social activism was starting to bloom then in what was still an essentially conservative time, and the Bagel Shop became a kind of rallying point for the disaffected. As such it was frequently the target of the police, who particularly had it in for a frequent patron, poet Bob Kaufman, an African American. That Kaufman was a poet was bad enough for the cops, but the fact that he was married to a white woman further drew their ire. Kaufman was arrested numerous times on flimsy charges.

By late 1960, with the Beat movement largely spent and with the continuing police scrutiny, the Co-Existence Bagel Shop closed—but not before someone painted a swastika on the police call box on the corner.

*Cross Green Street and go south on Grant Avenue. A few doors down on the right side is:*

### ⓭ 1353 Grant Avenue – Location of the Coffee Gallery
(1954–1980).

Originally bearing the rather prim name of Miss Smith's Tea Room, then later the Coffee Gallery, and still later the Lost and Found Saloon, this place went from being a tea room/coffeehouse to a folk music club to a raunchy rock bar before finally closing in 2000. (It has subsequently reopened). The venue was mainly noted for its rock clientele. Janis Joplin, Grace Slick, and Led Zeppelin are some of the performers and bands that played here.

### ⓮ 1339 Grant Avenue – Location of Coffee and Confusion
(c.1962–1969).

Just a few doors down the street, another coffeehouse of the era was the Coffee and Confusion. Its stage primarily hosted folk musicians, but Janis Joplin shook the place up in January 1963 when she first arrived in San Francisco from her home state of Texas. In town for barely 24 hours, she mounted the stage and wowed the crowd with her powerful vocals. A hat was passed after the performance—something that had never happened before—and $14 was collected.

---

*Continue the half block down Grant to Vallejo Street and turn right. The Gothic church at the intersection of Columbus is:*

---

### ⓯ 610 Vallejo Street – St. Francis of Assisi Church (1860).

The oldest building still extant in North Beach, St. Francis of Assisi Church, named for San Francisco's patron saint, was constructed between 1857 and 1860. The church—especially its interior—is a fine example of the Gothic Revival style that prevailed in the Victorian era. The surroundings certainly have changed in the last century and a half, but the church looks today much as it did then, the only major changes being that its red brick walls have been covered with cement and painted white, and dart-shaped spires have been added to the twin towers.

The site's origins as a place of worship actually go back to 1849, when services were first held here by a group of French Catholics in a simple wood-frame building that they had erected. Two years later

St. Francis of Assisi Church.

that structure was replaced by a chapel made of adobe. With Mission Dolores the only other Catholic place of worship until St. Mary's Cathedral was built at Grant Avenue and California Street in 1854, the St. Francis congregation grew rapidly: services were soon offered in English, Spanish, and Italian, as well as French. The original parishioners, wanting to maintain their own house, soon moved over to Bush Street, where they established Notre Dame des Victoires.

The 1906 earthquake left the walls of St. Francis of Assisi standing, but the ensuing fire gutted the interior. A steel frame was added, the church was refurbished, and it was rededicated in 1918. In 1994, after nearly a century and a half as an active parish, the church was closed as part of a downsizing move on the part of the Archdiocese. It reopened in the late 1990s with a new status, that of National Shrine of St. Francis of Assisi. (Shrines are places where religious relics are kept.)

---

*Cross over to the south side of Vallejo Street and walk the short distance to the southeast corner of Vallejo and Grant. From here you will have the best view of the façade of the church. The café on this corner is:*

---

### ⑯ 609 Vallejo Street – Caffe Trieste (since 1956).

Here since 1956, the Caffe Trieste is one of the few hangouts left from the Beat era. It's also notable because it's relatively unchanged from those days. Owned by the Giotta family since its opening, it was named for their native Trieste, Italy. The café is a favorite gathering place for locals and for poets and writers. Movie director Francis Coppola wrote parts of the screenplay for *The Godfather* here.

---

*Round the corner on Grant Avenue. Across Grant, on the northeast corner of Grant and Fresno Alley is:*

---

### ⑰ 1232 Grant Avenue – Location of Wagner's Beer Hall (1861–1884).

Opened in 1861 — and in continuous operation ever since — this is the oldest saloon in San Francisco. Originally called Wagner's Beer Hall, it was the namesake saloon of Ferdinand Wagner, an immigrant from the Alsace region of France who arrived in San Francisco in 1852 after a stint as a saloonkeeper in New Orleans. Forgoing the usual stab at gold mining, he worked first as a hotel manager and then as a fruit vendor before opening his saloon. Wagner, his wife, and two sons, one of whom continued on with the business after he retired, lived on the two floors above.

The building housing the present saloon on the site looks remarkably like it did in an 1870s photograph. And inside, the bar itself is the 1861 original. The establishment escaped destruction in 1906 when a U.S. Navy frigate berthed on the northern waterfront ran a hose over Telegraph Hill to this area and pumped water from the bay to fight the flames. It may have even been the same hose and crew that prevented the blaze from destroying Jackson Square and its wholesale liquor warehouses.

> A disproportionate number of liquor warehouses and saloons—including Wagner's Beer Hall—managed to survive the 1906 fire. Thirsty firefighters obviously had their priorities.

---

*Go down to Columbus Avenue to the corner of Broadway.*

---

### ⑱ 300 Columbus Avenue – The Condor (1959–1991).

The Condor was once the most famous of all the topless joints that clustered in the Broadway/Columbus area of North Beach in the 1960s. The topless craze, which soon spread to other cities, started here in San Francisco in 1964 when Carol Doda, a dancer at the club, was told to wear one of the new topless bathing suits that were all the rage that year. Flat-chested at the time, Doda soon began a series of silicone injections that inflated her breasts and the coffers of the club from patrons who came to have a look-see.

The topless mania was such that by 1967 close to 30 clubs in North Beach featured nudity. All vied to outdo the others. One, for example, headlined "Gaye Spiegelman - Topless Mother of Eight." Things went further in 1969 when even the G-strings were dispensed with and bottomless joined the list of firsts—started at the Condor, of course. Things eventually bottomed out, so to speak, in the 1970s. Changing times and tastes, and the invention of the VCR in 1975, which enabled people to watch nudity and sex in the privacy of their own homes, led to a lessening of the appeal of striptease. Carol Doda retired in 1982. The Condor continued as a strip joint until 1991. It then became a restaurant before reverting to striptease in 2007.

Inside the restaurant the top part of the Condor sign with its trademark red-light-bulb nipples has been preserved. On the walls in one section are photos of Doda and other strippers.

Before the Condor strip club ceased operations it was the scene of a bizarre accidental death. For the finale of her act in later years Carol Doda would stand on a baby grand piano that would be hoisted to the ceiling, where she would disappear through a small hole. By 1983 she had left the stage but the piano routine continued with other dancers. One night, after the show had closed, the club's manager and his girlfriend, one of the strippers, were lying on the piano when they accidentally hit the lever and were hoisted to the ceiling. The manager — who was clothed — was crushed to death. His traumatized girlfriend was discovered under him by the janitor the next morning.

---

*Go a half a block east on Broadway. On the northeast corner of Broadway and Romolo Alley is:*

---

### ⓲ 534 Broadway – Site of Old Broadway Jail (1851–1906) / Location of the Swiss-American Hotel (1910–1984).

Going back to the early days of San Francisco for a moment, this corner was the site, starting in 1851, of the Old Broadway Jail—the

City's first real prison. A three-story Norman-style brick and stone edifice, it was a damp and dark fortress that could hold up to 200 prisoners.

The shooting of newspaper editor James King of William in May 1856 and sites related to it are covered elsewhere in this book (see Financial District and Portsmouth

The Old Broadway Jail (at right) April 2, 1906.

Square walks), but part of that story happened at the jail. King's assassin, James Casey, was held here in the days after the shooting. Vigilance Committee members (a group made up largely of local merchants who banded together to combat what they saw as out-of-control lawlessness) mustered their forces and converged on the jail on May 18, 1856. As a large crowd of spectators watched, hundreds of Vigilance Committee members bearing rifles, shotguns, and whatever weapons were at hand, surrounded the jail. The Vigilance Committee's aim was to have Casey (and another prisoner, Charles Cora) turned over to them for trial. To prove they meant business a small brass cannon was stationed across the street and pointed at the jail, a lighted match at the ready. Faced with such overwhelming force, David Scannell, the sheriff, had no choice but to hand over the prisoners. Casey, who had requested that he not be dragged through the streets, went first and was led to a carriage waiting at the corner of Broadway and Dupont (now Grant Avenue). Despite the tension in the air and the gravity of the moment, one eyewitness recalled the utter silence that accompanied the drama. The only sound that could be heard, he said, was the crunch of the carriage's wheels as it rolled away from the scene.

A little over a hundred years later another person would cause some commotion here. He was not a murderer though. He was a comedian with a penchant for spewing four-letter and longer words. His name was Lenny Bruce. In 1965 he was at the end of his controversial career (and life for that matter; he died the following year).

The building that stands here now was then the Swiss-American Hotel. Bruce was staying here when early in the morning of March 29 he jumped or fell out of the second floor bow-fronted window closest to Romolo Street and landed on the sidewalk 25 feet below. He fractured bones in both ankles and one in his left hip. He was taken to San Francisco General Hospital, where the foul-mouthed comic managed to offend his handlers to the point that doctors had to tape his mouth shut.

Accounts vary as to why he jumped or fell. That he was high on drugs seems certain. But whether he was threatening Eric Miller, a guitar-player friend of his in the room, that he would jump out the window unless he kissed him, as Enrico Banducci stated in an interview some years ago, or he simply got carried away in an argument about censorship and accidentally fell, as a *Chronicle* news story had it, is unclear. Eric Miller did run downstairs right afterward and kissed his friend on the sidewalk. The *Chronicle* reporter quoted Bruce as saying: "We always kiss each other. It's not a sexual thing. We dig each other." So Banducci's version is probably the correct one.

---

*Just a few steps farther down Broadway is:*

---

**⑳ 504 Broadway – Enrico's** (since 1958).

Enrico's is a San Francisco institution—the closest thing the City has to a Montparnasse café. It was opened the day after Thanksgiving in 1958 by flamboyant impresario Enrico Banducci. Banducci, owner of the nationally renowned cabaret and nightclub, the hungry i (see the end of the chapter for more details), said he wanted a "sandals and sables" type of place as an accompaniment to his successful cabaret. And in the early days that pretty much described it, as artists, writers, and hookers and their pimps sometimes mixed with café society.

Enrico's is officially known as Enrico's Coffeehouse, the idea originally being that it would sell imported coffees, but that never took root and it has always been more of a bar and restaurant—with the emphasis on the former. A great number of celebrities, many of them drawn by their friendship with the ebullient proprietor, have graced its portals: writers Norman Mailer and Herb Gold; filmmakers John

Huston and Francis Coppola; performers Barbra Streisand and Bill Cosby, to name some. Those were the glory days. But Banducci sold the business in 1988, and the clientele has changed. A few regulars and local characters still call it home, but the crowd today, especially on weekends, is heavy on the dot-com types and the young who are discovering the City and making it their own, just as previous generations have done before them.

---

*Cross Kearny Street. A couple of doors up on the left is:*

---

**㉑ 498 Broadway – Location of the El Matador Nightclub** (1953–1963).

A popular nightspot of a bygone era was the El Matador, which was owned by artist, writer, and bullfight aficionado Barnaby Conrad. Herb Caen compared the place to Rick's in Casablanca because everyone went there. Certainly the big celebrities of the day did: Frank Sinatra, Marilyn Monroe, and John Wayne were among the stellar lights who drank, joked, and swapped stories here. (The place has changed hands, been renamed, and remodeled numerous times since the El Matador closed in 1963.) Conrad wrote a book of amusing stories, appropriately called *Name Dropping*, about the stars who visited his club.

---

*A few doors farther down is:*

---

**㉒ 440 Broadway – Location of Ann's Nightclub** (c.1953–1960).

Four-forty Broadway once housed Ann's, a nightclub with a lesbian clientele that in January 1958 took a chance on a virtually unknown comic named Lenny Bruce (1925–1966). Bruce, who had started his career doing imitations and other routine fare, by the late 1950s turned to the raw, emotionally charged, scatological, meant-to-shock brand of humor that soon became his trademark. It brought him great notoriety along with police busts in many cities for obscenity and illegal drug use.

Despite the City's reputation for tolerance, conservative mores were still the norm in the 1950s, even in San Francisco. Bruce's tryout of his new material at Ann's created a sensation and quickly brought him notice. *Chronicle* columnist Herb Caen and jazz critic Ralph J. Gleason wrote about him. Lawrence Ferlinghetti and the Beat poets came to watch. Another local who came to the club was Saul Zaentz, the chief executive at the time of Berkeley-based Fantasy Records. Zaentz signed Bruce to his first recording contract. (Zaentz later turned to movies, producing Academy Award winners *One Flew Over the Cuckoo's Nest, Amadeus,* and *The English Patient* among other films.) Even Hugh Hefner flew in from his mansion in Chicago to see what the fuss was about; he persuaded Bruce to come to Chicago and perform there.

Bruce quickly grew too big for Ann's, but he made appearances at other San Francisco clubs up until almost the time of his death.

### ㉓ 430 Broadway – Location of Mother's Nightclub
(1965–1966).

Originally a folk-music and then blues club called Sugar Hill which presented such legends of the blues as John Lee Hooker, T-Bone Walker, and Lightnin' Hopkins, Mother's changed its format in 1965 to psychedelic when rock became ascendant. The Lovin' Spoonful played here just as their first single, "Do You Believe in Magic," became a hit. They were shortly followed by two other local bands who became even bigger—Grace Slick (with The Great Society then), and the Grateful Dead. Its time as a rock venue was short; the club closed in 1966.

---

*A few doors farther down Broadway was:*

---

### ㉔ 412 Broadway – Location of Mr. D's (1967–1973) and The Stone (1980–1995).

Now an upscale strip club and much remodeled, this location was for nearly three decades one of the City's top venues for pop entertainment. Keeping step with the latest in musical trends, it booked a wide range of entertainment over the years. Originally called Mr. D's because it was partially owned at the time by Sammy Davis, Jr., it opened in 1967 with Tony Bennett as the headliner. By the early 1970s it had changed its format to soul, blues, and reggae. Bob Marley and the Wailers played here to sold-out houses in 1973 in their first major

U.S. gig. In 1980 the ownership and the name changed to The Stone. Many soul greats played here including James Brown, the Temptations, and the Four Tops. Later in the 1980s and into the early 1990s the club switched to booking heavy metal groups such as Metallica. The Stone closed in 1995.

---

*At Montgomery, cross to the south side of Broadway. On the corner is:*

---

**㉕ 401 Broadway – Location of Basin Street West** (1964–1973).

Basin Street West opened as a jazz club in 1964, but all sorts of talent has played here including some of the soul superstars of that time—Otis Redding, Smokey Robinson and the Miracles, and Ike and Tina Turner. Lenny Bruce, who did his act in a number of places in the 400 block of Broadway, also performed here. In fact, he had appeared here only hours before he fell out the window at the Swiss-American Hotel. In the spring of 1966 Bruce recorded his act here for the cameras. Since he died only a few months later, it remains the only surviving taped record of his nightclub routines.

Since closing as a nightclub in 1973 this venue has been variously a Korean restaurant and bars of different names. Yet the interior appears to have changed little since its nightclub days, with a platform stage and banquettes seating arrangement.

---

*Walk west on Broadway down to:*

---

**㉖ 473 Broadway – Location of the Jazz Workshop** (1957–1971).

San Francisco was once a great town in which to hear live jazz. Probably the premier club from the late 1950s to the late 1960s was the Jazz Workshop. Miles Davis, John Coltrane, and Cannonball Adderley are a few of the greats who played here. Lenny Bruce made news when he was arrested here on October 4, 1961—his first bust for obscenity. He won an acquittal—the only one of his life—but that didn't prevent cops in other cities from bringing similar charges. The last five years of his life, from this incident onward, proved a continuing series of arrests and trials on obscenity and drug charges.

*Continue west on Broadway to Columbus Avenue. Cross Columbus, take a
left, and stop in front of:*

**❷ 261 Columbus Avenue – City Lights Bookstore** (since 1953).

One of the landmarks of the Beat Era, and indeed of San Francisco itself, City Lights today enjoys a national and international reputation for both its publishing arm and its bookstore, which sells the best in great and experimental literature and poetry. It began modestly in 1953 when Lawrence Ferlinghetti and his then partner, Peter Martin, opened the store as a way of supporting their struggling literary magazine, *City Lights*. The magazine did not last, but the bookstore— said to be the first paperback only bookshop in the United States— was an immediate success. The original store, which occupied just the pie-shaped corner of the 1907 building it inhabits, has expanded over the years into the basement and next door as well. It recently added a poetry-only room upstairs.

City Lights made headlines and history in 1957 when owner Lawrence Ferlinghetti was arrested by San Francisco police for selling an allegedly obscene work, poet Allen Ginsburg's *Howl*, which Ferlinghetti had recently published and which he sold in his store. After a celebrated trial and a not-guilty verdict, in which the poem was ruled to have "redeeming social value" and was not obscene, Ferlinghetti became a First Amendment hero and a national figure.

The bookstore has been frequented over the years by local and visiting writers of all kinds. During its early years especially, many of the greats from the Beat era—Allen Ginsburg, Jack Kerouac, Neal Cassady, Michael McClure, and Philip Whalen, hung out here—giving meaning to the store's slogan, "A Literary Meetingplace Since 1953."

This location's literary associations actually go back to the time of the building's first occupancy, in 1907. The first tenant was A. Cavalli, an Italian-language bookstore whose clientele was North Beach's large Italian community. About 1921 Cavalli moved across the alley to where Vesuvio is today, and in 1934 moved from there to its present location on Stockton Street just off Columbus Avenue. Started in 1880, A. Cavalli is the oldest Italian-owned business in San Francisco today.

## ❷❽ 255 Columbus Avenue – Vesuvio Café (since 1949).

Just across Jack Kerouac Alley (the former Adler Place) from City Lights is Vesuvio Café. It was opened in 1949 by Henri Lenoir, a French émigré with a bohemian sensibility grounded in a sense of the absurd. After the term "beatnik" gained currency in the late 1950s, Lenoir put a sign in Vesuvio's window advertising a "Beatnik Kit," whose elements included a turtleneck, sunglasses, and sandals. "Don't Envy Beatniks. Be One!" blared the ad's headline. It was Lenoir's way of spoofing, of course, the uniform the coffeehouse idlers of the time were wearing.

Lenoir did have a knack for creating saloons that attracted artists, writers, and musicians. Cozy Vesuvio with its gas-fired chandelier (a real rarity in the age of electricity) and its bric-a-brac, antique shop décor creates just the sort of non-conformist atmosphere that appeals to many creative types. It especially found favor with the Beat writers for that reason, and the fact that it was just steps away from their literary Mecca, City Lights. Jack Kerouac, no slouch when it came to imbibing, felt at home here. The author of the classic

Henri Lenoir in front of Vesuvio.

*On The Road* came in for a drink one evening in 1960 before going to Big Sur to meet author Henry Miller, who had admired Kerouac's work and had invited him down to his coastal retreat. Kerouac called Miller several times that evening to let him know that he was still coming, but instead got drunk and spent the night in San Francisco. The two never did meet.

---

*Walk south on Columbus and cross Pacific Avenue. The brew pub on the corner is:*

---

## ❷❾ 155 Columbus Avenue (1907) - San Francisco Brewing Company – Formerly the Andromeda Saloon.

The interior of this bar (now a brew pub) is worth a look because the décor evokes a post-1906 Barbary Coast saloon—which is appropriate, since this corner was practically the heart of the old Barbary Coast. This saloon still has some of its original furnishings: the bar, which is made of one solid piece of mahogany; the ceiling, which appears to be made of pressed tin; and the cracked and stained tile drain, which wraps around the foot of the bar below the level of the floor. The latter made for ease of use in cleaning up since beer suds and floor debris could be easily swept into this gutter and then flushed away. Other pieces of décor that add to the atmosphere are the 1916 punkah-walla fan, powered by a small motor and spinning lazily overhead, and the circa-1907 upright piano.

"Legend has it..." is a common qualifier when a story is unverifiable or based on hearsay. When it comes to this saloon, legend has it that notorious gangster George "Baby Face" Nelson was once arrested here by the FBI. Inasmuch as Nelson was Public Enemy Number One on the FBI's Ten Most Wanted List in 1934 when he was on the lam in California for a couple of months, if he had been arrested here, not only would it have made the papers, it would have been front-page news. No such thing happened. But there is one interesting tidbit that lends credence to the fact that he might once have been in this bar. Nelson was killed in a vicious machine gun battle with FBI agents (he took two of them with him) in rural Illinois in November 1934. Two months later federal authorities arrested close to a dozen Bay Area residents and charged them with harboring Nelson when he was a fugitive. One of those arrested was a bartender here at 155 Columbus.

Legend also has it that famed prizefighter Jack Dempsey was once a bouncer here but that appears not to be true. When he first visited San Francisco in late 1916 or early 1917 he was married and already a professional boxer. Dempsey also stated in his autobiography that he never worked as a bouncer at a bar at any time in his life.

---

*Walk a few steps farther along Columbus Avenue past the bar's entrance.*

*The flatiron building with the distinctive copper-clad bay windows and tower on the gore intersection of Kearny Street and Columbus is:*

## ③ 916 Kearny Street – Columbus Tower (1907).

Under construction in 1906 when the earthquake hit, the Sentinel Tower, as this building was called then, suffered little damage and was completed in 1907. It was built by Abraham Ruef (1864–1936) a notorious political boss and fixer who was at his peak at the time. Ruef, who was the power behind Mayor Eugene Schmitz, extorted money from all sorts of people and organizations that had business with the City. Events soon caught up to him, however. He was convicted of extortion and sentenced to San Quentin prison. Upon his conviction, when a reporter asked the dapper Ruef how he'd fare exchanging his natty attire for prison stripes, he replied: "The zebra is one of the most beautiful and graceful of animals. Why, therefore, should I cavil at my attire." When he was released, in 1915, he set up a modest two-room real estate office on the fourth floor here. The name plate on the door read "A. Ruef. Ideas, Investments, and Real Estate."

The Columbus Tower has an extensive basement that has served a variety of purposes over the years. In the early days it housed a restaurant called Caesar's, and it was here, allegedly ("legend has it . . ."), that the Caesar salad was invented. During Prohibition it became a speakeasy called Neptune's Grotto. In 1949 the original hungry i opened here, and only moved to its new and most famous location at 599 Jackson Street (see next entry) when evicted by the fire marshal in 1953. In the 1960s the basement served as a recording studio; the Grateful Dead recorded their second album here.

In recent decades Columbus Tower's above-ground offices have attracted tenants associated with the performing arts—booking agents, talent scouts, etc. The building's ownership has perhaps had something to do with that. The Kingston Trio owned it in the 1960s. Today it is owned by filmmaker Francis Coppola.

---

*Cross Kearny Street and walk past Columbus Tower. Cross Jackson Street to the corner of Jackson and Kearny.*

### ❸ Jackson and Kearny streets – SE corner
### – Site of the hungry i nightclub (1953–1967).

This corner merits a place not only in San Francisco history but in the history of show business as well. In the 1950s and '60s it was the site of the hungry i nightclub, one of the nation's premier showcases of new talent. To say that it was physically unprepossessing would be an understatement. Located in the basement of a third-rate hotel housing mostly elderly Filipino bachelors, the décor consisted of bare brick walls with exposed, leaking pipes overhead. The audience sat on folding chairs. Yet it had such a reputation that major stars of the day such as Frank Sinatra and Gregory Peck could be found in the audience when they were in town.

Run by local impresario Enrico Banducci, the "i" presented new singers, comedians, and other entertainers, a large percentage of whom went on to become household names.

Two performers who would later be superstars, Woody Allen and Barbra Streisand, appeared on the same bill for three memorable weeks in 1961. Streisand, only 19 years old, carried herself with the aplomb of a veteran. But Allen, although he had a solid reputation as a writer of comedy material for others, was just starting out with his own stand-up act. He was facing one of his first audiences when he appeared at the hungry i, and his initial show was a disaster. Ten minutes into his routine he froze. The silence of the room combined with the drilling he was taking from two hecklers who had zeroed in on him proved too much. He turned his back to the audience and started mumbling to the brick wall. Banducci had to kill the lights to get Allen off the stage. He recovered by the next night, and he and Streisand proved to be smash hits, playing to capacity crowds by the end of their run.

The late 1950s and early 1960s was a golden era for the hungry i, but by the end of the '60s things had changed. The encroachment of television and the ascendancy of rock music altered the circumstances that had nurtured emerging talent. In December 1967 the hungry i shut its doors. It reopened in plusher surroundings at Ghirardelli Square in October 1968, but only lasted a little more than a year, closing for good on January 4, 1970. Only the name remains. Banducci sold that to a strip club on Broadway for $10,000.

# Enrico Banducci

## (1922–2007)

A legend in his own time is an overworked phrase but it really applied to the Bandooch!, the ebullient and colorful impresario and café owner who was a North Beach fixture for over half a century. Born Harry Charles Banducci in Bakersfield— he took the name Enrico from Enrico Caruso because it had more of a ring to it than Harry—he arrived in San Francisco in 1936 at age 14, a precocious itinerant violinist with show business in his blood. When he realized he wasn't going to make it as a professional violinist he turned to his other love, food, opening a restaurant, Enrico's Fine Foods, on Bush Street in the Tenderloin. It was there that he first donned his trademark beret. When a city health inspector came in one day and told him he had to have his head covered, Banducci grabbed the beret off the head of Luba, his wife at the time, and planted it on his own. (He doesn't seem ever to have been photographed without it.)

**Enrico Banducci.**

In 1950 Banducci purchased, on a shoestring, a struggling bar with a small performance stage called the hungry i, which was located in the basement of the Columbus Tower, a none-too-promising location. (Banducci always claimed the "i" stood for id but others, more plausibly, claimed it meant intellectual.) He somehow managed to stay afloat for a few years until forced out by the fire marshal; the hungry i moved a block away to 599 Jackson. There, over the next decade in his new basement cabaret, Enrico made his reputation as a man with an eye for talent as he booked any number of performers who were virtually unknown at the time but who went on to great success. Some of the names: Woody Allen, Barbra Streisand, Bill Cosby, Bob Newhart, Mort Sahl, Lenny Bruce, Phyllis Diller, Dick Gregory, Richard Pryor, Jonathan Winters.

In 1958 Enrico opened his namesake café, Enrico's, on Broadway, largely to give his vivacious fifth wife, Susie, a venue for her creative energies. But he spent plenty of time there holding court, and with his connections to the entertainment world the café proved a natural magnet for celebrities and those who wanted to rub shoulders with them.

Despite his success, the details of running a business were never a priority for Enrico Banducci. When he needed pocket money it was not unusual for him to grab a fistful of twenty dollar bills from the cash register and then walk out the door without even telling anyone how much he had taken. "It's my money," he would bellow, if anyone tried to stop him. Because of this cavalier attitude toward keeping the books Banducci sometimes found himself in trouble with the Internal Revenue Service. Several times both the hungry i and Enrico's were shut down for such things as failing to pay employees' withholding taxes. Only the financial assistance of Bill Cosby and a few other friends, who came through with last-minute loans, helped him reopen.

The hungry i closed for good in 1970 and Enrico sold his café in 1988 and retired. He joined his son, Gregory, in Richmond, Virginia for a time in the 1990s, where he helped him run a hot-dog stand. He returned to the Bay Area in 1999, where he spent his final years as the grand old man of a grand era of entertainment in San Francisco.

# Pacific Heights

**Length:** 1.3 miles / 2.1 kilometers.
**Time:** 1½ hours (3 hours or so total if you tour the Haas-Lilienthal House).
**Walk Rating:** Moderate.
**Hills:** California Street between Franklin and Gough, and Octavia Street between California and Sacramento, are slight to moderate uphill grades. It is also a moderate uphill climb from the entrance of Lafayette Park to its summit. Washington Street between Gough and Franklin (after stop 10) is a steep downhill.
**Public Transit:** Muni bus lines 47 and 49 run along Van Ness Avenue, the 22 goes along Fillmore, and the 12 runs east on Washington Street and west on Jackson through Pacific Heights.
**Parking:** Street parking is generally not too difficult, but there is a two-hour limit for those without residential parking stickers. Also check curbside street signs for street-cleaning days.
**Restrooms:** There is a public restroom in Lafayette Park just below the summit, to the east of the children's playground.

Pacific Heights today is one of San Francisco's choice residential districts. But in the early days of the City's history it was nothing more than a sandy void with occasional footpaths winding through the chaparral and underbrush. Incentive to settle the area didn't get its first boost until 1855–56 with the passage of the Van Ness Ordinance, under which city surveyors laid out a 500-block parcel between Larkin Street and Divisadero (which includes Pacific Heights), known as the Western Addition. More importantly, the ordinance granted legal title to squatters in the area, thus easing ownership concerns for those already there and for future settlers.

The real spur to development didn't come until the 1870s when cable car lines first extended west of Van Ness Avenue, initially on Clay and then on California Street. A Washington Street line came in 1887, and by 1900 most of the east-west streets leading from downtown into the district had transit lines on them.

Residential housing in the form of single-family homes came to the area starting in the 1870s, and from then until 1906 the well-to-do built large houses on corner lots while those of more modest means built on the lots in between. After the 1906 earthquake and fire

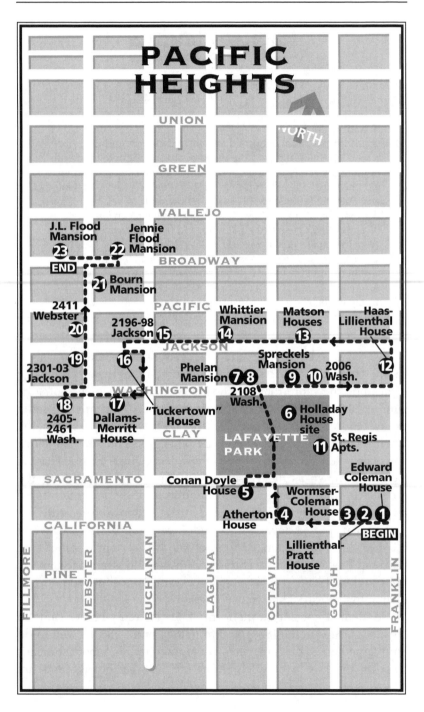

# PACIFIC HEIGHTS

UNION

GREEN

VALLEJO

**J.L. Flood Mansion** **23** **Jennie Flood Mansion** **22**

**END**

BROADWAY

**Bourn Mansion** **21**

**2411 Webster** **20**

PACIFIC

**Whittier Mansion** **14** **Matson Houses** **13** **Haas-Lillienthal House**

**2196-98 Jackson** **15**

JACKSON

**2301-03 Jackson** **19**

**16**

**Spreckels Mansion**

**Phelan Mansion** **7** **8** **9** **10** **2006 Wash.** **12**

WASHINGTON

**2108 Wash.**

**2405-2461 Wash.** **18** **Dallams-Merritt House** **17**

**"Tuckertown" House**

CLAY

**Holladay House site** **6**

LAFAYETTE PARK

**St. Regis Apts.** **11**

SACRAMENTO

**Conan Doyle House** **5**

**Edward Coleman House**

**Atherton House** **4** **Wormser-Coleman House** **3** **2** **1**

CALIFORNIA

**BEGIN**

**Lillienthal-Pratt House**

FILLMORE

PINE

WEBSTER

BUCHANAN

LAGUNA

OCTAVIA

GOUGH

FRANKLIN

# PACIFIC HEIGHTS

❶ 1701 Franklin Street - Edward Coleman House

❷ 1818 Franklin Street - Lilienthal-Pratt House

❸ 1834 Franklin Street - Wormser-Coleman House

❹ 1990 California Street - Atherton House

❺ 2151 Sacramento Street - Sir Arthur Conan Doyle House

❻ Lafayette Park - Site of Samuel Holladay House

❼ 2150 Washington Street - James Duval Phelan Mansion

❽ 2108 Washington Street

❾ 2080 Washington Street - Spreckels Mansion

❿ 2006 Washington Street

⓫ 1925 Gough Street - St. Regis Apartments

⓬ 2007 Franklin Street - Haas-Lilienthal House

⓭ 1950-60 Jackson Street - Matson Houses

⓮ 2090 Jackson Street - Whittier Mansion

⓯ 2196-98 Jackson Street

⓰ 2209 Jackson Street - "Tuckertown" House

⓱ 2355 Washington Street - Dallams-Merritt House

⓲ 2405 to 2461 Washington Street

⓳ 2301-03 Jackson Street

⓴ 2411 Webster Street

㉑ 2550 Webster Street - Bourn Mansion

㉒ 2120 Broadway - Cora Jane "Jennie" Flood Mansion

㉓ 2222 Broadway - James Leary Flood Mansion

destroyed most of the mansions on Van Ness Avenue, some of the elite, the Floods especially, built grand homes on Broadway. Because the wealthy had their own carriages and stables, Broadway became one of the few streets in Pacific Heights without public transit. The post-1906 building boom, however, proved to be a last hurrah for large single-family homes staffed with servants, since from then on more and more of them were demolished to make way for apartment buildings. Some of these early multi-story buildings, mostly from the 1920s, were well-constructed, even elegant, co-ops that contained just one unit per floor. After World War II more of the old Victorians fell to the wrecker's ball and were replaced by apartments, but these newer, multi-unit per floor buildings are of cheaper construction.

The neighborhood only received the appellation Pacific Heights—it sounds like a real estate promoter's made-up name—in the 1890s, and it initially applied to the blocks bounded by California, Broadway, Van Ness, and Fillmore. Today the area is considered to encompass Union Street to the north and Arguello Street to the west as well.

---

*Start this tour on the northwest corner of California and Franklin streets.*

---

### ❶ 1701 Franklin Street – Edward Coleman House (1895).

Not many Argonauts who came to California in search of gold became rich through the endeavor. Edward Coleman (1830–1913) was one of those who did. A native of Maine, Coleman emigrated to the Golden State in 1853. He and his brother John (more on him on the third stop on this walk) ended up owning and developing one of the richest mines in the Mother Lode, the Idaho—later called the Idaho-Maryland—mine in Grass Valley. After he and his brother sold it in 1893 and retired to San Francisco, Edward Coleman built this handsome house. A widower without children, he lived here with his sister until his death in 1913.

The house is a prime example of a Queen Anne-with-tower Victorian. It's lucky to still be standing: the 1906 fire, which was mainly halted at Van Ness Avenue, burned up to Franklin Street at this point, consuming the buildings across the street where the First Church of Christ, Scientist (1911) stands today.

Before moving on to the next stop, walk up Franklin Street a short distance for a look at the north side of the house to see one of the finest residential stained-glass windows in San Francisco. This large window of subtle colors and swirling patterns frames the staircase leading to the second floor. (It is best seen at night when the glow from the interior lights it up.)

---

*Walk west on California Street to the next house.*

---

### ❷ 1818 California Street – Lilienthal-Pratt House (1876).

This beautiful house, one of the finest free-standing, bay-windowed Italianate houses in San Francisco, was built by Louis Sloss, who made his fortune in mining and in the Alaskan sealskin fur trade. It was a wedding present to his daughter and her husband, Ernest Lilienthal. The Lilienthals lived here until 1907. In 1955 the house was purchased by Florine Bransten (widow of Edward Bransten, founder of MJB Coffee) together with the Edward Coleman house in order to safeguard the spacious yards adjoining them. Those

The Lilienthal-Pratt House.

acquisitions helped preserve the feeling of openness most of this block enjoys. Indeed, in San Francisco, where space has always been at a premium, these two houses (and the one further up the hill) with their full side yards are a rarity.

---

*Continue up California Street to the next house.*

---

### ❸ 1834 California Street – Wormser-Coleman House (1876, 1895).

This house is unusual in that it is really two houses melded into one. The eastern portion, done in the Italianate style popular during that period, was built in 1876 by Isaac Wormser, the "W" of S&W Fine Foods. In 1895 the property was purchased by John C. Coleman, brother of Edward Coleman, the owner of the previously mentioned 1701 Franklin Street. John Coleman (1823–1919) parlayed his gold-mining profits into successful investments in the California Street Cable Railroad, local utility companies, and many other businesses. In contrast to his childless brother, he and his wife had ten children—so he surely needed an extra large house. To accommodate his family he built a grander addition on the west half utilizing a large tower in the then prevailing Queen Anne style. The resulting combination gives the house an odd, unique look.

---

*Walk a block further west on California Street to the house on the northeast corner of California and Octavia streets.*

---

### ❹ 1990 California Street – Atherton House (1881, 1883).

This rambling house, now a 12-unit apartment complex, was built by Dominga de Goni Atherton, widow of Faxon Atherton, for whom the tony enclave of Atherton on the peninsula is named. Faxon Atherton was a New Englander who came to San Francisco from Chile in 1860 and became a successful importer and real estate speculator. A few years after his death in 1873, Dominga built this house as her city residence. (The Atherton name most people recognize is that of Gertrude Atherton, the writer and novelist. She was the daughter-in-law of Faxon and Dominga—married to their son George—but she never lived here.)

The house originally consisted of just the back portion of the building beyond where the current front entrance is, but critics derided the structure as not being impressive enough for a woman of Dominga's wealth (the original Atherton estate on the peninsula extended from the bay almost to the ocean). So in 1883 she added the front portion with its squat, round tower. The completed building, although it contains decorative elements of both Stick and Queen Anne, is an odd mélange of no particular style. One wag called the final result "pot luck monumental."

Walk around to the side of the house on Octavia Street. Look up at the semicircular eave and you will see under the curve the date 1881, the year the house—this portion anyway—was built. Commercial buildings sometimes feature the date of construction but it is rare for a private home to do so.

---

*Continue up Octavia and turn left on Sacramento Street. Go halfway down the block to:*

---

### ❺ 2151 Sacramento Street – Arthur Conan Doyle House (1921).

The most notable thing about this house is the brass plaque on the façade stating that Sir Arthur Conan Doyle once "occupied" this building. That's a bit of a stretch. Doyle spent a morning here and perhaps had breakfast, as a guest of its occupant, Dr. Albert Abrams, during the British author's only visit to San Francisco, in the late spring of 1923. Doyle, who had gained enduring fame as the creator of the legendary detective Sherlock Holmes, was visiting the U.S. that year on a lecture tour.

Dr. Abrams, who was known as a bit of a quack, married twice, both times to wealthy women, who left him their fortunes when they died. Abrams constructed this house in 1921 at a cost of $35,000. It replaced a two-story wood frame Victorian that dated from 1881. This Classical Baroque structure with its formal balustrade topped by seated lions, and its leaded-glass windows with their stained-glass escutcheons, makes the building look like a London gentleman's house. No doubt Sir Arthur felt right at home.

---

*Retrace your steps on Sacramento Street, cross over, and enter Lafayette Park between the two concrete stanchions at the Octavia Street entrance. Go up the path straight ahead to the summit.*

---

### ❻ Lafayette Park (landscaped 1890s) – Site of Samuel Holladay House (1869–1930s).

This pleasant park, today an oasis for sunbathers on nice days and for neighborhood dogs and their owners at all times of the year, was the scene of contentious litigation during the last four decades of the 19th century between an alleged squatter named Samuel Holladay and the City and County of San Francisco, which tried mightily to evict him.

Samuel Holladay (1823–1915) was a forty-niner and lawyer who quickly established himself after his arrival. After setting up a law practice he served a term in the California Assembly, in 1858, and was City Attorney from 1860 to 1863. Later in his career he was a judge.

He claimed that in 1851 he had purchased a plot of land stretching west from Van Ness Avenue up to the summit of the Clay Street Hill, as Lafayette Park was called at the time. He built a house for his family on the northwest corner of Van Ness and Clay Street at the eastern edge of his claim. The fur first started to fly in 1863 when Holladay started to fence in the Clay Street Hill portion of his property. The City sued, claiming that the land had been set aside for a public park and that Holladay was therefore a squatter. It was the first of four such suits, all of which the City lost, extending to 1896 when the U.S. Supreme Court ruled with finality that Holladay's claim was valid. One of the great ironies of the City's attempts to evict him is that when he was City Attorney in the 1860s Holladay had specialized in prosecuting squatters who claimed public land as their own. He apparently learned enough tricks of the trade to be able to fend off the authorities when it came time for them to move against him.

Meanwhile, Holladay in 1869 built a large, two-story white Victorian house with a barn and windmill at the summit of Lafayette Park. His little enclave became known as "Holladay Heights" and attracted leading literary and social figures of the day. He lived there peacefully until he died in 1915 at age 91. After Holladay's death the noted financier and real estate mogul Louis Lurie became interested in the property and in 1925 effected a swap with Holladay's son, exchanging some land Lurie owned in Oakland for several parcels of Lafayette Park. Lurie tried unsuccessfully to convince the City to extend Clay Street west past Gough Street into the park to provide access to his plots, which lay at the summit. His intention was to build apartment buildings. But opposition from surrounding property owners, who felt that the value of their homes would be diminished by housing in the park, as well as continued opposition from the City, torpedoed it. (One building was erected in the park – 1925 Gough Street. See stop #11 on this walk.)

At the summit of Lafayette Park the asphalt oval marks the site where Holladay's house stood. It was not demolished until the 1930s, finally allowing the City to claim the area some 70 years after it first tried to do so.

---

*Descend Lafayette Park to the north and exit it on the pathway between the two concrete stanchions on the Washington Street side. (Note the bronze plaque dedicated to Gertrude Atherton next to the pathway near the exit). Across the street to your left, the buff brick villa is:*

---

### ❼ 2150 Washington Street – Phelan Mansion (1915).

This Renaissance Revival house, designed by Charles Peter Weeks, was the home of James Duval Phelan (1861–1930) who was mayor of San Francisco from 1897 to 1902 and U.S. Senator from California from 1915 to 1921. Actually the house was registered in the name of his sister Mary, and both brother and sister, neither of whom ever married, lived there in separate suites until their deaths, attended by a live-in staff of seven.

**Despite his bachelor status, Phelan loved children and would come out of his house and talk to them when he would see them playing in the street.**

The wealthy Phelan, who gained a reputation as a reformer during a time when San Francisco politics was rife with corruption, left tangible legacies in the City and elsewhere in the Bay Area. He financed the Phelan Building on Market Street (on the gore lot at O'Farrell Street) and also served as the major fundraiser and contributor to the building of St. Ignatius Church on the campus of the University of San Francisco, his alma mater. A patron of the arts, he opened his Villa Montalvo estate down the peninsula in Saratoga to leading artists and writers of the day. Long after his death, Villa Montalvo is still used today as a venue for summer concerts and as an artists' retreat.

---

*Two doors to the east of the Phelan mansion is:*

---

### ❽ 2108 Washington Street (1888).

This red brick Georgian-style house is noteworthy because it used to be one block farther east on the lot where the Spreckels mansion now stands (see next entry). It was moved here in 1912 when Adolph and Alma Spreckels purchased the large plot of land for their new house, and had all six houses then standing on their property moved. This house was originally Victorian in style but was remodeled several times, most extensively by architect Lewis Hobart in 1925.

---

*Continue east on Washington Street to the corner of Octavia. The large white house on the northeast corner of Washington and Octavia is:*

---

### ❾ 2080 Washington Street – Spreckels Mansion (1913).

Alma de Bretteville was a determined woman. After she had snared a rich husband—Adolph Spreckels, son of a wealthy sugar magnate—she next wanted a grand house befitting her new status. Always proud of her French heritage, she wanted a home that would reflect that. So she selected architect George Applegarth, a graduate of Paris's Ecole des Beaux Arts, to design her dream house. The result was this grand French Baroque chateau. Three years under construction, it was completed in December 1913. Alma celebrated with a grand party attended by author Jack London and other celebrities.

Although still distinguished looking today the house is less impressive than in its early years. Originally the entrance was via a grand staircase from Washington Street that led to a bronze-canopied front door flanked by two huge stone urns. But all these were removed in the mid-1930s when Alma decided to subdivide her home into three apartments so that she could accommodate other family members and guests. The entrance was moved to the porte-cochere at the east end of the building, where it remains. (The original front entrance is marked by the high pillars in the middle of the Washington Street concrete wall.) The structure today suffers from a continuing deterioration of its limestone exterior finish. Limestone, which is rather porous, is a poor choice for foggy, windy, and sometimes rainy San Francisco.

The one block of Octavia Street between Washington and Jackson streets with its brick paving and curved sidewalks is also Alma Spreckels's doing. Her husband Adolph suffered from syphilis (although she didn't know what was wrong with him at the time), so she bullied the City into redoing this portion of a public street in the hopes that it would slow down and quieten the vehicles and thus not disturb her husband. Adolph's bedroom was on the opposite side of the house so it probably would have made no difference anyway, but Alma was protective of her husband and benefactor.

---

*Walk down the slope of Washington Street toward Gough Street. The salmon colored highrise is:*

---

## ❿ 2006 Washington Street (1925).

By the 1920s the wealthy were no longer building mansions in the city due to two factors: most of the choice land had already been built on and the old, more ostentatious lifestyle of large houses manned with servants was considered passé. So multiple unit highrises started to go up. Most were rental apartment buildings that catered to the less affluent, but 2006 Washington is a rare breed in San Francisco—a co-op. Co-ops differ from regular condos (in which each unit is individually owned) in that in a co-op the building is structured as a corporation in which the owners are shareholders. 2006 Washington was, and is, a luxury co-op: a couple of the original tenants were Dean Witter of the stock brokerage that bore his name exclusively until it was merged with Morgan Stanley, and members of the Schilling pepper and spice family.

---

*Walk down to the intersection of Washington and Gough streets. The six-story apartment building in the park a half a block down Gough Street to your right is:*

---

## ⓫ 1925 Gough Street – St. Regis Apartments (1908).

This handsome co-op, which would not look out of place in one of the nicer sections of Paris or London, is the last tangible legacy of the Samuel Holladay ownership of Lafayette Park. It was constructed between 1905 and 1908. The architect was C. A. Meussdorffer, who also designed 2006 Washington and its next-door neighbor, 2000 Washington.

The City had fought Holladay to keep structures out of the park, but Holladay, no doubt flush with his recent Supreme Court victory, had at some time prior to 1905 sold this parcel of land, apparently— the chain of title is unclear—to A. W. Wilson, a Swedish immigrant who was a real estate developer and restaurateur. Wilson built the St. Regis Apartments, and his descendants owned the building until 1963 when they sold it to a new owner who converted it from rentals to co-op ownership. Originally five-stories high—note the elaborate cornice above the fifth floor that marks the initial rooftop—a sixth floor was added in 1915, and in 1950 the penthouse was added.

Because it's a legacy of the dispute between a private individual and a local government, 1925 Gough is unique. It's the only privately owned building in a San Francisco park. Indeed, it may be the only such building in any public city park in the United States.

---

*Continue on Washington down the hill to Franklin Street and turn left. Halfway down the block on the left is:*

---

### ⑫ 2007 Franklin Street – Haas-Lilienthal House (1886).

Haas-Lilienthal House, circa 1887.

William Haas (1849–1916) was a Bavarian immigrant who came to the U.S. as a teenager and migrated to San Francisco where he established a successful wholesale grocery business. His youngest daughter, Alice, married into the Lilienthal family, hence the name attached to the house. Three generations of Haas's descendants lived here until 1972, when the house was donated to San Francisco's Architectural Heritage, a non-profit preservation group. They have their offices on the top floor, where the servants quarters used to be.

The house is a prime example of a late 19th-century upper-middle-class home. Construction costs for this 24-room (including seven and a half baths) house came to more than $18,000; certainly well below the million-dollar-plus range of the Nob Hill mansions but still a tidy sum when you consider that the average house of the time cost about $2,000.

Architecturally, the house is a combination of both the Stick style with its characteristic rectangular bay windows, and the Queen Anne Tower style—distinguished by the corner tower—popular during the 1880s and 1890s. Except for the chimneys and fireplaces on the south wall, which were added in 1898, the house looks much the same today as when it was built. Also in 1898 the lot adjoining the house to the south was purchased when a house that stood there was torn down. It was landscaped into the pleasant garden and lawn that remains today. That was a fortunate purchase, because the added space allows the house to be seen at full advantage as one approaches it from the south.

Inasmuch as the Haas-Lilienthal House is the only Victorian in San Francisco still with its original furnishings that is open to the public, if you happen to be by on a Wednesday or Sunday afternoon when it is open for tours, be sure and take one since the interior is well worth a look. Tours (call 415-441-3004) start in the ballroom in the basement and go through the first-floor living, dining room, and kitchen, and the second-floor bedrooms. Although some of the furniture was updated as 20$^{th}$-century residents decorated to suit their needs, the house strongly evokes what Victorian domestic life must have been like. A real highlight upstairs is the master bathroom with its original and elaborate plumbing, including a bidet, gas fixtures, and antique medicine bottles.

---

*Walk north to Jackson Street, turn left, and go one and a half blocks. On the right side of the street is:*

---

### ⓭ 1950–1960 Jackson Street – Matson Houses (1921, 1925).

Although this looks like one unit—which it now is—these Georgian Revival houses were originally separate. Both were built by Lillian Matson, widow of William Matson, a Swedish immigrant who founded the giant San Francisco-based Matson Navigation Steamship Line (see Market Street walk). Number 1950 Jackson was built by Lillian for herself; a few years later she built a similar home for her

daughter Lurline and son-in-law
William P. Roth. After Lillian's
death, the Roths purchased the
fabulous estate Filoli in 1946 and
moved there. These houses then
became the Swedish consulate—

**William Matson named his
daughter Lurline for his favorite
ship, the *Lurline*. Usually it's the
other way around—ships are
named for favored women.**

quite appropriate, given William Matson's Swedish heritage and the
fact that he was Swedish Consul-General for the last decade of his life.
In 1984 they became the German consulate.

Across the street is the back side of the Spreckels mansion. The
large arched door is the entrance to the garage, which can hold five
cars. During Alma Spreckels' ownership she irritated her neighbors
no end by holding a series of rummage sales out of this garage as fund
raisers for her various pet causes.

---

*Walk up to the intersection of Jackson and Octavia. From the northwest
corner there is a nice view of the upper levels of the back of the Spreckels
mansion. Walk one block to the house on the northeast corner of Jackson
and Laguna streets.*

---

### ⓮ 2090 Jackson Street – Whittier Mansion (1896).

William F. Whittier (1832–1917) was a native of Maine who came
to San Francisco in 1854. A merchant, he served as a member of the
Vigilance Committee two years later, and eventually he became a
partner in a firm that merged into the Fuller Paint Company. This fine
house was constructed between 1894 and 1896; Whittier, a widower,
moved in with his children and lived here until his death in 1917.

In April 1941 the house gained a bit of unwanted notoriety when
the Nazi government purchased it for their consulate. Only two
months later, however, it and the Italian consulate were both closed
by order of the U.S. government which ordered all propaganda
agents out of the country. In 1956 the house was purchased by the
California Historical Society and was used as their headquarters until
they sold it in 1994. The building is now privately owned.

The architect was Edward R. Swain, who also designed McLaren
Lodge in Golden Gate Park and who assisted on the Ferry Building.
Architecturally, it represents a transition between Queen Anne, with
its rounded corner towers, and Edwardian, with its Ionic-columned

portico and Classical temple-like façade centered above it. The interior is finished in rare marbles and exotic woods. The house has one of the first elevators installed in a residence in San Francisco.

The exterior is sheathed in a red sandstone that unfortunately, like the Spreckels mansion, has weathered badly. To protect it from further deterioration a protective coating has been applied. It has turned the original red finish to a shade of brown.

---

*Walk one block farther west to the northeast corner of Jackson and Buchanan streets.*

---

### ⓯ 2196–2198 Jackson Street (1900).

These two units, which share a common entry and were built at the same time, look so similar you would think that they were one unit—but they have always been two separate dwellings. The one on the right—2196—is a private home, while the one on the left—2198—is a bed-and-breakfast and time share. These buff brick buildings share a nice Romanesque arched entryway. Romanesque Revival architecture was quite popular at the turn of the century in major cities such as New York and Chicago, but was rarely employed in San Francisco.

---

*Cross Buchanan Street and then over to the south side of Jackson. Go west two doors down Jackson to:*

---

### ⓰ 2209 Jackson Street – "Tuckertown" House (1870).

This charming single-story house with a fenced-in front yard is the last remnant of "Tuckertown," the first planned housing development in Pacific Heights. It was the work of J. W. Tucker, a jeweler who had his office on Montgomery Street and who specialized in crafting highly polished chunks of granite embedded with gold. Tucker built homes similar to this one on the block bounded by Jackson, Buchanan, Washington, and Webster streets. This house has somehow managed to survive the nearly century and a half of changes that have transformed everything around it.

*Retrace your steps to Buchanan Street, turn right and go one block to Washington Street. Cross Washington to the south side of the street and go down about two-thirds of the block to:*

### ⑰ 2355 Washington Street – Dallams-Merritt House (1870).

This house, built by Richard Dallams, an importer of household products, brooms, tubs and such, originally stood at Sutter and Mason streets near Union Square. It was moved to this location in 1900 by its then owner, Dr. Emma Sutro (daughter of Comstock millionaire and San Francisco mayor Adolph Sutro), since the Union Square area was then changing from residential to business use. Dr. Sutro was using the house as her office at the Union Square location but converted it to her residence when she moved it here. The move spared the house from destruction; Union Square, like most of the rest of downtown, was consumed by the fire of 1906.

The house has an unusual mansard roof made up of multiple curved windows. Once popular, this is the last of its kind in San Francisco.

*Continue west on Washington Street. Cross Webster and go most of the way down the 2400 block for a look at this group of houses:*

### ⑱ 2405 to 2461 Washington Street (1888).

After the passage of more than a century, these eight houses, once virtually identical, provide a good example of how time works its changes. Only one of the eight looks much as it did originally — 2447 Washington. It is also the only one that still has its front yard and has not had a garage added, which makes it increasingly a rare bird these days.

The other houses have been remodeled in varying degrees, some quite severely. One of them — 2445 Washington — looks like modern construction completely, but a closer examination (look at the sides to see the Victorian horizontal wood siding) reveals that a totally new front, extending the structure out to the lot line, has been grafted on. Another one — 2409 Washington — has not only had all of its gingerbread amputated and replaced with stucco, it's no longer even a residence — it's been converted into a church.

*Retrace your steps on Washington Street to Webster, and turn left. Go
one block and stop on the northwest corner of Webster and Jackson streets.
This will give you a good look at the building on the southwest corner of the
intersection.*

**⑲ 2301–2303 Jackson Street** (c.1870s or 1880s).

Several nearby residents say that this nondescript building was
originally a stable. The almost total absence of decorative trim along
with the utilitarian look of this structure certainly lends credence to
that view. If it was, the large frame around what is now 2303 could
well have been the entrance for the horses. No record seems to exist
of when 2301–2303 was constructed, but its simple Italianate trim
would seem to point to the 1870s or perhaps the 1880s. The latter
decade was when the Victorians remaining on this block of Jackson
Street were built.

One story told about this building (by a former owner of the
corner grocery across the street), is that a local politician running for
the Board of Supervisors vowed to close down the smelly, noisy stable
if elected. He was indeed elected and the stable was converted into a
restaurant. After the restaurant failed the location became a grocery
store, but because of competition—there were groceries on two
nearby corners—it closed. At some point the building was converted
into its present two apartments.

*Continue north on Webster. A half a block on the left is:*

**⑳ 2411 Webster Street** (c.1915).

This Baroque Revival apartment building stands out due to its
elaborate ornamentation. The lions' heads brackets supporting the
first floor balcony, the French windows, and the lobby with its marble
floor and mirrored elevator doors all give it a certain grandeur. The
architect was James F. Dunn, a Francophile and a native San Franciscan, who designed at least three other small apartment buildings in
the City with a similar French/European flavor.

*Go one block farther north on Webster Street. In the middle of the block on the right is:*

### ❹ 2550 Webster Street – Bourn Mansion (1896).

This house was built during 1895–96 for William B. Bourn II (1857–1936), who at age 17 inherited the richest gold mine in California, the Empire. Before it closed in 1956, after more than a century of production, the Empire, located in Grass Valley, yielded over $100 million in gold. Bourn later added to his fortune as head of both the Spring Valley Water Company and the San Francisco Gas Company (one of the forerunners of Pacific Gas and Electric.) He also built Filoli, a grand country estate down the Peninsula in Woodside. Filoli was his primary residence; 2550 Webster served as his San Francisco pied-à-terre, his in-town location where he could receive city-based callers.

Both Filoli and this house were designed by architect Willis Polk. While Filoli has a more casual air to it, 2550 Webster bears the heaviness and formality of a competitive and ambitious capitalist, which Bourn certainly was. The dark red clinker bricks and the towering chimneys give this house an almost forbidding appearance. It resembles a New York City townhouse, and is quite out of character with San Francisco's Mediterranean feel with its predominately lighter-hued buildings. The Bourn mansion must have looked more impressive when it was first erected, because this house then stood as the centerpiece of a mostly empty block.

*Walk ahead to Broadway, turn right, and go half a block down for a look at:*

### ❷ 2120 Broadway – Cora Jane "Jennie" Flood Mansion (1901).

This handsome Italian Baroque-style mansion was originally built for James Leary Flood (1857–1926), son of James Clair Flood, the Comstock silver king. The junior Flood spent $340,000 on its construction—which included the bronze fence in front that is similar to the one his father built around his Nob Hill mansion—but he then went further and gave his interior decorator $1 million and carte blanche to finish it. The house boasts 13 fireplaces, each crafted from a different kind of marble, rooms paneled in oak, walnut, and mahogany, and wall coverings made of the finest brocade and silk. A "Red Room" on

**2120 Broadway, the "Jennie" Flood Mansion.**

the main floor was furnished entirely in a Chinese motif, with paneling of red lacquered wood, wall coverings of blue and silver patterned silk, and ceilings and beams with inlaid bamboo canes.

In 1906, after the fire, Flood's sister Cora Jane "Jennie" Flood (1855–1928), who was burned out of her father's Nob Hill brownstone, came to live with her brother and his wife, Maud. Jennie had been living alone at her father's mansion since his death in 1889. Partly because Maud and Jennie did not get along, James and Maud built a new house one block farther west (see next entry) and moved there in 1915. Jennie, who never married, continued on alone in this house from then until 1924, when she moved into an apartment at the Fairmont Hotel. She donated 2120 Broadway to the University of California in 1927; the following year the house was sold for $92,500 to the Hamlin School, a private secondary school for girls, which has occupied it ever since.

*Walk west one block on Broadway to see the last stop on this tour, the three mansions of The Society of the Sacred Heart.*

## ㉓ 2222 Broadway – James Leary Flood Mansion (1915).

James L. Flood's new mansion was perhaps the finest private home ever built in San Francisco. A Renaissance *palazzo*, modeled after a 16ᵗʰ-century Roman villa, it outstrips 2120 Broadway in its furnishings, workmanship, and attention to detail. The focal point of the façade is the front doorway, which is framed by two spiraled and slightly tapered Corinthian columns. Each of the figures on the door frame is unique and is hand carved. The exterior walls are of pink Tennessee marble; each huge block has been fitted so that the grains match as closely as possible with its neighbor. The interior reflects the same striving for perfection. The fireplaces and expansive floors are of marble and the walls are paneled in choice woods. A bow-windowed belvedere at the end of the main floor gallery offers panoramic views of the bay.

Three years under construction, the house was completed in 1915 as the Panama Pacific Exposition was being held on the flatlands below. Flood and has wife, attended to by a household staff of thirteen, lived in comfort, occasionally giving lavish parties. After James Flood died in 1926 Maud continued to live in the house until 1939 when she moved out and donated the mansion to The Society of the Sacred Heart, a Catholic school.

The Sacred Heart still occupies the building today; it serves as their girls high school. The organization subsequently purchased the two mansions flanking 2222 Broadway as well, which now bear the same address. The one to the right (as you face it) is the former mansion of Joseph Donohoe Grant (built 1910), who inherited his father's dry goods business. The Sacred Heart purchased this house in 1948 after Grant's widow died. It now serves as a girls elementary school. The brick house to the left is the former Andrew Hammond mansion (1905). Hammond made his money in railroads and lumber. Sacred Heart purchased it in 1956. It's now the Stuart Hall for Boys elementary school.

# Alma de Bretteville Spreckels
## (1881–1968)

Alma Emma Charlotte Corday le Normand de Bretteville, a woman with a grand name who became a grand dame, was born in poverty among the sand dunes of San Francisco's Sunset District in 1881. Her father, an idler who claimed descent from French royalty, instilled in his daughter a sense of entitlement, which young Alma converted into an iron will that she used her whole life to get what she wanted.

A six-foot-tall Rubenesque beauty with a Lillian Russell figure and a beautifully sculpted face, she attracted attention while still in her teens. To get noticed she started mod-

**Alma de Bretteville Spreckels.**

eling, even posing nude (a daring thing to do in her day), which gained her even more attention and notoriety. As a result, sculptor Robert Aitken chose her as his model for the Victory figure atop the monument to Admiral Dewey in Union Square. This in turn brought her to the attention of Adolph Spreckels, son of wealthy sugar magnate Claus Spreckels. After four years as his mistress, the determined Alma finally cajoled the long-time bachelor and playboy, twenty-six years her senior, into marrying her. She bore him three children but largely neglected them, leaving them in the care of a nanny.

Alma's great passion was fundraising for various causes and charities. She made enemies with her hard-charging, headstrong ways, but she was a person who got things done. Inspired by a trip she made to France when World War I started, Alma proved a dynamo at fund-raising for war relief. She personally called both Henry Ford and Teddy Roosevelt and got them to donate items for an auction benefiting war orphans and refugees.

She was nothing if not colorful, and her public and personal ventures provided good copy for San Francisco's newspapers for years. Once, almost on a whim, she eloped to Reno where she married a transvestite cowboy. (When the marriage ended her ex-husband married one of Alma's young nieces, much to her annoyance.) She also loved to shock people. The first time she met banker A. P. Giannini and paper magnate Harold Zellerbach it was at the front door of her house, and before she had even introduced herself she startled both men by announcing that she had just discovered her cook in bed with her butler.

Alma lived to be 87, an advanced age for an inveterate night owl who chain-smoked cigarettes and, until the final years of her life, kept a pitcher of martinis always within reach. Her greatest legacy is the California Palace of the Legion of Honor, the art museum that she and Adolph founded in Lincoln Park in 1924. Built around her collection of Rodin sculptures—the greatest assemblage of such pieces outside France—the museum's magnificent setting and fine collection make it one of San Francisco's jewels.

# Portsmouth Square

**Length:** 0.5 miles / 0.8 kilometers.
**Time:** ½ hour.
**Walk Rating:** Easy.
**Hills:** None. The tour goes mildly downhill from beginning to end.
**Public Transit:** Muni bus line 1 runs east on Clay Street and
    west on Sacramento. The 15 bus runs north on Kearny Street
    past Portsmouth Square.
**Parking:** The city-owned garage under Portsmouth Square (entrance is
    on Kearny via Clay) is relatively inexpensive. On weekend mornings
    street parking in the nearby financial district is usually easy to find,
    but look carefully at curbside signs since some streets are towaway
    zones at certain times.
**Restrooms:** There is a free public restroom in Portsmouth Square.

This small square, once the heart of San Francisco, has been the site of some of the most dramatic events in San Francisco history, especially in the early years. It has witnessed political rallies, funeral orations, Fourth of July and other celebrations (including one for statehood in 1850), and even a lynching. In 1906 it served for a few weeks as a temporary burying ground for victims of the earthquake.

Portsmouth Square has been called "the cradle of San Francisco" because it was here that the city of San Francisco was really born. It's first use was in 1833 when Candelario Miramontes, a resident of the Presidio, cleared the ground and used it as potato patch. In 1835 permanent human habitation was established when William A. Richardson built Yerba Buena's first civilian dwelling just west of the potato field. He was followed the next year by another early pioneer, Jacob Leese who, like Richardson, obtained a grant from the Mexican governor, and built his own house on a lot next door.

Within a few years more dwellings had risen in the vicinity, and in 1839 Jean-Jacques Vioget, a Swiss émigré who had some surveying experience, laid out a few streets and drew a map of the fledgling town. Central plazas were a primary feature of all Spanish/Mexican towns in the New World. Candelario Miramontes' potato patch was chosen as the plaza because it was a cleared piece of land and had no structures on it.

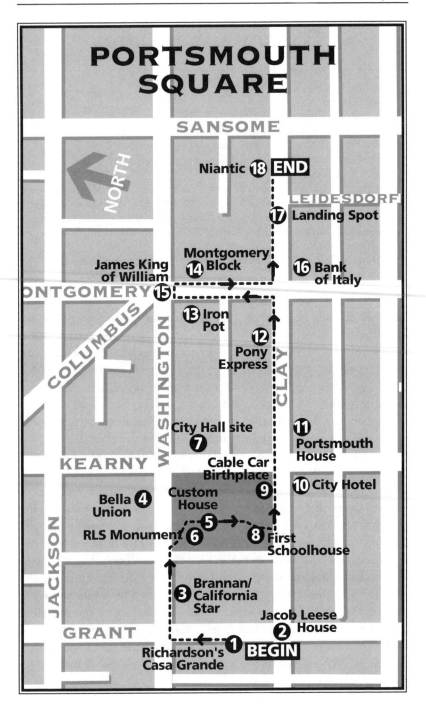

PORTSMOUTH SQUARE

SANSOME

NORTH

Niantic ⑱ **END**

LEIDESDORF

⑰ **Landing Spot**

James King
of William

Montgomery
⑭ Block

⑯ **Bank
of Italy**

ONTGOMERY ⑮

COLUMBUS

WASHINGTON

⑬ Iron
Pot

⑫
Pony
Express

CLAY

City Hall site
⑦

⑪
**Portsmouth
House**

KEARNY

Cable Car
Birthplace
⑨

⑩ **City Hotel**

Bella ④
Union

Custom
House

RLS Monument ⑥

⑤

⑧ **First
Schoolhouse**

JACKSON

Brannan/
③ California
Star

Jacob Leese
② House

GRANT

Richardson's
Casa Grande

① **BEGIN**

# PORTSMOUTH SQUARE

**①** 834 Grant Avenue - Site of William Richardson's "Casa Grande"

**②** Site of Jacob Leese House

**③** 743 Washington Street - Site of *California Star*

**④** 720 Washington Street - Site of Bella Union gambling house

**⑤** Site of Old Custom House

**⑥** Robert Louis Stevenson Monument

**⑦** Site of the El Dorado, the Parker House, Jenny Lind Theatre, City Hall, and Hall of Justice

**⑧** Site of First Public School House

**⑨** Clay Street - Birthplace of the Cable Car

**⑩** Site of City Hotel

**⑪** Site of Vioget House and Portsmouth House

**⑫** Site of Pony Express western terminus

**⑬** Site of Iron Pot Restaurant

**⑭** Site of Montgomery Block

**⑮** James King of William assassination site

**⑯** 580 Montgomery Street - former HQ of Bank of Italy

**⑰** Original shoreline and John B. Montgomery landing site

**⑱** Ship *Niantic* site

Developments came fast and furious starting in the 1840s. The war between the U.S. and Mexico brought California to the forefront. On July 9, 1846 Captain John B. Montgomery and a troop of sailors and marines from the *U.S.S. Portsmouth* anchored in the bay, landed, and raised the Stars and Stripes on the flagpole in the Plaza—which was renamed Portsmouth Square—and Yerba Buena (soon to be rechristened San Francisco) became U.S. territory. The following year, surveyor Jasper O'Farrell revamped and expanded Vioget's plan and gave names for the first time to the streets that had been laid out.

In January 1848 James Marshall made his epic gold discovery, and within a few months San Francisco started a dramatic transformation. Portsmouth Square was the center of town, and around it, shoulder-to-shoulder, buildings quickly sprang up, the vast majority of which were devoted to gambling. The square itself for the next few years was a hive of commercial and social activity, serving variously as a produce market, a corral for horses and cattle, and a gathering place for town meetings and political events. Physically it was a much abused piece of ground: muddy in the winters and dusty and windswept in the summers. Finally in 1854 vegetation was planted, pathways were laid out, and a plain wooden fence was put up around the perimeter. Two years later the wooden fence was replaced by an iron one.

Over the next century, although modifications were made to the park's layout and it was reduced in size a bit when Kearny Street was widened in 1866, it remained little changed until 1960 when the parking garage underneath was put in. What was formerly a pleasant green oasis became more of roof for the garage below, and in the ensuing decades of the 20th century the transformation became even greater as the grass was replaced by concrete and various structures, including a two-level children's playground. Now an integral part of Chinatown, Portsmouth Square little resembles the simple green common it once was.

---

*Start this tour on the west side of Grant Avenue between Clay and Washington streets. A bronze plaque (sometimes obscured by luggage from the Chinese-run store there) marks the location of:*

---

## ❶ 823 Grant Avenue – Site of William A. Richardson's "Casa Grande" (1837–1852).

This address in the heart of Chinatown was once the location of the first private dwelling at Yerba Buena Cove. Initially no more than a ship's sail stretched over four redwood posts, it was erected in June 1835 by William A. Richardson, an English sailor who had deserted his ship when it visited San Francisco Bay in 1822. In the interim, Richardson had become a Mexican citizen and had married the daughter of the commandant of the Presidio. Given a land grant by the Mexican governor he established himself as a waterfront trader, managing two schooners manned by Indian labor that collected produce, meat, hides, and tallow from the San Francisco and Santa Clara missions. These were then sold or exchanged for goods brought by the military and merchant ships that were starting to anchor with greater frequency in Yerba Buena Cove.

Within a few months of putting up his tent he improved it by adding rough board walls, but in 1837 he tore that structure down and replaced it with an imposing one-and-a-half-story building made of adobe bricks. Known as "Casa Grande" it was one of the largest buildings in Yerba Buena/San Francisco until 1848. Richardson and his family lived there only until 1842, when they moved to Sausalito (Richardson Bay there is named for him). The house had various owners over the next few years, and it seems to have served a variety of functions including that of meeting house/auditorium; in 1846 Sam Brannan and his Mormon flock held the first Protestant services conducted in California there. Casa Grande survived all of the fires that devastated San Francisco in the early 1850s. When it was torn down in 1852 because of damage done by winter rains it was the last building but one remaining in the city from before the discovery of gold.

The Casa Grande was situated at about a 30-degree angle to the northwest from the present day Grant Avenue. It was positioned that way likely because it paralleled a dirt trail about a block further down the slope that led to the Presidio. Richardson carved out a dirt path in front of his home and called it Calle de la Fundacion (Foundation Street). This in essence became San Francisco's first street. Although Vioget's town plan of 1839 made allowances for Richardson's angled boulevard it did not fit with Jasper O'Farrell's expanded layout of 1847, and the Calle de la Fundacion soon disappeared.

*Just a few yards to the south is:*

## ❷ Intersection of Grant Avenue and Clay streets – Site of Jacob Leese House (1836–c.1841).

A year after Richardson planted his flag at Yerba Buena Cove, Jacob Leese, an American from Monterey who also had become a naturalized Mexican citizen, received a land grant just to the southeast of Richardson. He built a 60- by 25-foot frame house that was completed just in time for a grand Fourth of July celebration he had planned for that day. Virtually the whole population of the Bay Area was invited. Mariano Vallejo came down from Sonoma, as did other Mexican landowners from their ranchos around the bay. They dined on broiled elk, barbecued beef, tortillas, and frijoles. Copious amounts of liquor were dispensed. It must have been quite a bash, for Leese noted in his diary that "our fourth ended on the evening of the fifth."

Leese soon married a Mexican woman, and in 1838 their daughter Rosalia became the first child of American parentage born in Yerba Buena. Leese moved to Sonoma in 1841 and sold his house and a trading post he had established on Montgomery Street on the shore of the cove. A few more settlers had taken up residence in Yerba Buena by then, but the area was still so wild that the year before Leese departed a mountain lion had come down off Nob Hill and carried off a small Indian boy who was playing in his yard.

Leese's house stood right about where the middle of the intersection of Grant Avenue and Clay Street is. It seems to have been torn down shortly after Leese left.

*Walk north on Grant Avenue and turn right on Washington Street. Just around the corner stop in front of the pagoda-like former Chinese Telephone Exchange Building (now a bank). A plaque embedded in concrete just to the right of the front door identifies this as:*

### ❸ 743 Washington Street – Site of *The California Star,* first newspaper in San Francisco (1847).

When Samuel Brannan and his Mormon flock arrived in Yerba Buena on the ship *Brooklyn* in 1846 they had with them a printing press. Brannan rented an existing house at this location, and built a small adobe structure behind it to house the press. On January 9, 1847 Brannan and his editor, Elbert P. Jones (for whom Jones Street is named), brought out the premier edition of the first newspaper in San Francisco, *The California Star.* Only two weeks later the *Star* printed Chief Magistrate Washington A. Bartlett's proclamation that the town of Yerba Buena would henceforth be known as San Francisco. It was a move Brannan opposed since he preferred the name Yerba Buena. He persisted in using Yerba Buena on the paper's masthead until late March when he finally relented and changed it to San Francisco. The *Star* continued in business on a weekly basis until it suspended operation in the spring of 1848 after the discovery of gold virtually emptied the town in the mad dash to the mines.

---

*Walk down Washington Street, cross Walter U. Lum Alley, and go a short distance into Portsmouth Square. Stop in the northwest corner about where the short flight of steps leads up from Washington Street. On the opposite side of Washington once stood:*

---

### ❹ 720 Washington Street – Site of Bella Union gambling house (1849–1868).

Where Buddha's Universal Church now stands was once the site of one of the more long-lived gambling parlors of early San Francisco. It opened in mid-1849 in the midst of a building boom fed by the gold rush, and although it initially offered a few theatrical performances it operated primarily as a casino. It was reputedly the first gambling house to feature women croupiers, which must have made it a big draw since women were still scarce in San Francisco then.

The Bella Union was destroyed by fire both in 1850 and 1851 but it was quickly rebuilt each time. Although gold-rush gambling fever peaked after only a few years, the Bella Union continued as a gaming establishment until 1856. It closed after the Second Vigilance Committee doings of that year but reopened shortly afterward as a melodeon (a music hall), which it remained until the building was torn down in 1868. It reopened around the corner on Kearny Street, where it became part of the Barbary Coast nightlife until it was destroyed in 1906.

This block also boasted what was allegedly San Francisco's first parlor house (although its exact location is not known). It opened during the summer of 1849 and was operated by a madam known as "The Countess." She employed eight girls and issued cards of invitation to the town's leading citizens—lawyers, merchants, physicians, and others—who would come to enjoy a good meal and fine wines and liquors along with any sexual entertainment that suited their pleasure.

### ❺ Portsmouth Square – NW corner – Site of the Old Custom House (1844–1851).

The corner where you are now standing was once the site of the town's first seat of government, the Old Custom House. Built in 1844 largely with Indian labor at the behest of the Mexican government, it was designed to serve as the office for Yerba Buena's alcalde (a combination mayor and judge). And as the name implies it was also used to inspect incoming goods and collect tariffs.

The building, which was one story with an attic, was made of adobe bricks and was capped by a Spanish tile roof. A shaded verandah extended around the structure with the exception of the back, or west side. It measured 56½ feet long by 22 feet wide.

In 1924 the San Francisco chapter of the Daughters of the American Revolution marked the site of the flagpole where Captain John B. Montgomery of the *U.S.S. Portsmouth* raised the American flag on July 9, 1846. (The concrete stand and bronze plaque nearby mark the spot.) The Mexican authorities had already fled, so Montgomery met no resistance when he and his troops entered the Plaza that day. Montgomery installed one of his officers, Washington A. Bartlett, as the new alcalde. After serving as the seat of government and as a military barracks the Old Custom House was rented out as office space to local lawyers and bankers. It was destroyed by the fire of June 22, 1851.

One of the more gruesome incidents in Portsmouth Square's history occurred in 1851 just 11 days before the Custom House burned.

**The hanging of John Jenkins at the Custom House.**

The Committee of Vigilance had formed that year in response to threats to law and order, and at 2 a.m. on June 11 they meted out frontier justice to an Australian ex-convict, John Jenkins, who had been caught stealing a safe from a store on Long Wharf just a few hours earlier. Jenkins was given a quick trial by the Committee in their Battery Street headquarters, was found guilty, and with a rope around his neck was marched to Portsmouth Square. The other end of the rope was thrown over a beam projecting from the south end of the Custom House, but before Jenkins could be hoisted up, some of his zealous prosecutors pulled on the rope and dragged him along the ground through the plaza, effectively strangling him before he could be strung up. As a warning to other lawbreakers, Jenkins was left hanging from the Custom House beam throughout the night, where his body was eerily illuminated by the lights from the gambling halls—still going full blast—surrounding the square.

---

*Set amidst the small green lawn here on the northwest corner is a granite shaft dedicated to author Robert Louis Stevenson.*

---

**❻ Robert Louis Stevenson Monument** (1897).

This granite shaft mounted with a cast bronze ship with gold-painted sails honors Scottish writer Robert Louis Stevenson (1850–1894). The author of such classics as *Treasure Island* and *The Strange Case of Dr. Jekyll and Mr. Hyde* spent six months in San Francisco during 1879–80. A woman he met and fell in love with at an artists' retreat near Paris, Fanny Osbourne, lived in Oakland, and he followed her here and waited for her divorce from her philandering husband to become final. They were married in San Francisco in May 1880, but in the interim he spent his time exploring the City. He especially enjoyed sitting on a park bench in Portsmouth Square where he read, wrote, or just watched the world go by. He was unknown at the time; his greatest works were still several years in the future.

Stevenson and his bride left for Europe shortly after their marriage, but they returned to San Francisco one last time in 1888 and chartered a yacht for a South Pacific voyage. The author fell in love with Samoa, where he purchased a 300-acre estate and where he died of tuberculosis at the age of 44. Three years after his death, poet Gelett Burgess and other local writers erected this monument in his memory. The thoughtful incised inscription painted in gold is from Stevenson's *Christmas Season*. The monument originally stood in the center of the square and was surrounded by a grove of trees, but it was moved here to the northwest corner during a subsequent landscaping.

---

*Walk south toward the center of the square. Look east across the square. The tall concrete highrise across Kearny Street on the southeast corner of Kearny and Washington is the Holiday Inn Hotel (1971).*

---

**❼ Kearny and Washington streets – SE corner – Site of the El Dorado** (1849–c.1855) **/ the Parker House** (1849–1850) **/ Jenny Lind Theatre** (1850–1852) **/ City Hall** (1852–1895) **/ Hall of Justice** (1895–1906, 1908–1970).

The corner where the Holiday Inn now stands is the site of several of the most historic buildings in San Francisco.

In 1849, when the gold rush was in full swing, gambling saloons sprang up all around Portsmouth Square. Two of the most famous were the El Dorado, which occupied the corner lot on Washington Street, and the Parker House right next door (which extended to Merchant Street). So great were the revenues from gambling that the El Dorado, which initially was nothing more than a modest canvas tent, leased for $40,000 a year. Its neighbor, the Parker House, a more substantial two-story frame structure, commanded a rent of $10,000 *a month*. Both buildings were destroyed several times by the fires that savaged the city between 1849 and 1851, and were rebuilt.

The Parker House was replaced by the Jenny Lind Theatre, an imposing four-story brick and stone building with a classical façade. In 1852 the City purchased it for $200,000 (which caused a scandal because even in those boom times the price was considered exorbitant), gutted it and converted it into a city hall. About 1855 the adjoining El Dorado was purchased and turned into a hall of records. Both buildings were demolished in 1895 as the new city hall complex at the Civic Center was finally ready for occupancy after more than 20 years of construction.

The site became the location of the first Hall of Justice, containing the police department, prison courts, the coroner, and the morgue. The building was destroyed in 1906 and replaced by a handsome new Hall of Justice. Renaissance inspired, it had an arcaded façade and was fitted out with marble floors and mahogany paneling. Sadly, that building was torn down in 1970 and replaced the following year by a Holiday Inn (now a Hilton), a less than worthy successor with its concrete tower and a virtually unused footbridge connecting it to Portsmouth Square. The combination of this building and the parking garage put in below the park a decade earlier forever altered the almost garden-like atmosphere that Portsmouth Square had maintained for over a century.

---

*Continue toward the corner of the square near Clay Street. Look for the sandstone base with a bronze plaque embedded in it.*

---

### ❽ Portsmouth Square – SW corner – Site of First Public School House (1848).

As the plaque states, this was the location of San Francisco's—and

California's—first public school. The building housing it was a single-story frame structure that was constructed in late 1847 and was used initially as a meeting hall for various religious and fraternal organizations. It opened as a public school in April 1848 but held classes only for about two months because as word of the riches of the gold fields started to spread, local parents decamped for the diggings and took their kids with them. The school closed and the schoolmaster locked the door and joined the rush too. The building was torn down in 1850.

---

*Exit Portsmouth Square and go down the sidewalk to northwest corner of Clay and Kearny streets.*

---

### ❾ Clay Street – Birthplace of the Cable Car (1873).

One of San Francisco's signature symbols, the cable car, got its start on Clay Street adjacent to Portsmouth Square. At 4 a.m. on August 2, 1873 inventor Andrew Hallidie (1836–1900) guided the first cable car down Clay Street from Jones Street atop Nob Hill to Kearny Street and back up again in a successful demonstration of this new form of transportation. (The early-morning test was done to disguise the fact that Hallidie had missed the deadline of August 1—he was in danger of forfeiting his franchise.)

The smooth first ride belied the difficulty Hallidie faced in bringing this project to fruition. Although cable wire rope technology had previously been used for transporting ore in Mother Lode mines, this was the first time it was employed to move people up and down steep hills. Hallidie had trouble raising money for the project—investors and others were skeptical. And some were downright fearful. On the morning of the first demonstration, Hallidie's original gripman lost his nerve before setting the car in motion, so the inventor himself had to take the controls. But with his successful first run under his belt Hallidie gave a more public demonstration that same afternoon for city officials. They lauded this great new invention. Even with a fare costing only five cents Hallidie's cable car proved popular and profitable. Lines quickly spread elsewhere, and horse-drawn cars, which had been the main mode of transportation prior to this, soon faded into memory.

*Across Clay Street was:*

## ⑩ Clay and Kearny streets – SW corner – Site of the City Hotel (1846–1851).

In 1846 William A. Leidesdorff built a large one-and-a-half story adobe on this corner. It had a verandah and a peaked roof with dormer windows and served as both an office and a store for Leidesdorff. In November of that year he converted the attic portion of it into the City Hotel. He leased it to John Henry Brown, an Englishman who had come overland to California in 1845. Brown soon became one of the foremost innkeepers of San Francisco and because of that the City Hotel was sometimes known as Brown's Hotel.

**The Old City Hotel.**

With the advent of the gold rush Brown became one busy hotel proprietor. During the winter of 1848–49 some 90 miners crowded the hotel waiting out the seasonal rains. Flush with gold dust and bored with playing billiards they clamored to have the place turned into a gambling den. The main rooms were soon set up with tables for roulette and popular card games of the time such as faro and monte.

The action was fast and furious: thousands of dollars sometimes changed hands on the turn of a single card. Brown couldn't have objected too strongly to the games of chance because he collected huge sums in rents from the gamblers. His main problem lay in supplying his tenants with food, drink, and other amenities. Local sources of supply were still scarce, so it was necessary to import the needed items. To that end he once gave a ship's captain departing for Hawaii (then called the Sandwich Islands) bottles of gold dust weighing 20 *pounds* to pick up supplies to bring back on his return journey.

The City Hotel lasted until the fire of May 3–4, 1851 swept it away.

---

*Cross Kearny Street to the northeast corner of the intersection.*

---

**⓫ Clay Street just east of the SE corner of the intersection – Site of the Vioget House** (c.1840–1846) **/ the Portsmouth House** (1846–c.1851).

About 70 feet east of Kearny on the south side of Clay Street, Jean-Jacques Vioget in either 1840 or 1841 put up a wooden structure that served as a saloon and billiard parlor. Vioget had, as noted, laid out the first town plan in 1839. Behind his bar he kept the original drawing showing the streets and buildings; he would amend it as needed to show new buildings and owners.

> A Russian, I. G. Voznesensky, who was visiting from Ft. Ross in the early 1840s, noted that a few apartments within the Vioget House were set aside for travelers, making it the first hotel in Yerba Buena, and thus in California.

With the hurly-burly of the Bear Flag Revolt and the arrival of Sam Brannan's more than two hundred Mormons during the summer of 1846, the need for more sleeping quarters was obvious, so Vioget expanded his operation soon after to meet the demand. Mormon carpenters crafted the beds, apparently assuming that one size fits all. One morning the innkeeper, John H. Brown (who soon left to manage the City Hotel), greeted guest Robert Semple, who was 6 feet 7 inches, and asked him how he had slept. Semple drily inquired if Brown had any chickens he'd like to roost: there was plenty of room on his legs, which had stuck way out over the end of the bed.

The Vioget House changed its name to the Portsmouth House in

1846 after some crew members of the Portsmouth offered to paint a sign for the establishment free of charge if he would change the name to honor their ship.

---

*Continue down Clay Street. About three-quarters of the way down the block are several bronze plaques on the side of the building that relate to the Pony Express.*

---

### ⑫ Clay Street near Montgomery – Site of Pony Express western terminus (1860–1861).

There are more bronze plaques here than for any other single historic site in San Francisco, which is ironic since the fabled Pony Express lasted only a year and a half and really only merits a footnote in the City's history. San Francisco was not even the real terminus – Sacramento was – but when the first rider from St. Joseph, Missouri arrived in April 1860 he and his horse were ferried down the bay by river steamer and a grand celebration was held on Montgomery Street near the local offices of the company. The Pony Express, with its hell-bent-for-leather riders spurring their horses on, cut the time for delivering mail to 10 to 13 days from about 23 days, from the next fastest way, the overland stage. But with the invention of the telegraph the legendary delivery service with its tales of derring-do quickly faded into history.

---

*At Montgomery Street turn left and, if you're here during business hours, go into the lobby of 655 Montgomery Street, the highrise just past Merchant Street.*

---

### ⑬ 655 Montgomery Street – Site of the Iron Pot Restaurant (c.1950–1981).

Display cases on the 14th floor of this high rise contain artifacts from buildings that once stood on this block of Montgomery Street. Two of the most notable are the Montgomery Block (see next section) and the Iron Pot Restaurant, which stood where 655 Montgomery is today for close to three decades (and elsewhere before that).

The Iron Pot, along with the Black Cat, which was located a block away at 710 Montgomery and had a mostly gay clientele, were two favorite bohemian hangouts for artists and writers of the mid-20th century. The walls were adorned with paintings by local artists. Henri Lenoir, who later opened the favorite Beat watering hole Vesuvio in North Beach, was in charge of "Art and Publicity" at the Iron Pot. It enabled him to showcase his antic wit. He annotated a 1943 Iron Pot menu (not on display) with: "The male customers who need a haircut are not artists," and "The paintings and prints here are for sale. Limit one dozen to a customer. But don't ask the help to explain them to you. They don't understand them either."

---

*Cross Montgomery Street to the Transamerica Pyramid (1972).*

---

### ⓮ Montgomery Street between Washington and Merchant streets – East side – Site of the Montgomery Block
(1853–1959).

Where the northern half of the Transamerica Pyramid now stands was the site for over a century of perhaps the most renowned office building in San Francisco — the Montgomery Block. When completed in 1853 it was four stories high and was the tallest and grandest building west of the Mississippi River.

It was the brainchild of Henry Halleck, a U.S. Army captain in the engineering corps and a lawyer to boot. (With the start of the Civil War, Halleck became General-in-Chief of the Union Army.) Halleck had seen what the fires of 1850 and 1851 had done and he was deter-mined that his building would withstand anything — earthquake or fire — that could be thrown at it.

For the foundation, redwood logs floated over from the East Bay were dovetailed into tiers, linked with iron clamps, and sunk to a depth of 22 feet — a savvy solution to the problem of how to provide stability to an area that was once unstable shoreline. On this base, surrounding a central courtyard, rose a square building that, not sur-prisingly given Halleck's reputation as a military engineer, resem-bled a fort. Three-foot-thick brick walls were covered with stucco and punctuated with deep-set windows, and to guard against fire, were covered with double iron shutters. Large water tanks were installed in the basement. As a security measure, foot-thick iron doors fronted the entrance of the banking and express office of the prime tenant, Adams & Company.

The interior was not neglected either. The glass and mirrors were imported from Belgium, gas was fed by pipes into every room, and the lobby and common areas were decorated with potted palms, red velvet sofas, and shiny brass cuspidors. The ground floor on the northwest corner housed one of the more storied saloons in San Francisco history—The Bank Exchange. Its signature drink, Pisco Punch—made with a secret recipe from Peruvian brandy—was so potent that proprietor Duncan Nicol limited patrons to two apiece. When The Bank Exchange opened along with the Montgomery Block in 1853 it was the last word in barroom ambience: black and white checkered marble floors, mahogany bar, overstuffed cowhide chairs, and Wedgewood porcelain beer pumps.

The building was originally called the Washington Block after George Washington, but the name Montgomery Block was applied early and stuck, even after a bust of the first president was placed over the front entrance. In the early days it housed a lot of lawyers, including Halleck and his part-

**The Montgomery Block, circa 1856.**

ners who became wealthy handling the many lengthy and tangled land title claims stemming from the change from Mexican to U.S. ownership after the end of the war with Mexico in 1848.

The Montgomery Block started to develop a reputation even in the 19th century as a bohemian hangout for artists and writers. Bret Harte and Mark Twain were two of the leading literary lights who either worked there or patronized its facilities. It was in the basement steam bath in fact that Mark Twain met a fireman named Tom Sawyer. Twain used the name for his famous novel, and Sawyer, who later opened a saloon on Mission Street, allegedly capitalized on his immortality by advertising his tavern as "the Original Tom Sawyer's."

The bohemian tradition continued into the 20th century as Ambrose Bierce, Jack London, George Sterling, and others passed through its portals. The tradition became more pronounced during the Depression, when the Monkey Block—as it was fondly called—

turned into a haven for those practicing the creative arts. As many as 75 artists and writers lived there in the 1930s, attracted by rents as low as $5 a week.

The sturdy Montgomery Block, which survived the 1906 earthquake with nary a scratch, was torn down in 1959. The space was used for parking until the Transamerica Pyramid was built in 1972.

### ⓯ Intersection of Montgomery and Washington streets – Site of the Assassination of James King of William (1856).

What was probably the most famous street shooting of early San Francisco occurred at the intersection of Montgomery and Washington streets on May 14, 1856. The killer was James Casey and the victim was James King of William.

Both men were newspaper editors in an age when vitriol and personal attacks in newsprint were common fare. Barbs had been traded back and forth between Casey's *Sunday Times* and King's *Evening Bulletin*. Matters came to a head when King published the news that Casey had served time in New York's notorious Sing Sing prison prior to coming to California. Casey confronted King in his office and angry words were exchanged. After King left his office that day and neared the northwest corner of the intersection, Casey stepped forward and shot King in the chest at close range. Mortally wounded, King was taken into the Montgomery Block where he died six days later. The outrage was such that King's murder led to the formation of the Second Committee of Vigilance (see the Financial District chapter) and the hanging of Casey by vigilantes on the day of King's funeral, May 22.

---

*Walk south on Montgomery past the Transamerica Pyramid to the northeast corner of the intersection with Clay Street. The building on the southeast corner is:*

---

### ⓰ 550 Montgomery Street – Former Headquarters of Bank of Italy (1908–1921).

This handsome building served as the headquarters for A. P. Giannini's Bank of Italy (predecessor of the Bank of America) from 1908 to 1921. Giannini founded his bank in 1904 just a stone's throw away at

One Columbus Avenue (see the Jackson Square walk). The structure on that site was destroyed in 1906 and when the city was rebuilt after the earthquake, Giannini erected this nine-story Renaissance Revival edifice. It was from here that he pioneered the concept of branch banking that led to his firm's rapid expansion. The once humble Bank of Italy was renamed Bank of America in 1930 and went on to become the largest commercial bank in the world by the 1940s.

Much of the bank's interior adornment is still original and provides a visual treat. Especially noteworthy are the massive vault, the veined marble walls, and the brass teller cages. On the latter, look for the sailing ship, the *Portsmouth,* which has long served as an emblem for the bank, since troops from the vessel landed very near this spot on July 9, 1846 prior to raising the U.S. flag over Yerba Buena. Also note the entwined B and I at the bottom of the cage windows, which stand, of course, for Bank of Italy.

---

*Walk east on Clay Street until you are across from the end of Leidesdorff Alley on the other side of the street.*

---

**⑰ Leidesdorff and Clay streets – Original shoreline and site of the landing of John B. Montgomery and troops from the U.S.S. *Portsmouth* on July 9, 1846.**

It is impossible to pinpoint with precision where the original shoreline was at this point, but prior to 1848 a short, little-used pier extended from an embankment at Montgomery and Clay streets over a stretch of beach to about where Leidesdorff Street is now. It was likely at this pier that Captain John B. Montgomery and his troops landed and marched up Clay Street to the Plaza, where on July 9, 1846 he raised the American flag and claimed Yerba Buena for the United States.

---

*Continue east on Clay Street almost to the corner of Sansome. A bronze plaque on the wall of the building to your left marks this as the location of:*

---

**⑱ Clay Street between Sansome and Leidesdorff – North side – Site of the remains of the ship *Niantic*.**

The *Niantic*—named for a tribe of Indians in Rhode Island—was a whaling ship that was operating in the Pacific in 1849 when it received word of the gold rush and of Argonauts in Panama who were clamoring for passage to San Francisco. It left Panama loaded beyond capacity with 248 gold seekers, including "four Negroes with their southern owners," and sailed up the coast, arriving in San Francisco Bay on July 5, 1849. The passengers quickly departed and the ship's owners sold the *Niantic* to speculators who, at high tide, attached empty oil casks to the ship's bottom and floated it to its final resting place on the northwest corner of Clay and Sansome streets. Once beached, the vessel was covered with a shingle roof, the deck was partitioned into stores and offices, and doors were cut into the hull, which was turned into storage. Rentals brought in $20,000 a month.

The ship burned to the waterline in the fire of May 3–4, 1851 but eight feet of the hull that was below ground was spared. Its contents were covered over and thus preserved, and have been dug up during several subsequent excavations. San Francisco was always in a hurry to rebuild after fires, and within a few months a wooden three-story structure, the Niantic Hotel, had been erected over the ship's remains. When the hotel was demolished in 1872, numerous bottles of champagne were unearthed from the mud below.

A four-story brick office building, the Niantic Block, rose in place of the old hotel, and when the earthquake of 1906 destroyed it more champagne was discovered when the foundations were dug for its replacement, the Niantic Building, a four-story reinforced concrete structure. In 1978 during excavation for the present building—called the Pacific Mutual not the Niantic—a more thorough excavation of the site was undertaken. This time in addition to more intact bottles of champagne being recovered, of the Jacquesson-Fils label (a French firm still in business today), other artifacts found included a percussion cap rifle, bolts of cloth believed to be an early type of linoleum, and a brass duck's-head paperholder. Also saved before construction resumed was a portion of the *Niantic's* stern and rudder with most of its original copper sheathing still nailed in place. It is on display at the Maritime Museum at the foot of Polk Street.

It could well be that more artifacts from the *Niantic* still lie buried here. The ship was 120 feet long and it is estimated that about 30 feet of the bow portion, which was not excavated, extends under Redwood Park next to the Transamerica Pyramid.

# Russian Hill

**Length:** 0.6 miles / 1.0 kilometers.
**Time:** 1 hour.
**Walk Rating:** Easy to Strenuous.
**Hills:** There is a steep downhill on Taylor between Vallejo and
 Broadway and then a steep uphill from the bottom at Taylor up
 Broadway to Florence, although cement steps lead all the way up.
 Vallejo Street from Florence to the summit is a moderate uphill.
**Public Transit:** The closest lines are the Powell Street cable car line,
 which runs along Mason Street one block east of Taylor; and the
 41 bus line, which runs along Union Street one block north of Green.
**Parking:** No garages or parking lots nearby. Street parking is difficult to
 find. Two-hour limits for those without residential parking permits.
**Restrooms:** No public restrooms in the area.

Although in close proximity to downtown,
Russian Hill was slow to develop as a residential neighborhood.
Through most of the late 19$^{th}$ century, while the city expanded to the
south and far to the west, the crest of the hill mostly remained in
splendid isolation due to its inaccessibility. Three hundred and forty
feet high at its peak, it was simply too steep for horse-drawn vehicles
hauling building materials.

A couple of hardy souls did put up frame houses on the north
slope of the hill near Broadway and Taylor streets in the early 1850s.
And about 1861 an observatory with a winding staircase, which from
a distance looked like a giant corkscrew, was erected on the summit.
It was known as Jobson's Tower after its owner/builder David Jobson, who charged 25 cents to climb to the top to peer through a
telescope at the panoramic views it afforded. But it was only in the
late 1880s that the summit area (the blocks bounded by Taylor, Broadway, Jones, and Green streets), which had largely remained an untouched field of wild mustard, succumbed to residential development.

The houses that went up over the next two decades and the earlier
ones dating from the 1850s, survived the flames of 1906. The same
inaccessibility that had made Russian Hill late to develop helped save
it from the 1906 holocaust.

How Russian Hill got its name has never been precisely deter-

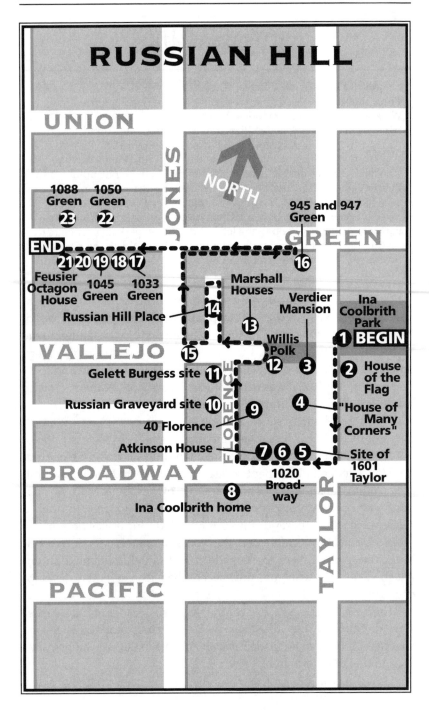

# RUSSIAN HILL

UNION

1088 Green **23**    1050 Green **22**

JONES

NORTH

945 and 947 Green **16**

GREEN

**END**

**21 20 19 18 17**

Feusier Octagon House    1045 Green    1033 Green

Russian Hill Place

**14**

Marshall Houses **13**

Verdier Mansion

Ina Coolbrith Park

**1 BEGIN**

VALLEJO

**15**

Willis Polk **12**    **3**

**2** House of the Flag

Gelett Burgess site **11**

**9**

**4**    "House of Many Corners"

Russian Graveyard site **10**

FLORENCE

40 Florence

Atkinson House

**7 6 5**

Site of 1601 Taylor

**8**

1020 Broad-way

BROADWAY

Ina Coolbrith home

TAYLOR

PACIFIC

# RUSSIAN HILL

**1** Ina Coolbrith Park

**2** 1652 Taylor Street - House of the Flag

**3** 1001 Vallejo Street - Hanford/ Verdier mansion

**4** 1637 Taylor Street - House of Many Corners

**5** Site of 1601 Taylor Street

**6** 1020 Broadway

**7** 1032 Broadway - Atkinson House

**8** 1067 Broadway - Ina Coolbrith home

**9** 40 Florence Alley

**10** 35, 37, 39 Florence Alley - Site of Russian graveyard

**11** Gelett Burgess House site

**12** 1013-1019 Vallejo Street - Willis Polk House

**13** 1034-1036 Vallejo Street - Marshall Houses

**14** Russian Hill Place

**15** Jones-Vallejo ramp

**16** 945 and 947 Green Street

**17** 1033 Green Street

**18** 1039-1043 Green Street

**19** 1045 Green Street

**20** 1055 Green Street

**21** 1067 Green Street - Feusier Octagon House

**22** 1050 Green Street

**23** 1088 Green Street

mined. The most credible explanation is that it was named for Russian sailors who were buried there. The Russians had established settlements in the Bodega Bay/Fort Ross area north of San Francisco as early as 1812, and their ships made regular calls at Yerba Buena to trade for meat and grain until 1841, when they sold out to John Sutter and returned to Alaska. It could be that they buried their dead there for two reasons: the hard clay of the hill made for a better burial ground than the shifting sands of most of the rest of the area, and there is a tradition of sailors interred on land being buried in sight of the sea. The Pacific Ocean is not visible from Russian Hill, but the bay — which would qualify as a substitute — certainly is.

Or the name could be derived from the story of the Russian sailor who, after a drinking spree one night in Yerba Buena in 1847, fell into a well and drowned. His comrades carried his body up the hill to the west where his resting place became known as "the Russian's hill."

Burials continued on the hill until the early 1850s, when the bodies were either disinterred and moved to Yerba Buena Cemetery (where the Civic Center now is), or more likely they were simply forgotten — the wooden grave markers disappeared and the graves were built over as housing went up.

Once settlement did take place, Russian Hill almost from the start developed a bohemian cast as writers and artists found inspiration in its isolation and area-wide views. Cheap rents were also likely a factor. The hill was not considered a desirable place to live until street paving in the 20th century improved access. Today, with accessibility no longer an issue, Russian Hill is one of the City's choicest — and most expensive — residential districts. It also has some of the most varied architecture of any San Francisco neighborhood.

---

*Start this tour at the entrance to Ina Coolbrith Park just off Taylor Street.*

---

## ❶ Taylor and Vallejo streets – NE corner – Ina Coolbrith Park

This hilltop park with great views of downtown through the trees is dedicated to Russian Hill resident and poet Ina Coolbrith. A bronze plaque embedded in a stone cairn near the entrance provides some basic facts about her. Unfortunately there are a few mistakes: she came overland in 1851 not 1852; she was the first poet laureate of California, not the United States; and she died in Berkeley, not Oakland.

Coolbrith favored Russian Hill as a residence toward the end of her life. From 1902 to 1906 she lived at what was 1604 Taylor Street near the northeast corner of Taylor and Broadway, one block down the hill from here. After the 1906 fire she lived briefly at 15 Macondray Lane (then called Lincoln Street) and then moved to 1067 Broadway (a stop later on this walk).

---

*Adjacent to Ina Coolbrith Park on the southeast corner of Taylor and Vallejo is:*

---

## ❷ 1656 Taylor Street – the House of the Flag (1864).

Called the "House of the Flag," this structure is famous in San Francisco lore for the way it survived the 1906 fire. As flames were approaching it the house's owner, before evacuating, stuck an American flag on the roof. Soldiers from the Twentieth Infantry Regiment, seeing this act of defiance, hurried to the site and with water stored in the house's bathtubs, seltzer bottles, and wet sand from a construction site, managed to save the house from destruction.

The core of this house dates from 1864. It likely was a traditional Italianate Victorian. In 1903 a new front was added and it was remodeled into a shingle-style dwelling. In the 1980s new construction in the back converted it into a condominium complex.

**The House of the Flag., circa 1907.**

---

*The big house directly across Taylor Street is:*

---

## ❸ 1001 Vallejo Street – the Hanford-Verdier Mansion (1906).

This tall and sprawling Tudor-style residence was under construction and just nearing completion when the 1906 disaster struck. It survived unscathed—the fire was stopped across the street. It was one of the first houses in San Francisco covered with stucco, a material employed by its architect, Houghton Sawyer, at least partly to blend in with the adjacent chalky hillside.

The house was erected by Robert G. Hanford who had mining interests in the Mother Lode and had previously owned several of San Francisco's street railways before selling out for a large sum. He built the mansion for his new bride, Gabrielle Cavalsky, a woman he had met at the Del Monte golf course. She was an amateur singer, and as a nod to her musical skills the house contained a large ballroom with a balcony from which she sang with accompaniment from musicians below.

Hanford's marriage did not last long, and he sold the house to Felix Verdier, the grandson of the founder of the City of Paris, one of the City's then-premier department stores. During World War II the house was used by the military as an officers club. Later it was subdivided into apartments. Today, after recent remodeling, it is a two-family dwelling.

---

*Walk south down the east side of Taylor Street. About half way down the hill you can get the best look across the street at the house next to the Hanford-Verdier house:*

---

## ❹ 1637 Taylor Street – the "House of Many Corners" (1854).

A bit hard to see through the trees, this house was one of the earliest on the hill and was known as the "House of Many Corners" for its staggered setbacks, each wall of which was had its own window, the object presumably being to allow maximum light into the interior. In the 1890s the house underwent a drastic remodeling. It was owned by Everard Morgan, who was a swindler and blackmailer. As his problems mounted he and his wife divorced. As part of the settlement the house was sawed in half. The southern half of the house—which is what remains—was left with his wife on the lot. Morgan took the northern half and moved it to some unknown location. The empty northern lot was sold to Robert Hanford who used it for part of his gargantuan house next door.

In 1911 the "House of Many Corners" was divided into flats and rented out. It attracted artistic and literary people as tenants, including the painter Maynard Dixon and his wife, photographer Dorothea Lange, who lived there from 1926 until the early or mid-1930s. In the 1950s the façade of 1637 Taylor was substantially remodeled, and that is the house you see today—although the "many corners" aspect is still discernible.

---

*Go to the bottom of the hill and cross Taylor Street to the northwest corner. Above the concrete retaining wall on this corner is:*

---

❺ **Site of 1601 Taylor Street** (1853–1910).

Northwest corner of Broadway and Taylor, 1870s.

The first people to build on the summit of Russian Hill were contractors, men who already had the materials and skills to put up buildings. One of them was Charles Homer, who built the mammoth U.S. Marine Hospital at Rincon Point in 1853, the same year he built his own home, a three-story frame Victorian, here on this corner. Homer had purchased the six 50-vara lots bounded by Taylor, Broadway, Jones, and Vallejo streets for a total of $5,000 that year, a bargain considering that within a few months he sold most of the other

50-vara lots for $4,000 apiece. It was a nice profit but not nearly as much on a percentage basis as the previous owner, William Squire Clark, had made. Clark had purchased these same six parcels four and a half years earlier for only $225.

In 1866 Taylor Street between Broadway and Vallejo was graded to make it more accessible. But it effectively lowered the street level here to the point where a shear wall of earth was left exposed and in danger of subsiding into the street, so a stone and concrete retaining wall was put up. Most of the wall from the corner to about halfway up Taylor Street is original from that time. Additionally, the remains of the stone ramp that was once the base of the stairs leading up to 1601 Taylor are still visible under the foliage that cascades over the wall from above.

The Homer house was torn down in 1910. The corner location was left vacant to make a garden for two other homes, 1629 Taylor and 1020 Broadway, both of which are still standing. They were erected on opposite corners of the same lot the previous year by Lillian and Ethel Parker, the granddaughters of Charles Homer.

---

*Go up the Broadway steps to see the next two houses on this walk. To view them better you might want to briefly cross the street.*

---

### ❻ 1020 Broadway (1909).

Set back amidst the foliage and a bit hard to see, this shingled Craftsman home is known as the Sara Bard Field house after the feminist poet who lived there in the 1920s.

It is hard to envision today, but between this house and its neighbor at 1032 Broadway there was once an official city street. Originally called Charles Street it, was changed later to Sweet Street. It was apparently a "street" in name only since photographs show it as no more than a dirt trail winding up the hill between the two houses. Sweet Street likely disappeared in 1894 when the massive concrete retaining wall on this side of the street was put up after this block of Broadway was graded.

### ❼ 1032 Broadway – Atkinson House (1853).

One of the lots Charles Homer sold for $4,000 was this one just up the hill. It was purchased by Joseph H. Atkinson, a fellow contractor and part owner of the Lone Mountain cemetery, which was located at the western edge of the city just past where Presidio Avenue is today. In 1853 Atkinson constructed this Italianate villa-style house. It is the oldest house extant on Russian Hill today.

The house still strongly resembles its 1853 appearance, but some changes have taken place over the past century and a half. In 1893 architect Willis Polk remodeled the first-floor interior, and the following year he did the fine classical balustrade atop the wall as well as the wrought-iron entrance gate near the top of the steps. The house's exterior was originally clapboard siding, but early in the 20th century, perhaps influenced by the Hanford/Verdier House around the corner, it was replaced by stucco. More recent changes include the installation of a picture window in the 1970s, and in 2000 a two-car garage was punched through the wall beneath the house.

The Atkinson house was one of the centers of Russian Hill's literary tradition. Mark Twain may have visited the house during the mid-1860s, since he was friends with Almarin B. Paul, one its residents at the time. But its heyday was in the 1890s when poet Gelett Burgess (more on him shortly), sculptor Bruce Porter, and others who were associated with the literary magazine *The Lark*, and who were known as *Les Jeunes* (the young ones), gathered here for talk, meals, and songfests.

---

*Go to the top of the steps. There is a fine view of downtown and the bay from here. Across the street about halfway to Jones Street is:*

---

### ❽ 1067 Broadway – Home of Ina Coolbrith (1909–1919).

After living at 1604 Taylor Street and 15 Macondray Lane, Ina Coolbrith made this her last home on Russian Hill. This two-flat house was purchased for her through a fundraiser held at the Fairmont Hotel by local novelist Gertrude Atherton and other supporters. Coolbrith requested that the dwelling look like the one next door at 1073 Broadway.

California's soon-to-be poet laureate lived in the upper flat and rented out the lower one. Here she presided over an informal literary salon where she offered encouragement to local writers. On her walls were pictures of Mark Twain, Gertrude Atherton, the painter William Keith, and others of her long association with California's literary and artistic community.

Coolbrith lived here from the time the house was built in 1909 to at least 1919. From 1922 until her death in 1928 she lived with her niece in Berkeley.

---

*On the north side of Broadway across from the Coolbrith house climb the steps leading to Florence Street. Halfway along Florence on the right is:*

---

### ❾  40 Florence Street (1854).

Buried inside this house, which has been remodeled a number of times, is a single-story dwelling first erected in 1854 by contractor David M. Morrison. In the 1870s the home was jacked up and another floor was added beneath it; the original first-floor porch became a second-story balcony. In 1889 Horatio P. Livermore, whose family ended up owning much of the summit of Russian Hill, purchased it as an investment property. It sat vacant until 1891, when architect Willis Polk moved in. In exchange for free rent he remodeled the first floor's interior. During the year he spent here he worked on the design for 1015–1019 Vallejo Street around the corner.

In 1897 Horatio Livermore, who owned the Sacramento Electric, Gas and Railway Company, which he had inherited from his father, moved with his family into 40 Florence (the address was then 1023 Vallejo Street). Due to financial reverses Livermore had had to give up his Rockridge estate in Oakland and move here. He soon made further alterations to the house, virtually obliterating any exterior visual traces of the original Morrison dwelling. In 1988 post-modern architect Robert A. M. Stern revamped the entire structure, giving it the appearance you see today.

---

*On the other side of Florence Street, which was named for Florence Paul, youngest daughter of Almarin B. Pa.......*

---

### ❿  35, 37, 39 Florence Street (1912–1916) – Site of Russian graveyard (1840s).

This grouping of Pueblo Revival-style houses was designed in the

1910s for Horatio Livermore's son Norman by architect Charles F. Whittlesey. Whittlesey, who had spent time in Albuquerque, was no doubt influenced by the adobe structures there.

This location—the block bounded by Florence, Vallejo, Jones, and Broadway—was the site of the Russian graveyard. Bodies may still be buried here.

---

*Walk up to the corner of Florence and Vallejo streets.*

---

### ⓫ Florence and Vallejo streets – SW corner – Site of Gelett Burgess residence (1894–1897).

The present address is 1071 Vallejo Street, but prior to 1906 this was 1031 Vallejo, an 1860s plain box of a house, one-and-a-half stories high, nicknamed by its occupant "The Peanut Shell." It was the home from 1894 to 1897 of poet Gelett Burgess (1866–1951). Burgess, bespectacled, slight of build, and a bit of a dandy, lived here when he started *The Lark*, a monthly literary magazine of playful intent that published lighthearted poetry and prose. The first issue, in May 1895, carried what became Burgess's best-known work, his poem "The Purple Cow":

> "I never saw a Purple Cow
> I never hope to see one
> But I can tell you anyhow
> I'd rather see than be one."

The work was republished so many times that Burgess came to regret the notoriety it brought him. He later penned a bookend to it:

> "Ah yes, I wrote the 'Purple Cow'
> I'm sorry, now, I wrote it
> But I can tell you anyhow
> I'll kill you if you quote it."

*The Lark* folded after two years and Burgess left for New York and other literary endeavors. He wrote more nonsensical verse and a few novels but never achieved real fame, although he rubbed elbows with Franklin D. Roosevelt, Henry James, and Picasso, among others. He visited Russian Hill one last time shortly before his death in 1951. It must have been a nostalgic visit after the glory days of his youth over a half century before. "The Peanut Shell" was long gone but the

Atkinson house at 1032 Broadway and a few other familiar structures still remained.

*Walk up the south side of Vallejo Street to the crest of the hill for a look at:*

## ⓬ 1015–1019 Vallejo Street – Willis Polk house (1892).

In 1892, up-and-coming architect Willis Polk (1867–1924), was joined on Russian Hill by his parents and brother and sister who moved to San Francisco from Kansas City. His mother, Endie, purchased a 20-foot-wide lot at the top of Vallejo Street just east of a 40-foot-wide lot that was sold at the same time to artist Dora Williams, widow of Virgil Williams, one of the founders of the Bohemian Club. (Polk was a Bohemian Club member.)

He contracted with Dora Williams to build a house with a roof that covered both residences—a duplex, in effect, separated by a common wall. What was built, and stands there now almost unaltered, is the most distinctive house on Russian Hill, one most appropriate for its setting. Rustic, made of unpainted redwood,

**1015–1019 Vallejo Street.**

the house has been described as a modern variation of a European medieval row house. Its most distinctive feature is its curvilinear Gothic window under the main gable. The house looks deceptively small, but in back on the Polk side at 1013 it drops down the hillside for six stories, offering spectacular views of downtown San Francisco.

Polk was only 25 years old when he designed this house, in conjunction with his building-contractor father and architect brother. Willis was clearly the star of the firm of Polk and Polk, and throughout the 1890s he burnished his reputation, mainly designing residences. In 1901 Polk left San Francisco for Chicago and a two-year stint with the prestigious firm of Daniel Burnham & Company. He returned in 1903, and for the next two decades, and especially after the 1906 earthquake, Polk put his stamp on San Francisco with numerous buildings, including his masterpiece, the Hallidie Building at 130 Sutter Street (see the Financial District walk).

Robert Louis Stevenson died in Samoa in December 1894, and in May the following year his widow, Fanny, and her two children came to stay at 1019 Vallejo with her friend Dora Williams. It was Dora who had urged Fanny to marry the writer right away after her divorce, rather than waiting one year as was the custom then. Fanny caught the eye of Gelett Burgess down the street and the two soon began an affair. It did not last long—Fanny and her kids left for Hawaii in November 1895—but the romance resumed a few years later when both were traveling in England.

---

*Cross over to the north side of Vallejo Street for a closer look at:*

---

## ⓭ 1034 and 1036 Vallejo Street – Marshall Houses (1889).

These two wood-shingled buildings set back behind fences are two survivors of what were three nearly identical structures that were erected during 1888–1889. Known as the Marshall houses after the first owner of the property, they were designed by Joseph Worcester (1836–1913), a shy yet influential minister of the Swedenborgian Church located in Pacific Heights. He was also an amateur architect. While a passion for religion and architecture might seem an incongruous mix at first glance, in Worcester's case they proved beneficial because Swedenborgian doctrine, at its most elemental, seeks union between the spiritual and natural worlds. So Worcester's basis for his architecture was tied to his belief that buildings should appear to spring as organically as possible from their surroundings. To that end he designed these shingle houses made from untreated redwood.

The value of these houses in architectural history is that they were virtually the first in the Bay Area, and for that matter in the U.S., to attempt a deliberate harmony between the natural and the built environment. They also notably signaled the first shift away from the prevailing High Victorian architecture.

While the Marshall houses had an affect on other architects—they no doubt influenced Willis Polk when he designed 1013–1019 Vallejo three years later—the stylistic details could have better suited the site. Sharply peaked roofs are just not necessary in San Francisco, where snowfall is never an issue, and the houses stacked side by side with their few and small windows do not take full advantage of this top-of-the-hill location that cries out for picture windows to go with the panoramic views.

This grouping originally had a third house, 1032 Vallejo, which stood just to the east. And just to the east of that, although up against the front of the lot line so as not to restrict the views of the other three, stood Worcester's own house, 1030 Vallejo, where he lived rent-free courtesy of David and Emilie Marshall as payment for his uncompensated services as minister of the Swedenborgian Church (of which the Marshalls were members). The 1984 Hermitage apartments, a rustic design with a Willis Polk-type classical balustrade, occupy the land where these two houses once stood.

---

*Walk down Vallejo a short distance to Russian Hill Place.*

---

### ⓮ 1, 3, 5, 7 Russian Hill Place (1916).

These four stucco-covered Mediterranean-style villas with Spanish tile roofs were designed by Willis Polk and contracted during 1915–1916 on land owned by Norman Livermore, son of Horatio. Their front entrances on Russian Hill Place make them seem small, but in the back, on the Jones Street side, they descend a full three stories. Elegant and sophisticated, these homes epitomize urban living at its best.

The brick-paved street itself, one of the few such streets remaining, was a private lane until Livermore deeded it to the City in 1926.

---

*Walk down the ramp, or down the stairs in the center, and cross Jones Street to the corner for a better look at the ramp itself and the buildings flanking it.*

---

### ⓯ The Jones / Vallejo ramp (1914).

From this vantage point the entry to the summit of Russian Hill, with its stucco dwellings topped by Spanish tile roofs and tall chimneys, resembles an Italian hill town. This is no accident, since it was inspired by a trip Horatio P. Livermore and his family made to Italy during 1908–1909. Livermore and Willis Polk had discussed improving the Vallejo/Jones approach to the summit prior to 1906, but it was only after the earthquake and the trip to Italy that any action was taken. Horatio and his son Norman started by buying the lots on the Jones Street frontage. They then turned the design over to Polk. Polk's ramp, which was constructed in 1914 and replaced a simple wooden stairway that had previously offered the main access to this side of the summit, reinforced the Italian feel with its classical balustrade: it was a reiteration of the one he had done for 1032 Broadway two decades earlier.

---

*Walk north on Jones Street to Green and turn right. Go to the end of Green Street at the cul-de-sac where the two high-rise towers stand side by side.*

---

### ⓰ 945 Green Street and 947 Green Street (late 1920s).

Like the notorious spite fence that Charles Crocker placed around a property owner who refused to sell to him on Nob Hill, these two buildings also involve a tale of revenge. The building to the west, 947 Green, went up first. But the tower blocked the view of its neighbor behind it, 1000 Vallejo. To get even, that owner erected an even taller tower—945 Green—on the lot right next to it. It was not only taller by two stories but it was configured in an L shape that wrapped around to the south to make sure that 947 Green lost all of its eastern views.

Both of these buildings have just one unit per floor and were originally rental apartments. In the 1970s they converted to individual ownership; 945 Green is a co-op, 947 Green is condominiums.

---

*Retrace your steps on Green Street to Jones. Cross Jones Street and proceed along the south side of Green and stop in front of:*

---

### ⓱ 1033 Green Street (1868).

Known as the Bayley house after the man who built it—a portrait photographer named William Bayley—this home originally stood on Taylor Street near Jackson on Nob Hill. Bayley sold it in 1883 to a prosperous tailor, Oliver Nordwell, who moved it to the lot he owned here on Green Street, since he wanted to build a new house at the Nob Hill location. It's fortunate that he did, because this side of Green

Street in this block managed to escape the flames of 1906. This house was spared, whereas Nordwell's Nob Hill house burned.

### ⑱ 1039–1043 Green Street (1885).

This three-flat Victorian with the unusual staircase leading to the second floor appears to date from 1885, because the San Francisco Water Department shows a hookup at this site then. One of the owners in the 1960s however, thought that these units originally stood on Van Ness Avenue and were moved here after the 1906 earthquake.

The building was designed by the Newsom Brothers, whose signature building is the Carson mansion in Eureka. Why the unusual exterior staircase was employed has never been determined, but the formal entry on the second floor suggests that this may once have been a two-story structure that had an additional unit shoved underneath it at a later date, necessitating the winding stairway.

### ⑲ 1045 Green Street (c.1867).

This little dwelling, which with its windowless cupola resembles a schoolhouse, was built in the Italianate style about 1867. Around 1910 the son of one of the first owners added the cupola and the dark wood shingles, apparently to bring it more in line with the new Craftsman-style of design then prevailing.

### ⑳ 1055 Green Street (1866, 1916).

Next door is a home that has changed its appearance drastically since it was built in 1866. Originally it was a rather plain clapboard-sided Italianate with a front porch. Wooden steps led from the center of the porch to the sidewalk. In 1916, noted architect Julia Morgan completely revamped it by removing the top floor, shaving off the front porch, and moving the front entrance over to the side. She resurfaced it with stucco, and using classical decorative elements, such as the urns garlanded with flowers under the arched windows where the front entrance used to be, gave it a Beaux Arts look in keeping with the style of the times.

### ㉑ 1067 Green Street – Feusier Octagon House (c.1857).

This eight-sided dwelling is one of the most unusual residences in San Francisco. Octagonal houses enjoyed a brief vogue during the mid-19<sup>th</sup> century, since they were supposed to provide a more healthy living environment for their occupants. The extra walls, with windows in each, were designed to admit more light—sunshine was deemed to be beneficial. At one time there were about half a dozen octagonal houses in San Francisco, including one that once stood on the northwest corner of Green and Jones where the high rise is today. Today only the Feusier House and the Octagon House at Union and Gough streets still stand. (The latter is open to the public.)

The Feusier House gets it name from Louis Feusier, a French immigrant who arrived in San Francisco in the early 1850s but who spent much of the 1850s and 1860s in Nevada, where he supposedly was pals with Mark Twain. Feusier became a commission merchant for a wholesale produce business and purchased this house in 1875. The house remained in the Feusier family until 1954.

A number of alterations have been made to the house over the years. It has always had a cupola, but probably during the 1880s the third story mansard roof with the fish-scale shingles and the dormer windows was added and the cupola was remodeled and seemingly enlarged. And like the Julia Morgan house next door, the entrance was moved from the center—where the double windows with the balustraded balcony are today—around to the side.

---

*Across the street are:*

---

### ㉒ 1050 Green Street (1913).

A little touch of Paris in San Francisco, this elegant five-story edifice set back from the street behind a manicured green lawn reflects the classical training of its Ecole des Beaux Arts-educated architect Lewis P. Hobart. Originally apartments, the building is now condominiums with just one unit on each of the upper four floors.

### ㉓ 1088 Green Street (1907).

This "Tudor Revival Swiss Chalet"-style structure was built in

1907 and opened in June 1908 as a city firehouse. The firemen lived upstairs, while the three-horse team was stabled on the ground floor. You can still see the original fire pole just to the left of the front entryway.

Partly because Russian Hill was relatively isolated, this firehouse also functioned as a kind of community center. Neighborhood children would come to pet the horses and help oil the leather fire helmets. In return the firemen would render simple first aid and fix the kids' bicycles. This community spirit continued even into World War II, when local residents would bring food and gather in the firehouse during blackouts.

In 1952 the firehouse closed and the building was declared surplus. Five years later Mr. and Mrs. Ralph K. Davies bought it at auction for $17,300. They used it as a city pied-a-terre, and also would lend it to various local organizations for charity events. In 1978 Mrs. Davies (who was widowed by then) deeded it to the National Trust for Historic Preservation. In 1997 the Trust sold the building to the Society of St. Andrews, a benevolent organization that promotes Scottish arts and culture in northern California. The Society maintains a library in the building and holds its monthly meetings here. The Society of St. Andrews was founded in San Francisco in 1863. John McLaren, longtime caretaker of Golden Gate Park, was one of its first presidents.

# Ina Coolbrith

## (1841–1928)

Ina Coolbrith was California's leading woman poet of her day—perhaps the leading poet of either sex. Although her poetry occasionally plumbed the darker themes of loss and regret, she mainly wrote lyric poems about the joys of life and the natural beauty of California. In 1915 the state legislature named her California's first poet laureate.

As a person, Coolbrith was reserved and not given to self-revelation. Although she lived a long, eventful life she never wrote an autobiography, claiming: "Were I to write what I know, the book would be too sensational to print; but were I to write what I think proper, it would be too dull to read." The first part of that statement is certainly true.

She was born Josephine D. Smith in Nauvoo, Illinois, the daughter of Agnes Coolbrith and Don Carlos Smith, the younger brother of Mormon founder and prophet Joseph C. Smith. Her father died when she was only four months old. Her mother, who was opposed to the polygamy established by Joseph C. Smith, left the sect and moved to St. Louis, where she remarried. In 1851 the family joined the migration to California. They nearly perished crossing the Sierra, but through a chance encounter they met the legendary mulatto fur-trapper and mountain man Jim Beckwourth, who guided them safely on through. If the lore is to be believed, young Coolbrith rode perched on Beckwourth's saddle.

Ina Coolbrith.

After only a brief stay in northern California the family moved to Los Angeles. At age 17, the tall, pretty, dark-haired Coolbrith married Robert B. Carsley, a partner in an iron works company and a sometime minstrel-show actor. Carsley proved to be temperamental and unstable. Pathologically jealous, he accused his young wife of infidelity. Coolbrith retreated to the house of her stepfather, William Pickett, where Carsley followed, calling her "a whore." After threatening her with a knife and pistol, Carsley took a shot at her with a rifle. Pickett fired back and hit Carsley in the hand, damaging it severely enough that it had to be amputated. Not surprisingly, Coolbrith was granted a divorce and she and her family moved to San Francisco to put the dreadful experience behind them. She never remarried.

Coolbrith, who had already had a few poems published in a Los Angeles paper under her pen name of Ina Coolbrith, settled into the San Francisco literary scene, where her new poems quickly found an audience. She became assistant editor to Bret Harte at the *Overland Monthly* and, along with other writers, (whom in later years she called "the boys,"—Mark Twain, Charles Warren Stoddard, Joaquin Miller), she became an integral part of the vibrant literary scene of 1860s San Francisco. The men in her circle recognized her talent and treated her as an equal.

Poetry rarely pays the bills however, so Coolbrith first became a school teacher and then, more famously, head librarian at the Oakland Public Library, where she introduced a youngster by the name of Jack London to the world of books. Later she became librarian for the Bohemian Club and was voted an honorary member, the only woman of her time to receive the honor from the all-male bastion. She was burned out of her first Russian Hill abode in 1906, but returned shortly afterward and lived most of her remaining years there, where she served as den mother of an informal literary salon.

# South of Market – Rincon Hill

---

**Length:** 1.3 miles / 2.1 kilometers.

**Time:** 1½ hours.

**Walk Rating:** Easy

**Hills:** The last block of the tour along Federal Street to the end of Rincon Street at Bryant is a mild uphill.

**Public Transit:** The 15 bus runs south on Second Street and north on Third, as do the 30 and 76 buses. The 42 bus goes west on Brannan and east on Townsend streets. For those coming up from the peninsula by train, the Caltrain terminal is located at Fourth and Townsend streets.

**Parking:** There are a few parking garages along Townsend Street to accommodate Giants baseball fans, but street parking is relatively easy to find. Check street signs however, since some zones are one-hour only. Don't drive to this area and try to find parking when either the Giants are playing at home (the stadium is between Second and Third streets just south of Townsend) or weekdays after about 2 p.m. Commuter traffic trying to get on the Bay Bridge to leave the City can lead to congestion.

**Restrooms:** There are no public restrooms and few commercial establishments along this route.

---

No section of San Francisco has undergone more change than the Rincon Hill area, south of Market Street. (The name was derived from Rincon Point, a knob of land at Harrison and Spear streets that formed the southern corner of the original shoreline of Yerba Buena Cove. *Rincón* is Spanish for "corner.") It has been an elite residential area, an industrial/warehouse district, and most recently has become, along with much of the rest of South of Market, the area of choice for multimedia and internet companies as the former warehouses have been converted to offices and live/work lofts. Physically the hill has been transformed, most dramatically in 1869 when the notorious "Second Street Cut" was gouged through and then again in the 1930s when the hill was leveled some more to provide for the anchorage for the Bay Bridge.

In the 1850s, in the wake of the gold rush, San Francisco's wealthy citizens started building magnificent homes in the area bounded by Folsom, Fremont, Bryant, and Third streets. They chose this location because it was not as windy or foggy as most other parts of the city, it

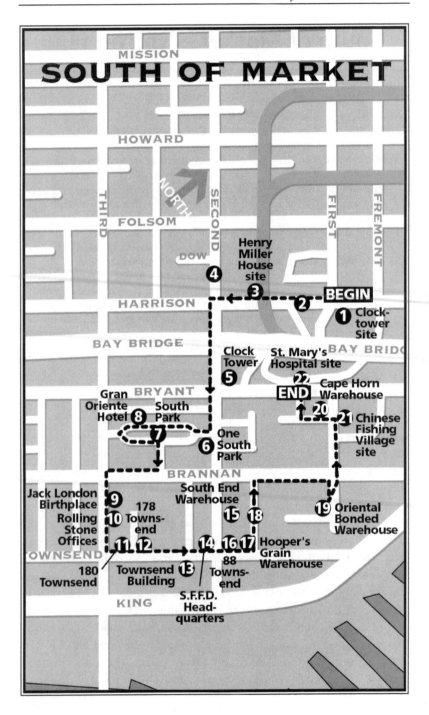

# SOUTH OF MARKET

**❶** 425 First Street - Bank of America Clocktower

**❷** 500 block of Harrison Street

**❸** Site of Henry Miller home

**❹** Second Street between Harrison and Folsom streets

**❺** 461 Second Street - Clock Tower Lofts

**❻** One South Park

**❼** South Park

**❽** 106 South Park

**❾** 601 Third Street - Jack London Birthplace

**❿** 625 Third Street - Rolling Stone Offices

**⓫** 180 Townsend Street

**⓬** 178 Townsend Street

**⓭** 123 Townsend Street - Townsend Building

**⓮** 698 Second Street - S.F.F.D. Headquarters

**⓯** 625 Second Street

**⓰** 699 Second Street

**⓱** 64 Townsend Street - Hooper's South End Grain Warehouse

**⓲** Colin P. Kelly, Jr. Street

**⓳** 650 Delancey Street - Oriental Bonded Warehouse

**⓴** 540 First Street - Cape Horn Warehouse

**㉑** Federal Street - Site of Chinese fishing village

**㉒** Site of Old St. Mary's Hospital

was close to downtown and the waterfront, and it was at an elevation of up to 100 feet above the surrounding locale, thus affording superb views. San Francisco mayors, U.S. senators, bank presidents, leading merchants and industrialists, and senior military officers built show-place homes here. To add a sense of class, many of the alleys carved through the large blocks were given English names—Hawthorne, Essex, Dover, Vassar, Laurel (now Lansing).

The hill retained its prestige until 1869 when the mound on which it sat was bored through at Second Street largely between Folsom and Bryant streets. The impetus was to provide a level path between downtown and the Pacific Mail and other company docks clustered around the end of Second Street. What became known as the "Second Street Cut" was spearheaded by John Middleton, a real estate broker and legislator who owned a house on the southeast corner of Second and Bryant streets. He rammed a bill through the state legislature authorizing the Cut in the expectation that easier access to the southern wharves would increase the value of his property (and others he may have been fronting for). But in a classic example of the realization of the law of unintended consequences, real estate values on Rincon Hill quickly declined instead of rising. The huge gash carved through Second Street left adjoining homes some 50 feet to 75 feet above the street level and perilously close to toppling over. A wooden bridge had to be constructed on Harrison Street to span the chasm. Worse, the area became home to young ruffians who perched on top and hurled rocks at Chinese immigrants below on their way from the docks to downtown.

The Cut was the beginning of the end for Rincon Hill as a desirable residential district. Although some homeowners stayed on, many moved on to new plots of land in the Western Addition; others switched to Nob Hill, which after the invention of the cable car in 1873 became newly accessible. In 1906 the fire swept the area up to the northern border of Brannan and Townsend, where a few warehouses near First and Second streets were spared. But every single one of the remaining grand homes was obliterated.

Rincon Hill was rebuilt as an industrial area after 1906. Ware-houses and factories were erected on the sites of former mansions. In the 1930s, major change came again when the San Francisco anchor-age and ramps for the Bay Bridge were laid down in the blocks between Harrison and Bryant streets. After the Great Depression of the 1930s, World War II led to a revival of business for the remaining warehouses, and the waterfront and nearby businesses hummed with activity for several more decades.

Change came again in the 1960s when containerization—the shipment of goods in huge ships holding railroad-size boxcar containers—led to the decline of waterfront activity in San Francisco, where the piers were not equipped to handle such large loads. And with trucking having replaced shipping and railroads as the favored method of transportation, by the early 1970s many of the warehouses had fallen into disuse and become vacant.

In the early 1980s the turnaround, which is still continuing, started the transition of the area into what it is today, a mixture of office, retail, and residential use. Virtually all of the warehouses in what is now known as the South End Historic District have been refurbished to accommodate their new tenants.

---

*Start this tour on the northwest corner of First and Harrison streets. Across the intersection on the southeast corner was the site of one of the City's more notable landmarks.*

---

### ❶ First and Harrison – SE corner – Clock Tower site.

For much of the 20th century the southeast corner of First and Harrison streets was the site of a distinctive triangular clock tower. Designed by architect Lewis Hobart in 1940 for the Union Oil Company, the original clock tower was a 138-foot-high Modernist structure that served as a beacon for the newly erected Bay Bridge. In 1954 Hobart's tower was demolished and a newer triangular one of 190 feet was put up in its place. The orange and blue Union 76 symbol, which was a familiar sight for Bay Bridge motorists for four decades, came down in 1995 when the Bank of America bought the building. They slapped their logo on and replaced the weathered white enameled porcelain steel panels with new ones. The tower, which was torn down in 2005 to make way for condominiums, stood on what was just about the summit of the original Rincon Hill. The one-way First Street on-ramp curving around the site leading on to the bridge was, prior to 1958, an off-ramp, because until that time the bridge carried two-way traffic on both decks.

## ❷ 500 block of Harrison Street.

You would never know it today, but the 500 block of Harrison Street was once the most fashionable address in San Francisco. The thunderous traffic on the Bay Bridge directly behind it has totally changed the ambience of what was once a quiet residential street whose homes had commanding views of the bay and downtown.

A number of San Francisco's leading citizens lived on this street during its prime in the 1860s and '70s. Number 500 Harrison, where the Union 76 service station is now, was once the site of a large three-story Italianate Victorian with a mansard roof that was the home of Charles McLane, a general agent for Wells Fargo & Company. Next door, at 526 Harrison, was the mansion of banker Joseph A. Donohoe, which boasted a household staff of five servants and a coachman. Next door to Donohoe lived publisher and historian Hubert Howe Bancroft (see Market Street walk for more on Bancroft). Across Harrison Street on the south side of the block lived similarly illustrious people in mansions worthy of their station.

---

*Walk west down the slope of Harrison to the northeast corner of Harrison and Essex streets. Across Essex stood:*

---

## ❸ Harrison and Essex – NW corner – Site of Henry Miller home (1877–1906).

Wealthy landowner Henry Miller, known as the "Cattle King" for his vast holdings of cattle ranches spread over three states, once lived on this corner in what was by all appearances the largest house ever built on Rincon Hill, a baronial edifice with a mansard roof. The concrete Fremont Street off-ramp from the Bay Bridge you see above runs through about where Miller's living room would have been. (Essex Street was graded, lowered, and widened in 1936 to accommodate traffic to the bridge. Prior to 1958, Essex was two-way traffic for trucks only.)

Miller built his mansion here in 1877 after earlier purchasing and tearing down an Italian-style villa that had been erected in 1861. He was home on the morning of April 18, 1906, and after being awakened by the quake he dressed and walked downtown. Soldiers prevented him from reaching his office on California Street so he returned home.

With fires starting to break out (South of Market was one of the first areas to burn) the widower—his wife had died the previous year—loaded his crippled adult son into a horse-drawn wagon and set off for the Third Street train depot, hoping to rendez-vous with his daughter who lived down the pen-

Henry Miller's Rincon Hill home, 1882.

insula. There were no trains however, so he proceeded across the Third Street Bridge to Butchertown where he spent the next few nights in a cheap hotel waiting for the fire to end.

Miller's Essex Street house burned to the ground. His German insurance company initially refused to pay, claiming that the fire was caused by the earthquake and that there was no insurance for earthquake damage. Miller sued and won his case when the jury agreed with his argument that the fire was not directly caused by the earthquake but by the carelessness of others. The "Ham and Eggs" fire, which was started by a woman cooking breakfast for her family and which quickly got out of control, was cited as an example.

---

*Continue down Harrison Street to the northwest corner of Second Street.*

---

### ❹ Second Street between Harrison and Folsom.

Here at the intersection of Harrison and Second Street is the center of where the Second Street Cut was cleaved through the heart of Rincon Hill. The street level prior to the Cut in 1869 ranged from about 50 feet to as much as 75 feet higher in the two-block stretch of Second Street between Folsom and Bryant than it is today. Look up at the modern office building on the east side of Second between Harrison and Folsom and count up between five and seven stories, and then try to imagine houses sitting up this high above the current street level and you will get an idea of how drastic the Second Street Cut was.

**The Second Street Cut, 1869.**

On the west side of Second in this block stood the residences of several people well known to San Francisco history. Poet Charles Warren Stoddard lived for a time post-Cut in a house halfway down the block on the southwest corner of Second and Dow Street. His friend Robert Louis Stevenson, who lived briefly in the City, visited Stoddard here in 1880. Stevenson surveyed Stoddard's crumbling estate: cypress trees with their roots in the air, a shaky wooden stairway leading to the dwelling, and the house itself seemingly about to pitch over into the chasm below. "What a background for a novel!" Stevenson exclaimed.

On the other side of Dow Street stood the houses of Joseph Folsom, for whom Folsom Street is named, and Henry Halleck, who lived on the corner of Second and Folsom and who built the famed Montgomery Block (see Portsmouth Square walk). Both men lived here in the early 1850s however, well before the Second Street Cut transformed the neighborhood.

---

*Walk one block south on Second Street to the southwest corner of Second and Bryant streets. Across the intersection on the northeast corner is:*

## ❺ 461 Second Street - Clock Tower Lofts (1907) – Site of Peter Donahue House (1860–1889).

No location on Rincon Hill better illustrates the changes that have occurred in the last century and a half than the northeast corner of Second and Bryant streets. Occupying this corner from 1860 to 1889 was the grand Victorian home of industrialist Peter Donahue (see also Market Street walk). Donahue was the founder of what became the city's largest iron works, its first gas works, and builder of the state's second railroad, the San Francisco-San Jose Railroad. The house, which fronted on Bryant Street, occupied several city lots and was flanked on both sides by formal gardens.

By 1902 the Schmidt Lithograph Company had established a factory here. Max Schmidt was a German immigrant who, starting from scratch, built his enterprise into the largest printer of labels for canned goods in the United States. The current building replaced his previous plant after the 1906 disaster. The six-story clock tower portion at the north end was added in 1920. In the 1930s, when the original plan for the Bay Bridge called for it to cut across the roof of his building, he allegedly protested to City Hall and threatened to move his business out of San Francisco. This perhaps explains why the bridge curves at this point and skirts the north end of his clock tower.

By the 1980s the company, which through several mergers had become Stecher, Traung & Schmidt, had vacated for greener pastures. In the early 1990s the building was renovated and converted from industrial use to live/work lofts, which it remains today.

---

*Walk one-half block farther south on Second Street to the entrance of South Park. On the southern corner of South Park and Second Street is:*

---

## ❻ One South Park (1913).

This building was erected for the use of the Tobacco Company of California, and served originally as a tobacco warehouse. It was unusual for warehouses of any kind to incorporate decorative elements in their design but this one did—note the Indian head medallions below the first floor cornice. Indians have served as symbols of tobacco since the days of the first American colonists, and that no doubt was the reason for their use here. The medallions look as if they are made of plaster but they are in fact cast bronze painted white. Also noteworthy here are the sections of railroad tracks leading toward the loading dock. These are some of the very few remnants of the Belt Line Railroad spur tracks that brought goods offloaded from ships at the Embarcadero directly into warehouses.

---

*Walk west into the park that starts between One and Two South Park and start down the right side.*

---

### ❼ South Park (1854).

This oval park planted with sycamore trees and surrounded by low-rise buildings holding a mix of businesses, residences, and cafés brings a delightfully European feel to an area of town that still evokes its industrial past despite its ongoing conversion to other uses.

It was developed as a planned community in the early 1850s by an entrepreneur named George Gordon, an English migrant to San Francisco who established one of the city's most successful iron foundries, the Vulcan Iron Works, and built a profitable sugar refinery among other endeavors. He and his architect, another Englishman, George Goddard, modeled South Park after similar parks and mews in London. By the end of 1854 he had constructed, on speculation, 17 Regency-style townhouses standing shoulder-to-shoulder on the northwest quad of the oval. His plan was to sell the remaining lots to buyers who would build houses of the same type. At a time when land was still widely available and those with money could built mansions to suit their tastes, Gordon's creation of South Park was a leap of faith.

The first auction of houses and lots was held in January 1855. His timing couldn't have been worse; San Francisco's gold-rush-driven economy was just starting to experience its first big recession. Several big banks failed and nearly 200 businesses went bankrupt. Despite the gloomy economic conditions most of the lots with houses sold, mainly to the city's elite, men such as Lloyd Tevis, president of Wells Fargo Bank, U.S. Senator William Gwin, and Robert Woodward, owner of the What Cheer House hotel and later developer of Woodward's Gardens, a popular resort in the Mission District. What drew them in part was that their neighbors were men of like standing, the houses were of brick and stone and thus seen to be fireproof, and the development was far removed from the brothels and gambling joints of downtown. To insure peace and quiet and to discourage riffraff, Gordon had also stipulated that in South Park no saloons were to be allowed within its confines. And in another attempt to make South Park a prestigious place to live, the oval park was made private and was only for the use of the surrounding homeowners. It was encircled by a high iron fence with locked gates: only the residents had keys.

One of the more amusing incidents in the early annals of San Francisco occurred here on November 26, 1855 and serves to illustrate the young city's attempt to establish the proper decorum while still struggling with its rowdy and more playful instincts. On that date a party was held in South Park to celebrate the defeat during the Crimean War of the Russians at Sebastopol by forces from England, France, Turkey, and Sardinia (as Italy was known then). A large tent, decorated with the flags of the Allies, was erected and a magnificent banquet was laid on. In the center, on a table, sat a huge cake. A band played, an ox, sheep, and pigs were roasted, and wine and champagne flowed in copious amounts. After the ladies retired, things started to get out of hand. A few diners, bored with the after-dinner speeches, started throwing dinner rolls at the cake. Several men then put their shoulders to the cake and toppled it. As a food fight erupted men stood on chairs and tables waving their countries' flags and

The Crimean War fete held at South Park in 1855.

singing their national songs. When partygoers started cutting holes in the tent it collapsed and the whole affair literally came to a crashing end.

South Park never fulfilled its promise despite George Gordon's best efforts. After the initial sales the rest of the lots sold very slowly, and when they did the unity of design that Gordon hoped would carry over into the new houses built on the oval did not materialize. South Park declined along with the rest of Rincon Hill after the Second Street Cut. By the 1880s the fence around the park was gone; the oval became a public city park in 1897. The 1906 fire turned all of South Park's real estate to ashes.

For most of the 20th century South Park remained a hidden away and forgotten enclave fronted by small factories, machine shops, and rooming houses. By the 1970s it had hit its nadir and was even dangerous to visit. Drug dealers and the mentally ill camped in the oval and kept bonfires built from scrap wood going to keep themselves warm at night. But in the 1980s the turnaround came as several European-style bistros and cafés opened on the oval. Today South Park serves as a magnet for all the local workers in the area who populate the cafes or sprawl on the park's grass at the noon hour and eat their lunches.

---

*Start walking around the park to your right. Stop when you get to:*

---

## ❽ 106 South Park (1907) – Gran Oriente Filipino Hotel
(since 1921).

Sandwiched in between two cafés is a remnant from an earlier era. The Gran Oriente is a rooming house for elderly low-income Filipinos. The rooms are small and the accommodations spare. The toilets and showers are down the hall. Almost all the residents are men and many are former merchant seamen who saw service during World War II. Their predecessors bought this building in 1921 for $6,000 to serve as a boarding house for their seafaring members. The name Gran Oriente derives from their fraternity of the same name back in the Philippines.

In 1940 the organization bought 43 and 49 South Park across the oval as additional housing, and in 1951 erected their own Masonic

Lodge temple behind it on Center Place (now named Jack London in honor of the author).

---

*Continue around the oval and up the other side to Jack London Place. The buildings on the SE corner are the just mentioned Gran Oriente properties. Go down London Place, turn right at Brannan, and go the half block to Third Street. Cross Third to the southeast corner of the intersection.*

---

### ❾ 601 Third Street – Birthplace of Jack London.

A bronze plaque on the side of this commercial building identifies this as the birthplace in 1876 of writer Jack London. The area then was residential rather than commercial. (The two-story Victorian house where London was born — the address was 615 Third Street — stood not where the plaque is but about 60 feet farther south on Third Street, right about where this building ends and the adjoining red brick building starts.)

Jack London, who would become internationally famous as the author of such classics as *Call of the Wild* and *The Sea Wolf,* became newsworthy, in a sense, before he was even born. The sole progeny of a brief union between "Professor" William H. Chaney, an itinerant astrologer, and Flora Wellman, a music teacher and "spiritualist," his parents split up because of his conception. A domestic row ensued when Flora found out that she was pregnant and her husband refused her request for lighter duties around the house. When she refused to have an abortion, as Chaney insisted, he walked out, never to see her again. Distraught by her sudden abandonment, Flora Wellman tried to kill herself, first by taking opium, and then by shooting herself with a revolver. She only suffered a flesh wound from the latter when the bullet grazed her forehead. (It left a permanent scar.) This whole "fiasco of the hearthstone" was reported as a news item in the *San Francisco Chronicle* on June 4, 1875. A little over seven months later Flora's baby, John Chaney, was born. Eight months later she married a new acquaintance, John London, who raised his stepson as his own child. To distinguish the new father from the son, the boy was called Jack.

The family moved to Oakland before Jack London's third birthday. London returned only occasionally to the city of his birth, most notably as a journalist to report what he saw in the immediate aftermath of the 1906 earthquake and fire.

---

*Continue down Third Street to the large brick building:*

---

## ⑩  625 Third Street (1908) – *Rolling Stone* Magazine offices (1970–1977).

This large brick structure was built post-earthquake as a warehouse for the Transcontinental Freight Company. Its main claim to fame today is that from 1970 to 1977 it housed the offices of *Rolling Stone* magazine. This was of course long before South of Market became a hot area and chic address. *Rolling Stone* got its start in San Francisco in 1967—in a building around the corner on Townsend Street—chronicling the nascent rock scene spawned in Haight-Ashbury. After a decade in San Francisco, publisher Jann Wenner decided that the City was a little too provincial and moved the operation to New York.

At the time the magazine was located here the address was 645–47 Third Street. You can still vaguely see those numbers on the shields flanking the north entrance to the building.

---

*Continue south on Third Street and take a left on Townsend. The first building on your left on the north side of the street is:*

---

## ⑪  180 Townsend Street (1905).

Completed just before the 1906 quake this building not only survived that temblor but the fire as well since the flames were stopped just behind it at Brannan Street. The building is given a touch of class by the circular stone insets that are spaced at intervals on the façade below the cornice. The third story was added in 1921. The building's first tenant was the California Wine Association. Later the MJB Coffee Company used it.

## ⑫  178 Townsend Street (1888).

Across Clarence Place is another quake survivor, this one from the 19th century. It was built for the California Electric Light Company, which first provided electricity to San Franciscans in 1879. In 1888 the company was awarded a contract for supplying electricity to the city's outlying districts; this was probably built in response to that need. After 1906 and at least until 1915 the former power plant was converted to a warehouse for storing hay and grain.

The segmental arched parapet atop the front façade makes this building more distinctive than most of the typical box warehouses in the area.

---

*Walk east on Townsend until you are at Stanford Alley across from:*

---

### ⑬ 123 Townsend Street – Townsend Building (1904).

Starting in the 20$^{th}$ century as real estate increased in value, warehouses grew in height. This handsome six-story building with a peaked roofline was the tallest in the area at the time. It was built by Southern Pacific as a warehouse to supplement its transportation operations along the nearby waterfront. Tracks from SP trains went right into the building.

123 Townsend Street.

Other uses for the warehouse were for storing Chinese fireworks and coffee beans. Like its neighbors, it was subsequently remodeled into office space. The new tenants would tell of coffee beans occasionally falling out of the rafters.

*Rolling Stone*'s first offices were located here on the sixth floor. They published their first issue on November 9, 1967. In early 1970 the magazine moved to the previously mentioned 625 (then 645) Third Street.

Long before *Rolling Stone* or the Southern Pacific planted its flag here however, the block bounded by Second and Third and Townsend and King streets on which 123 Townsend stands was the site of the Citizens Gas Company works, erected in 1865. It was a large brick building that housed the company's offices, and there was a separate gas tank that was 40 feet high and 90 feet in circumference. A 50-foot-high wooden coal depot facing the wharves in back of the building rounded out the complex. The company produced the coal gas that lighted San Francisco's streets until electricity started replacing gas in the late 19$^{th}$ century.

---

*On the northwest corner of Townsend and Second Street is:*

---

### ⓮ 698 Second Street (1910) - San Francisco Fire Department Headquarters (since 1998).

The 1906 fire revealed many deficiencies in the City's fire-fighting capabilities. One of them was the failure to take full advantage of water from the bay to protect wharves and waterfront buildings from destruction. So in 1910 this unusual structure, which somewhat resembles a Greco-Roman temple, was constructed to serve as a salt-water pumping station. The building houses eight turbine engines, which were originally steam-driven but are now diesel-powered. A large tunnel extends under Townsend Street to the bay and would feed water to these pumps in the event of a fire. The building is still meant to serve its original fire-fighting function even though in 1998 the fire department brass made this their headquarters as well.

If you are on this tour on a weekday during business hours, inside the building in the lobby is a fine and historic relic from the City's early days, the original fire engine from Knickerbocker Company #5. The long wooden poles on top, which are the pumping arms, were the longest ever made when this was built in 1855. This steam-driven machine could throw a stream of water over 200 feet.

The person most associated with Knickerbocker #5 is Lillie Hitchcock Coit (see Telegraph Hill walk), who with her enthusiasm for fire-fighting was adopted as the company's "mascot." She sat on top of this very machine during parades and official functions. When the City's fire department was changed from volunteer status to professional in 1866 this piece was sold to the Virginia City, Nevada Fire Department. After it finished out its useful life there, friends of Lillie Coit's bought it and gave it to the de Young Museum. Directly before it was placed here it sat in the Fire Department Museum on Presidio

Avenue. (At the dedication of Coit Tower in 1933 this engine was hauled up to Telegraph Hill as part of the ceremonies.)

---

*From the corner of Townsend and Second streets, look north to the tall brick warehouse halfway up Second Street on the east side of the street. This is:*

---

## ⓰ 625 Second Street (1905).

Built just before the 1906 earthquake and fire, 625 Second Street was a lucky survivor in that the flames were halted just yards away. And with so many buildings destroyed and warehouse space at a premium it operated at capacity in the years right after the fire. It also benefited from recent improvements in warehouse design: railroad tracks led right into the building. Up to seven freight cars could be unloaded at once. The original owner, the South End Warehouse Company, was one of the two (along with Haslett) big warehouse companies that were prominent along the southern waterfront well into the 20th century.

---

*Walk across Second Street to the northeast corner of Second and Townsend. The building on this corner is:*

---

## ⓱ 699 Second Street (1882).

This former tea warehouse was built in 1882 on land owned by Palace Hotel owner Senator William Sharon and a partner. At the time of construction it boasted that it was the only warehouse where railroad cars could unload right inside the building. By 1900, spur tracks leading into warehouses were a common feature, as has been seen with 123 Townsend and 625 Second Street, but two decades earlier this was the height of innovation.

This building was also originally just a two-story affair. Rising real estate values and a crying need for more housing in San Francisco have led to an innovative new use for this venerable building: over 100 new residential units have been created with the addition of several new stories above the original structure.

---

*Next door to 699 Second on its east side on Townsend Street is:*

---

## ⑰ 72 Townsend Street – Hooper's South End Grain Warehouse (1874).

A one-story building with very high ceilings, this former warehouse is the second oldest in the district. It was built in 1874 by John Hooper, a member of a family with an extensive lumber business, to hold a high grade wheat known as "California Gold." From the 1860s into the 1890s huge grain harvests from California's interior valleys regularly made their way to San Francisco docks and warehouses such as this one before being exported to Europe and elsewhere. This building is a rare survivor and reminder of that era. It was untouched by the 1906 fire; its contents survived intact.

This aging brick structure, covered with stucco, was vacant for many years before being reinforced and restored, starting in 2001. Retail establishments, which had been added to the Townsend Street side by 1911, are being remodeled into modern glass storefronts.

---

*The street next to 72 Townsend Street is:*

---

## ⑱ Colin P. Kelly, Jr. Street (c.1870s).

This alley was originally named Japan Street by the Pacific Mail Steamship Company (which similarly named China Basin and the Oriental Warehouse) in honor of the firm's extensive trade with Asia. In the 1940s during World War II, when anything having to do with Japan anathema, the name was changed to Colin P. Kelly, Jr. Street to honor the first U.S. aviator to sink a Japanese warship.

Before you leave the corner to walk north on Colin Kelly note the sidewalk near the fire hydrant where there is a bronze marker embedded between undulating borders that says "1857 SHORELINE." As you walk up Colin Kelly on the west sidewalk, you will see several other bordered "waves" denoting the 1857 shoreline. This shows that much of this street and everything to your right was once part of the bay. For all practical purposes the shoreline of 1857 was the shoreline that existed when gold was first discovered, since this area didn't start to be filled until the 1860s.

*Go to the end of Colin Kelly Street and turn right at Brannan Street. Go the half block to First Street (this part of First is now called Delancey), turn right, and walk about ten steps for a look down the street to your right at:*

## ⑲ 650 Delancey Street – Oriental Bonded Warehouse (1867).

The large brick building off to your right is the Oriental Bonded Warehouse. It is the oldest structure on the southern waterfront and one of the most historic buildings in San Francisco. After more than a century of use as a warehouse, in the mid-1990s the structure was converted to live/work condominiums. To stand here and look at the remaining brick wall on the north side and see the stainless steel frame of the new lofts inside provides an arresting juxtaposition between the past and the present.

The building was constructed in 1867 as part of a complex of warehouses and wharves in this area for the Pacific Mail Steamship Company. PMSS (as the name was commonly abbreviated) originally started in the late 1840s as a transportation company carrying mail and cargo from the East Coast through Panama to San Francisco. Starting in the 1860s the company built huge wooden steamships and began trans-Pacific service between San Francisco and China and Japan carrying mail, cargo, and people.

From the 1860s until 1910 the PMSS First Street Wharf served as the chief U.S. entry point for the vast majority of Chinese immigrants arriving on the West Coast. The newcomers typically came down the gangway with all their worldly possessions slung over their shoulders at the ends of their bamboo poles. They were lodged in the wharf's wooden sheds before being transported to Chinatown. As far as is known no immigrants were lodged in the Oriental Warehouse itself, but the storage facility held a variety of goods over the years, among them such things as beans, rice, tea, dried fish, liquor, and silk.

In 1910 the seawall and the new curved Embarcadero—construction had begun in the Fisherman's Wharf area in the 1870s—finally reached this area. As a result the First Street Wharf was demolished, thus cutting the Oriental Warehouse's direct ties to the waterfront. That same year Chinese immigrants were shifted to a new immigration station that opened on Angel Island.

The building continued to serve as a warehouse well into the 20th century. Prior to its conversion to residential lofts in 1996 it was vacant for a number of years and suffered as a result. It was damaged by fires in 1988 and 1994 and also by the Loma Prieta earthquake of 1989. Threatened with demolition, it nevertheless managed to survive and its walls stand today—silent witnesses to much San Francisco history.

---

*If you haven't already walked up to the front of the building for a closer look do so, and then retrace your steps, cross over Brannan Street, and walk two-thirds of the way down the next block toward Bryant Street to Federal Street, a narrow alley. Stop here for a look at the building on the northwest corner of Federal and First streets.*

---

### ⚫ 540 First Street – Cape Horn Warehouse (1907).

This three-story brick building was erected as a warehouse in 1907 to replace three dwellings on this site that were destroyed in 1906. Called Cape Horn Warehouse it first stored bulk paper. It continued its association with that trade well into the 1980s by serving as a storage facility for local printers, engravers, and lithographers. At some point early on and continuing until about 1945 it became part of the South End Warehouse Company, hence the name "South End Warehouses" still stenciled in white on the façade. In the mid-1990s the building was seismically upgraded and renovated, and in 1997 was converted into 16 new residential units known as the Cape Horn Lofts.

---

*Walk up Federal Street. A short way up you will see on both sides of the street "1857 SHORELINE" markers once again.*

---

### ⚫ Federal Street – Site of a Chinese fishing village
(c.1853-c.1865).

This was the approximate location of a Chinese fishing village in the 1850s and early 1860s. A cluster of dwellings sat on what was then a bluff about 20 to 40 feet above the bay. Wooden stairs leading down the side of the embankment connected the Chinese to their fishing boats on the beach below. This was just one of many Chinese camps that once dotted the shores of San Francisco Bay. They primarily netted shrimp, which they either sold live to local markets or dried for export to China.

---

*Continue up Federal Street and take a right at Rincon Alley. Go up Rincon to Bryant Street. Across the street is:*

---

## ❷ Bryant and Rincon streets – NE corner – Site of Old St. Mary's Hospital (1861–1906).

Directly across the street, until it was demolished in 2008, there remained the foundation wall of a vanished building. Affixed to the cement-covered brick wall was a bronze plaque that described how Rincon Hill was a fashionable neighborhood and the home of many of the city's illustrious residents, including William Ralston, Hubert Howe Bancroft, and William Tecumseh Sherman. That foundation retaining wall belonged to St. Mary's Hospital.

St. Mary's was founded by a group of Irish Catholic nuns who were forced by necessity to become nurses when they arrived in San Francisco in 1855 during an outbreak of cholera. In 1857 they founded the first St. Mary's Hospital, on Stockton Street near Broadway. In 1861 they opened a landmark four-story hospital here on the crest of Rincon Hill. It was known as the "Hospital on the Hill," and besides sweeping views it had the latest in hospital appurtenances—interior basins and slabs were all of marble and the two antiseptic rooms were tiled floor to ceiling.

The original main part of the hospital actually stood on the northwest corner of Bryant and First streets; a new west wing was added in 1891. The foundation wall that recently stood here was from that 1891 addition.

The hospital survived the 1906 earthquake virtually undamaged, but the fire totally consumed it. Not one of the 170 patients died however since they were carried to the shore before the flames reached here and were ferried across the bay to Oakland on a freighter. With Rincon Hill totally destroyed, St. Mary's reestablished itself in 1911 on Stanyan Street across from Golden Gate Park, where it remains today.

St. Mary's was not the only hospital on Rincon Hill. Every nationality in the early days had their own hospital. There was a German Hospital, a French Hospital, British Hospital, and so forth. But the biggest of all the medical facilities in the area was the landmark U.S. Marine Hospital (later called the Sailors' Home). Located on Harrison Street between Main and Beale streets, a few blocks from St. Mary's, it had opened in 1853. It was a grandiose H-shaped structure four stories high. It survived the 1906 earthquake and continued in use until 1912 before being demolished in 1919.

# Henry Miller
## (1827–1916)

Henry Miller is a perfect example of the classic rags-to-riches story. He arrived in San Francisco in 1850 with six dollars in his pocket. Forty years later he was the largest private landowner in the United States and was worth in excess of $40 million.

He was born Heinrich Alfred Kreiser near Heidelberg, Germany in 1827, the son of the town butcher. He learned his father's trade and emigrated to New York at age 19, where he found employment slaughtering and dressing pork 16 hours a

Henry Miller.

day for $8 a month. With gold fever raging in California a friend of his—named Henry Miller—planned to take passage via the isthmus of Panama; Heinrich would follow as soon as he had saved enough money. On the day he was set to depart however, Miller changed his mind and sold his ticket at a reduced price to Heinrich, who took the ticket—and the name Henry Miller—and sailed for San Francisco.

Upon arrival, and unswayed by the siren song of gold, he had no trouble finding work as a butcher since there was a strong demand for fresh meat. Miller worked hard, saved his money, established his own butcher shop, and soon bought a few cattle of his own. In exploring the area south of San Jose he quickly saw where the real gold lay—in the vast and empty former rancho lands in the Central Valley and beyond. After buying some land with the profits of his thriving meat business, he soon partnered with a competitor, Charles Lux, and over the next 30 years they assembled huge parcels of land, primarily in California's Central Valley.

But it was Miller who was the driving force of the duo. While Lux spent his time in San Francisco running the office, Miller was in the field overseeing everything and making acquisitions. One contemporary compared him to an old-style general, and he did resemble Alexander the Great somewhat, on a smaller scale of course, in the way he gobbled up territory, in the way he outmaneuvered and bought out those who stood in his path and then left them to run their operations—but with him firmly in charge as the owner—and in the loyalty he inspired in his "troops," the ranch foremen, cooks, and cattle drovers with whom he rode, ate, and sometimes slept among on the hard ground. Miller's genius lay in his ability to convert raw land to productive use. He pioneered the building of canals for irrigation and was one of the first to grow rice, alfalfa, and cotton in California.

His battles over land and water rights came at a cost, however. He was involved in litigation of one sort or another almost his entire career. It led to his most famous utterance: "I have made three fortunes. One for myself, one for my partner, and one for my lawyers." And he suffered personal tragedy. His first wife died in childbirth. He had three children with his second wife but his only son was born a cripple and died in middle age, and his youngest daughter was killed at age 12 when she fell from a horse.

Henry Miller once confessed that he did not know how much land he owned, but it was estimated to be in excess of one million acres spread over the states of California, Oregon, and Nevada. When he died in 1916 at age 89 he had outlived his partner, his wife, and his children except for his oldest daughter. After his death, the firm of Miller and Lux continued under a trusteeship, but after hard times in the 1930s when many of the holdings had to be sold at distress prices, allegations of mismanagement and fraud ensued. After much litigation and numerous appeals it was not until 1965 that the firm of Miller and Lux was liquidated and its assets finally distributed to Miller's heirs.

# Telegraph Hill

**Length:** 0.6 miles / 1.0 kilometers.
**Time:** 1½ hours (longer if you take the elevator to the top of Coit Tower.)
**Walk Rating:** Strenuous.
**Hills:** Union Street from Calhoun to Montgomery is a short but steep uphill. The Filbert Street steps make for a good aerobic workout. Montgomery Street from Julius's Castle to Filbert is a moderate uphill. More steps lead from Filbert and Montgomery up to Telegraph Hill Boulevard. From Coit Tower to the Marconi Monument is a moderate downhill.
**Public Transit:** The 39 bus line runs from Fisherman's Wharf and Washington Square to Coit Tower. The line's southern terminus is at Montgomery and Union streets near the start of this tour.
**Parking:** Parking at Coit Tower is limited to 30 minutes. Street parking is difficult to find; two-hour limits for non-residents.
**Restrooms:** There is a coin-operated (25 cents) public toilet at Coit Tower.

Originally called Loma Alta or "High Hill" by the Spanish, then subsequently Windmill Hill and Signal Hill, Telegraph Hill got its present name in 1850 when a semaphore telegraph was erected at the summit. It consisted of a pole with wooden arms attached to it that could be manipulated to indicate to the populace below what kind of ship would soon be arriving at Yerba Buena Cove. In 1853 this simple device was superceded by a real telegraph line, which was strung from Pt. Lobos on the ocean directly to downtown.

The hill originally covered a larger area than it does today. Almost from day one, gravel and rock from its base were taken as ballast for outbound ships. Starting in the 1880s, quarrying, particularly of its eastern slope, began in earnest when the Gray Brothers, local contractors, started dynamiting its sides to loosen rock to be used in construction of the seawall and for paving city streets. They continued their efforts until about 1914, by which time a number of houses on the hill had tumbled to ruin.

Habitation began on the hill in the early 1850s, primarily by poor Irish and later Italian and other immigrants whose livelihoods principally depended upon activity centered upon the nearby wharves.

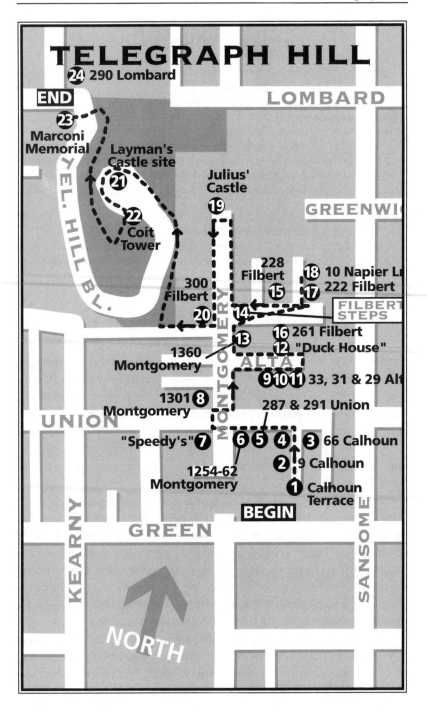

# TELEGRAPH HILL

**24** 290 Lombard

LOMBARD

**END**

**23**

Marconi
Memorial

Layman's
Castle site

**21**

Julius'
Castle

**19**

GREENWI

TEL. HILL BL.

**22**
Coit
Tower

228
Filbert

**18** 10 Napier L
**17** 222 Filbert

300
Filbert

**15**

FILBERT
STEPS

**20**

**14**

**13**

**16** 261 Filbert
**12** "Duck House"

1360
Montgomery

ALTA

**9 10 11** 33, 31 & 29 Al

1301 **8**
Montgomery

287 & 291 Union

UNION

"Speedy's" **7**

**6 5 4** **3** 66 Calhoun

**2** 9 Calhoun

1254-62
Montgomery

**1** Calhoun
Terrace

**BEGIN**

KEARNY

GREEN

SANSOME

NORTH

# TELEGRAPH HILL

**❶** **Calhoun Terrace**

**❷** **9 Calhoun Terrace**

**❸** **66 Calhoun Terrace**

**❹** **265 Union Street**

**❺** **287 and 291 Union Street**

**❻** **1254-62 Montgomery Street**

**❼** **301 Union Street - "Speedy's" New Union Grocery**

**❽** **1301 Montgomery Street**

**❾** **33 Alta Street**

**❿** **31 Alta Street**

**⓫** **29 Alta Street**

**⓬** **60 Alta Street - "Duck House"**

**⓭** **1360 Montgomery Street**

**⓮** **Filbert Street Steps**

**⓯** **228 Filbert Street**

**⓰** **261 Filbert Street**

**⓱** **222 Filbert Street**

**⓲** **10 Napier Lane**

**⓳** **Julius' Castle**

**⓴** **300 Filbert Street**

**㉑** **Coit Tower parking lot - Site of Layman's Castle**

**㉒** **Coit Tower**

**㉓** **Guglielmo Marconi Memorial**

**㉔** **290 Lombard Street**

They were primarily longshoremen, stevedores, fishermen, and warehouse workers who competed for low-paying scarce jobs. They built modest dwellings on the hill's slopes; some of them still exist today. The area remained largely working-class until the early decades of the 20<sup>th</sup> century. Throughout its history the hill has also enjoyed a reputation as a haven for artists, writers, and bohemians of all sorts who have been attracted by its views, cozy charm, and—until the latter part of the 20<sup>th</sup> century—its affordable housing costs.

Telegraph Hill was one of the few downtown enclaves to survive the 1906 fire. Local residents managed to stave off the flames with a combination of hoarded water and homemade wine that the area's Italians had produced and stored. Despite the summit having survived the disaster, the hill remained a relative backwater until the 1930s, largely due to its inaccessibility. (Goats grazed freely here until banished by a city ordinance in 1928.) Its steep slopes were largely bypassed by the city's transit lines. There was no need to serve its relatively few cliff-dwelling inhabitants, and active commerce was located on the flatlands below. But street paving during the Depression years led to increased accessibility and new housing. Alta Street and Montgomery Street between Union and Greenwich were graded and paved in 1931. During 1939–40 the same was done for the intersection of Calhoun and Union streets.

In terms of building styles found here there was a long hiatus between the hill's early development in the 1850s and 1860s when Carpenter Gothic and Italianate prevailed, and the 1930s when a few new Moderne and International-style buildings were erected. This gap has meant that there are no Stick or Queen Anne-style Victorians here nor any of the bay window buildings that are so prevalent elsewhere in San Francisco. This architectural anomaly makes for a contrasting yet actually quite harmonious blend.

Telegraph Hill today, in contrast to its down-at-the-heels roots, is one of the City's choice residential neighborhoods. Its breathtaking views of the bay, its stairway gardens, and human scale architecture give it a unique ambience.

---

*Start this walk at the south end of upper Calhoun Terrace (enter from Union Street).*

---

## ❶ Calhoun Terrace (1851).

Called Calhoun Street until 1942, this now two-level dead-end alley once connected with Green Street to the south until the late 19th century when the notorious Gray Brothers started quarrying the eastern slope of Telegraph Hill. Their continued eating away of the hill cut Calhoun off from Green and undermined and collapsed all seven of the houses that once stood on the east side of the street here. Calhoun originally was just a dirt trail, and even as late as the 1930s it was nothing more than a narrow planked thoroughfare. Finally during 1939–40 it was graded, divided into two levels, and paved.

The views of the Embarcadero and the bay from here give a good idea of why this is such an attractive location. If you look straight down and to the right you will see a two-story flat-roofed industrial building on the northwest corner of Green and Sansome streets. This was the site of the Gray Brothers rock crusher while they were carving away the hillside. (See the Embarcadero walk).

A few buildings worth noting on this street are:

## ❷ 9 Calhoun Terrace (1854).

This Gothic Revival structure, somewhat obscured by trees, is the oldest house still extant on this block. It was erected in 1854 by David G. "Yankee" Robinson, a popular actor and theater impresario. It went through several changes of ownership over the next two decades, then remained in the same family from 1877 to 2000.

## ❸ Calhoun and Union streets – SE corner – 66 Calhoun Terrace (1939).

A fine example of the International Style, this three-story white building with the horizontal bands of windows on all floors was one of the early efforts of architect Richard Neutra. It was built for investment banker Sidney P. Kahn as a single-family residence. It was later divided into flats.

## ❹ Calhoun and Union streets – SW corner – 265 Union Street (1962).

From the early 20th century until it was torn down in 1961 this was the site of a structure known as "The Compound." Up until about World War II the place was known as a haven for artists, writers, and musicians of various kinds. After the war the building attracted better-paying tenants in the form of lawyers, secretaries, and flight attendants. The Compound was noted for its party atmosphere. In 1962 the present apartment building, designed by noted local architect Gardner Dailey, was erected.

---

*Walk up Union Street a few steps for a look at:*

---

❺ **287 Union Street** (c.1853) **and 291 Union Street** (c.1851).

Two ninety-one Union Street is one of the two oldest structures on Telegraph Hill. Records show that the lot was purchased in 1850 by Irish immigrant John Cooney. Cooney, who married an English-woman, originally emigrated to Australia but moved his family to San Francisco when word of the gold rush reached there. After erecting their house the Cooneys ran a small grocery store out of the first floor. Sometime before 1880 the top floor Italianate false front was added, giving the building a more imposing appearance. Cooney family descendants continued to live in this house until 1937.

In 1852 John Cooney purchased the lot next door and erected the Gothic Revival-style 287 Union as two rental units. This building has had its windows modernized but it still retains its gable bargeboards, features that the main Cooney house once had but which were removed when it was remodeled into an Italianate.

---

*Up on the southeast corner of Union and Montgomery streets is:*

---

❻ **1254–62 Montgomery Street** (1861, 1880s).

Aside from the Pioneer Park platform where Coit Tower stands, the southeast corner of the intersection here is the highest point on Telegraph Hill. That made it a good place to catch the prevailing winds, a desirable condition since the first structure to occupy this site was a windmill that was used to operate the grinders for a coffee mill run by an H. C. Hudson. The building that stands here now was erected in 1861. Originally it was just a one-story affair that was two units wide, but in the late 1880s it was enlarged and converted into a hotel, operated by a Vincenzo Davalle. Apparently it did not last long as a hotel for it was converted into apartments by the early 20$^{th}$ century.

---

*Across the street on the southwest corner of this intersection is:*

---

## ❼ 301 Union Street – "Speedy's" New Union Grocery (1915).

A neighborhood institution and the only local market remaining on the summit, "Speedy's" got its name from its longtime proprietors the Spediacci family who owned the building and ran the store almost continuously from 1915 to 1954. Known for their neighborliness, the close-knit Italian family also made its own homemade wine in the basement of the building. They crushed the grapes using the traditional method of stomping on them with their bare feet.

The store's roots go back to 1860 when a grocery first opened on this corner. By 1880 it had been converted to a butcher shop, which it remained until just a few years prior to 1906. The fire that year just managed to reach this corner and destroy the building that was here at the time. (The other three corners of this intersection were spared.) This building was erected during 1914–15 and was remodeled in 1955. The exterior was stuccoed over and the entrance to the store, which used to be on the corner, was perhaps changed then to its present location on Union Street.

---

*Across Union Street from Speedy's on the northwest corner of the intersection is:*

---

## ❽ 1301 Montgomery Street (c.1851).

This unprepossessing and easily overlooked structure is arguably the most historic building on Telegraph Hill. Underneath the stucco façade of this two-story edifice with the deep recessed windows is an all-brick structure, the only such one on the hill and one of the three oldest brick buildings in the City (one or two in Jackson Square may be older). Either it or 291 Union can claim the title as the oldest on Telegraph Hill. Its exact date of construction is impossible to pinpoint but it seems to have been here at least by February 1852 since a

**1301 Montgomery Street, 1865.**

building—almost surely this one—appears at this location on the U.S. Coast Survey map of that year.

In a photo of it taken in 1865 it looks like a scene out of the Old West—a simple brick building with a second-floor balcony (long since removed) on the Montgomery Street side supported by four wooden pillars anchored to a wood plank sidewalk at street level. A man and a woman dressed in their Sunday best pose stiffly on the balcony, while down below on the dirt pathway that was Montgomery Street a couple of two-wheeled carts without horses, stand forlornly at the curb.

Unlike all of its neighbors, this building was certainly intended solely as a commercial enterprise, perhaps to take advantage of traffic visiting the semaphore/telegraph on the hill behind it. Its first documented use was as a grocery store, starting in 1854. It continued as such under various owners through much of the 19th century. Sometime in the early 20th century the building was stuccoed over—perhaps as an earthquake proofing measure—and it became variously a barber shop, a pool hall, and a soft-drink dispensary. It then was converted to residential use, which it still is.

---

*Cross over to the east side of Montgomery Street and walk a half block down to Alta Street, a deadend. Halfway down Alta on the right side are three side-by-side gable-roof houses that date from the mid-nineteenth century.*

### ❾ 33 Alta Street (c.1865).

The gable portion of this two-story wood-frame Gothic Revival house dates from about 1865, while the flat roof half attached to the west side is more modern, dating from about 1930. The windows on the lower floor in the older portion have also been remodeled, and thus this house provides a good example of how dwellings change over time to suit various owners. The first owner of the house was a James Harrington, a warehouseman.

### ❿ 31 Alta Street (c.1853).

This three-story frame house on a brick foundation/basement is the most distinctive house on the block since it has two balconies. It is also the oldest, having been built around 1853. The first owner was apparently a Captain A. Andrews, a jewelry store owner and dealer in diamonds. A subsequent owner in the 1860s and 1870s was an R. Andrews, a stevedore by trade and perhaps a relative of the captain.

During the late 1920s this house gained a bit of notoriety when resident Myrtle Sawvelle opened a tea room and night club in the basement called the "Telegraph Hill Tavern." She distributed flyers advertising her establishment as having "all the atmosphere of the Montmartre with a Marine View." Since Myrtle was serving home-made beverages with a bit more kick than tea, and this was during Prohibition, the police raided the place and hauled Myrtle off to jail. She spent 90 days behind bars (the metal kind). Not long after her release, Myrtle and her husband decamped permanently for Carmel, and San Francisco heard of them no more.

### ⓫ 29 Alta Street (c.1876).

This house is the third of three gable-roofed Victorians on this side of the street. The last of the three built, it also has been extensively remodeled (in this case in 1955).

---

*Across the street is:*

---

### ⓬ 60 Alta Street – the "Duck House" (1936).

Because of the steep slope here, the north side of Alta Street in this block was not developed until well into the 20th century. Construction of housing only really became feasible after a concrete retaining wall was put in in 1931 in preparation for the street paving, which was done in conjunction with paving Montgomery Street.

A notable building here, and part of the housing boom that was facilitated by the street paving, is #60, also known as the "Duck House." Built for artist Helen Forbes by architect William Wurster, the dwelling got its name from the frescoes of ducks that Ms. Forbes painted on the west exterior under the eave while the building was under construction. Forbes painted frescoes for the San Francisco Zoo and elsewhere in northern California. Mrs. Eleanor Roosevelt visited the Duck House's second owner, Mayris Chaney Martin, on several occasions.

---

*Walk back up Alta, turn right on Montgomery, and stop at the corner of the Filbert Street steps. The apartment building on the southeast corner is:*

---

### ⓫ 1360 Montgomery Street (1936).

This beautiful Moderne apartment house (condos since 1983), now such an integral part of Telegraph Hill, was the subject during its construction of protests and vandalism by area residents, who thought that the building was out of scale relative to its smaller neighbors. The etched-glass window over the entrance, with its palm trees and undulating waves, the sgraffito exterior wall panels (fashioned by carving through several layers of cement) of heroic figures of California, and the streamline ocean liner-style detailing give the building a distinctive character. Its decorative elements make it one of the few buildings to place San Francisco in context as belonging to the Pacific Rim. This effect is emphasized by the vegetation planted in front—the large palm fronds, the bougainvillea, and the Japanese maple tree are all natives of countries bordering the Pacific Ocean.

Because of its styling and its location it has drawn notable residents, such as Hiram Johnson, former governor of California and U.S. Senator who lived here from 1937 to 1945. It has also served as the backdrop for several movies, including *Dark Passage* in 1947 starring Humphrey Bogart (hence the Bogart cutout usually visible in the second-floor window) and Lauren Bacall, and the more recent *Nine Months*, starring Hugh Grant.

## ⓴ The Filbert Street steps.

Often thought of as quintessential Telegraph Hill, this block of Filbert between Montgomery and Sansome Street (way down below) is an official city street, but it is so steep that it is only accessible by stairways. It's a sylvan glade of vegetation today, but prior to 1950, when local resident and ace gardener Grace Marchant took charge, the slope here was a dumping ground for refuse. Ms. Marchant devoted the next 30 years of her life to beautifying the area. She died in 1982 at age 96. A signpost plaque near the head of the gardens praises her for her work. Even though this is city property, the gardens are still today privately maintained.

---

*Walk down the steps for a better look at these stairway gardens and to see three dwellings bordering the gardens. The stairway curves to your left as you descend. A short distance down on the left is:*

---

## ⓯ 228 Filbert Street (1882).

This fine Carpenter-style cottage embellished with a sculpted bargeboard and Gothic window frames was completed in 1882, having replaced a simpler structure on the same site. The house was built by Philip Brown, a native of the Isle of Jersey in the English Channel. After spending time at sea, Brown established a stevedoring business in San Francisco and settled on Telegraph Hill to be close to the waterfront. Brown died in 1901, but his descendants continued to own the property as late as 1959.

---

*Across the way the three-story shingle-covered dwelling with the slanted windows on the two upper floors is:*

---

## ⓰ 261 Filbert Street (1941).

Designed by architect Gardner Dailey, who did the previously mentioned 296 Union Street apartment building, the original owner of 261 Filbert was Helen Forbes of the Duck House on Alta Street. She had planned to build two other dwellings in the area, but World War II intervened and the plans fell through. The exterior of this building was covered with shingles in 1971, altering its character somewhat.

*A little farther down the steps on the northeast corner of Napier Lane is:*

**⓱ 222 Filbert Street** (c.1879).

This rather plain wood-shingled Italianate with a simple cornice bracket as virtually its only decoration was built about 1879 by Michael Thornton, an Irish immigrant who lived here and ran a grocery store out of the lower floor until his death in 1918. He might also have operated the place as a "blind pig," or an unlicensed saloon, in the early years.

*The plank-laid thoroughfare at the side of 222 Filbert is Napier Lane, a charming deadend whose dwellings mostly date from the 1860s and 1870s. The first house to the right is:*

**⓲ 10 Napier Lane** (c.1857, c.1887).

If you look closely down the right side of this single-story Italianate cottage you can see a different, slightly higher roof line about ten feet farther back. The back portion of this house seems to date from the mid-1850s, when it was likely just a modest working-man's shack that was apparently built by two brothers, Mortimer and John Clark, who worked respectively as a teamster and laborer at the nearby Greenwich Dock Warehouse. About 1887 the front portion of the house, with the Italianate façade, was added.

*After exploring the rest of Napier Lane return to the Filbert Street steps. The garden across the way at this location is especially beautiful, with many bunches of long-stemmed roses rising skyward. Go back up the steps to Montgomery Street and turn right. At the end of the street is:*

**⓳ 1541 Montgomery Street – Julius' Castle** (1922).

A Telegraph Hill institution known more for its views than its food, Julius' Castle restaurant dates from 1922. The site had originally played host to a combination grocery/liquor store as early as 1889. Toward the end of World War I, when it burned down, the structure there served as a residence. Julius Roz, an Italian immigrant from Turin and the restaurant's namesake, erected this crenellated structure on the ruins of the burned-out building. Before Montgomery Street north of Alta was paved, in 1931, that stretch was little more than a dirt trail just wide enough for one car. To accommodate patrons arriving by automobile, a turntable was installed in front of the restaurant and a local teenage boy was employed to park the cars and turn them around.

---

*Walk back on Montgomery Street on the upper level one block to Filbert Street and go up the first flight of steps.*

---

## ❷⓪ 300 Filbert Street

Nestled among the roses in the garden of 300 Filbert Street is a small statue of a group of male and female nude figures, which until recently, was covered with many layers of paint. This work is titled "Creation," and is a studio model for the much larger final version of a statue of the same name that graced the Golden Gate International Exposition world's fair held on Treasure Island during 1939–40. The nudity of the figures, sculpted by local artist Haig Patigian, caused controversy at first. The many coatings of paint might have been applied to quiet those who were offended.

---

*Walk up the concrete Filbert Steps to Telegraph Hill Boulevard. Take the paved walkway to the right and follow its curve past the boulder wall up to the Coit Tower parking lot.*

---

## ❷① Coit Tower parking lot – Site of Layman's Castle
(1882–1903).

The northern half of Coit Tower's parking lot was once the site of an L-shaped building with a crenellated octagonal tower, known as Layman's Castle after its developer, Frederick Layman. Opened in 1882, it served as a restaurant and observatory. The hilltop attraction never proved very popular, largely due to the hill's inaccessibility. Several things were tried in an attempt to drum up business. For

**A jousting tournament on Telegraph Hill, 1886.**

about a year in the mid-1880s there were weekly jousting contests, in which two armor-clad combatants on horseback charged at each other with swords flying. And a cable-car line was run up Greenwich Street to the summit in 1884 in an attempt to increase access and traffic, but the line never turned a profit and was discontinued after only a few years. By the 1890s the castle was a scene of neglect. In 1903 a fire damaged the structure. The remainder, beyond repair, was dismantled and carted off for firewood.

The statue of Christopher Columbus, which was the result of a proposal by the Italian consul general, was dedicated by the City's Italian community and others on Columbus Day, October 12, 1957. It marks the line of the southern wall of Layman's Castle.

## ㉒ Coit Tower (1933).

Coit Tower is the result of a bequest left by Lillie Hitchcock Coit. Coit, who died in 1929, visited Telegraph Hill a few years before her death and mused about donating money for an observatory to be built at the summit. But in her will she simply decreed that the roughly $120,000 she left as a gift to the City "be expended in an appropriate manner for the purpose of adding to the beauty of the city which I have always loved."

Among a number of designs considered for the project, the winning entry was submitted by Henry T. Howard of the firm of Arthur Brown Jr., which had designed both City Hall and the Opera House. Howard's choice of a fluted tower pierced by open windows at the top proved ideal for the site. The polygonal form makes the tower visually appealing from any angle, and the vertical flutes in the way that they capture light and shadow add to what could have been a sterile column. Although some at the time claimed that the tower resembles a fire hose nozzle, architect Howard emphatically denied any such intent. He claimed that the fluted tower idea was *sui generis*, although interestingly the Battersea Power Station in London, which had been completed a few years before Coit Tower got underway, had four similar looking towers and may have been a subconscious influence.

---

*Enter the tower for a look at the murals on the ground floor.*

---

When Coit Tower was dedicated in October 1933, the original plans called for a restaurant on the ground floor. Instead, the space was first used to exhibit artifacts and pictures from San Francisco's pioneer days, an idea apparently suggested by the land on which Coit Tower sits—Pioneer Park.

The idea of murals for Coit Tower was given birth by artist George Biddle, a classmate of President Franklin D. Roosevelt, who was familiar with the works of such great muralists as Diego Rivera and Jose Clemente Orozco and the colorful murals that they had created for Mexican government buildings in the 1920s. Biddle wrote to his chum FDR, proposing that something similar be undertaken in this country. The idea took root and a new federal agency was established, the Public Works Art Project. The timing was perfect, for the newly completed Coit Tower became the first project of a program that was soon expanded nationwide.

A couple of dozen local artists were hired to do the Coit Tower murals, the subject of which was to be "the contemporary American scene in all its various aspects." This was later modified to just scenes of California and San Francisco. Most of the artists did their work in fresco (the Italian word for "fresh") which is paint applied to wet plaster. They employed a contemporary style during the Depression years known as Social Realism, in which biting political and social commentary was woven into art. They succeeded all too well. The scenes here show unsmiling workers toiling grimly at their labors. The feeling of oppression these figures are experiencing from mechanized, industrial society is palpable.

When finished, the murals caused controversy. Many of the artists were left-leaning politically, and certain manifestations of those beliefs found their way into their art: newspapers for sale at a newsstand include *The New Masses* and *The Daily Worker*; a man reaches high on a shelf for a book by Karl Marx; a hammer and sickle symbol bordered the slogan "Workers of the World Unite." This last bit of expression was too much—it was expunged before the murals were opened to the public in late 1934. (It was located above the west windows on fresco #4.)

Like a fly in amber, the murals today are very much of their time. The art captures the sentiments of a turbulent era that may seem especially remote to younger people today.

---

*After viewing the murals go around to the back of the tower and take the paved path spiraling down through the trees to the base of the hill on the north side. When you finish descending the last staircase, cross Telegraph Hill Boulevard— watch for cars—and take a look at the stone bench embedded with the bronze medallion.*

### ㉓ Guglielmo Marconi memorial (1939).

Certainly appropriate here at the base of Telegraph Hill, this stone bench pays tribute to Guglielmo Marconi (1874–1937), the Nobel-prize-winning inventor of wireless telegraphy. A man ahead of his time, Marconi had originally envisioned a two-way wireless telephone complete with video pictures instead of just the one-

The Marconi memorial.

way broadcast radio that made him famous. (The technology of his day was not advanced enough to achieve his vision.) In 1898 he became the first to send a wireless communication over a large body of water when he made a transmission across the English Channel.

The Latin inscription under the bronze relief of Marconi in profile says: "Outstripping the lightning, the voice races through the empty sky."

---

*The tall apartment building across Lombard Street on the northeast corner of Lombard and Kearny Street is:*

---

### ㉔ 290 Lombard Street (1940).

This seven-story building, constructed in 1940 by a wife of a descendant of chocolate king Domingo Ghirardelli, raised an outcry after it was completed in 1940 because it was much taller than its neighbors. Afraid that their views would be blocked by further such construction, area residents led by architect Gardner Dailey pressed for a 40-foot height limit, a restriction that was duly passed by the Board of Supervisors. A very desirable building because of its Art Deco styling and unimpeded views, 290 Lombard has attracted a number of prominent residents, among them the late *Chronicle* columnist Herb Caen, who lived here for a few years during the early 1960s.

# Lillie Hitchcock Coit
## (1843–1929)

Lillie Hitchcock Coit was one of San Francisco's most colorful characters. Anything but a prim Victorian and dutiful housewife, Lillie smoked cigars, drank bourbon, and played poker. She delighted in dressing like a man, sometimes going on late-night excursions with male friends to men-only hangouts; on at least one occasion she went disguised as a man with her husband to a cockfight near Washerwoman's Lagoon. And because women were not allowed to attend prizefights she once paid two pugilists to stage a boxing match for herself and a few friends in her suite in the Palace Hotel.

Lillie Hitchcock Coit.

Other eccentricities included dying her hair, and then when her husband complained or she grew bored with the new color she'd shave her head and wear wigs until her hair grew back. Not a great beauty, she craved attention and seemed to have been charismatic enough to have gotten it, since she was always surrounded by beaux when single and was constantly demanding the attention of her husband when married. In hindsight she comes off as narcissistic. She was once quoted as saying: "Women are angry if they are gazed at by men, but are disappointed if they are not."

Lillie Hitchcock came to San Francisco at age eight in 1851 with her mother and father, an army surgeon who had been transferred to the Presidio from the East. An only-child tomboy, she was rescued as a young girl from a burning building by one of the local volunteer fire companies, Knickerbocker #5. The experience left her with an enduring fascination with fire fighting and an unshakable loyalty to the engine company that had saved her life. She became Knickerbocker #5's mascot and benefactor, and frequently rode along with the boys on their way to fight city blazes. She even added a "5" at the end when signing her name. During the Civil War, Lillie and her mother, who were southern sympathizers, retreated to Paris, where Lillie, fluent in French, translated Confederate documents at the court of Napoleon III. After returning to San Francisco, Lillie, after flirtations with a number of eligible bachelors, in 1870 married Howard Coit, a wealthy stockbroker. The union was opposed by Lillie's parents, and the couple separated after a few years—perhaps partially due to her mother's meddling. But they never divorced, and when Howard died prematurely of heart disease at age 47 in 1885 he left his wife his entire estate of $250,000, a considerable sum.

Lillie Coit spent the rest of her days alternately in Paris and San Francisco, being paid court by a series of gentlemen but never remarrying. One day in 1904, while she was living in the Palace Hotel, a minor functionary of hers, Alexander Garnett, burst into her suite with a gun and shot and killed her financial manager, with whom she was conferring. Garnett's apparent target was Lillie herself. The whole affair so unnerved her that she decamped for Paris and did not return to San Francisco until 1924, after word had reached her that Garnett had died in the insane asylum where he had been confined.

Shortly after her return to a much changed San Francisco (she had left before the 1906 earthquake), Lillie Hitchcock Coit suffered a disabling stroke. She lingered until 1929. Her name is forever linked today to Coit Tower, the memorial that was built with the money she left as a bequest to "beautify the city I loved."

# Photo/Illustration Credits

# Select Bibliography

## Books

Abeloe, William N. *Historic Spots in California.* 3d ed. rev. Stanford, CA: Stanford University Press, 1966.

Altrocchi, Julia Cooley. *The Spectacular San Franciscans.* New York: E. P. Dutton, 1949.

Arts Commission of San Francisco. *San Francisco Civic Art Collection: A Guided Tour to Publicly Owned Art of the City and County of San Francisco.* San Francisco: The San Francisco Arts Commission, 1989.

Asbury, Herbert. *The Barbary Coast: An Informal History of the San Francisco Underworld.* Garden City, NY: Garden City Publishing, 1933.

Asher, Don. *Notes From a Battered Grand, A Memoir: Fifty Years of Music From Honky-Tonk to High Society.* New York: Harcourt Brace Jovanovich, 1992.

Baird, James Armstrong, Jr. *Time's Wondrous Changes: San Francisco Architecture 1776–1915.* San Francisco: California Historical Society, 1962.

Bakalinsky, Adah. *Stairway Walks in San Francisco.* Berkeley, CA: Wilderness Press, 1995.

Bancroft, Hubert Howe. *History of California.* Vol. 5, *1846–1848.* San Francisco: The History Company, 1886.

Barker, Malcolm E. *More San Francisco Memoirs, 1852–1899: The ripening years.* San Francisco: Londonborn Publications, 1996.

———. *San Francisco Memoirs, 1835–1851: Eyewitness accounts of the birth of a city.* San Francisco: Londonborn Publications, 1994.

———. *Three Fearful Days: San Francisco Memoirs of the 1906 earthquake and fire.* San Francisco: Londonborn Publications, 1998.

*The Bay of San Francisco: The Metropolis of the Pacific Coast and its Suburban Cities: A History.* Vol. 2. Chicago: The Lewis Publishing Co., 1892.

Benet, James. *A Guide to San Francisco and the Bay Region.* New York: Random House, 1963.

Bernhardi, Robert C. *Great Buildings of San Francisco: A Photographic Guide.* New York: Dover Publications, 1980.

Blaisdell, F. William, and Moses Grossman. *Catastrophes, epidemics, and neglected disasters: San Francisco General Hospital and the evolution of public care.* San Francisco: San Francisco General Hospital Foundation, 1999.

Bloomfield, Arthur. *The San Francisco Opera, 1922–1978.* Sausalito, CA: Comstock Editions, 1978.

Blumenson, John J-G. *Identifying American Architecture: A Pictorial Guide to Styles and Terms, 1600–1945.* New York: W. W. Norton & Co., 1981.

Bode, William. *Lights and Shadows of Chinatown.* San Francisco: H. S. Crocker, 1896.

Boessenecker, John. *Against the Vigilantes: The Recollections of Dutch Charley Duane.* Norman, OK: University of Oklahoma Press, 1999.

Bonnett, Wayne. *Victorian San Francisco: The 1895 Illustrated Directory.* Sausalito, CA: Windgate Press, 1996.

Brammer, Alex. *Victorian Classics of San Francisco.* Sausalito, CA: Windgate Press, 1987.

Browning, Peter, ed. and comp. *Yerba Buena, San Francisco: From the Beginning to the Gold Rush, 1769–1849.* Lafayette, CA: Great West Books, 1998.

Bugliosi, Vincent, and Curt Gentry. *Helter Skelter: The True Story of the Manson Murders.* New York: W. W. Norton & Co., 1974.

Burke, Marie Louise. *Swami Trigunatita: His Life and Work.* San Francisco: Vedanta Society of Northern California, 1997.

Byington, Lewis Francis. *The History of San Francisco.* Vol. 2. Chicago: The S. J. Clarke Publishing Co., 1931.

Caen, Herb. *Baghdad By The Bay.* 1949. Reprint. Sausalito, CA: Comstock Editions, n.d.

———. *Baghdad 1951.* Garden City, NY: Doubleday & Co., 1950.

———. *One Man's San Francisco.* Garden City, NY: Doubleday & Co., 1976.

Chamberlin, Jane and Hank Armstrong. *The Great and Notorious Saloons of San Francisco.* Santa Barbara, CA: Capra Press, 1982.

Clarke, Dwight L. *William Tecumseh Sherman: Gold Rush Banker.* San Francisco: California Historical Society, 1969.

Conrad, Barnaby. *Name Dropping: Tales From My San Francisco Nightclub.* San Francisco: Wild Coconuts Publishing, 1997.

deFord, Miriam Allen. *They Were San Franciscans.* Caldwell, ID: The Caxton Printers, Ltd., 1947.

Delehanty, Randolph. *In The Victorian Style.* San Francisco: Chronicle Books, 1991.

———. *San Francisco: The Ultimate Guide.* San Francisco: Chronicle Books, 1995.

Dillon, Richard. *San Francisco: Adventurers and Visionaries.* Tulsa, OK: Continental Heritage Press, 1983.

———. *Humbugs and Heroes: A Gallery of California Pioneers.* Garden City, NY: Doubleday & Co., 1970.

———. *North Beach: The Italian Heart of San Francisco.* Novato, CA: Presidio Press, 1985.

Dobie, Charles Caldwell. *San Francisco's Chinatown.* New York: D. Appelton-Century Co., 1936.

Dwinelle, John W. *The Colonial History of San Francisco.* 1867. Reprint. Berkeley, CA: Ross Valley Book Co., 1978.

Eldridge, Zoeth S. *The Beginnings of San Francisco.* Vol. 1. *1774–1850.* San Francisco: Zoeth S. Eldridge, 1912.

Fardon, George Robinson. *San Francisco Album: Photographs 1854–1856.* With an introduction by Jeffrey Frankel and Hans P. Kraus, Jr. San Francisco: Chronicle Books, 1999.

Farnsworth, Elma G. *Distant Vision: Romance and Discovery on an Invisible Frontier: Philo T. Farnsworth, Inventor of Television.* Salt Lake City: Pemberly Kent Publishers, 1990.

Ferlinghetti, Lawrence and Nancy J. Peters. *Literary San Francisco: A Pictorial History from Its Beginnings to the Present Day.* San Francisco: City Lights Books, 1980.

Fisher, Anne Reeploeg. *Exile of a Race.* Seattle: F & T Publishers, 1965.

The Foundation for San Francisco's Architectural Heritage. *Splendid Survivors: San Francisco's Downtown Architectural Heritage.* San Francisco: California Living Books, 1979.

French, Warren. *The San Francisco Poetry Renaissance, 1955–1960.* Boston: Twayne Publishers, a division of G. K. Hall & Co., 1991.

Friedman, Myra. *Buried Alive: The Biography of Janis Joplin.* New York: William Morrow & Co., 1973.

Garraty, John A. and Mark C. Carnes, eds. *American National Biography.* New York: Oxford University Press, 1999.

Gebhard, David, Eric Sandweiss, and Robert Winter. *The Guide to Architecture in San Francisco and Northern California.* Salt Lake City: Peregrine Smith Books, 1985.

Gentry, Curt. *The Dolphin Guide to San Francisco and the Bay Area, Present and Past.* Garden City, NY: Doubleday & Co., 1962.

———. *The Madams of San Francisco: A hundred years of the city's secret history.* 1964. Reprint. Sausalito, CA: Comstock Editions, 1977.

Glasscock, C. B. *Lucky Baldwin: The Story of an Unconventional Success.* Reno, NV: Silver Syndicate Press, 1993.

Goulart, Ron, ed. *Encyclopedia of American Comics: From 1897 to the Present.* New York: Facts on File, 1990.

Goldman, Albert, and Laurence Schiller. *Ladies and Gentlemen Lenny Bruce!!* New York: Random House, 1971.

Gumina, Deanna Paoli. *The Italians of San Francisco.* New York: Center for Migration Studies, 1978.

Hansen, Gladys. *San Francisco Almanac: Everything You Wanted to Know About Everyone's Favorite City.* San Francisco: Chronicle Books, 1995.

Harris, David, with Eric Sandweiss. *Eadweard Muybridge and the Photographic Panorama of San Francisco, 1850–1880.* Montreal: Canadian Centre for Architecture, 1993.

Hart, Ann Clark. *Clark's Point: A Narrative of the Conquest of California and the Beginning of San Francisco.* San Francisco: Pioneer Press, 1937.

Hart, James D. *A Companion to California.* New York: Oxford University Press, 1978.

Herron, Don. *The Literary World of San Francisco and its Environs.* San Francisco: City Lights Books, 1985.

*Hills of San Francisco.* (Compiled from articles in the *San Francisco Chronicle*.) San Francisco: Chronicle Publishing Co., 1959.

Hittell, J. S. *A History of The City of San Francisco and Incidentally of the State of California And A Guide Book to San Francisco.* 1878. Reprint. Berkeley, CA: Berkeley Hills Books, 1999.

Hittell, Theodore H. *History of California.* Vol. 3. San Francisco: N. J. Stone & Co., 1897.

Holdredge, Helen. *Firebelle Lillie.* New York: Meredith Press, 1967.

Horn, Maurice, ed. *The World Encyclopedia of Comics.* New York: Chelsea House, 1999.

Hunt, Rockwell D. *California's Stately Hall of Fame.* Stockton, CA: College of the Pacific, 1950.

Jackson, Joseph Henry, ed. *The Western Gate: A San Francisco Reader.* New York: Farrar, Straus and Young, 1952.

Jewett, Masha Zakheim. *Coit Tower, San Francisco: Its History and Art.* San Francisco: Volcano Press, 1983.

Johnson, Paul C. and R. R. Olmsted. *Mirror of the Dream: An Illustrated History of San Francisco.* San Francisco: Scrimshaw Press, 1976.

Jones, Idwal. *Ark of Empire: San Francisco's Montgomery Block.* Garden City, NY: Doubleday & Co., 1951.

Kahn, Edgar M. *Cable Car Days in San Francisco.* San Francisco: The Friends of the San Francisco Public Library, 1976.

Kostura, William. *Russian Hill: The Summit, 1853–1906.* San Francisco: Aerie Publications, 1997.

Lewis, Donovan. *Pioneers of California: True Stories of Early Settlers in the Golden State.* San Francisco: Scottwall Associates, 1993.

Lewis, Oscar. *The Big Four.* 1938. Reprint. Sausalito, CA: Comstock Editions, 1971.

———. *San Francisco: Mission to Metropolis.* San Diego: Howell-North Books, 1980.

———. *Silver Kings.* New York: Alfred A. Knopf, 1947.

Lewis, Oscar, and Carroll D. Hall. *Bonanza Inn.* 1939. Reprint. New York: Ballantine Books, 1971.

Lewis, Richard. *Poor Richard's Guide to Non-Tourist San Francisco.* San Francisco: Unicorn Publishing Co., 1958.

Lick, Rosemary. *The Generous Miser: The Story of James Lick of California.* The Ward Ritchie Press, 1967.

Lloyd, B. E. *Lights and Shades in San Francisco.* 1876. Reprint. Berkeley, CA: Berkeley Hills Books, 1999.

Logan, Lorna E. *Ventures in Mission: The Cameron House Story.* Castro Valley, CA: Self-published, 1976.

London, Joan. *Jack London and His Times: An Unconventional Biography.* 1939. Reprint. Rev. ed. Seattle: University of Washington Press, 1974.

Longstreth, Richard. *On the Edge of the World: Four Architects in San Francisco at the Turn of the Century.* New York, and Cambridge, MA: The Architectural History Foundation and the MIT Press, 1983.

Malone, Dumas. *Dictionary of American Biography.* New York: Charles Scribners & Sons, 1935.

Martin, Mildred C. *Chinatown's Angry Angel: The Story of Donaldina Cameron.* Palo Alto: Pacific Books, 1977.

McSweeney, Thomas Denis. *Cathedral on California Street: The Story of St. Mary's Cathedral, San Francisco.* Fresno, CA: Academy of California Church History, 1952.

Mullen, Kevin J. *Let Justice Be Done: Crime and Politics in Early San Francisco.* Reno, NV: University of Nevada Press, 1989.

Muybridge, Eadweard, and Mark Klett. *One City / Two Visions: San Francisco Panoramas, 1878 and 1990.* San Francisco: Bedford Arts, Publishers, 1990.

Nash, Gerald D. *A. P. Gianinni and the Bank of America.* Norman, OK: University of Oklahoma Press, 1992.

Nash, Jay Robert. *Bloodletters and Badmen.* New York: Warner Books, 1975.

O'Brien, Robert. *This Is San Francisco.* New York: Whittlesey House, a div. of McGraw-Hill, 1948.

Olmsted, Nancy. *The Ferry Building: Witness to a Century of Change, 1898–1998.* San Francisco and Berkeley, CA: The Port of San Francisco and Heyday Books, 1998.

Olmsted, Roger, and T. H. Watkins. *Here Today: San Francisco's Architectural Heritage.* San Francisco: Chronicle Books, 1973.

Perry, Charles. *The Haight-Ashbury: A History.* New York: Vintage Books, 1985.

Phillips, Catherine Coffin. *Portsmouth Plaza: The Cradle of San Francisco.* San Francisco: John Henry Nash, 1932.

Pickelhaupt, Bill. *Shanghaied in San Francisco.* San Francisco: Flyblister Press, 1996.

Polledri, Paolo, ed. *Visionary San Francisco.* San Francisco: San Francisco Museum of Modern Art, 1990.

Richards, Rand. *Historic San Francisco: A Concise History and Guide.* San Francisco: Heritage House Publishers, 2001.

Robinson, W. W. *Land in California: The Story of Mission Lands, Ranchos, Squatters, Mining Claims, Railroad Grants, Land Scrip, Homesteads.* Berkeley, CA: University of California Press, 1979.

Scharlach, Bernie. *Big Alma: San Francisco's Alma Spreckels.* San Francisco: Scottwall Associates, 1995.

Selvin, Joel. *San Francisco: The Musical History Tour: A guide to over 200 of the Bay Area's most memorable music sites.* San Francisco: Chronicle Books, 1996.

Shilts, Randy. *The Mayor of Castro Street: The Life and Times of Harvey Milk.* New York: St. Martin's Press, 1982.

Shumate, Albert. *The California of George Gordon and the 1849 sea voyages of his California Association.* Glendale, CA: The Arthur H. Clark Co., 1976.

Shumate, Albert. *Rincon Hill and South Park: San Francisco's Early Fashionable Neighborhood.* Sausalito, CA: Windgate Press, 1988.

Soulé, Frank, John H. Gihon, and James Nisbet. *The Annals of San Francisco.* 1855. Reprint. Berkeley, CA: Berkeley Hills Books, 1998.

Stillwell, B. F. *San Francisco Business Directory and Mercantile Guide for 1864–65.* San Francisco: B. F. Stillwell & Co., 1864.

Stoddard, Tom. *Jazz on the Barbary Coast.* Berkeley, CA: Heyday Books, 1998.

Stryker, Susan. *Gay by the Bay: A History of Queer Culture in the San Francisco Bay Area.* San Francisco: Chronicle Books, 1996.

Swasey, W. F. *The Early Days of Men of California.* Oakland, CA: Pacific Press Publishing Co., 1891.

Taper, Bernard, ed. and intro. *Mark Twain's San Francisco*. New York: McGraw-Hill, 1963.

Tchen, John Kuo Wei. *Genthe's Photographs of San Francisco's Old Chinatown*. New York: Dover Publications, 1984.

Tong, Benson. *Unsubmissive Women: Chinese Prostitutes in Nineteenth Century San Francisco*. Norman, OK: University of Oklahoma Press, 1994.

Treadwell, Ernest. *The Cattle King: The Biography of Henry Miller, Founder of the Miller and Lux Cattle Empire*. Santa Cruz, CA: Western Tanager Press, 1981.

Wagner, Jack. *Gold Mines of California*. Berkeley, CA: Howell-North Books, 1970.

Waldhorn, Judith Lynch, and Sally B. Woodbridge. *Victoria's Legacy*. San Francisco: 101 Productions, 1978.

Walker, Franklin. *San Francisco's Literary Frontier*. New York: Alfred A. Knopf, 1939.

Watkins, T. H., and R. R. Olmsted. *Mirror of the Dream: An Illustrated History of San Francisco*. San Francisco: Scrimshaw Press, 1976.

Willard, Ruth Hendricks. *Sacred Places of San Francisco*. Novato, CA: Presidio Press, 1985.

Wilson, Carol Green. *Chinatown Quest: One Hundred Years of the Donaldina Cameron House, 1874–1974*. San Francisco: California Historical Society with Donaldina Cameron House, 1974.

Woodbridge, Sally B., John M. Woodbridge, and Chuck Byrne. *San Francisco Architecture: The Illustrated Guide to Over 1,000 of the Best Buildings, Parks, and Public Artworks in the Bay Area*. San Francisco: Chronicle Books, 1992.

Yenne, Bill. *The Lions By The Golden Gate: Sarah Dix Hamlin and The History of the Hamlin School*. San Francisco: The Hamlin School, 1990.

Young, John P. *San Francisco: A History of the Pacific Coast Metropolis*. Vol. 1. The S. J. Clarke Publishing Co., San Francisco, 1912.

## Manuscripts, Pamphlets, Pocket Guides, Theses, Dissertations

Bloomfield, Anne, and William Kostura. *Pocket Guide to the Historic Districts of San Francisco*. San Francisco: San Francisco Convention and Visitors Bureau and The Victorian Alliance, 1993.

Carlisle, Henry C. *San Francisco Street Names: Sketches of the Lives of the Pioneers for Whom San Francisco Streets Are Named*. San Francisco: American Trust Co., 1954.

Caughey, John Walton. "Hubert Howe Bancroft, Historian of Western America." Reprint from the *American Historical Review*, n.d.

Delehanty, Randolph. *Victorian Sampler: A Walk in Pacific Heights and the Haas-Lilienthal House*. San Francisco: The Foundation for San Francisco's Architectural Heritage, 1979.

Dow, Gerald Robert. "Bay Fill in San Francisco: A History of Change." Master's thesis, San Francisco State University, 1973.

Draper, Joan Elaine. "The San Francisco Civic Center: Architecture, Planning, and Politics." Ph.D. diss., Montana State University, 1979.

"Eureka Valley Victorians." San Francisco State University, Geography 699, Spring 1975.

Fitzhamon, E. G. *The Streets of San Francisco*. First published as articles in the *San Francisco Chronicle*, 1928–1929.

*Golden Gate Pocket Guide and Souvenir*. San Francisco: Golden Gate Guide Publishing Co., August, 1904.

"Haight-Ashbury Victorian Inventory." San Francisco State University, Geography 699, Fall 1974.

Hubbard, Anita Day. *Cities Within The City*. First published as articles in the *San Francisco Bulletin*, 1924.

Kow, Jasmine. "San Francisco Chinatown Alleyways." Master's thesis, U. C. Berkeley, 1993.

Levinsohn, John P. *Cow Hollow: Early Days of a San Francisco Neighborhood from 1776*. San Francisco: San Francisco Yesterday, 1976.

Morphy, Edward. *San Francisco Thoroughfares*. First published as articles in the *San Francisco Chronicle*, 1919–1920.

*North Beach San Francisco: An Architectural, Historical, Cultural Survey*. Sacramento, CA: State Office of Historic Preservation, 1982.

O'Day, Edward F. *Old San Francisco: A Beautiful, Romantic, Historic Picture Story of "The City."* First published as articles in the *San Francisco News*, 1920s.

Olmsted, Roger R., Nancy L. Olmsted, and Allen Pastron. *San Francisco Waterfront*. San Francisco: San Francisco Wastewater Management Program, 1977.

Patterson, Bill. "San Francisco Street By Street." Typescript manuscript, n.d. [c.1980].

*A Record of the Proceedings of the Ayuntamiento or Town Council of 1849–1850*. San Francisco: Town & Bacon, 1860.

*San Francisco 1878: Eadweard Muybridge's Portrait of the City*. 1979. Revised. San Francisco: Wells Fargo Bank, 1987.

*San Francisco Street and Avenue Guide*. San Francisco: Charles F. Hoag, Publisher, 1905.

Schimmel, Jerry F. *The Old Streets of San Francisco: Early Street Names on Some Brass Tokens*. San Francisco: Pacific Coast Numismatic Society, 1993.

Shumate, Albert. *A Visit to Rincon Hill and South Park*. San Francisco: Yerba Buena Chapter, E Clampus Vitus, 1963.

Silver, Mae. *Jose de Jesus Noe: The Last Mexican Alcalde of Yerba Buena*. Privately printed, 1991.

St. Laurence, Ronald A. "The Myth and the Reality: Prostitution in San Francisco, 1880–1913." Masters thesis, California State University, Hayward, 1974.

Topham, Edward, M.D. *St. Mary's Hospital and the Sisters of Mercy, 1903-1949*. San Francisco: Privately printed, 1950.

Waldhorn, Judith. *An Amateur's Guide: Victorian Research in San Francisco.* Stanford Research Institute, 1974.

*Walking Tour Guidebook: A Tour Leader's Guide to "Take a Walk Through Mission History."* Stanford Research Institute, 1973.

Watson, Douglas. *An Hour's Walk Through Yerba Buena.* San Francisco: Yerba Buena Chapter, E Clampus Vitus, 1937.

Wheeler, Alfred. *Land Titles in San Francisco and the Laws Affecting Same.* San Francisco: Alta California Steam Printing Establishment, 1852.

Woolley, L. H. *California 1849–1913, Or The Rambling Sketches and Experiences of Sixty-Four Years Residence in That State.* Oakland, CA: DeWitt and Shelling Publishers, 1913.

Yip, Christopher. "San Francisco's Chinatown: An Architectural and Urban History." Ph.D. diss. U.C. Berkeley, 1985.

## Newspapers

*Alta California* (San Francisco)
*Bay Area Reporter* (San Francisco)
*Daily Alta* (San Francisco)
*The Independent* (San Francisco)
*New York Times*
*Noe Valley Voice* (San Francisco)
*San Francisco Bay Guardian*
*San Francisco Bulletin*
*San Francisco Call*
*San Francisco Chronicle*
*San Francisco Examiner*
*San Francisco Herald*
*San Francisco News Letter*
*San Francisco Progress*
*San Jose Pioneer*

## Magazines, Journals, and Periodicals

*Archaeology*
*The Argonaut*
*The Argonaut* (Journal of the San Francisco Historical Society)
*California Historical Society Quarterly*
*Ebony*
*Life*
*The New Yorker*
*The New Fillmore*
*Newsweek*
*Nob Hill Gazette*
*Overland Monthly*
*Pacific Magazine*

*Pacific Coast Mining Review*
*Pacific Marine News*
*Real Estate Journal* (1890s)
*San Francisco Focus*
*San Francisco Magazine*
*San Francisco Water* (1920s)
*Society of Architectural Historians Journal*
*Time*
*U. S. Catholic Historian*

## Miscellaneous Sources

Block Books for 1894, 1901, 1906, 1909, 1910.
City Directories (San Francisco), various years.
City Guides tours.
*Edwards Abstracts*
Maps of San Francisco for various years. Especially helpful were: U. S. Coast
   Survey maps for 1852 and 1857 and Sanborn Fire Insurance maps for
   1886–1893, 1899–1900, 1913–1915.
*Real Estate Circular*
*San Francisco Municipal Reports*
Spring Valley Water Company tap records (started 1861).

## Author Interviews

Ward Dunham (bartender at Enrico's Café since 1967), January 10, 2001.
Michael Feno, at Lucca Ravioli, June 24, 2000.
Lawrence Ferlinghetti (by phone), March 8, 2001.
Enid Ng Lim, at the Donaldina Cameron House, September 19, 1999.
Ben Nerone, at McAllister Tower, April 28, 2000.
Seizo Oka, at the Japanese American History Archive, March 26, 2001
Reggie Pettus, at the New Chicago Barbershop, March 30, 2001.
John Valentini, at A. Cavalli & Co., December 27, 2000.

## Videos

Levy, Pam Rorke, producer. *The Mission*. San Francisco: KQED, 1994.
Schweichen, Richard, producer. *The Times of Harvey Milk*. Cinecom Films,
   1986.
Stein, Peter L., producer. *The Castro*. San Francisco: KQED, 1997.
Stein, Peter L., producer. *The Fillmore*. San Francisco: KQED, 1999.

# Index

# About the Author

Rand Richards is the author of the highly praised, local best-selling book, *Historic San Francisco: A Concise History and Guide.* He has been interviewed on radio and television and is a sought after speaker and tour guide.

In 1995 Rand received a coveted invitation to the Gorbachev Foundation's State of the World Forum for world leaders held at the Fairmont Hotel. He met Mikhail Gorbachev, gave a presentation at the conference on San Francisco history, and led tour groups around the city.

Rand has lived in San Francisco since 1972 except for a year spent at Schiller

Rand Richards.

College in Paris, France where he taught international marketing. He has a B.A. degree in History from the University of Minnesota and an MBA degree from San Francisco State University. He is a member of the California Historical Society and of several local historical associations.